Algebra 1

JM EDU

PREFACE

Joseph Pak was born and raised in South Korea and moved to the United States during his teenhood. Joseph graduated from high school in Texas, where he discovered his knack for studying mathematics. He received his Bachelor's degree in mathematics at the University of Texas at Austin. Subsequently, Joseph passed a content examination(135 Mathematics 8−12), which certified him to work as a mathematics instructor at Texas Public High School.

Joseph has been teaching U.S. mathematics to students in Seoul, South Korea, for over a decade, during which time he realized a desperate need for high−quality workbooks for his students. He has been researching and developing exquisite content for his workbooks to educate his students more effectively, and to mostly alleviate the hardships students often encounter when trying to tackle new concepts in mathematics.

After years of exhaustive research in math education methodology, Joseph has finally put out a series of comprehensive workbooks that include all of the following aspects:

1. 5−step systematic workbook.
   "Concept → Example → Check Point → Review Exercise → Chapter Test"

2. Detailed explanation for each topic and easy−to−understand problem−solving methods that provide a thorough understanding of the materials.

3. Step−by−step problem structure that enables students to study on their own.

4. Problems that foster creativity and thinking skills, based on a concrete understanding of the concepts.

5. A reliable and effective reference guide to preparing for standardized exams as well as school exams.

6. Detachable solution manual for ease and convenience for students.

Author's Words:

A well−structured workbook plays a critical role in students' learning experience. It serves as a very influential guide for students. I hope this book helps you realize all your inner−inquisitivity in learning mathematics, as well as contribute to the advancement of U.S. mathematics at large.

As a final note, I am thrilled that you've chosen this book to help you on this journey, and please do not hesitate to reach out to us to share your challenges, concerns, and successes. Wish you all the best of luck!

Joseph Pak
JM EDU
B.A. Mathematics −University of Texas at Austin, 2006

Chapter 1. Linear Equations

    1. Variable and Expressions | 10

    2. Solving Linear Equations, Part 1 | 22

    3. Solving Linear Equations, Part 2 | 31

    4. Applications of Linear Equations | 37

    5. Chapter Test | 50

Chapter 2. Graphing Lines

    1. Introduction to Graphing Linear Equations | 60

    2. Two Forms of the Lines | 69

    3. Parallel and Perpendicular Lines | 80

    4. Chapter Test | 86

Chapter 3. System of Linear Equations

    1. Solving System of Linear Equations, Part 1 | 98

    2. Solving System of Linear Equations, Part 2 | 108

    3. Application of Linear Systems | 116

    4. Chapter Test | 126

Chapter 4. Linear Inequalities

1. Solving Linear Inequalities, Part 1 | 136

2. Solving Linear Inequalities, Part 2 | 144

3. Graphing Linear Inequality | 150

4. Application of Linear Inequality | 155

5. Chapter Test | 162

Chapter 5. Manipulating Polynomials

1. Addition and Subtraction of Polynomials | 170

2. Multiplication of Polynomials, Part 1 | 178

3. Multiplication of Polynomials, Part 2 | 186

4. Chapter Test | 194

Chapter 6. Factoring

1. Factors and Prime Factorization | 202

2. Factoring Binomials | 210

3. Factoring Trinomials | 214

4. Chapter Test | 223

Chapter 7. Quadratic Equations

1. Solving Basic Quadratic Equations | 230
2. Completing the Square | 238
3. The Quadratic Formula and the Discriminant | 242
4. Chapter Test | 250

Chapter 8. Rational Expressions

1. Simplify Rational Expressions | 260
2. Addition and Subtraction | 269
3. Rational Equations | 274
4. Chapter Test | 279

Chapter 9. Radical Expressions

1. Simplifying Radical Expressions | 286
2. Operations with Radical Expressions | 294
3. Radical Equations | 303
4. Chapter Test | 306

Solutions Manual

Chapter 1

Linear Equations

1. Variable and Expressions
2. Solving Linear Equations, Part 1
3. Solving Linear Equations, Part 2
4. Applications of Linear Equations
5. Chapter Test

1 Variable and Expressions

01 Vocabulary

Definition	Examples
Constant: A number	$3, -2, \dfrac{1}{3}$
Variable: A symbol, usually a letter, that represents the value(s)	x, y
Expression: A mathematical phrase that includes one or more constants or variables	$2x+3, 3x-4y+1$
Term: A constant, a variable, or the product of a number and one or more variables	In the expression $3x-4y+1$, $3x$, $-4y$, and 1 are considered terms.
Coefficient: The constant factor of each term	Coefficient of $3x$ is 3.
Expression in Simplest Form: An expression that has no like terms or parentheses	Not Simplified: $2(3x-x+5)$ Simplified: $4x+10$

02 Multiplication and Division, Part 1

1. Constant × Monomial or Monomial × Constant

   After multiplying numbers, write the number before the variable.

   Concept Check

   $3 \times (-4x) = (3 \times (-4)) \times x = (-12) \times x = -12x$

   $(-4x) \times 3 = ((-4) \times 3) \times x = (-12) \times x = -12x$

2. Monomial ÷ Constant

(1) Convert division to multiplication $\Rightarrow A \div B = A \times \dfrac{1}{B}$

(2) After multiplying numbers, write the number before the variable.

Concept Check

$(-4x) \div 8 = (-4x) \times \dfrac{1}{8}$ → Convert division to multiplication

$ = \left((-4) \times \dfrac{1}{8}\right) \times x$ → Multiply the numbers

$ = -\dfrac{1}{2}x$ → Simplify

Example 1

Simplify the expression.

① $5 \times 6x$

② $(-4x) \times (-9)$

③ $(-12x) \div 4$

④ $\dfrac{3}{8}x \div (-6)$

Solution

① $5 \times 6x = (5 \times 6) \times x = 30x$

② $(-4x) \times (-9) = (-4 \times (-9)) \times x = 36x$

③ $(-12x) \div 4 = (-12x) \times \dfrac{1}{4} = \left(-12 \times \dfrac{1}{4}\right) \times x = -3x$

④ $\dfrac{3}{8}x \div (-6) = \dfrac{3}{8}x \times \left(-\dfrac{1}{6}\right) = \left(\dfrac{3}{8} \times \left(-\dfrac{1}{6}\right)\right) \times x = -\dfrac{1}{16}x$

Check Point 1

Simplify the expression.

① $36x \times \left(-\dfrac{1}{12}\right)$

② $(-2) \times (-13x)$

③ $(-25y) \div \dfrac{5}{3}$

④ $(-28y) \div \left(-\dfrac{7}{2}\right)$

03 Multiplication and Division, Part 2

1. **Distributive Property**

   For the three numbers a, b, and c,
   $$a(b+c) = ab + ac \text{ and } (a+b)c = ac + bc$$

2. **Constant × Expression or Expression × Constant**

   (1) Use the distributive property to simplify the product.

   (2) If $-$ is multiplied outside parentheses, $-$ must be multiplied by all terms in parentheses.
   $$-a(b+c) = -ab - ac \text{ and } (a+b)(-c) = -ac - bc$$

   Concept Check

   $-2(3x+4) = (-2 \times 3x) + (-2 \times 4) = -6x - 8$

   $(3x+4) \cdot (-2) = (3x \times (-2)) + (4 \times (-2)) = -6x - 8$

   Be careful that $-2(3x+4) \neq -6x + 8$.

3. **Expression ÷ Constant**

   (1) Convert division to multiplication.

   (2) Use the distributive property to simplify the product.
   $$(a+b) \div c = (a+b) \times \dfrac{1}{c} = \dfrac{a}{c} + \dfrac{b}{c}$$

Chapter 1. Linear Equations

Concept Check

$(-4x+8) \div 2 = (-4x+8) \times \dfrac{1}{2}$ → Convert division to multiplication

$\qquad = \left(-4x \times \dfrac{1}{2}\right) + \left(8 \times \dfrac{1}{2}\right)$ → Use the distributive property

$\qquad = -2x+4$ → Simplify

Example 2

Simplify the expression.

① $4(5x-2)$

② $-6\left(5x - \dfrac{5}{12}\right)$

③ $(24x-18) \div 9$

④ $(-64x+14) \div (-4)$

Solution

① $4(5x-2) = (4 \times 5x) + (4 \times (-2)) = 20x - 8$

② $-6\left(5x - \dfrac{5}{12}\right) = ((-6) \times 5x) + \left((-6) \times \left(-\dfrac{5}{12}\right)\right) = -30x + \dfrac{5}{2}$

③ $(24x-18) \div 9 = (24x-18) \times \dfrac{1}{9}$

$\qquad = \left(24x \times \dfrac{1}{9}\right) + \left(-18 \times \dfrac{1}{9}\right) = \dfrac{8}{3}x - 2$

④ $(-64x+14) \div (-4) = (-64x+14) \times \left(-\dfrac{1}{4}\right)$

$\qquad = \left(-64x \times \left(-\dfrac{1}{4}\right)\right) + \left(14 \times \left(-\dfrac{1}{4}\right)\right) = 16x - \dfrac{7}{2}$

Check Point 2

Solutions_Page 2

Simplify the expression.

① $-4\left(-\dfrac{3}{2}x+8\right)$

② $\dfrac{1}{3}(-12x-36)$

③ $(14y+63) \div \left(-\dfrac{7}{2}\right)$

④ $\left(\dfrac{15}{4}y - 25\right) \div \dfrac{5}{2}$

04 Like Terms

1. Definition

    Terms that have the same variable factors are called like terms or similar terms. For example, $2x$ and $-3x$ are like terms. Terms that do not have the same variable factors are called unlike terms or dissimilar terms.

    Concept Check

Terms	Variable Factors	Like or Unlike Terms
$2x$ and $-5x$	x and x	Like Terms
$2x$ and $-5y$	x and y	Unlike Terms
$-3a^2$ and $2a^2$	a^2 and a^2	Like Terms
$4ab$ and $-b$	ab and b	Unlike Terms

2. Addition and Subtraction of Like Terms

    Use the distributive property to add or subtract like terms.
    $$ax+bx=(a+b)x,\ ax-bx=(a-b)x$$

    Concept Check

    (1) $2x+5x=(2+5)x=7x,\ 2x-5x=(2-5)x=-3x$

    (2) $3x+7-4x-6$

    $\quad = 3x-4x+7-6 \quad \rightarrow$ Group the x terms and constants separately

    $\quad = (3-4)x+(7-6) \quad \rightarrow$ Use the distributive property

    $\quad = -x+1 \quad\quad\quad\quad\ \ \rightarrow$ Simplify

05 Addition and Subtraction

1. Solving Parentheses

    (1) If there is a $+$ in front of the parentheses, leave the sign in parentheses.

    $A+(B+C)=A+B+C$

    $A+(B-C)=A+B-C$

    (2) If there is a $-$ in front of the parentheses, reverse the sign in parentheses.

    $A-(B+C)=A-B-C$

    $A-(B-C)=A-B+C$

    Concept Check

    (1) $4x+(2x-5)=4x+2x-5$

    (2) $4x-(2x-5)=4x-2x+5$

2. Order of Addition or Subtraction

    (1) Solve the parentheses using the distributive property.

    (2) Group like terms.

    (3) Simplify.

    Concept Check

    (1) $(3x+4)+2(5x-1)$

    $=3x+4+10x-2$ → Solve the parentheses

    $=3x+10x+4-2$ → Group the x terms and constants separately

    $=13x+2$ → Simplify

    (2) $4(2a+1)-3(3a+2)$

    $=8a+4-9a-6$ → Solve the parentheses

    $=8a-9a+4-6$ → Group the a terms and constants separately

    $=-a-2$ → Simplify

Example 3

Simplify the expression.

① $7x+5-4x-9$ ② $12x+2(5x-3)$

③ $3(6x-1)-4(x+9)$ ④ $\frac{1}{2}(4x+6)+4(-3x+1)-\frac{2}{3}(6x-9)$

Solution

① $7x+5-4x-9 = 7x-4x+5-9$
$= 3x-4$

② $12x+2(5x-3) = 12x+10x-6$
$= 22x-6$

③ $3(6x-1)-4(x+9) = 18x-3-4x-36$
$= 18x-4x-3-36$
$= 14x-39$

④ $\frac{1}{2}(4x+6)+4(-3x+1)-\frac{2}{3}(6x-9) = 2x+3-12x+4-4x+6$
$= 2x-12x-4x+3+4+6$
$= -14x+13$

Check Point 3

Simplify the expression.

① $-11x+14-6x+3$ ② $-3(4x+7)+4(x-3)$

③ $\frac{5}{6}(12x-24)-7(-2x-3)$ ④ $4x-3(-2x-5)-\frac{3}{2}(6x+10)$

06 Addition and Subtraction in Fraction Form

1. Steps to Add or Subtract Expressions

    (1) First, find the common denominator of each term. The common denominator should be LCM(Least Common Multiple) of each denominator.

    (2) Keep the denominator the same and then add or subtract the numerator.

    (3) Solve parentheses on the numerator using the distributive property.

    (4) Group like terms and then simplify.

    Concept Check

    $\dfrac{x-2}{2} - \dfrac{2x-5}{3}$

    $= \dfrac{x-2}{2} \cdot \dfrac{3}{3} - \dfrac{2x-5}{3} \cdot \dfrac{2}{2}$ → LCM of 2 and 3 is $2 \cdot 3 = 6$

    $= \dfrac{3(x-2)}{6} - \dfrac{2(2x-5)}{6}$ → Simplify

    $= \dfrac{3(x-2) - 2(2x-5)}{6}$ → Keep the denominator the same and then subtract the Numerator

    $= \dfrac{3x - 6 - 4x + 10}{6}$ → Solve parentheses in the numerator

    $= \dfrac{3x - 4x - 6 + 10}{6}$ → Group like terms

    $= \dfrac{-x+4}{6}$ or $-\dfrac{x-4}{6}$ → Simplify

2. Note the following

    (1) If the numerator is an expression with two or more terms, enclose it in parentheses.

    Concept Check

    $\dfrac{x-2}{2} - \dfrac{x+1}{4} = \dfrac{x-2}{2} \cdot \dfrac{2}{2} - \dfrac{x+1}{4} = \begin{cases} \dfrac{2(x-2) - x + 1}{4} & \to \text{Incorrect} \\ \dfrac{2(x-2) - (x+1)}{4} & \to \text{Correct} \end{cases}$

(2) The numerator can be divisible when all the terms of the numerators are divisible by the denominator.

Concept Check

$\dfrac{2x-5}{4} = \dfrac{\cancel{2}x-5}{\cancel{4}} = \dfrac{x-5}{2}$ → Incorrect

$\dfrac{2x-6}{4} = \dfrac{\cancel{2}x-\cancel{6}}{\cancel{4}} = \dfrac{x-3}{2}$ → Correct

Example 4

Simplify the expression.

① $\dfrac{x+3}{5} - \dfrac{2x-7}{2}$

② $2x + \dfrac{x-4}{3} - \dfrac{3x-1}{4}$

Solution

① LCM of 5 and 2 is 10.

$\dfrac{x+3}{5} - \dfrac{2x-7}{2} = \dfrac{x+3}{5} \cdot \dfrac{2}{2} - \dfrac{2x-7}{2} \cdot \dfrac{5}{5}$

$= \dfrac{2(x+3) - 5(2x-7)}{10}$

$= \dfrac{2x+6-10x+35}{10}$

$= \dfrac{-8x+41}{10} = -\dfrac{8x-41}{10}$

② LCM of 3 and 4 is 12.

$2x + \dfrac{x-4}{3} - \dfrac{3x-1}{4} = \dfrac{2x}{1} \cdot \dfrac{12}{12} + \dfrac{x-4}{3} \cdot \dfrac{4}{4} - \dfrac{3x-1}{4} \cdot \dfrac{3}{3}$

$= \dfrac{24x + 4(x-4) - 3(3x-1)}{12}$

$= \dfrac{24x + 4x - 16 - 9x + 3}{12}$

$= \dfrac{19x - 13}{12}$

Check Point 4

Simplify the expression.

① $-\dfrac{2x+1}{5}+\dfrac{x-2}{3}$

② $\dfrac{2x-5}{4}-\dfrac{x+1}{6}+2$

Review Exercise

01 Which of the following is NOT true?

(A) $24x \times \left(-\dfrac{3}{4}\right) = -18x$

(B) $\left(-\dfrac{9}{5}x\right) \div (-6) = \dfrac{3}{10}x$

(C) $\dfrac{2}{3}(-6x+9) = -4x+6$

(D) $(12x-15) \div \dfrac{5}{3} = \dfrac{4}{5}x - 9$

(E) None of the above

02 Which of the following expression is equal to $-4\left(2x - \dfrac{3}{4}\right)$?

(A) $4\left(2x + \dfrac{3}{4}\right)$

(B) $-2(4x-3)$

(C) $\left(-2x + \dfrac{3}{4}\right) \div \dfrac{1}{4}$

(D) $(4x-3) \div \left(-\dfrac{1}{2}\right)$

(E) None of the above

03 Find the value of $a-b$ from the expression
$$\left(-\dfrac{6}{5}x - 4\right) \div \left(-\dfrac{2}{5}\right) = ax + b.$$

04 Find the value of $a+b$ from the expression given below.

(1) $5(3x-1) - 4(x-2) = ax + b$

(2) $\dfrac{1}{2}(6x-10) - 3(x+4) - 5x = ax + b$

05 Simplify the expression $2(x-3y) - 5(3x+y)$.

Challenging

06 The coefficient of x is m and the constant is n when the expression
$4x - 2(ax + 3a) + \dfrac{2}{3}(3x-9)$ is simplified. What is the value of $2m - n$ in terms of a?

07 Find the value of $a+b+c$ from the equation given below.

(1) $\dfrac{5x-4}{2} - \dfrac{2x+3}{5} = \dfrac{ax+b}{c}$

Challenging
(2) $\dfrac{x-5}{4} - \dfrac{4x-2}{3} + \dfrac{x+3}{2} = -\dfrac{ax+b}{c}$

08 Assuming $A=3x-4$ and $B=2x+1$, simplify the expression $\dfrac{5}{3}A - \dfrac{1}{2}(B-5)$ in terms of x.

Challenging
09 Assuming $A=4x+2$, $B=5y-3$, and $C=3x-4y+2$, simplify the expression $3B-2(A-C)$ in terms of x and y.

2 Solving Linear Equations, Part 1

01 Definition of One-Variable Linear Equations

An equation is a statement of equality containing one or more variables.
By solving an equation, it means finding all value of the variable for which the equation is true. A one-variable linear equation is an algebraic equation in which each term is either a constant or the product of a constant and the first power of a single variable.

Concept Check

The following are one-variable linear equations:
$3x-4=11$, $2a+\frac{1}{2}=4a$, and $14y=\frac{3y}{2}-2$

The following are NOT one-variable linear equations:
$3x^2-4=11$, $\frac{1}{2}=4\sqrt{a}+3$, and $\frac{4}{y^2}+10=8$

02 Solving One-Step Linear Equations

1. Equivalent Equations

    Equivalent equations are equations that have the same solution. When we perform the same inverse operation on each side of an equation, we get an equivalent equation.

2. Addition and Subtraction Properties of Equality

    (1) Addition Property of Equality: Adding the same number to each side of an equation produces an equivalent equation.

For any real numbers a, b, and c,
$$a=b$$
$$a+c=b+c$$

Concept Check

Solve the equation $x-4=5$.

Solution

$x-4=5$ → Write the original equation
$x-4+4=5+4$ → Add 4 to each side
$x=9$ → Simplify

The solution is $x=9$

(2) Subtraction Property of Equality: Subtracting the same number to each side of an equation produces an equivalent equation.

For any real numbers a, b, and c,
$$a=b$$
$$a-c=b-c$$

Concept Check

Solve the equation $x+4=5$.

Solution

$x+4=5$ → Write the original equation
$x+4-4=5-4$ → Subtract 4 to each side
$x=1$ → Simplify

The solution is $x=1$

3. Multiplication and Division Properties of Equality

(1) Multiplication Property of Equality: Multiplying the same nonzero number to each side of an equation produces an equivalent equation.

For any real numbers a, b, and c,
$$a=b$$
$$a \cdot c = b \cdot c$$

Concept Check

Solve the equation $\frac{x}{3}=4$.

Solution

$\frac{x}{3}=4$ → Write the original equation

$\frac{x}{3} \cdot 3 = 4 \cdot 3$ → Multiply each side by 3

$x=12$ → Simplify

The solution is $x=12$

(2) Division Property of Equality: Dividing the same nonzero number to each side of an equation produces an equivalent equation.

For any real numbers a, b, and c, $\quad \begin{array}{c} a=b \\ \frac{a}{c}=\frac{b}{c} \end{array}$

Concept Check

Solve the equation $4x=20$.

Solution

$4x=20$ → Write the original equation

$\frac{4x}{4}=\frac{20}{4}$ → Divide each side by 4

$x=5$ → Simplify

The solution is $x=5$

Example 1

Solve the equation.

① $x-8=4$ ② $x+5=-6$
③ $\frac{x}{3}=9$ ④ $-2x=16$

Solution

① $x-8=4$
   $x-8+8=4+8$
   $x=12$

   $x=12$

② $x+5=-6$
   $x+5-5=-6-5$
   $x=-11$

   $x=-11$

③ $\dfrac{x}{3}=9$

$\dfrac{x}{3} \cdot 3 = 9 \cdot 3$

$x=27$

$x=27$

④ $-2x=16$

$\dfrac{-2x}{-2}=\dfrac{16}{-2}$

$x=-8$

$x=-8$

> **Check Point 1**

Solutions_Page 5

Solve the equation.

① $x+13=5$

② $x-7=-14$

③ $-\dfrac{x}{7}=15$

④ $-11x=-121$

03 Solving Multi-Step Linear Equations

To solve a multi−step linear equation with one variable, follow a few simple steps below:

1. Remove parentheses using distributive property, if there is(are) any.

2. Simplify both sides of the equation by combining like terms on each side.

3. Move all the terms with the variable to one side and all the constants to the other using addition and subtraction.

4. Eliminate the coefficient of the variable by applying inverse operation.

> **Concept Check**

1. Solve the equation $2x-1+4x=3x+5-15$.

> **Solution**

$2x-1+4x=3x+5-15$	→ Write original equation
$6x-1=3x-10$	→ Simplify each side
$6x-3x-1=3x-3x-10$	→ Subtract $3x$ to each side
$3x-1=-10$	→ Simplify
$3x-1+1=-10+1$	→ Add 1 to each side
$3x=-9$	→ Simplify

Chapter 1. Linear Equations 25

$$\frac{3x}{3} = \frac{-9}{3}$$ → Divide each side by 4

$x = -3$ → Simplify

The solution is $x = -3$

2. Solve the equation $3(2x-5)+1 = 4(x+2)-18$.

Solution

$3(2x-5)+1 = 4(x+2)-18$ → Write original equation
$6x-15+1 = 4x+8-18$ → Remove parentheses
$6x-14 = 4x-10$ → Simplify each side
$6x-4x-14 = 4x-4x-10$ → Subtract $4x$ to each side
$2x-14 = -10$ → Simplify
$2x-14+14 = -10+14$ → Add 14 to each side
$2x = 4$ → Simplify
$\frac{2x}{2} = \frac{4}{2}$ → Divide each side by 2
$x = 2$ → Simplify

The solution is $x = 2$

Example 2

Solve the equation.

① $3x+5 = x+9$

② $6x = 3x-2+2x$

③ $4x-2(x+1) = 6x-8$

④ $2(3x-4)+3x = 3(x+2)-2$

Solution

①
$3x+5 = x+9$
$3x-x+5 = x-x+9$
$2x+5 = 9$
$2x+5-5 = 9-5$
$2x = 4$
$\frac{2x}{2} = \frac{4}{2}$
$x = 2$

②
$6x = 3x-2+2x$
$6x = 5x-2$
$6x-5x = 5x-5x-2$
$x = -2$

$x = -2$

$x = 2$

26 Chapter 1. Linear Equations

③ $\quad 4x-2(x+1)=6x-8$
$\quad\quad 4x-2x-2=6x-8$
$\quad\quad\quad 2x-2=6x-8$
$\quad 2x-6x-2=6x-6x-8$
$\quad\quad\quad -4x-2=-8$
$\quad -4x-2+2=-8+2$
$\quad\quad\quad\quad -4x=-6$
$$\frac{-4x}{-4}=\frac{-6}{-4}$$
$$x=\frac{3}{2}$$

$$x=\frac{3}{2}$$

④ $\quad 2(3x-4)+3x=3(x+2)-2$
$\quad\quad 6x-8+3x=3x+6-2$
$\quad\quad\quad 9x-8=3x+4$
$\quad 9x-3x-8=3x-3x+4$
$\quad\quad\quad 6x-8=4$
$\quad\quad 6x-8+8=4+8$
$\quad\quad\quad\quad 6x=12$
$$\frac{6x}{6}=\frac{12}{6}$$
$$x=2$$

$$x=2$$

Check Point 2

Solve the equation.

① $5-3x=5x-35$

② $13-4x-5=7x-5x+2$

③ $3x-4+2(1-x)=-8$

④ $4-2x=-4(3-x)-5(x-1)$

Review Exercise

01 Solve the equation.

(1) $x+5=-19$

(2) $\dfrac{x-6}{2}=12$

(3) $3x-7=14$

(4) $x+4=3x-8$

02 Solve the equation.

(1) $x-5+6x=4+4x$

(2) $6x-4x+9=7+7x-3$

(3) $3x-14=24-16x$

(4) $15x-9-7x=18+6-3x$

03 Solve the equation.

(1) $4x-4=2(x+3)$

(2) $10-4(x+1)=2(x+5)$

(3) $2(2x-7)-x=2-3x$

(4) $4x-(2-3x)=\dfrac{1}{2}(2x-5)+\dfrac{3}{2}$

$4-2(3x-5)=3x-(4-x)$ → Given
$4-6x+10=3x-4-x$ → Step 1
$-6x+14=2x-4$ → Step 2
$-6x-2x=-4-14$ → Step 3
$-8x=-18$ → Step 4
$x=\dfrac{9}{4}$ → Step 5

04 Which is the first <u>incorrect</u> step in the solution shown above?

(A) Step 1
(B) Step 2
(C) Step 3
(D) Step 4
(E) Step 5

05 If $x=-3$ is the solution to the equation $2(x-3k)+1=4k-3(4-x)$, what is the value of k?

Review Exercise

Challenging

06 The equation $ax+5=x+a$ and $5x+3=3(x-1)$ have the same solution x. What is the value of a?

Challenging

08 In some expression, $3(6x-5)$ should be added to A, but subtracted from A by mistake. If the resulting expression is $-4x+1$,

(1) Find the expression A.

(2) Find the correct expression.

Challenging

07 $7(x+3)-\boxed{}=4(2x-3)+3x$

Write the correct expression in $\boxed{}$ above.

3 Solving Linear Equations, Part 2

01 Solving Complicated Linear Equations

To solve a complicated linear equation with one variable, follow a few simple steps below:

1. Eliminate fractional coefficients by multiplying both sides of the equation by the least common multiple (LCM).
2. Eliminate decimals by multiplying both sides of the equation by a power of 10.
3. Solve the equation in the same way we solved the multi-step linear equations.

Concept Check

1. Linear Equation with Fractional Coefficients

$\frac{1}{2}x - 2 = \frac{2}{3}x + \frac{1}{4}$ → The LCM of 2, 3, and 4 is 12

$\left(\frac{1}{2}x - 2\right) \cdot 12 = \left(\frac{2}{3}x + \frac{1}{4}\right) \cdot 12$ → Multiply each side by 12

$6x - 24 = 8x + 3$ → Simplify each side

$-2x - 24 = 3$ → Subtract $8x$ to each side

$-2x = 27$ → Add 24 to each side

$x = -\frac{27}{2}$ → Divide each side by -2

The solution is $x = -\frac{27}{2}$

2. Linear Equation with Decimals

$0.6x + 1 = 0.4(2x - 3)$

$(0.6x + 1) \cdot 10 = (0.4(2x - 3)) \cdot 10$ → Multiply each side by 10

$6x + 10 = 4(2x - 3)$ → Simplify each side

$6x + 10 = 8x - 12$ → Remove parentheses on the right side

$-2x + 10 = -12$ → Subtract 8x to each side

$-2x = -22$ → Subtract 10 to each side

$x = 11$ → Divide each side by -2

The solution is $x = 11$

Example 1

Solve the equation.

① $\frac{1}{3}x+5=\frac{11}{6}x-4$

② $\frac{x+1}{2}-\frac{2x+5}{3}=\frac{3x-1}{4}$

③ $0.1x+0.9=0.3x+0.5$

④ $0.3x+0.2(1-x)=-0.4$

Solution

① $\frac{1}{3}x+5=\frac{11}{6}x-4$

The LCM of 3 and 6 is 6.
So, multiply each side by 6.

$\left(\frac{1}{3}x+5\right)\cdot 6=\left(\frac{11}{6}x-4\right)\cdot 6$

$2x+30=11x-24$

$-9x+30=-24$

$-9x=-54$

$x=6$

② $\frac{x+1}{2}-\frac{2x+5}{3}=\frac{3x-1}{4}$

The LCM of 2, 3, and 4 is 12.
So, multiply each side by 12.

$\left(\frac{x+1}{2}-\frac{2x+5}{3}\right)\cdot 12=\left(\frac{3x-1}{4}\right)\cdot 12$

$6(x+1)-4(2x+5)=3(3x-1)$

$6x+6-8x-20=9x-3$

$-2x-14=9x-3$

$-11x-14=-3$

$-11x=11$

$x=-1$

$x=6$

$x=-1$

③ $0.1x+0.9=0.3x+0.5$

Multiply each side by 10.

$(0.1x+0.9)\cdot 10=(0.3x+0.5)\cdot 10$

$x+9=3x+5$

$-2x+9=5$

$-2x=-4$

$x=2$

④ $0.3x+0.2(1-x)=-0.4$

Multiply each side by 10.

$(0.3x+0.2(1-x))\cdot 10=(-0.4)\cdot 10$

$3x+2(1-x)=-4$

$3x+2-2x=-4$

$x+2=-4$

$x=-6$

$x=2$

$x=-6$

Check Point 1

Solutions_Page 8

Solve the equation.

① $\frac{x}{8}+\frac{1}{2}=\frac{3}{8}x-1$

② $\frac{3x-4}{3}+\frac{x}{2}=\frac{x+2}{2}-\frac{1}{3}$

③ $0.2(2x-7)=0.2-0.4x$

④ $0.4(3-x)+0.5x=0.9x-2$

02 Special Linear Equations

1. Linear Equation with Infinitely Many Solutions

   If the equation is in the form of $ax=b$ and, $a=0$ and $b=0$, then there are infinitely many solutions to the equation.

   Concept Check

$4+6x=2(3x+2)$	→ Given
$4+6x=6x+4$	→ Remove parentheses
$4+6x-6x=4$	→ Subtract $6x$ to each side
$6x-6x=4-4$	→ Subtract 4 to each side
$(6-6)x=4-4$	→ $6x-6x=(6-6)x$
$0 \cdot x=0$	→ Simplify

   This means that the equation is always true for all x.

   Therefore, the equation has infinitely many solutions.

2. Liner Equation with No Solution

   If the equation is in the form of $ax=b$ and, $a=0$ and $b \neq 0$, then there are no solutions to the equation.

   Concept Check

$5x-4=5x+4$	→ Given
$5x-5x-4=4$	→ Subtract $5x$ to each side
$5x-5x=4+4$	→ Add 4 to each side
$(5-5)x=4+4$	→ $5x-5x=(5-5)x$
$0 \cdot x=8$	→ Simplify

   This means that the equation is always false for all x.

   Therefore, the equation has no solution.

Example 2

Solve the equation.

① $6x-4-3(3+2x)=-13$

② $5(2x-3)+2=7x-3(2-x)$

Solution

① $6x-4-3(3+2x)=-13$
$6x-4-9-6x=-13$
$6x-13-6x=-13$
$6x-6x=-13+13$
$(6-6)x=0$
$0 \cdot x=0$

There are infinitely many solutions

② $5(2x-3)+2=7x-3(2-x)$
$10x-15+2=7x-6+3x$
$10x-13=10x-6$
$10x-10x=-6+13$
$(10-10)x=7$
$0 \cdot x=7$

There is no solution

Check Point 2

① $3-\dfrac{5-3x}{4}=\dfrac{7}{8}+\dfrac{3}{4}x$

② $1.8(x-1)+0.5=3.6\left(1+\dfrac{x}{2}\right)-4.9$

Review Exercise

01 Solve the equation.

(1) $\dfrac{2x-1}{3}-2=\dfrac{x}{3}+6$

(2) $\dfrac{3x+1}{2}+\dfrac{2x-1}{3}=3x-4$

02 Solve the equation.

(1) $1.6x+0.5=0.8x-2.7$

(2) $0.25x-0.2=2(0.45-0.05x)+1$

03 Find a if $x=2$ is a solution to the equation $\dfrac{x+a}{2}=\dfrac{3a-x}{4}$.

04 Which of the following equation has infinitely many solutions?

(A) $0.4x-0.9=0.2x+0.9$

(B) $\dfrac{6x+4}{5}=x+0.2$

(C) $\dfrac{1}{2}(4x+8)=-2(3-x)$

(D) $2(x+1)-\dfrac{5}{4}x=\dfrac{3x+8}{4}$

(E) None of the above

Review Exercise

05 If the equation $\dfrac{ax+5}{2}-\dfrac{2}{3}=\dfrac{5}{6}x-\dfrac{1}{3}b$ is true for all x, what is the value of a and b?

06 For what value of b does the equation $2(x-2)=3bx-7$ have no solutions for x?

Challenging

07 For what value of a and b does the equation $\dfrac{3x+4}{5}=\dfrac{ax}{2}-2b$ have infinitely many solutions for x?

Challenging

08 Solve the equation $\dfrac{2x-1}{3}-0.9=x-\dfrac{x+2}{4}$.

4. Application of Linear Equations

01 Introduction

Applications of linear equations are real-life tasks. In this topic, linear equations start to become useful. The key to solving application problems is converting the words into mathematical equations. Refer to the following steps.

1. Understand thoroughly what the problem is asking you to do.
2. Represent one of the unknown quantities with a variable.
3. Form an equation that will relate known quantities to the unknown quantities.
4. Solve the equation.

02 Number Problems

(1) Let x be the number.
(2) Write the equation for x.
(3) Solve the equation for x.

Example 1

Four more than twice a number is equal to three times the number minus two. What is the number?

Solution

Let x be the number. Four more than twice a number is $2x+4$ and three times the number minus two is $3x-2$. Since these two quantities are equal, we have $2x+4=3x-2$. Now solve the equation for x.

$$2x+4=3x-2$$
$$-x+4=-2$$
$$-x=-6, \ x=6$$

The number is 6.

Check Point 1

Solutions_Page 11

There are two numbers whose sum is 21. If four times the first number is 6 more than twice the second number, what are two numbers?

03 Consecutive Integers Problems

Let x be the integer.

(1) Two consecutive integers: $x, \ x+1$ (or $x-1, \ x$)

(2) Three consecutive integers: $x-1, \ x, \ x+1$ (or $x, \ x+1, \ x+2$)

(3) Two consecutive even(or odd) integers: $x, \ x+2$ (or $x-2, \ x$)

(4) Three consecutive even(or odd) integers: $x-2, \ x, \ x+2$ (or $x, \ x+2, \ x+4$)

Example 2

The sum of the three consecutive integers is 54. What are the values of the three integers?

Solution

Let three consecutive integers be $x-1$, x, and $x+1$. Since the sum of three integers is 54, we have $(x-1)+x+(x+1)=54$. Now solve the equation for x.

$$(x-1)+x+(x+1)=54$$
$$x-1+x+x+1=54$$
$$3x=54, \ x=18$$

Since $x=18$, $x-1=18-1=17$ and $x+1=18+1=19$.

The three consecutive integers are 17, 18, and 19.

Check Point 2

Solutions_Page 11

The sum of three consecutive integers is 17 more than twice the least of the integers. Find the least integer.

04 Age Problems

Let x be the age of A.
(1) The age of A after a years $\Rightarrow x+a$
(2) B is a years older than A $\Rightarrow B=x+a$
(3) B is a years younger than A $\Rightarrow B=x-a$
(4) B is a times as old as A $\Rightarrow B=ax$

Example 3

David's age is 12 more than three times Justin's age. If the sum of their ages is 48, what are their ages?

Solution

Let x be Justin's age. Then, David's age is $3x+12$. Since the sum of their ages is 48, we have $(3x+12)+x=48$. Now solve the equation for x.

$$(3x+12)+x=48$$
$$4x+12=48$$
$$4x=36,\ x=9$$

Therefore, Justin's age is 9 years old and David is $3x+12=3(9)+12=39$ years old.

Justin is 9 years old and David is 39 years old.

Check Point 3 Solutions_Page 11

Currently, John is 14 years old and his father is 38 years old. In how many years will his father be twice as old as John will be?

05 Coin Problems

(1) Penny: 1 cent
(2) Nickel: 5 cents
(3) Dime: 10 cents
(4) Quarter: 25 cents

Example 4

Jason has some coins in his pocket consisting of nickels and dimes only. If the total value of the coins is $3.60 and there are 9 more nickels than dimes, how many nickels and dimes are there?

Solution

Let x be the number of dimes. Then, the number of nickels is $x+9$. Since the total value of the coins is \$3.60(360 cents), we have $10x+5(x+9)=360$. Now solve the equation for x.

$$10x+5(x+9)=360$$
$$10x+5x+45=360$$
$$15x+45=360$$
$$15x=315, \ x=21$$

Therefore, there are 21 dimes and $x+9=21+9=30$ nickels.

30 nickels and 21 dimes

Check Point 4

Annie has some coins in her pocket consisting of nickels, dimes, and quarters. There are twice as many nickels as quarters and the number of dimes is one less than the number of quarters. If the total value of the coins is \$2.15, how many nickels, dimes, and quarters are there?

06 Rate, Time and Distance Problems

The relationship between rate(speed), distance, and time

$$\text{Speed} = \frac{\text{Distance}}{\text{Time}}$$

is used to solve uniform motion problems. The units of speed depend on the units used for the distance and time. The above formula can be rearranged as follows.

$$\text{Speed} = \frac{\text{Distance}}{\text{Time}} \Leftrightarrow \text{Time} = \frac{\text{Distance}}{\text{Speed}} \Leftrightarrow \text{Distance} = \text{Speed} \times \text{Time}$$

Example 5

Two cars A and B started from the same point, traveling in opposite directions at 60 miles per hour and 70 miles per hour, respectively. After how many hours will they be 520 miles apart?

Solution

Let x be the time each car traveled. Then, the distance car A traveled is $60 \times x = 60x$ and the distance car B traveled is $70 \times x = 70x$, as shown in the figure below.

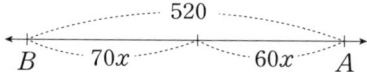

Since two cars are 520 miles apart, we have $60x + 70x = 520$. Now solve the equation for x.
$$60x + 70x = 520$$
$$130x = 520, \quad x = 4$$
Therefore, they will be 520 miles apart after 4 hours.

4 hours

Check Point 5

Two cars are 340 miles apart and moving directly towards each other. One car is moving at a speed of 64 miles per hour and the other at 72 miles per hour, respectively. Assuming that the cars start moving at the same time, how long does it take for the two cars to meet?

07 Mixture Problems

Let's take saline solution as an example.

(1) The percent of salt $=\dfrac{\text{The amount of salt}}{\text{The amount of solution}} \times 100\%$

(2) The amount of solution = The amount of salt + The amount of water

(3) The amount of salt $=\dfrac{\text{The percent of salt}}{100} \times$ The amount of solution

Example 6

How many gallons of a 40% saline solution must be added to 10 gallons of a 13% saline solution to make a 25% saline solution?

Solution

Let x be the amount of a 40% saline solution. Create a table as shown below.

	40% saline solution	13% saline solution	25% saline solution
The amount of solution	x	10	$x+10$
The amount of salt	$\dfrac{40}{100}x = 0.4x$	$\dfrac{13}{100} \cdot 10 = 1.3$	$\dfrac{25}{100}(x+10) = 0.25(x+10)$

Because the sum of the salts of a 40% saline solution and a 13% saline solution is the same as that of a 25% saline solution, we have $0.4x + 1.3 = 0.25(x+10)$. Now solve the equation for x.

$$0.4x + 1.3 = 0.25(x+10)$$
$$(0.4x + 1.3) \cdot 100 = (0.25(x+10)) \cdot 100$$
$$40x + 130 = 25(x+10)$$
$$40x + 130 = 25x + 250$$
$$15x + 130 = 250$$
$$15x = 120, \quad x = 8$$

8 gallons of a 40% saline solution

> **Check Point 6**
> Solutions_Page 12
>
> How many liters of an 18% acid−solution must be added to 8 liters of a 12% acid−solution to make a 15% acid−solution?

08 Plane Geometry Problems

(1) The perimeter of a rectangle equals to the sum of two widths and two lengths.

(2) A square has four equal sides.

(3) The sum of the three angles of any triangle equals 180°.

Example 7

The perimeter of the rectangle is 300 inches. If the length of the rectangle is 24 inches longer than twice the width, what are the dimensions of the rectangle?

Solution

Let x be the width of the rectangle. Then the length of the rectangle is $2x+24$. Since the perimeter of the rectangle is 300 inches, we have $2x+2(2x+24)=300$. Now solve the equation for x.

$$2x+2(2x+24)=300$$
$$2x+4x+48=300$$
$$6x+48=300$$
$$6x=252, \ x=42$$

Therefore, the width is 42 inches and the length is $2x+24=2(42)+24=108$ inches.

The rectangle is 42 inches wide and 108 inches long

Check Point 7

The first angle of a triangle is three times the second, and the third is 12 less than twice the second. Find the three angles.

09 Finance Problems

1. Investment Problems

   The investment problem involves three basics.
   (1) P: The amount of money invested (called the "principal")
   (2) r: The interest rate
   (3) I: The interest on the original amount, where $I = P \times r$

2. Other Finance Problems

   Represent one of the unknown prices with a variable.

Example 8

Chris plans to invest $8,000. He invests a certain amount in the bank which pays 4 percent interest and the remainder in stocks which pays a 6 percent yearly return. How much did he invest in each if his yearly income from the two investments was $380?

Solution

Let x be the amount in dollars invested at 4%. Then the amount in dollars invested at 6% is $8000 - x$. Create a table as shown below.

	Bank	Stock
The amount invested	x	$8000-x$
The interest earned	$\frac{4}{100}x = 0.04x$	$\frac{6}{100}(8000-x) = 480 - 0.06x$

Since his yearly income from the two investments was $380, we have $0.04x + (480 - 0.06x) = 380$. Now solve the equation for x.

$$0.04x + (480 - 0.06x) = 380$$
$$(0.04x + (480 - 0.06x)) \cdot 100 = (380) \cdot 100$$
$$4x + 100(480 - 0.06x) = 38000$$
$$4x + 48000 - 6x = 38000$$
$$-2x = -10000, \quad x = 5000$$

Therefore, Chris invested $5,000 in the bank and $8000 - x = 8000 - 5000 = \$3,000$ in stocks.

$5,000 in the bank and $3,000 in stocks

Check Point 8

Solutions_Page 12

A man invested $500 more in Bank X, which pays 5% interest than Bank Y, which pays 4% interest. If the interest earned by both banks was $133, how much did he invest in each bank?

46 Chapter 1. Linear Equations

Review Exercise

01 There are two numbers whose difference is 13. If twice the larger number is 1 less than five times the smaller number, what are two numbers?

02 Half of the larger of two consecutive even integers is equal to seven less than the smaller. Find the two integers.

03 Ken is twice as old as Nick. The sum of their ages five years ago was 26. How old are they now?

04 Steven is 28 years younger than his mother, Emily. If Emily is twice as old as Steven 15 years later, how old is Steven now?

05 David has some coins in her pocket consisting of pennies, nickels, dimes, and quarters. There are four times as many dimes as nickels and the number of quarters is one more than the number of dimes. If there are 4 pennies and the total value of the coins is $6.09, how many nickels, dimes, and quarters are there?

Review Exercise

06 Linda drove at a rate of 55 miles per hour for 3 hours. He stopped for dinner then drove for another 2 hours to reach his destination. If the total distance she traveled is 275 miles, at what rate did Linda drive for the last two hours?

07 Two buses are 96 miles apart and start moving to the right at the same time. The bus on the left is moving at twice the speed as the bus on the right. 3 hours after starting, the bus on the left catches up with the bus on the right. How fast was each bus moving?

08 Ben walks and jogs to work each day. He averages 3 miles an hour walking and 5 miles an hour jogging. The distance from home to work is 5 miles and Ben makes the trip in 1 hour 20 minutes. How far does Ben walk?

09 Justin's science teacher distributes 65 balloons to his students in his laboratory. When he gives 4 balloons to each of his students, 1 balloon will remain. How many students are in the laboratory?

10 How many liters of water must be added to 12 liters of a 25% acid-solution to make a 15% acid-solution?

12 Samuel invested $10,000 in stocks and bonds. Suppose he earned 5 percent on stocks and 7 percent on bonds. If he earned $196 more on bonds than on stocks, how much did he invest in each?

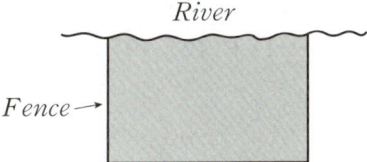

11 Paul has 74 feet of fencing and wants to fence off a rectangular field that borders a straight river, as shown in the figure above. If the length of the field is 14 feet more than three times the width, what are the dimensions of the field if no fencing is needed along the river?

13 At a concert, adult tickets were sold at $27 each and students tickets at $19. If the total amount of revenue from tickets sold was $4,000 and there were 160 people in attendance, how many of each ticket were sold?

Chapter Test — Level 1

01 Which of the following expression is NOT equal to $\frac{2}{15}\left(10x-\frac{5}{4}\right)$?

(A) $-\frac{2}{15}\left(-10x+\frac{5}{4}\right)$

(B) $\left(10x-\frac{5}{4}\right)\div\frac{15}{2}$

(C) $\left(-\frac{5}{2}x+5\right)\div\left(-\frac{15}{8}\right)$

(D) $\frac{2}{3}\left(2x-\frac{1}{4}\right)$

(E) $\left(-\frac{5}{4}x+\frac{5}{32}\right)\div\left(-\frac{15}{16}\right)$

02 Find the value of ab from the expression $-3(2x+1)+(12x-9)\div 3=ax+b$.

03 The coefficient of x is 6 and the constant is 4 when the expression $\frac{1}{4}(ax-8)-\frac{1}{3}(9x+2b)+5$ is simplified. What is the value of $a\div b$?

04 Find the value of $a+b+c$ from the expression $\dfrac{3x-4}{6}+\dfrac{5x-1}{2}=\dfrac{ax+b}{c}$.

05 Assuming $A=x-\dfrac{1}{2}$ and $B=2x+3$, simplify the expression $4\left(A+\dfrac{5}{2}\right)-3(B-2)$ in terms of x.

06 If the solution of $5x+3=12x-3(2x-2)$ is $x=a$ and the solution of $\dfrac{x-2}{3}=\dfrac{3x-1}{2}-6$ is $x=b$, what is the value of ab?

07 Solve the equation $0.6x-0.08=0.2+0.1(2x-4)$.

Chapter Test — Level 1

08 If both of the equation $\dfrac{3-(x-6)}{2}=-2(3x-4)+13$ and $0.4(2x-3k)-1=0.5(-x+4)$ has the same solution, what is the value of k?

09 If the equation $6(3x-2a)+4=-2(bx+5)-8x$ is true for all x, what is the value of $6a-b$?

10 For what value of k does the equation $4-\dfrac{1}{6}(4x+5)=2kx+6$ have no solutions for x?

11 For what value of m does the equation $\dfrac{6x-3m}{2}=4(1+x)-x$ have infinitely many solutions for x?

12 Chris is now 36 years old, and his daughter Helen is 6 years old. In how many years will Chris be twice as old as Helen?

13 A pharmacist has a 45% saline solution and a 20% saline solution. How much of each must be mixed to make 20 liters of a 30% saline solution?

14 There are two different squares. The length of one side of the larger square is 3 centimeters longer than the length of one side of the smaller square. If the sum of the perimeters of the two squares is 68 centimeters, what is the length of one side of the larger square?

Chapter Test — Level 2

01 If $24-3x$ is 8 less than twice of 10, what is the value of $5x$?

02 Find the value of $a+b+c$ from the expression $\dfrac{2x+3}{6}+\dfrac{x-2}{8}-\dfrac{3x-1}{12}=\dfrac{ax+b}{c}$.

03 Assuming $A=3x-1$, $B=2x+y-3$, and $C=-2y+2$, simplify the expression $\dfrac{1}{2}(A+4B)-2(B+C)$ in terms of x and y.

04 If $x=k$ is the solution to the equation $\dfrac{3(x-3)+1}{4}=\dfrac{2(5x+4)}{3}-4x+1$, what is the solution of the equation $0.4(3k-5)+0.5x=\dfrac{x+6}{4}$?

05 Solve the equation $1.4-(1-x)=\dfrac{4}{3}(x-3)$

06 In some expression, $\dfrac{1}{2}(-4x+5)$ should be subtracted from A, but added to A by mistake. If the resulting expression is $\dfrac{3}{2}x-4$,

(1) Find the expression A.

(2) Find the correct expression.

07 If both of the equation $4x-2a=-(3x+1)+2$ and $\dfrac{1}{3}(bx+6)+1=\dfrac{5-3x}{6}$ have the solution $x=5$, what is the value of a and b?

Chapter 1. Linear Equations 55

Chapter Test — Level 2

08 For what value of a and b does the equation $0.4(-2x-5a)=\dfrac{bx+3}{6}-\dfrac{1}{5}$ have infinitely many solutions for x?

09 $\dfrac{3x-4}{2}-\dfrac{\boxed{}}{3}=\dfrac{4x+1}{6}$

Write the correct expression in $\boxed{}$ above.

10 The sum of three consecutive even integers is 144. What is the largest even integer?

11 Stephen took a taxi to the airport. The taxi driver charges a basic fare of $6 plus $1.2 per mile. If Stephen paid a total of $70 including a tip of $10, what is the distance he traveled to the airport?

12 In K high school, the number of male students increased by 15% and the number of female students decreased by 5% compared to last year. If the total number of students last year was 700 and this year has increased by 41 compared to last year, what was the number of male students last year in K high school?

Chapter 2

Graphing Lines

1. Introduction to Graphing Linear Equations
2. Two Forms of the Lines
3. Parallel and Perpendicular Lines
4. Chapter Test

1 Introduction to Graphing Linear Equations

01 The Coordinate Plane

We can plot points on the coordinate plane (sometimes called the Cartesian plane or xy-plane). The horizontal and vertical number lines are each called the x-axis and y-axis, respectively. From the ordered pair of the form (x, y), the first number is the x-coordinate and corresponds to the numbers horizontal. The second is the y-coordinate and corresponds to the numbers vertical. Also, the point of intersection of two axes is called the origin, which has an ordered pair of $(0, 0)$. Refer to the following figure below.

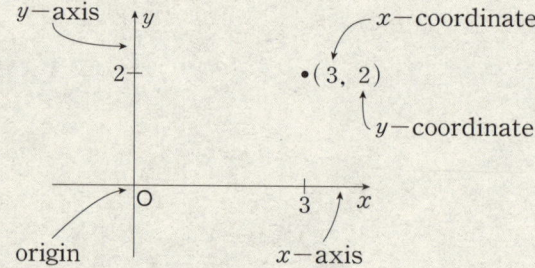

Two axes $x-$ and $y-$axis usually called the coordinate axes, divide the plane into four regions called quadrants. The quadrants are numbered counterclockwise using Roman numerals I, II, III, and IV. The signs of the coordinates differ from quadrant to quadrant, indicated below.

$$
\begin{array}{c|c}
\text{II} & \text{I} \\
(-, +) & (+, +) \\
\hline
\text{III} & \text{IV} \\
(-, -) & (+, -)
\end{array}
$$

02 Standard Form

The standard form of a linear equation $Ax+By=C$, where A, B, and C are constants, and A and B are not both zero, is a straight line. We can use the $x-$ and $y-$intercepts to draw the graph.

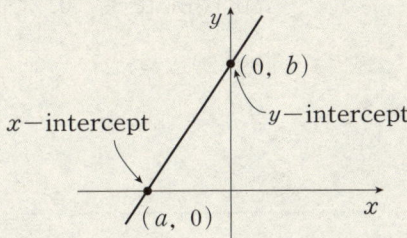

1. The $x-$intercept

    (1) The $x-$intercept of the line is the point at which the line crosses the $x-$axis.

    (2) It is the value of x coordinate when $y=0$.

    (3) If the $x-$intercept is a, the coordinate is $(a, 0)$.

2. The $y-$intercept

    (1) The $y-$intercept of the line is the point at which the line crosses the $y-$axis.

    (2) The value of y coordinate when $x=0$.

    (3) If the $y-$intercept is b, the coordinate is $(0, b)$.

Concept Check

Find the $x-$ and $y-$intercepts of the line $-3x+5y=15$.

For $x-$intercept, let $y=0$ and then solve for x.

For $y-$intercept, let $x=0$ and then solve for y.

$$-3x+5y=15$$
$$-3x+5(0)=15$$
$$-3x=15$$
$$x=-5$$

The x-intercept is $x=-5$ and its coordinate is $(-5, 0)$.

$$-3x+5y=15$$
$$-3(0)+5y=15$$
$$5y=15$$
$$y=3$$

The y-intercept is $y=3$ and its coordinate is $(0, 3)$.

Example 1

Graph the equation $2x+5y=10$ using $x-$ and $y-$intercepts.

Solution

The x-intercept: let $y=0$.
$2x+5(0)=10$
$2x=10$, $x=5$
The y-intercept: let $x=0$.
$2(0)+5y=10$
$5y=10$, $y=2$
Draw a line through two points $(5, 0)$ and $(0, 2)$ as shown on the right.

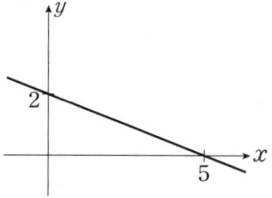

Check Point 1

Solutions_Page 22

Graph the equation using $x-$ and $y-$intercepts.

① $4x-3y=-12$

② $2x-\dfrac{y}{4}=6$

03 Slope of a Line

The slope(or gradient) of a line is a measure of its steepness. It is the ratio of the difference in y values to the difference in x values. So the slope is often called the average rate of change. The difference in y values is usually written Δy, and it's often called the rise. In the same way, the difference in x values is usually written Δx, and it's often called the run.

$$\text{Slope} = \frac{\text{difference in } y \text{ values}}{\text{difference in } x \text{ values}} = \frac{\Delta y}{\Delta x} = \frac{\text{rise}}{\text{run}}, \text{ where } \Delta x \neq 0$$

The slope, usually denoted by the letter m, of a line passing through the points (x_1, y_1) and (x_2, y_2) is given by $m = \frac{\Delta y}{\Delta x} = \frac{y_2 - y_1}{x_2 - x_1}$, where $x_2 - x_1 \neq 0$

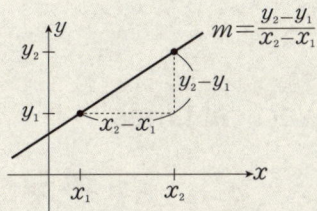

1. A line with a positive slope increases from left to right.
2. A line with a negative slope decreases from left to right.

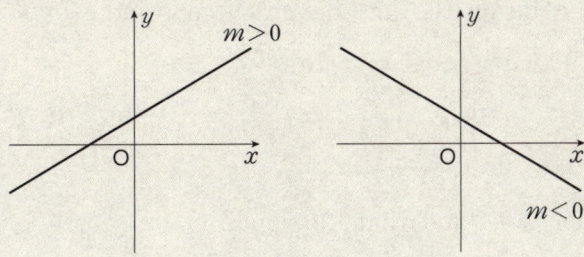

Example 2

Find the slope of the line that passes through the points (1, 5) and (5, 7).

Solution

Let $(x_1, y_1) = (1, 5)$ and $(x_2, y_2) = (5, 7)$.

The slope $m = \dfrac{y_2 - y_1}{x_2 - x_1} = \dfrac{7-5}{5-1} = \dfrac{2}{4} = \dfrac{1}{2}$.

The slope of the line is $\dfrac{1}{2}$.

Check Point 2

Solutions_Page 22

Find the slope of the line that passes through the points.

① (3, 5) and (0, −1)   ② (−2, 5) and (3, −4)

04 Horizontal and Vertical Lines

1. Horizontal Lines

   (1) A horizontal line is a line whose equation is of the form $y = k$ where k is a constant.

   (2) All points that lie on the line have a y coordinate of k.

   (3) The slope is always equal to zero.

   Concept Check

   Graph the equation $y = 4$ and find its slope.

   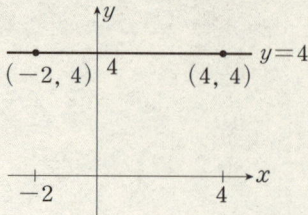

Let $(x_1, y_1) = (-2, 4)$ and $(x_2, y_2) = (4, 4)$.

The slope $m = \dfrac{y_2 - y_1}{x_2 - x_1} = \dfrac{4 - 4}{4 - (-2)} = \dfrac{0}{6} = 0$.

The slope of the horizontal line is 0.

2. Vertical Lines

   (1) A vertical line is a line whose equation is of the form $x = h$ where h is a constant.

   (2) All points that lie on the line have a x coordinate of h.

   (3) The slope is always undefined.

Concept Check

Graph the equation $x = 2$ and find its slope.

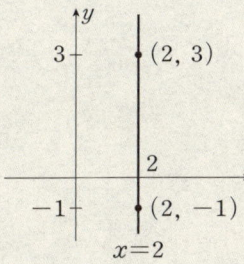

Let $(x_1, y_1) = (2, -1)$ and $(x_2, y_2) = (3, -1)$.

The slope $m = \dfrac{y_2 - y_1}{x_2 - x_1} = \dfrac{3 - (-1)}{2 - 2} = \dfrac{4}{0} =$ undefined.

The slope of the vertical line is undefined.

Example 3

Graph each equation and find its slope.

① $y=-5$ ② $x=3$

Solution

①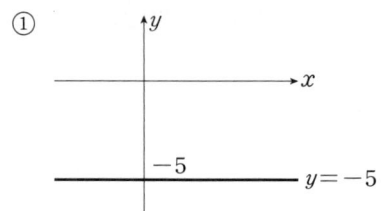

The slope of the line is 0.

②

The slope of the line is undefined.

Check Point 3

Solutions_Page 22

Graph each equation and find its slope.

① $x=-4$ ② $y=2$

Review Exercise

01 Which point lies on the line defined by $4x-5y=-3$?

(A) $(-2, -1)$
(B) $(-1, -2)$
(C) $(2, 1)$
(D) $(1, 2)$
(E) $(2, -1)$

02 Graph the equation using $x-$ and $y-$intercepts.

(1) $6x-4y=12$

(2) $2x+3y=-9$

03 Find the slope of the line that passes through the points

(1) $(0, -2)$ and $(4, 6)$

(2) $\left(-\dfrac{3}{2}, 5\right)$ and $(1, -10)$

04 Find the slope of the line.

(1)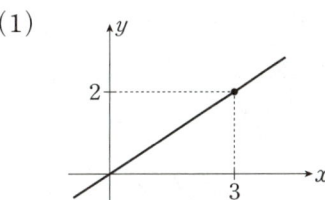

(2)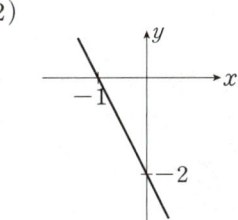

(3)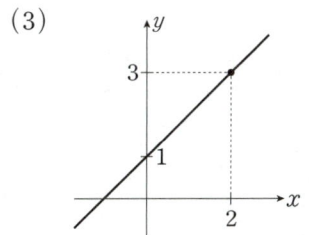

Review Exercise

(4)
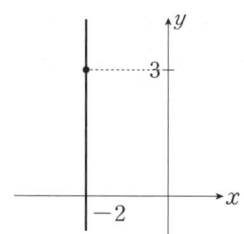

(5)
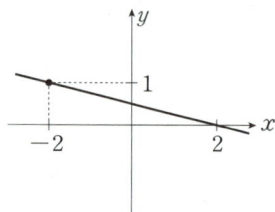

(6)
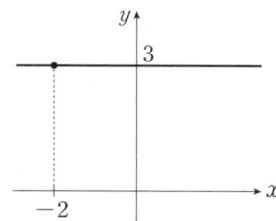

(2) $\left(a, \dfrac{1}{2}\right)$, $(3, -8)$; $m=4$

(3) $(-2, b)$, $(2, -7)$; $m=0$

(4) $\left(-\dfrac{1}{2}, \dfrac{5}{2}\right)$, $\left(a, \dfrac{3}{4}\right)$; $m=$ undefined

Challenging

06 If the slope of the line that passes through the points $(k+1, 4)$ and $(2, 3k-1)$ is 2, what is the value of k?

05 Each pair of points lies on a line with the given slope m. Find a or b.

(1) $(4, 7)$, $(-2, b)$; $m=-\dfrac{1}{3}$

Challenging

07 If the three points $(1, 4)$, $(-2, 3a+1)$, and $(2, 2a-3)$ lie on the same line, what is the value of a?

2 Two Forms of Equation in Line

01 Point-Slope Form

The point−slope formula for finding the equation of a line is

$$y - y_1 = m(x - x_1)$$

where m is the slope and (x_1, y_1) is a point on the line.

Concept Check

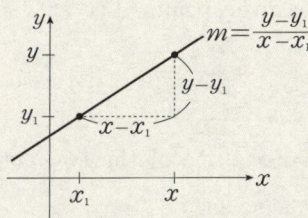

If the point (x, y) is on the line with slope m through the point (x_1, y_1), then we have

$\dfrac{y - y_1}{x - x_1} = m$ → The slope of the line passing through (x, y) and (x_1, y_1)

$y - y_1 = m(x - x_1)$ → Multiply both sides of the equation by $x - x_1$

Example 1

Find the equation of the line through $(3, 1)$ that has a slope of -2.

Solution

$y - y_1 = m(x - x_1)$ → The point−slope form
$y - 1 = -2(x - 3)$ → $(x_1, y_1) = (3, 1)$ and $m = -2$

$$y - 1 = -2(x - 3)$$

Check Point 1

Find the equation of the line through $(-2, -5)$ that has a slope of 3.

Example 2

Write the equation of the line that passes through the points $(4, -3)$ and $(-2, 5)$.

Solution

First, we need to find the slope using the given points. Let $(x_1, y_1) = (4, -3)$ and $(x_2, y_2) = (-2, 5)$. Then the slope is

$$m = \frac{y_2 - y_1}{x_2 - x_1} = \frac{5 - (-3)}{-2 - 4} = \frac{8}{-6} = -\frac{4}{3}$$

Now, write the equation $y - y_1 = m(x - x_1)$ using one of the two points.

$y - y_1 = m(x - x_1)$ → The point–slope form

$y - (-3) = -\frac{4}{3}(x - 4)$ → $(x_1, y_1) = (4, -3)$ and $m = -\frac{4}{3}$

$y + 3 = -\frac{4}{3}(x - 4)$ → Simplify the left side

$$y + 3 = -\frac{4}{3}(x - 4)$$

Note: You can also use the point $(x_2, y_2) = (-2, 5)$ to find the equation of the line.

Check Point 2

Write the equation of the line that passes through the points $(1, 4)$ and $(3, -3)$.

Example 3

Graph the equation of the line $y + 4 = -3(x - 2)$.

Solution

The equation is in point–slope form, $y - y_1 = m(x - x_1)$. A point $(x_1, y_1) = (2, -4)$ and the slope is $m = -3$.

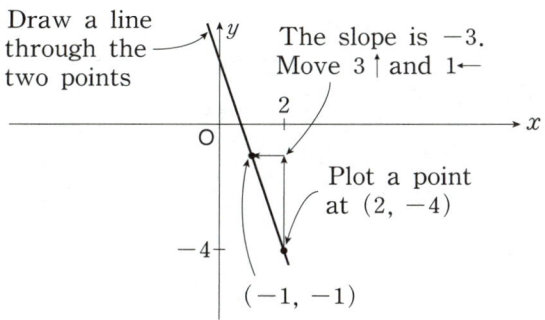

Draw a line through the two points

The slope is -3. Move $3\uparrow$ and $1\leftarrow$

Plot a point at $(2, -4)$

$(-1, -1)$

Check Point 3

Solutions_Page 25

Graph the equation of the line $y+2=\dfrac{1}{2}(x+3)$.

02 Slope-Intercept Form

The slope-intercept form of the equation is

$$y=mx+b$$

where m is the slope and b is the y-intercept of the line.

Concept Check

If we let (x_1, y_1), and (x_2, y_2) are two point on the line $y=mx+b$, we have two following equations $y_1=mx_1+b$ and $y_2=mx_2+b$. Therefore, the slope of the line is

$$\dfrac{y_2-y_1}{x_2-x_1}=\dfrac{mx_2+b-(mx_1+b)}{x_2-x_1}$$
$$=\dfrac{mx_2-mx_1}{x_2-x_1}=\dfrac{m(x_2-x_1)}{x_2-x_1}=m$$

The y-intercept of the line has x coordinate $x=0$. When $x=0$, $y=m(0)+b=b$. Therefore, $y=b$ is the y-intercept of the line.

Chapter 2. Graphing Lines

Example 4

Find the slope and y-intercept of the graph $y=3x+5$.

Solution

$y=mx+b \Leftrightarrow y=3x+5$

The slope is 3 and the y-intercept is 5.

Check Point 4

Solutions_Page 25

Find the slope and y-intercept of the graph $y=-4x+6$.

Example 5

Find the equation of the line that has a slope of 4 and y-intercept -3.

Solution

$y=mx+b$ → The slope-intercept form
$y=4x-3$ → Substitute 4 for m and -3 for b

$y=4x-3$

Check Point 5

Solutions_Page 25

Find the equation of the line that has a slope of $-\dfrac{2}{3}$ and y-intercept 3.

Example 6

Graph the equation of the line $y=\frac{3}{2}x-2$.

Solution

The equation is in slope−intercept form, $y=mx+b$. The slope is $m=\frac{3}{2}$ and the y−intercept is -2.

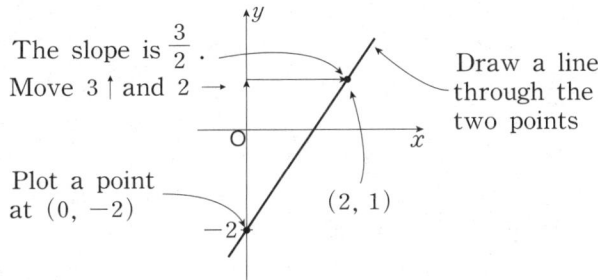

The slope is $\frac{3}{2}$. Move 3 ↑ and 2 →

Draw a line through the two points

Plot a point at $(0, -2)$

$(2, 1)$

Check Point 6

Solutions_Page 25

Graph the equation of the line $y=-2x+3$.

03 Intersection of Two Lines

When two lines intersect at one point, the $x-$ and $y-$coordinates of the intersection point are the same as shown below.

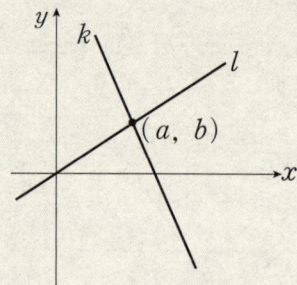

Intersection (a, b) is on both lines k and l.

Example 7

Fine the intersection point of two lines $y=3x-4$ and $y=-2x+11$.

Solution

At the intersection point, two lines have the same $x-$ and $y-$coordinates. So, let
$$3x-4=-2x+11$$
$$5x=15,\ x=3$$
Now, substitute 3 for x in the equation of either line.
$$y=3x-4$$
$$y=3(3)-4=5$$

Therefore, the intersection point is $(3, 5)$.

Check Point 7

Fine the intersection point of two lines $y=-\dfrac{1}{2}x+6$ and $y=3x-22$.

04 Application

The key to solving application problems is converting the words into mathematical equations. Refer to the following steps.

1. Identify the meaning of the problem and set the variables x and y.
2. Establish an equation of the relationship between x and y.
3. Solve the equation.
4. Make sure that the solution you find fits the meaning of the problem.

Example 8

Hours Worked	Wage
10	$220
20	$400
30	$580
40	$760

The table above shows the amount of time Lillian works and her total wage.

① What equation in a point−slope form that gives Lillian's wage at any time?

② What does the slope represent?

③ What does the y−intercept represent?

Solution

① Let x be the number of hours and y be the total wage. Then we can use two points, such as $(x_1, y_1) = (10, 220)$ and $(x_2, y_2) = (20, 400)$ to find the slope

$$m = \frac{y_2 - y_1}{x_2 - x_1} = \frac{400 - 220}{20 - 10} = \frac{180}{10} = 18.$$

Now, write the equation in point−slope form.

$$y-y_1=m(x-x_1)$$
$$y-220=18(x-10)$$

$$y-220=18(x-10)$$

② The slope with the units is
$$m=\frac{\$400-\$220}{(20-10)\text{hours}}=\frac{\$180}{10\text{ hours}}=\$18/\text{hour}$$
Therefore, the meaning of the slope is her hourly pay rate (she earns $18 per hour).

③ The y-intercept is her total wage when she worked zero hours.
So it represents a fixed amount of income per pay period.

Review Exercise

01 Write an equation in point–slope form of the line that passes through the given point and with the given slope m. Then write the equation in slope–intercept form.

(1) $(1, -4)$; $m=-3$

(2) $\left(-\dfrac{3}{2}, 4\right)$; $m=5$

02 Write an equation in point–slope form of the line that passes through the given points. Then write the equation in slope–intercept form.

(1) $(-5, 3)$, $(-3, -1)$

(2) $\left(2, -\dfrac{1}{2}\right)$, $\left(-\dfrac{3}{2}, 3\right)$

03 Graph the equation of the line.

(1) $y-3=(x-1)$

(2) $y-2=-\dfrac{3}{2}(x+2)$

(3) $y=-3x+2$

(4) $y=\dfrac{3}{4}x-3$

Review Exercise

04 Find the value of k such that the graph of the equation has the given slope m.

(1) $y = -3kx - 8$, $m = 2$

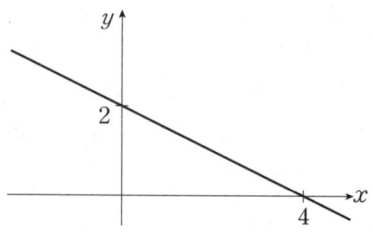

06 The graph above has the equation $y = mx + b$. Find the value of mb.

(2) $4x - 3ky = 12$, $m = -\dfrac{3}{2}$

05 A line in the xy-plane passes through the point $(6, 2)$ and has a slope of $-\dfrac{2}{3}$. Which of the following points lies on the line?

(A) $(-1, -6)$
(B) $(1, 4)$
(C) $(0, 5)$
(D) $(3, -4)$
(E) $(-3, 8)$

07 In the graph of $y = mx - 4$, the value of y decreases by 6 units as the value of x increases by 2 units. What is the value of m?

Challenging

08 If two graphs, $y=-4x+a$ and $y=bx-\frac{1}{2}$, are identical, what is the value of ab?

Challenging

09 Find the area bounded by three lines $y=x+1$, $y=-\frac{1}{2}x+4$, and y-axis.

10 A car repair service charges $65 for diagnosis and $40 per hour for repairs. How much will be charged if a certain car is repaired for 8 hours?

Renting a DVD

Days	Cost in dollars
3	$7
5	$13
7	$19

11 The data in the table shows the cost of renting a DVD by the day. Assuming the cost increases constantly as the number of days a DVD is rented, what is the cost if a DVD is rented for 10 days?

3. Parallel and Perpendicular Lines

01 Slope of $Ax+By=C$

The standard form of a linear equation is $Ax+By=C$, where A, B, and C are constants. If $B\neq 0$, then the slope and y-intercept of the graph $Ax+By=C$ are

$$Ax+By=C\,(B\neq 0) \Rightarrow y=-\frac{A}{B}x+\frac{C}{B} \Rightarrow \begin{cases} \text{Slope: } m=-\dfrac{A}{B} \\ y\text{-intercept: } b=\dfrac{C}{B} \end{cases}$$

Concept Check

The graph of linear equation $2x+3y=5$ has the slope $m=-\dfrac{2}{3}$ and the y-intercept $b=\dfrac{5}{3}$.

02 Parallel Lines

Two or more lines that never intersect each other are called parallel lines. Non-vertical lines are parallel when they have the same slope and different y-intercepts. Vertical lines are parallel when they have different x-intercept.

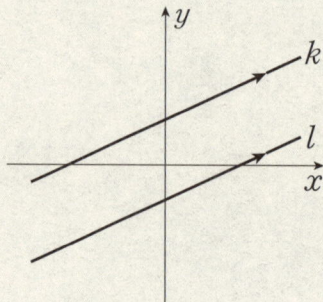

Concept Check

1. The graph of the lines $y=2x+1$ and $y=2x-3$ are parallel because they have the same slope $m=2$ and different y-intercepts.

2. The graph of the lines $y=3x+1$ and $y=2x-3$ are NOT parallel because they have different slope.

3. If two lines k and l are parallel, we write $k \parallel l$.

Example 1

Find the equation in slope-intercept form of the line that passes through $(3, -2)$ and is parallel to the line $5x-2y=4$.

Solution

Step 1 The slope of the line $5x-2y=4$ is $m=-\frac{5}{-2}=\frac{5}{2}$. The parallel lines have the same slope.

Step 2 Write an equation of the line in point-slope form that passes through $(x_1, y_1)=(3, -2)$ with slope $m=\frac{5}{2}$.

$$y-y_1=m(x-x_1) \quad \rightarrow \text{The point-slope form}$$
$$y-(-2)=\frac{5}{2}(x-3) \quad \rightarrow (x_1, y_1)=(3,-2) \text{ and } m=\frac{5}{2}$$
$$y+2=\frac{5}{2}x-\frac{15}{2} \quad \rightarrow \text{Simplify each side}$$
$$y=\frac{5}{2}x-\frac{19}{2} \quad \rightarrow \text{Subtract 2 to each side}$$

$$y=\frac{5}{2}x-\frac{19}{2}$$

Check Point 1 Solutions_Page 29

Find the equation in slope-intercept form of the line that passes through $(-4, 5)$ and is parallel to the line $-2x+4y=1$

03 Perpendicular Lines

Two lines that forms right angle when they intersect are called perpendicular lines. If two non-vertical lines are perpendicular, then the product of their slopes is −1. Two numbers whose product is −1 are opposite reciprocals. Also, a vertical line and a horizontal line are perpendicular lines.

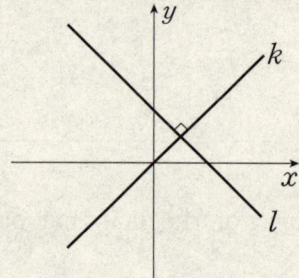

Concept Check

1. The graph of the lines $y=\frac{2}{3}x+1$ and $y=-\frac{3}{2}x+5$ are perpendicular because the product of their slopes is $\frac{2}{3}\times\left(-\frac{3}{2}\right)=-1$.

   $\Rightarrow -\frac{3}{2}$ is the opposite reciprocal of $\frac{2}{3}$ and also $\frac{2}{3}$ is the opposite reciprocal of $-\frac{3}{2}$.

2. The graph of the lines $y=2x+1$ and $y=-2x-3$ are NOT perpendicular because the product of their slopes is $2\times(-2)=-4\neq-1$.

3. If two lines k and l are perpendicular, we write $k \perp l$.

Example 2

Find the equation in slope-intercept form of the line that passes through $(-1, 5)$ and is perpendicular to the line $3x+6y=1$.

> **Solution**

Step 1 The slope of the line $3x+6y=1$ is $m=-\frac{3}{6}=-\frac{1}{2}$. The opposite reciprocal of $-\frac{1}{2}$ is 2. Therefore, the perpendicular line has a slope of 2.

Step 2 Write an equation of the line in point−slope form that passes through $(x_1, y_1)=(-1, 5)$ with slope $m=2$.

$y-y_1=m(x-x_1)$ → The point−slope form
$y-5=2(x-(-1))$ → $(x_1, y_1)=(-1, 5)$ and $m=2$
$y-5=2x+2$ → Simplify the right side
$y=2x+7$ → Add 5 to each side

$$y=2x+7$$

> **Check Point 2** Solutions_Page 29

Find the equation in slope−intercept form of the line that passes through $(3, 0)$ and is perpendicular to the line $6x-4y=5$.

Review Exercise

01 Write an equation in slope−intercept form of the line that passes through the given point and is <u>parallel</u> to the line of the given equation.

(1) $(3, -4)$; $y=4x-5$

(2) $\left(-\dfrac{1}{2}, \dfrac{3}{4}\right)$; $4x+2y=3$

02 Write an equation in slope−intercept form of the line that passes through the given point and is <u>perpendicular</u> to the line of the given equation.

(1) $(-3, -8)$; $y=-x+6$

(2) $\left(5, \dfrac{1}{3}\right)$; $2y-5x=4$

03 Which equation represents the line that passes through $(2, 5)$ and is perpendicular to the graph of $y=-2x+3$?

(A) $x-2y=-8$

(B) $2x-y=-1$

(C) $2x-2y=-6$

(D) $2x+2y=14$

(E) $2x+y=9$

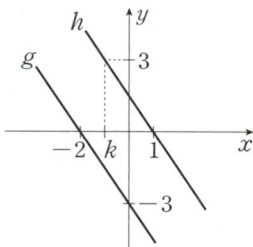

04 If line g is parallel to the line h in the graph above, what is the value of k?

84 Chapter 2. Graphing Lines

05 The equation of line k is $3x+4y=11$, and the equation of line p is $4x-3y=9$. Which statement about the two lines is true?

(A) Lines k and p have the same x-intercept.

(B) Lines k and p have the same y-intercept.

(C) Lines k and p are parallel.

(D) Lines k and p are perpendicular.

(E) Lines k and p are two identical lines.

Questions 6 and 7

Refer to the following graph.

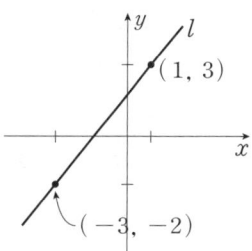

06 Which of the following is an equation of the line that is parallel to line l?

(A) $5x+4y=3$

(B) $4x+5y=3$

(C) $5x-4y=-3$

(D) $-4x+5y=-3$

(E) None of the above.

07 Which of the following is an equation of the line that is perpendicular to line l?

(A) $5x+4y=3$

(B) $4x+5y=3$

(C) $5x-4y=-3$

(D) $-4x+5y=-3$

(E) None of the above.

Chapter Test — Level 1

01 If the $x-$ and $y-$intercepts of the graph $3x+12y=36$ is a and b, respectively, what is the value of ab?

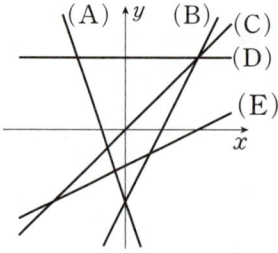

02 In the figure above, which line has the smallest slope?

03 If the slope of the line that passes through the points $(-2,\ a+1)$ and $(2a-3,\ 6)$ is 3, what is the value of a?

04 Suppose the line k is horizontal that passes through the point $(b, -5)$ where b is a real number. Find the equation of the line.

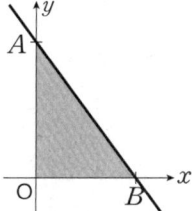

05 If the equation of the line that passes through A and B above is $7x+5y=21$, what is the area of $\triangle AOB$?

06 Write an equation in slope–intercept form of the line that passes through the points $(3, -4)$ and $(-1, -9)$.

Chapter Test — Level 1

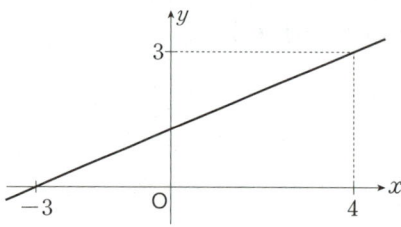

07 The graph above has the equation $y=mx+b$. Find the value of $m+b$.

08 If two graphs, $y=(4m+n)x+5$ and $y=mx-(3n+7)$, are identical, what is the value of mn?

09 Write an equation in slope–intercept form of the line that passes through the point $(2, 8)$ and is parallel to the line $y=-\dfrac{3}{2}x+1$.

10 Write an equation in slope−intercept form of the line that passes through the point $(-3, 0)$ and is perpendicular to the line $3x+4y=10$.

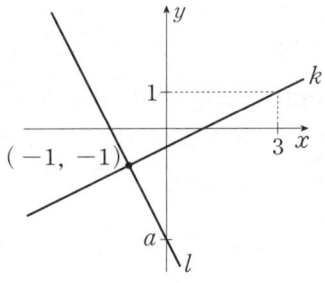

11 If line k is perpendicular to the line l in the graph above, what is the value of a?

Chapter Test — Level 1

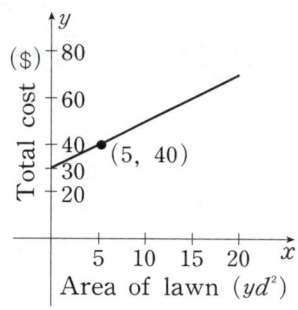

12 Samuel is hiring a company to mow the lawn in his backyard. The company charges a one−time fee plus a certain amount per square yard of mowing. The graph above shows the relationship between the number of square yards of mowing and the total cost, in dollars.

(1) Which of the following quantity represent the cost per square yard of mowing?

(A) x−intercept
(B) y−intercept
(C) Slope
(D) Point−slope form
(E) Slope−intercept form

(2) Find the equation of the line in slope−intercept form.

13 The total cost y in dollars of renting a certain premium car for x days is given by equation $y=150+70x$. If the total cost was $570, for how many days was the car rented?

14 Andrea is an urban planner. As an independent contractor, she charges a $160 fee plus $30 per hour for each contract with the city. Find the total amount she charges for 12 hours project.

15 In 2016, City A had only 16,000 trees. Starting in 2017, the city has been planting 50 trees each month. At this rate, how many trees will City A have in 2025?

Chapter Test — Level 2

01 If the line $5x-2y=-\dfrac{3}{2}$ has the x-intercept a, the y-intercept b, and the slope c, what is the value of $\dfrac{ac}{b}$?

02 Let k be the line that passes through the points $(a, 0)$ and $(2, 4)$. Find the equation in point-slope form of the line k in terms of a.

03 Suppose the line passing through the origin also passes through the two points $(a-3, 4)$ and $(3a+2, -2)$. What is the value of a?

04 If the slope and the y-intercept of the line $2ax-5y=b$ is 2 and 6 respectively, what is the value of $a+b$?

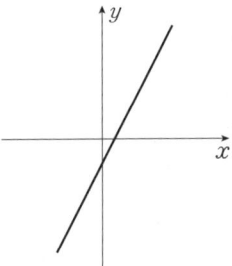

05 The line in the figure above has the equation $y=mx+b$. In which quadrant(s) does the graph of line $y=-\dfrac{b}{m}x-bm$ not pass?

(A) I (B) II (C) III (D) IV (E) I and II

06 Find the area bounded by three lines $y=x+3$, $4x+3y=16$, and x-axis.

Chapter Test — Level 2

07 The graph of a line in the xy-plane has slope -4 and contains the point $(1, -3)$. The graph of a second line passes through the point $(2, 10)$ and has x-intercept of $-\dfrac{1}{2}$. If the two lines intersect at the point (m, n), what is the value of $m \div n$?

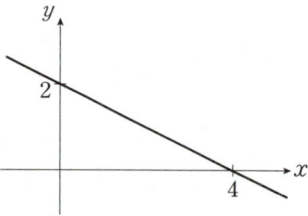

08 Write an equation in slope-intercept form of the line that has the x-intercept at $x = -2$ and is perpendicular to the line shown above.

09 Suppose the line $y = mx - 2$ is parallel to the line $y = -\dfrac{2}{3}x + 1$ and intersects with the line $y = kx + 3$ at the x-axis. What is the value of $m + k$?

10 If the two parallel lines $y=\frac{2}{3}x+5$ and $y=mx+b$ intersect the x-axis at the points A and B respectively and $\overline{AB}=12$, what is the value of mb?

11 At a video game center, g games are played by adding q quarters. If $g=2q+1$, how many additional quarters are needed to play 6 additional games?

12 To edit a college essay, Mr. Jackson charges $30 for the first 3 pages and $14 per page after the first 3 pages. How much does Mr. Jackson charge if he edits 23 pages of a college essay?

13 Luke starts a car wash service. He spends $80 on supplies. He plans to charge $9 for each car wash service. What is his profit if he has done 20 car wash services?

memo

Chapter **3**

System of Linear Equations

1. Solving System of Linear Equations, Part 1
2. Solving System of Linear Equations, Part 2
3. Application of Linear Systems
4. Chapter Test

Solving System of Linear Equations, Part 1

01 Introduction to System of Linear Equations

1. Definition

    The general form of a system of linear equations in two variables is written as
    $\begin{cases} a_1x + b_1y = c_1 \\ a_2x + b_2y = c_2 \end{cases}$

    Concept Check

    $\begin{cases} 2x+y=4 \\ x-3y=1 \end{cases}$ and $\begin{cases} x-2y=0 \\ x+y=2 \end{cases}$ are examples of the system of linear equations in two variables.

2. The Solutions to the System

    A solution of the system is an ordered pair that is a solution of each equation in the system. Not all the systems have one solution. They sometimes have no solutions or infinitely many solutions. A linear system is said to be consistent if it has solutions, and inconsistent otherwise.

    Concept Check

    The ordered pair $(2, 3)$ is the solution to the system $\begin{cases} x+y=5 \\ x+2y=8 \end{cases}$ because
    $\begin{cases} 2+3=5 \\ 2+2(3)=8 \end{cases} \Rightarrow \begin{cases} 5=5 \\ 8=8 \end{cases}$

Example 1

If the solution to the system $\begin{cases} ax+y=2 \\ 3x-by=1 \end{cases}$ is $(1, 3)$, what is the value of $a+b$?

Solution

Substitute $(1, 3)$ into the system of equations $\begin{cases} ax+y=2 \\ 3x-by=1 \end{cases}$. Then, we have

$$a(1)+(3)=2 \quad \text{and} \quad 3(1)-b(3)=1$$
$$a+3=2 \qquad\qquad\qquad 3-3b=1$$
$$a=-1 \qquad\qquad\qquad -3b=-2$$
$$b=\frac{2}{3}$$

Therefore, $a+b=-1+\frac{2}{3}=-\frac{1}{3}$.

$$a+b=-\frac{1}{3}$$

Check Point 1

If the solution to the system $\begin{cases} 4x-my=8 \\ nx+3y=-4 \end{cases}$ is $(-1, -2)$, what is the value of $m-n$?

02 Graphical Interpretation of Solutions

A system of two linear equations can be solved graphically, by graphing both equations in the same coordinate plane. The solution of a system of linear equations in two variables is the point of intersection of their graphs.

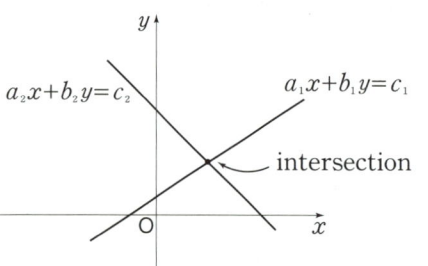	1. There is one intersection. 2. There is one solution. 3. The system is consistent and independent.
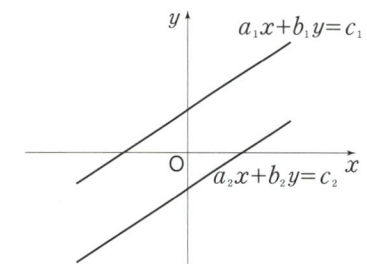	1. Two lines are parallel, which means that is no intersection. 2. There is no solution. 3. The system is inconsistent.
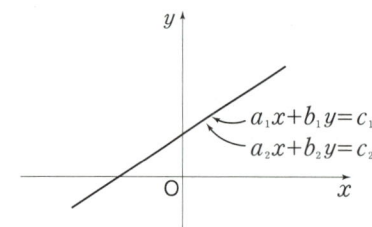	1. Since two lines are identical, there are infinitely many intersections. 2. There are infinitely many solutions. 3. The system is consistent and dependent.

03 Solving Systems using Substitution

Here are the basic steps of the substitution method.

1. Take one of the equations and solve for either x or y.
2. Substitute the expression for the variable into the other equation. This gives us an equation with only one variable.
3. Solve the equation to find the value of the variable.
4. Substitute this value into one of the earlier equations and solve it to find the value of the second variable.

Example 2

Solve the system $\begin{cases} x-y=4 \\ 2x+y=5 \end{cases}$ using the substitution method.

Solution

Step 1 Solve one of the equations for one of the variables.

$x-y=4$ → The first equation
$x=y+4$ → Solve the equation for x

Step 2 Substitute $y+4$ for x in the other equation and solve for y.

$2x+y=5$ → The second equation
$2(y+4)+y=5$ → Substitute $y+4$ for x
$2y+8+y=5$ → Simplify
$3y=-3$ → Subtract both sides by 8
$y=-1$ → Divide both sides by 3

Step 3 Substitute -1 for y in either equation and solve for x.

$x-(-1)=4$ → Substitute $y=-1$ back into the equation $x-y=4$.
$x+1=4$ → Simplify
$x=3$ → Subtract both sides by 1

Therefore, the solution is $(3, -1)$.

Check Point 2

Solve the following systems using the substitution method.

① $\begin{cases} x-2y=-6 \\ 2y-2x=9 \end{cases}$

② $\begin{cases} 3x+y=4 \\ 2x-5y=14 \end{cases}$

04 Solving Systems using Elimination

Here are the basic steps of the elimination method.

1. Multiply or divide one or both equations so that one variable has coefficients of the same size in both equations.
2. Eliminate this variable by either adding or subtracting one equation from the other.

Example 3

Solve the system $\begin{cases} x-2y=-1 \\ 2x+3y=12 \end{cases}$ using the elimination method.

Solution

Step 1 Eliminate one of the variables. Multiply $x-2y=-1$ by 2 and then subtract.

$\begin{cases} (x-2y=-1)\cdot 2 \\ 2x+3y=12 \end{cases} \Rightarrow \begin{array}{r} 2x-4y=-2 \\ -\underline{2x+3y=12} \\ -7y=-14 \\ y=2 \end{array}$

→ Subtract the equation
→ Divide both sides by -7

Step 2 Solve for the eliminated variable using one of the equations.

$x-2y=-1$ → The first equation
$x-2(2)=-1$ → Substitute 2 for y
$x=3$ → Solve for x

Therefore, the solution is $(3, 2)$.

Check Point 3

Solve the following systems using the elimination method.

① $\begin{cases} x-2y=12 \\ 3x-y=-4 \end{cases}$
② $\begin{cases} 4x+y=-5 \\ 3x-2y=-12 \end{cases}$

05 Linear Systems with Infinitely Many Solutions

Some systems of two linear equations have an infinite number of solutions. This means that every solution of one equation is also a solution to the other equation.

1. When one of the variables is eliminated, we have the equation $0 \cdot x = 0$ and $0 \cdot y = 0$.

2. In the system $\begin{cases} a_1 x + b_1 y = c_1 \\ a_2 x + b_2 y = c_2 \end{cases}$, if $\dfrac{a_1}{a_2} = \dfrac{b_1}{b_2} = \dfrac{c_1}{c_2}$, two equations are exactly equal so that there are infinitely many solutions to the system.

Example 4

Solve the system $\begin{cases} 2x-y=2 \\ 4x-2y=4 \end{cases}$.

Solution

Method 1:

$\begin{cases} 2x-y=2 \\ 4x-2y=4 \end{cases} \Rightarrow y = 2x - 2$

Substitute $2x-2$ for y in the second equation.

$4x - 2(2x-2) = 4$
$\quad 4x - 4x + 4 = 4$

$$4x - 4x = 4 - 4$$
$$0 \cdot x = 0$$

Method 2:

From $\begin{cases} 2x - y = 2 \\ 4x - 2y = 4 \end{cases}$, we have $\dfrac{2}{4} = \dfrac{-1}{-2} = \dfrac{2}{4}$.

Therefore, the system has infinitely many solutions.

Check Point 4

Solutions_Page 38

Solve the system $\begin{cases} 2x - y = 3 \\ -6x + 3y = -9 \end{cases}$.

06 Linear Systems with No Solutions

Some systems of two linear equations have no solutions. This means that no ordered pair satisfies both of the equations in the system.

1. When one of the variables is eliminated, we have the equation $0 \cdot x \neq 0$ and $0 \cdot y \neq 0$.

2. In the system $\begin{cases} a_1 x + b_1 y = c_1 \\ a_2 x + b_2 y = c_2 \end{cases}$, if $\dfrac{a_1}{a_2} = \dfrac{b_1}{b_2} \neq \dfrac{c_1}{c_2}$, two lines are parallel, and there are no solutions to the system.

Example 5

Solve the system $\begin{cases} 2x + y = 1 \\ 6x + 3y = 4 \end{cases}$.

Solution

Method 1:

$$\begin{cases} 2x+y=1 \\ 6x+3y=4 \end{cases} \Rightarrow y=-2x+1$$

Substitute $-2x+1$ for y in the second equation.

$6x+3(-2x+1)=4$
$\quad 6x-6x+3=4$
$\quad\quad 6x-6x=4-3$
$\quad\quad\quad 0\cdot x=1 \;\rightarrow\; 0\cdot x \neq 0$

Method 2:

From $\begin{cases} 2x+y=1 \\ 6x+3y=4 \end{cases}$, we have $\dfrac{2}{6}=\dfrac{1}{3}\neq\dfrac{1}{4}$.

Therefore, the system has no solution.

Check Point 5

Solve the system $\begin{cases} -x+2y=3 \\ 3x-6y=-8 \end{cases}$.

Review Exercise

01 If the solution to the system
$\begin{cases} 1 - \frac{by}{4} = 4 \\ 6ax + 2y = 42 \end{cases}$ is $\left(\frac{3}{2},\ 12\right)$,
what is the value of ab?

(2) $\begin{cases} x - 12y = 4 \\ 3x = 20y + 28 \end{cases}$

(3) $\begin{cases} 6x - 4y = -12 \\ 2x - y = -7 \end{cases}$

02 If the x-coordinate of the solution to the system $\begin{cases} 2x - y = 9 \\ 3ax + ay = 11 \end{cases}$ is 4, what is the value of a?

(4) $\begin{cases} 5x + 4y = 2 \\ 3x + y = 4 \end{cases}$

03 Solve the system using the substitution method.

(1) $\begin{cases} 3x - 5y = -1 \\ x + 2y = 7 \end{cases}$

04 Solve the system using the elimination method.

(1) $\begin{cases} 3x - 4y = -9 \\ -3x + 5y = 6 \end{cases}$

(2) $\begin{cases} 3x+2y=13 \\ 4x-4y=-1 \end{cases}$

(3) $\begin{cases} 4x+6y=12 \\ -2x-3y=-6 \end{cases}$

(4) $\begin{cases} -x-6y=17 \\ 5x-3y=14 \end{cases}$

06 For what values of a and b does the system $\begin{cases} x+4y=a \\ 2x=by+10 \end{cases}$ have infinitely many solutions?

07 For what values of a does the system $\begin{cases} x=ay+2 \\ 3x-4y=5 \end{cases}$ have no solution?

Challenging

05 If $x=2$ and $y=-1$ is solution to the system $\begin{cases} ax-by=5 \\ bx+ay=-2 \end{cases}$ what is the value of a?

2 Solving System of Linear Equations, Part 2

01 Linear Systems with Parentheses

Eliminate the parentheses first and then solve the system.

Concept Check

$$\begin{cases} 2(3-x)+3(x+y)=2 \\ 5(x+2y)-x=3 \end{cases} \xrightarrow{\text{Eliminate the parentheses}} \begin{cases} 6-2x+3x+3y=2 \\ 5x+10y-x=3 \end{cases}$$

$$\xrightarrow{\text{Simplify}} \begin{cases} x+3y=-4 \\ 4x+10y=3 \end{cases}$$

Example 1

Solve the system $\begin{cases} 2(x-3)+3y=-9 \\ 2(5-y)-x=11 \end{cases}$.

Solution

$$\begin{cases} 2(x-3)+3y=-9 \\ 2(5-y)-x=11 \end{cases} \Rightarrow \begin{cases} 2x-6+3y=-9 \\ 10-2y-x=11 \end{cases}$$

$$\Rightarrow \begin{cases} 2x+3y=-3 \\ -2y-x=1 \end{cases} \rightarrow x=-2y-1$$

Substitute $-2y-1$ for x in the first equation.
$$2(-2y-1)+3y=-3$$
$$-4y-2+3y=-3$$
$$-y=-1$$
$$y=1$$

Substitute 1 for y in the equation $x=-2y-1$.
$$x=-2(1)-1=-3$$

The solution is $(-3, 1)$.

Check Point 1   Solutions_Page 41

Solve the following system.

① $\begin{cases} x+5=3y \\ 2(x+3y)=4x+10 \end{cases}$ ② $\begin{cases} 3(x+y)-y=-6 \\ 5x-4(x+y)=5 \end{cases}$

02 Linear Systems with Fractional Coefficients

Multiply both sides of the equation by least common multiple (LCM).

Concept Check

$\begin{cases} \frac{x}{4} - \frac{y}{3} = 1 \\ \frac{x}{3} + \frac{y}{2} = \frac{1}{3} \end{cases}$ $\xrightarrow{\text{Multiply both sides by 12}}$ $\begin{cases} 3x - 4y = 12 \\ 2x + 3y = 2 \end{cases}$

Example 2

Solve the system $\begin{cases} \frac{x}{3} + \frac{y}{2} = 1 \\ \frac{2x}{3} - \frac{y}{4} = 2 \end{cases}$.

Solution

$\begin{cases} \frac{x}{3} + \frac{y}{2} = 1 \\ \frac{2x}{3} - \frac{y}{4} = 2 \end{cases} \Rightarrow \begin{cases} \left(\frac{x}{3} + \frac{y}{2} = 1\right) \times 6 \\ \left(\frac{2x}{3} - \frac{y}{4} = 2\right) \times 12 \end{cases}$

$\Rightarrow \begin{cases} 2x + 3y = 6 \\ 8x - 3y = 24 \end{cases}$

Add two equations to eliminate y.

$$\begin{array}{r} 2x + 3y = 6 \\ +\ 8x - 3y = 24 \\ \hline 10x = 30 \end{array}$$

$x = 3$

Substitute 3 for x in the equation $2x + 3y = 6$.

$2(3) + 3y = 6$
$6 + 3y = 6$
$3y = 0$
$y = 0$

The solution is $(3, 0)$.

Check Point 2

Solve the following system.

① $\begin{cases} x - \dfrac{y}{3} = \dfrac{1}{3} \\ -\dfrac{x}{2} + \dfrac{2y}{5} = 1 \end{cases}$

② $\begin{cases} \dfrac{2x}{3} - \dfrac{3y}{2} = 5 \\ \dfrac{x}{2} - \dfrac{3y}{4} = 3 \end{cases}$

Solutions_Page 41

03 Linear Systems with Decimal Coefficients

Multiply both sides of the equation by a power of 10.

Concept Check

$\begin{cases} 0.2x + 0.5y = 0.4 \\ x + 0.6y = 1.2 \end{cases}$ $\xrightarrow{\text{Multiply both sides by 10}}$ $\begin{cases} 2x + 5y = 4 \\ 10x + 6y = 12 \end{cases}$

Example 3

Solve the system $\begin{cases} 0.1x + 0.2y = 0.4 \\ 0.4x - 0.4y = -2 \end{cases}$.

Solution

$\begin{cases} 0.1x + 0.2y = 0.4 \\ 0.4x - 0.4y = -2 \end{cases} \Rightarrow \begin{cases} (0.1x + 0.2y = 0.4) \times 10 \\ (0.4x - 0.4y = -2) \times 10 \end{cases}$

$\Rightarrow \begin{cases} x + 2y = 4 \\ 4x - 4y = -20 \end{cases} \rightarrow x = 4 - 2y$

Substitute $4 - 2y$ for x in the second equation.

$4(4 - 2y) - 4y = -20$
$16 - 8y - 4y = -20$
$-12y = -36$
$y = 3$

Substitute 3 for y in the equation $x = 4 - 2y$.

$x = 4 - 2(3) = -2$

The solution is $(-2, 3)$

Chapter 3. System of Linear Equations

Check Point 3

Solve the following system.

① $\begin{cases} 1.2x - 0.4y = 0.3 \\ 4x + y = -\dfrac{4}{3} \end{cases}$

② $\begin{cases} \dfrac{y}{3} - \dfrac{x+y}{5} = -1 \\ 0.1x + 0.2y = 1.3 \end{cases}$

04 Linear Systems with a Variable on Denominators

Substitute the reciprocal of a variable with some other letter.

Concept Check

$\begin{cases} \dfrac{1}{x} - \dfrac{1}{y} = 2 \\ \dfrac{1}{x} + \dfrac{1}{y} = 1 \end{cases}$ Let $\dfrac{1}{x} = A$ and $\dfrac{1}{y} = B$ $\longrightarrow$ $\begin{cases} A - B = 2 \\ A + B = 1 \end{cases}$

Example 4

Solve the system $\begin{cases} \dfrac{1}{x} - \dfrac{1}{y} = 2 \\ \dfrac{1}{x} + \dfrac{1}{y} = 1 \end{cases}$.

Solution

$\begin{cases} \dfrac{1}{x} - \dfrac{1}{y} = 2 \\ \dfrac{1}{x} + \dfrac{1}{y} = 1 \end{cases}$ Let $\dfrac{1}{x} = A$ and $\dfrac{1}{y} = B$ $\longrightarrow$ $\begin{cases} A - B = 2 \\ A + B = 1 \end{cases}$

Add two equations to eliminate B.

$$+\begin{array}{r} A - B = 2 \\ A + B = 1 \\ \hline 2A = 3 \end{array}$$

$A = \dfrac{3}{2}$ $\rightarrow$ $\dfrac{1}{x} = \dfrac{3}{2}$

$$x = \frac{2}{3}$$

Substitute $\frac{3}{2}$ for A in the second equation $A+B=1$.

$$\frac{3}{2}+B=1$$

$$B=-\frac{1}{2} \quad \rightarrow \quad \frac{1}{y}=-\frac{1}{2}$$

$$y=-2$$

The solution is $\left(\frac{2}{3}, -2\right)$.

Check Point 4

Solutions_Page 42

Solve the system $\begin{cases} \frac{2}{x}-\frac{3}{y}=-\frac{1}{2} \\ \frac{3}{x}+\frac{1}{2y}=\frac{11}{12} \end{cases}$.

05 Equation in the form, $A=B=C$

For the equation $A=B=C$, convert it to the system of

$\begin{cases} A=B \\ A=C \end{cases}$, $\begin{cases} A=B \\ B=C \end{cases}$ or $\begin{cases} A=C \\ B=C \end{cases}$.

Since the solution satisfies all of A, B, and C, we can choose any one of these three systems.

Concept Check

$2x+3y=4x-y=7 \Rightarrow \begin{cases} 2x+3y=4x-y \\ 2x+3y=7 \end{cases}$, $\begin{cases} 2x+3y=4x-y \\ 4x-y=7 \end{cases}$ or $\begin{cases} 2x+3y=7 \\ 4x-y=7 \end{cases}$

Choose one of three systems above and solve for x and y.

Example 5

Solve the equation $2x+y=x+4y=12$.

Solution

$$2x+y=x+4y=12 \Rightarrow \begin{cases} 2x+y=x+4y \\ 2x+y=12 \end{cases}, \begin{cases} 2x+y=x+4y \\ x+4y=12 \end{cases}, \begin{cases} 2x+y=12 \\ x+4y=12 \end{cases}$$

we can choose any one of three systems above. Let's solve the first system.

$$\begin{cases} 2x+y=x+4y \\ 2x+y=12 \end{cases} \rightarrow \begin{cases} x=3y \\ 2x+y=12 \end{cases}$$

Substitute $3y$ for x in the second equation.

$$2(3y)+y=12$$
$$7y=12$$
$$y=\frac{12}{7}$$

Substitute $\frac{12}{7}$ for y in the equation $x=3y$.

$$x=3\left(\frac{12}{7}\right)=\frac{36}{7}$$

The solution is $\left(\frac{36}{7}, \frac{12}{7}\right)$.

Check Point 5

Solve the equation $7x+2y=4x+y=2x-y-4$.

Review Exercise

01 Solve the following system.

(1) $\begin{cases} 2(3x+y)=4+4y \\ 4x-3(y-1)=4 \end{cases}$

(2) $\begin{cases} x+\dfrac{y-1}{3}=1 \\ \dfrac{2x+6}{5}-\dfrac{y+2}{2}=2 \end{cases}$

02 Solve the following system.

(1) $\begin{cases} 0.2x-0.1y+0.5=1.2 \\ \dfrac{5x}{3}-\dfrac{y}{2}=\dfrac{11}{2} \end{cases}$

(2) $\begin{cases} 3x-5=\dfrac{3(1-y)}{2}+x \\ 0.3y-0.2x=0.1 \end{cases}$

03 Solve the following system.

(1) $\begin{cases} \dfrac{6}{x}+\dfrac{5}{y}=7 \\ \dfrac{3}{x}-\dfrac{5}{y}=-4 \end{cases}$

(2) $\begin{cases} \dfrac{1}{2x}-\dfrac{1}{3y}=\dfrac{5}{36} \\ \dfrac{2}{5x}+\dfrac{3}{y}=\dfrac{6}{5} \end{cases}$

04 Solve the equation
$\dfrac{2x+y}{2}=1-2x=\dfrac{4y-2}{3}$.

Challenging

05 If the solution of the equation $2x+y+7=x-3y=4x+5y+9$ satisfies the equation $3x-ay=7$, what is the value of a?

Challenging

06 If both systems $\begin{cases} 4x-ay=7 \\ 5x+y=13 \end{cases}$ and $\begin{cases} 2x-3y=-5 \\ bx-4y=9 \end{cases}$ have the same solution, what are the values of a and b?

3. Application of Linear Systems

Just like the application from linear equations we have studied in the previous chapter, this section will repeat the same type of examples. This time they will be worked using two unknowns, usually x and y, and two equations solved simultaneously. The advantage of using two unknowns is that we have greater flexibility to solve higher-level problems. The key to solving application problems is converting the words into mathematical equations. Refer to the following steps below.

1. Understand thoroughly what the problem is asking you to do.
2. Represent unknown quantities with two variables.
3. Form a system of equations that will relate known quantities to the unknown quantities.
4. Solve the system of equations.

Example 1

The sum of two numbers is 25. Three less than four times the larger number is equal to one more than twice the smaller. Find two numbers.

Solution

Let x and y be the larger and smaller number, respectively. Then, we have

$x+y=25$ and $4x-3=2y+1$. Now, solve the system $\begin{cases} x+y=25 \\ 4x-3=2y+1 \end{cases}$.

$$\begin{cases} x+y=25 \\ 4x-3=2y+1 \end{cases} \Rightarrow \begin{cases} y=-x+25 \\ 4x-2y=4 \end{cases}$$

Substitute $-x+25$ for y in the second equation.

$$4x-2(-x+25)=4$$
$$4x+2x-50=4$$
$$6x=54, \ x=9$$

Now, substitute 9 for x in the equation $y=-x+25$.
$$y=-(9)+25=16$$

Therefore, two numbers are 9 and 16

Check Point 1

Solutions_Page 45

The difference between the two numbers is 13. If the sum of twice the larger number and one more than three times the smaller number 62, what are two numbers?

Example 2

Andrew is four years younger than twice Brian's. If the sum of their ages after 5 years is 45, how old are they now?

Solution

Let x and y be Andrew and Brian's current age, respectively. Then we have $x=2y-4$ and $(x+5)+(y+5)=45$. Now, solve the system $\begin{cases} x=2y-4 \\ (x+5)+(y+5)=45 \end{cases}$.

$$\begin{cases} x=2y-4 \\ (x+5)+(y+5)=45 \end{cases} \Rightarrow \begin{cases} x=2y-4 \\ x+y=35 \end{cases}$$

Substitute $2y-4$ for x in the second equation.
$$(2y-4)+y=35$$
$$3y=39, \ y=13$$

Now, substitute 13 for y in the equation $x=2y-4$.
$$x=2(13)-4=22$$

Therefore, Andrew is now 22 years old and Brian is now 13 years old.

Check Point 2

Solutions_Page 45

Jason is currently three times as old as his daughter. After seven years, Jason will be four years older than twice his daughter. How old are they now?

Chapter 3. System of Linear Equations

Example 3

Suppose Victoria has 28 coins in dimes and nickels only and has a total of $1.65. How many coins does she have each?

Solution

Let x and y be the number of dimes and nickels, respectively. Since $1.65 is equal to 165 cents, we have

$x+y=28$ and $10x+5y=165$. Now, solve the system $\begin{cases} x+y=28 \\ 10x+5y=165 \end{cases}$.

$$\begin{cases} x+y=28 \\ 10x+5y=165 \end{cases} \Rightarrow \begin{cases} x=-y+28 \\ 2x+y=33 \end{cases}$$

Substitute $-y+28$ for x in the second equation.

$$2(-y+28)+y=33$$
$$-2y+56+y=33$$
$$-y=-23, \ y=23$$

Now, substitute 23 for y in the equation $x=-y+28$.

$$x=-23+28=5$$

Therefore, Victoria has 5 dimes and 23 nickels.

Check Point 3

Solutions_Page 46

Laurie has some coins in her pocket consisting of dimes and quarters only. If the total value of the coins is $3.35 and the number of dimes is two more than twice the number of quarters, how many dimes and quarters are there in Laurie's packet?

Example 4

An airplane flies with a tail wind from New York to Los Angeles, a distance of 2550 miles, in 5 hours. On the return trip against the same wind, the airplane flies back in 6 hours. Find the speed of the airplane in still air and the speed of the wind.

Solution

Let x and y be the speed of the airplane and wind, respectively.

	Distance (mile)	Time (hour)	Speed (mile/hour)
From N.Y. to L.A.	2550	5	$x+y$
From L.A. to N.Y.	2550	6	$x-y$

Since the distance is equal to speed times time, we have $(x+y)5=2550$ and $(x-y)6=2550$.

Now, solve the system $\begin{cases}(x+y)5=2550\\(x-y)6=2550\end{cases}$

$$\begin{cases}(x+y)5=2550\\(x-y)6=2550\end{cases} \Rightarrow \begin{cases}x+y=510\\x-y=425\end{cases}$$

Add two equations to eliminate y and solve for x.

$$+\begin{array}{r}x+y=510\\x-y=425\\\hline 2x=935\end{array}$$

$$x=467.5$$

Substitute 467.5 for x in the first equation.

$$467.5+y=510$$
$$y=42.5$$

Therefore, the speed of the airplane and wind is 467.5 miles per hour and 42.5 miles per hour, respectively.

Check Point 4   Solutions_Page 46

Two cars started at the same time, traveling in opposite directions. The difference in the speed of two cars is 5 miles per hour. If two cars are 500 miles apart after 4 hours, how fast did each car travel?

Example 5

A chemist has a 16% saline solution and a 25% saline solution. How many liters of the 16% and 25% solution must be mixed to make 36 liters of a 20% saline solution?

Solution

Let x and y be the liters of a 16% and 25% saline solution, respectively.

	16% solution	25% solution	20% solution
The amount of solution	x	y	36
The amount of salt	$0.16x$	$0.25y$	$0.2(x+y)$

We have the system $\begin{cases} x+y=36 \\ 0.16x+0.25y=0.2(x+y) \end{cases}$. Now, solve the system.

$$\begin{cases} x+y=36 \\ 0.16x+0.25y=0.2(x+y) \end{cases} \Rightarrow \begin{cases} x+y=36 \\ 16x+25y=20(x+y) \end{cases}$$

$$\Rightarrow \begin{cases} x+y=36 \\ 16x+25y=20x+20y \end{cases}$$

$$\Rightarrow \begin{cases} x+y=36 \\ 5y=4x \end{cases} \rightarrow y=\frac{4}{5}x$$

Substitute $\frac{4}{5}x$ for y in the first equation.

$$x+\frac{4}{5}x=36$$

$$\frac{9}{5}x=36, \quad x=20$$

Now, substitute 20 for x in the equation $y=\frac{4}{5}x$.

$$y=\frac{4}{5}(20)=16$$

20 liters of a 16% solution and 16 liters of a 25% solution.

Check Point 5

Solutions_Page 46

Mrs. Johnson has a 12% solution of boric acid and a 18% solution of boric acid. How many gallons of the 12% and 18% solution must be mixed to make 12 gallons of a 16% solution of boric acid?

Example 6

The perimeter of rectangle is 64 inches. If the length of the rectangle is 4 inches less than twice the width, what is the area of the rectangle?

Solution

Let x and y be the width and length of the rectangle, respectively. Since the perimeter is 64 inches, $2x+2y=64$. Also, since the length of the rectangle is 4 inches less than twice the width, $y=2x-4$. Now, solve the system $\begin{cases} 2x+2y=64 \\ y=2x-4 \end{cases}$.

$$\begin{cases} 2x+2y=64 \\ y=2x-4 \end{cases} \Rightarrow \begin{cases} x+y=32 \\ y=2x-4 \end{cases}$$

Substitute $2x-4$ for y in the first equation.
$$x+(2x-4)=32$$
$$3x=36, \ x=12$$

Now, substitute 12 for x in the equation $x+y=32$.
$$(12)+y=32, \ y=20$$

Therefore, the width is 12 inches and the length is 20 inches.

Check Point 6

Solutions_Page 47

The perimeter of the rectangle is 24 feet. When the rectangle is doubled in length and tripled in width, the perimeter of the new rectangle will be 10 feet longer than twice the perimeter of the original rectangle. Find the width and length of the original rectangle.

Example 7

Jenny plans to invest $9,000. He invests a certain amount in the bank which pays 4 percent interest and the remainder in stocks which pays a 3 percent yearly return. How much did she invest in each if her yearly income from the two investments was $308?

Solution

Let x and y be the amount in dollars invested in the bank and stocks, respectively.

Then we have $x+y=9000$ and $0.04x+0.03y=308$. Now, solve the system $\begin{cases} x+y=9000 \\ 0.04x+0.03y=308 \end{cases}$.

$$\begin{cases} x+y=9000 \\ 0.04x+0.03y=308 \end{cases} \Rightarrow \begin{cases} y=-x+9000 \\ 4x+3y=30800 \end{cases}$$

Substitute $-x+9000$ for y in the second equation.
$$4x+3(-x+9000)=30800$$
$$4x-3x+27000=30800$$
$$x=3800$$

Now, substitute 3800 for x in the equation $y=-x+9000$.
$$y=-(3800)+9000=5200$$

Jenny invested $3,800 in the bank and $5,200 in stocks.

Check Point 7

Solutions_Page 47

Ethan invested $1,000 more in Bank M, which pays 3% interests than Bank K, which pays only 2.5% interests. If the interest earned by both banks was $305, how much did he invest in each bank?

Review Exercise

01 Three times the larger of two integers is equal to 19 more than twice the smaller. If the difference between two integers is 2, what are the two integers?

02 Jonathan has a total of 50 quarters and dimes. If the total value of the coins is $10.55, how many dimes does he have?

03 Jason bought a shirt and a pair of pants for his homecoming party. The sum of the prices before the sales tax was $76. There was an 8% sales tax on the shirt and a 5% sales tax on the pants. If the total amount Jason paid including the sales tax was $81, what was the price of each item?

04 A chemist mixed some 20%−saline solution with some 35%−saline solution to obtain 8 liters of a 25%−saline solution. How much of the 20%−saline solution and 35%−saline solution did the chemist use in the mixture?

Review Exercise

05 If 4 burgers and 3 soft drinks cost $26 and 3 burgers and 6 soft drinks cost $27, how much is a burger and soft drink each?

06 Two cars started at the same time, traveling in opposite directions. The difference in the speed of two cars is 8 miles per hour. If two cars are 360 miles apart after 3 hours, how many miles per hour did each car travel?

07 Mike, who runs the restaurant, ordered 20 packages of buns from a wholesaler. Some packages include 12 buns each, some of them 8 buns each. If he has a total of 188 buns, how many packages of 8 buns Mike ordered?

08 Admission tickets for adults and students at the museum were sold for $15 and $9 respectively. If the total revenue of the tickets sold was $2,250 and there were 170 attendees, how many adult tickets were sold?

09 Kevin is 22 years older than his son, Paul. If Kevin is twice as old as Paul in 7 years, how old is Paul now?

10 Charles bought several dozen pencils and pens at the local mart. The pencils cost $4.50 per dozen, and the pens cost $6.50 per dozen. If Charles bought 8 dozen pencils and pens a total of $42, how many dozens of pencils did he buy?

11 The perimeter of the rectangle is 40. When the rectangle is doubled in width and halved in length, the perimeter of the new rectangle will be 12 more than half the perimeter of the original rectangle. What is the area of the original rectangle?

Chapter Test — Level 1

01 Solve the system using any method that seems easier to use.

(1) $\begin{cases} x = -2y - 2 \\ 3x + 5y = -3 \end{cases}$

(2) $\begin{cases} 2x - 3y = 6 \\ -4x + 6y = 12 \end{cases}$

(3) $\begin{cases} 2x - 5y = 1 \\ 3x - 15y = 3 \end{cases}$

(4) $\begin{cases} 5x - y = 5 \\ 6x - 4y = -8 \end{cases}$

02 If the y-coordinate of the solution to the system $\begin{cases} 2kx+3y=1 \\ 5x-2y=-16 \end{cases}$ is 3, what is the value of k?

$$\begin{cases} 3x+4y=-2 & \to (1) \\ 4x-2y=7 & \to (2) \end{cases}$$

03 In the system above, which of the following is needed to eliminate x?

(A) $(1) \times 2 + (2)$ (B) $(1) + (2) \times 2$ (C) $(1) \times 3 - (2) \times 4$

(D) $(1) \times 4 - (2) \times 3$ (E) $(1) \times 3 + (2) \times 4$

$$\begin{cases} x-4y=7 \\ 8y=2x-15 \end{cases}$$

04 How many solutions (x, y) are there to the system of equations above?

(A) Zero
(B) One
(C) Two
(D) Three
(E) Infinitely many solutions

Chapter Test — Level 1

05 If $(2, 1)$ is the solution to the equation $3ax-by=ax-2by-7=x+4y+1$, what is the value of $a+b$?

06 For what values of a and b does the system $\begin{cases} ax+2y=6 \\ 8x-by=-12 \end{cases}$ have infinitely many solutions?

07 For what values of k does the system $\begin{cases} kx+5y=12 \\ 3x-2y=4 \end{cases}$ has no solution?

$$\begin{cases} my-12x=-21 \\ 4x-3y=n \end{cases}$$

08 In the system of equations above, m and n are constants. If the system has infinitely many solutions, what is the value of m and n?

09 Jason has some $5 bills and some $10 bills. If he has 22 bills worth $155, how many bills does he have each?

10 Mr. Henderson wants to make 1.5 liters of 35% orange juice by mixing 20% orange juice and 60% orange juice. How many milliliters of a 60% orange juice does he need to add? (Note: 1 liter is equal to 1,000 milliliters)

11 The relationship between the Fahrenheit(F) scale and the Celsius(C) scale is $F = \frac{9}{5}C + 32$. Find the temperature of Fahrenheit when the Celsius temperature is equal to 20% of the Fahrenheit temperature.

Chapter Test — Level 2

01 If (x, y) is the solution to the system of equations $\begin{cases} 1.3x+y=0.7 \\ -0.02x-0.1y=0.04 \end{cases}$, what is the value of $x+y$?

02 If the ordered pair $(1, 2)$ is a solution to the system $\begin{cases} x+ay=-3 \\ 3x+by=5 \end{cases}$, which of the following is true?

(A) $a>0$ (B) $b<0$ (C) $a=2b$
(D) $a=-2b$ (E) $a^2+b^2=4$

03 If the x-coordinate of the solution to the system $\begin{cases} 4x-5y=c \\ 2x+6y=-8 \end{cases}$ is one greater than twice the y-coordinate, what is the value of c?

04 If (x, y) is the solution to the system of equations $\begin{cases} x+2y=k+2 \\ 2x-y=k \end{cases}$ and $x+y=10$, what is the value of k?

05 If the solution of the equation $\begin{cases} kx+0.5y=13 \\ \dfrac{5}{6}x+\dfrac{3}{2}y=8 \end{cases}$ satisfies the equation $x-2y=2$, what is the value of k?

06 Solve the system $\begin{cases} 15x-28y=123 \\ 13x-27y=123 \end{cases}$.

Chapter Test — Level 2

07 If both systems $\begin{cases} 3x-y=11 \\ \dfrac{a}{2}x-by=1 \end{cases}$ and $\begin{cases} ax-\dfrac{5b}{3}y=3 \\ 2x-y=7 \end{cases}$ have the same solution, what is the value of $a+b$?

08 For which of the following values of a and b does the system $\begin{cases} 2x+6y=a \\ 3x-by=6 \end{cases}$ have no solutions?

(A) $a \neq 4,\ b=-9$ (B) $a=4,\ b \neq -9$ (C) $a=-9,\ b=4$
(D) $a \neq -9,\ b=4$ (E) $a=-9,\ b \neq 4$

09 Find x and y if $\sqrt{x}+2\sqrt{y}=12$ and $4\sqrt{x}-3\sqrt{y}=4$.

10 A company has 200 tablets PCs in stock, of which 60 percent are 10 inches and 40 percent are 8 inches in size. The entire tablet PCs are either black or white. If 150 of the tablet PCs are black and 90 of the black tablet PCs are 10 inches, how many of the tablet PCs are both white and 8 inches?

11 John spent a total of $8.4 for fresh salmon and pork. The salmon cost 1.5 times as much per pound as the pork, and John bought 2 times as many pounds of pork as pounds of salmon. How much, in dollars, did the John spend on pork?

memo

Chapter 4

Linear Inequalities

1. Solving Linear Inequalities, Part 1
2. Solving Linear Inequalities, Part 2
3. Graphing Linear Inequality
4. Application of Linear Inequality
5. Chapter Test

1 Solving Linear Inequalities, Part 1

01 Introduction to Inequalities

Inequality is a relation that holds between two values when they are different. For example, expressions such as $2x+4>5$, $x-5<21$, and $x\geq 4$ are inequalities. There are four notations for inequalities, as shown below.

1. $x<y$ means that x is less than y.
2. $x>y$ means that x is greater than y.
3. $x\leq y$ means that x is less than or equal to y.
4. $x\geq y$ means that x is greater than or equal to y.

And, blow are the same expressions.
1. "less than or equal to" = "not greater than" = "at most."
2. "greater than or equal to = "not less than" = "at least."

02 Solutions of Inequalities

We can write the solution of inequality as an interval or we can graph the solution on the number line. The inequality $x<2$ represents the interval where the numbers are less than 2. Similarly, $x\geq 3$ represent all real numbers greater than or equal to 3 on the number line. The numbers 2 and 3 in these examples represent the endpoints of the interval of the number line. However, $x\geq 3$ includes the endpoint 3, while $x<2$ excludes the endpoint 2.

Concept Check

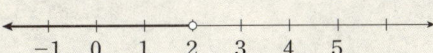

(1) Endpoint 2 is not part of the interval.
(2) This is called an open interval.
(3) The interval notation is $(-\infty, 2)$.

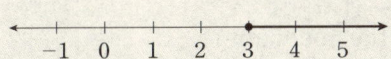

(1) Endpoint 3 is included in the interval.
(2) This is called a closed interval.
(3) The interval notation is $[3, \infty)$.

03 Properties of Inequalities

Inequalities are governed by the following properties. Assume a, b, and c are real numbers.

Property	Examples
Converse Property: 1. If $a<b$, then $b>a$	1. If $2<5$, then $5>2$ 2. If $-3<4$, then $4>-3$
Transitivity Property: 1. If $a<b$ and $b<c$, then $a<c$ 2. If $a>b$ and $b>c$, then $a>c$	1. If $2<5$ and $5<7$, then $2<7$ 2. If $2>-1$ and $-1>-6$, then $2>-6$
Addition and Subtraction Properties: 1. If $a<b$, then $a\pm c<b\pm c$ 2. If $a>b$, then $a\pm c>b\pm c$	1. If $2<5$, then $2+3<5+3$ 2. If $4>2$ then $4-5>2-5$
Multiplication and Division Properties: 1. If $a<b$ and $c>0$, then $ac<bc$ and $\frac{a}{c}<\frac{b}{c}$ 2. If $a<b$ and $c<0$, then $ac>bc$ and $\frac{a}{c}>\frac{b}{c}$	1. If $1<3$ and $c=2$, then $1\cdot 2<3\cdot 2$ and $\frac{1}{2}<\frac{3}{2}$ 2. If $1<3$ and $c=-2$, then $1(-2)>3(-2)$ and $\frac{1}{-2}>\frac{3}{-2}$
Additive Inverse Property 1. If $a<b$, then $-a>-b$ 2. If $a>b$, then $-a<-b$	1. If $2<4$, then $-2>-4$ 2. If $3>-2$, then $-3<2$
Multiplicative Inverse Property 1. If $0<a<b$, then $\frac{1}{a}>\frac{1}{b}$	If $2<5$, then $\frac{1}{2}>\frac{1}{5}$

✔ These properties also hold true for inequalities involving $\leq$ and $\geq$.

Example 1

Solve the inequality.

① $3x-4 > 2x-7$ ② $x+2 \leq 4x-10$

Solution

① $3x-4 > 2x-7$ → Given
   $3x-4-2x > 2x-7-2x$ → Subtract both sides by $2x$
   $x-4 > -7$ → Simplify each side
   $x-4+4 > -7+4$ → Add both sides by 4
   $x > -3$ → Simplify each side

The solution in the interval notation: $(-3, \infty)$
The graph on the number line:

② $x+2 \leq 4x-10$ → Given
   $x+2-4x \leq 4x-10-4x$ → Subtract both sides by $-4x$
   $-3x+2 \leq -10$ → Simplify each side
   $-3x+2-2 \leq -10-2$ → Subtract both sides by 2
   $-3x \leq -12$ → Simplify each side
   $\dfrac{-3x}{-3} \geq \dfrac{-12}{-3}$ → Divide both sides by -3. $\leq$ changes to $\geq$
   $x \geq 4$ → Simplify each side

The solution in the interval notation $[4, \infty)$
The graph on the number line:

Check Point 1

Solutions_Page 56

Solve the inequality.

① $3x-2 \geq 16$ ② $x-3 < -15+4x$

③ $4x-1 \leq 9-x$ ④ $\dfrac{1}{3}x - \dfrac{1}{2} < -\dfrac{4}{3}x + 7$

04 Solving Multi-Step Inequalities

Here are useful steps to solve more complicated inequality problems.

1. Remove parentheses, if there is(are) any.
2. Simplify each side of the inequality.
   - ✔ Eliminate fractional coefficients by multiplying both sides of the equation by the least common multiple (LCM).
   - ✔ Get rid of decimals by multiplying both sides of the equation by a power of 10.
3. Move all the terms with the variable to one side and all the constants to the other using addition and subtraction.
4. Divide both sides by the variable's coefficient.

Example 2

Solve the inequality.

① $2(x-4)+3(1-2x) \geq 2x+13$

② $\dfrac{x-2}{2}+\dfrac{2x+1}{3} > 1$

Solution

① $2(x-4)+3(1-2x) \geq 2x+13$ → Given
$2x-8+3-6x \geq 2x+13$ → Remove parentheses
$-4x-5 \geq 2x+13$ → Simplify each side
$-6x-5 \geq 13$ → Subtract both sides by $2x$
$-6x \geq 18$ → Add both sides by 5
$x \leq -3$ → Divide both sides by -6.
Change the direction of the inequality sign

The solution in the interval notation: $(-\infty, -3]$
The graph on the number line:

② $\quad \dfrac{x-2}{2}+\dfrac{2x+1}{3}>1$ → Given

$\left(\dfrac{x-2}{2}+\dfrac{2x+1}{3}\right)\cdot 6>1\cdot 6$ → Multiply both sides by 6 (The LCM of 2 and 3).

$3(x-2)+2(2x+1)>6$ → Simplify

$3x-6+4x+2>6$ → Remove parentheses

$7x-4>6$ → Simplify each side

$7x>10$ → Add both sides by 4

$x>\dfrac{10}{7}$ → Divide both sides by 7

The solution in the interval notation : $\left(\dfrac{10}{7},\ \infty\right)$
The graph on the number line :

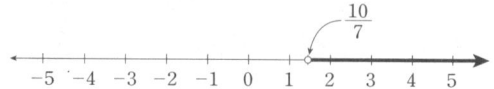

Check Point 2

Solutions_Page 56

Solve the inequality.

① $4-12x\geq 2(x+6)$

② $3(x-2)>4x-3(2x+1)$

③ $\dfrac{2x-4}{3}+2\leq 3x-11$

④ $1.2x-4.8<-0.6x+2.4$

Review Exercise

01 Solve the inequality.

(1) $5x < 3x - 12$

(2) $3x + 4 > 2x - 8$

(3) $-8 - 4x \geq x - 23$

(4) $13x - 8 \leq 32 - 7x$

02 Solve the inequality.

(1) $2(x-4) < -3x + 7$

(2) $-3x + 5 > 4(x-3) + 7$

(3) $5(3x-1) + 4 < 4(5x+1)$

(4) $2x - 6(3-x) \geq 3(x+2)$

Review Exercise

03 Solve the inequality.

(1) $3 - \dfrac{x-2}{4} > 3x+1$

(2) $\dfrac{x+1}{2} + \dfrac{x-1}{3} \leq \dfrac{2x+1}{6}$

(3) $2 + \dfrac{x-2}{2} \geq \dfrac{x+2}{10} - \dfrac{3}{5}$

(4) $\dfrac{2}{3}x - \dfrac{5}{2} > \dfrac{7}{3} - \dfrac{1}{4}x$

04 Solve the inequality.

(1) $0.4x + 0.6 > 0.8x - 1$

Challenging
(2) $0.5(3x-1) \geq \dfrac{x-4}{5} + 0.4$

05 Which of the following numbers is NOT a solution of the inequality $3x - 5 \geq -2(4-x) + 1$?

(A) -3
(B) -1
(C) 0
(D) 1
(E) 3

06 Solve the inequality $ax-2a<5$ in terms of a where $a<0$.

Challenging

07 If $4(2-y)\leq 3y-\dfrac{1}{3}(y+6)$, what is the smallest possible value of $2y+1$?

2 Solving Linear Inequalities, Part 2

01 Compound Inequalities

A compound inequality is an inequality that combines two simple inequalities.

1. Conjunction Inequality: A compound inequality that uses the word "and" is known as a conjunction inequality. This inequality is true only if both inequalities are true.

   Concept Check

   Consider the inequality $-2 < x \leq 5$. This is equivalent to $-2 < x$ and $x \leq 5$ where the word "and" implies an intersection(overlap) of the solutions from each part.

   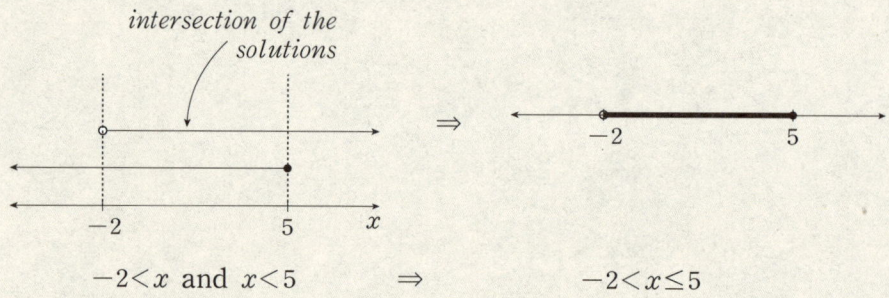

   $-2 < x$ and $x < 5$ $\Rightarrow$ $-2 < x \leq 5$

   The solution in the interval notation: $(-2, 5]$

2. Disjunction Inequality: A compound inequality that uses the word "or" is known as a disjunction inequality. This inequality is true if one or more of the inequalities is true.

   Concept Check

   Consider the inequality $x < -2$ or $x \geq 5$. The word "or" implies an union of the solutions from each part.

   $x < -2$ or $x \geq 5$

   The solution in the interval notation: $(-\infty, -2) \cup [5, \infty)$

Example 1

Solve the inequality.

① $-5 < 2x-1 \leq 11$

② $3x+1 \leq -11$ or $\frac{1}{3}x-1 > 2$

Solution

①
$-5 < 2x-1 \leq 11$ → Given
$-5+1 < 2x-1+1 \leq 11+1$ → Add all three sides by 1
$-4 < 2x \leq 12$ → Simplify each side
$\dfrac{-4}{2} < \dfrac{2x}{2} \leq \dfrac{12}{2}$ → Divide all three sides by 2
$-2 < x \leq 6$ → Simplify each side

The solution in the interval notation: $(-2, 6]$
The graph on the number line:

②
$3x+1 \leq -11$ or $\frac{1}{3}x-1 > 2$

$3x+1-1 \leq -11-1$ or $\left(\frac{1}{3}x-1\right) \cdot 3 > 2 \cdot 3$

$3x \leq -12$ or $x-3 > 6$

$x \leq -4$ or $x-3+3 > 6+3$

$x > 9$

The solution in the interval notation: $(-\infty, -4] \cup (9, \infty)$
The graph on the number line:

Check Point 1

Solutions_Page 58

Solve the inequality.

① $-4 < 3x-6 < 9$

② $3 \leq \frac{1}{2} - \frac{3}{2}x \leq 8$

③ $\dfrac{2-x}{3} > 2$ or $2x-5 > 9$

④ $\frac{3}{5}x+2 \leq x - \frac{5}{2}$ or $-7-2x \geq 2$

02 Absolute Value Inequalities

An inequality involving absolute value can be solved by first rewriting it as a compound inequality. There are two forms of absolute value inequalities as shown below.

1. If $|x|<a$, then $-a<x<a$, where a is positive number

   $|x|<a$ means that x is restricted to points on the number line less than a units from 0 in either the positive or negative direction.

2. If $|x|>a$, then $x<-a$ or $x>a$, where a is positive number

   $|x|>a$ means that x is restricted to points on the number line more than a units from 0 in either the positive or negative direction.

✔ These properties also hold true for inequalities involving $\leq$ and $\geq$.

Concept Check

1. If $|x|<4$, then $-4<x<4$
2. If $|x|>4$, then $x<-4$ or $x>4$

Example 2

Solve the absolute value inequality.

① $|2x-3|<5$

② $\left|\dfrac{1}{2}x-1\right|-4\geq 4$

Solution

① $\quad |2x-3|<5 \quad \rightarrow$ Given
$\quad -5<2x-3<5 \quad \rightarrow$ Write the inequality as a conjunction
$\quad -2<\ 2x\ <8 \quad \rightarrow$ Add all three sides by 3
$\quad -1<\ x\ <4 \quad \rightarrow$ Divide all three sides by 2

The solution in the interval notation: $(-1,\ 4)$
The graph on the number line:

② $\left|\dfrac{1}{2}x-1\right|-4\geq 4 \quad \rightarrow$ Given

$\quad \left|\dfrac{1}{2}x-1\right|\geq 8 \quad \rightarrow$ Add both sides by 4

$\dfrac{1}{2}x-1\leq -8$ or $\dfrac{1}{2}x-1\geq 8 \quad \rightarrow$ Write the inequality as a disjunction

$\dfrac{1}{2}x\ \leq -7$ or $\dfrac{1}{2}x\ \geq 9 \quad \rightarrow$ Add each side by 1

$x\ \leq -14$ or $x\ \geq 18 \quad \rightarrow$ Multiply each side by 2

The solution in the interval notation: $(-\infty,-14]\cup[18,\ \infty)$
The graph on the number line:

Check Point 2

Solutions_Page 58

Solve the inequality.

① $|2x+5|\leq 13$

② $|4-3x|\geq 11$

③ $\left|\dfrac{1}{2}x-1\right|-4<4$

④ $6+\dfrac{1}{4}|3x+2|\geq 31$

Chapter 4. Linear Inequalities 147

Review Exercise

01 Solve the inequality.

(1) $8 < 2x-4 < 14$

(2) $-8 \leq 6-x \leq -4$

(3) $-4 \leq \dfrac{4x-2}{3} \leq 1$

(4) $-4 \leq 2(3-x) < 10$

02 Solve the inequality.

(1) $x-3 > 9$ or $2x+5 < -3$

(2) $4x-9 \geq -1$ or $\dfrac{1}{2}x-3 \leq -3$

(3) $4-x < \dfrac{1}{3}$ or $\dfrac{3-x}{2} - \dfrac{5}{3} \geq \dfrac{4}{3}$

(4) $\dfrac{x-3}{6} + 1 \geq x$ or $\dfrac{x-6}{3} - x \geq 4$

Challenging

03 Solve the inequality.

(1) $-3 < \dfrac{3x+4}{3} - \dfrac{x-3}{2} \leq 2$

(2) $-2 < x-4 < 3$ or $-5 \leq 5x-8 \leq 12$

04 Solve the inequality.

(1) $|2x-5| > 8$

(2) $|4x+1| - 1 \leq 2$

(3) $\dfrac{|x-2|}{2} + 2 < 8$

(4) $\dfrac{3|5x+1|}{2} - 2 \geq 7$

Challenging

05 Solve the inequality $1 < |x| < 6$.

06 For what value of x is $|2x-1|+2$ equal to 1?

(A) 0 (B) 1

(C) 2 (D) 3

(E) There is no such value of x

07 How many integer values of x satisfy the inequality $2x-1 < 7$ and $2-3x < 11$?

3. Graphing Linear Inequality

01 Graphing Linear Inequality

The solution set for inequality is described as an area of the coordinate plane called a half−plane. All points in that region are solutions of the inequality. An equation defines the boundary of the half−plane. To graph a linear inequality, rearrange the equation for y first. Then, assume that the inequality to be the equal sign and then graph the line.

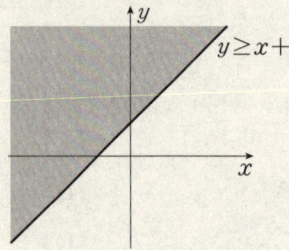

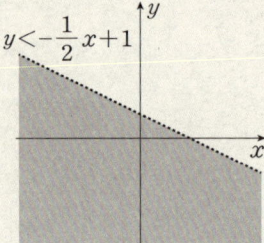

1. Every point on a solid line is a solution.
2. A solid line is used for inequalities with $\leq$ or $\geq$.
3. If $y>$ or $y\geq$, the region of the solution is above the line.

1. Every point on a dashed line is NOT a solution.
2. A dashed line is used for inequalities with $<$ or $>$.
3. If $y<$ or $y\leq$, the region of the solution is below the line.

Example 1

Graph the inequality $4x-2y\leq 8$.

Solution

Step 1 Rearrange the equation for y.

$\quad\quad 4x-2y\leq 8 \quad\quad \rightarrow$ Given
$\quad\quad -2y\leq -4x+8 \quad \rightarrow$ Subtract both sides by $4x$
$\quad\quad y\geq 2x-4 \quad\quad \rightarrow$ Divide both sides by -2

Step 2 Graph $y=2x-4$ as a solid line

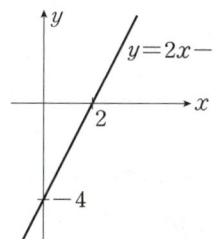

Step 3 Shade the area above the line since y is greater than or equal to $2x-4$.

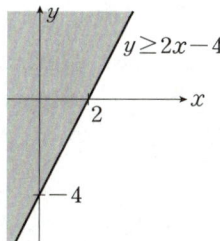

Check Point 1 Solutions_Page 61

Graph the inequality.

① $y > \dfrac{1}{2}x - 2$ ② $2x + 4y \leq 6$

02 System of Linear Inequalities

A system of linear inequalities in two variables consists of at least two linear inequalities in the same variables. Solving systems of linear inequalities means graphing each inequality, and then finding the overlap of the solutions.

Example 2

Graph the system of inequalities $\begin{cases} y \geq x+1 \\ y < -\frac{1}{2}x+1 \end{cases}$.

Solution

First, graph each inequality separately. The solution to the system is the region where the shadings from each inequality overlap one another.

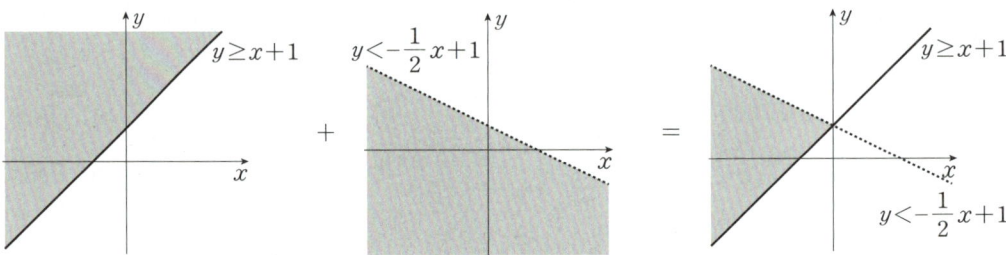

Check Point 2

Solutions_Page 61

Graph the system of inequalities.

① $\begin{cases} y < \frac{6}{5}x+3 \\ y \geq -3x-6 \end{cases}$

② $\begin{cases} y < \frac{1}{2}x+2 \\ y \geq x-1 \end{cases}$

Review Exercise

01 Graph the inequality.

(1) $y \geq -2x+1$

(2) $y < \dfrac{1}{2}x - 1$

(3) $3x + 2y \leq 4$

(4) $2x - 3y < 6$

02 Write a linear inequality that represents the graph.

(1)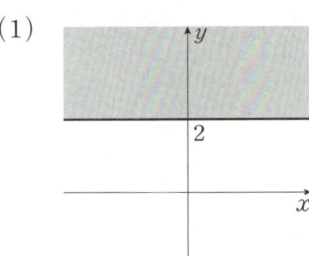

(2)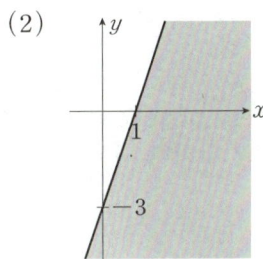

Review Exercise

03 Graph the system of inequalities.

(1) $\begin{cases} y < -x+2 \\ y \geq \dfrac{1}{3}x - 2 \end{cases}$

(2) $\begin{cases} 2x - y \leq 3 \\ x + 3y \geq -2 \end{cases}$

04 Write a system of inequalities that represents the graph.

(1)

(2)

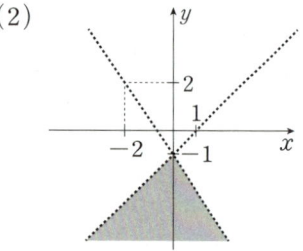

$\begin{cases} 2x - 3y > -1 \\ -x + 5y \leq 3 \end{cases}$

05 Which of the following points does not lie in the solution region of the system of inequalities above?

(A) (1, 2) (B) (1, −2)

(C) (−1, −2) (D) (2, 1)

(E) (2, −1)

$\begin{cases} y \geq -2 \\ x \geq 1 \\ 2x + y \leq 6 \end{cases}$

06 For the system of linear inequalities above, find the area of the solution region.

154 Chapter 4. Linear Inequalities

Application of Linear Inequality

Refer to the following steps.
1. Understand thoroughly what the problem is asking you to do.
2. Represent one of the unknown quantities with a variable.
3. Form an inequality that will relate known quantities to the unknown quantities.
4. Solve the inequality.

Example 1

Mike received 80, 90, and 87 in his first three exams in his chemistry class this semester. What is the minimum score Mike can get on the fourth exam to get an average of 85 or more?

Solution

Let x be the score of the fourth exam. Since Mike needs to get an average of 85 or more, we have the following inequality:

$$\frac{80+90+87+x}{4} \geq 85$$
$$80+90+87+x \geq 340$$
$$257+x \geq 340$$
$$x \geq 83$$

Therefore, the minimum score Mike must receive on the fourth exam is 83.

Check Point 1

Solutions_Page 64

Jeffery made an average of 88 on his last three tests in his algebra 1 class. To get an A, the average of his four test must be between 90 and 100, inclusive. What is the minimum score on the fourth test he must receive to get an A in Algebra 1 class?

Example 2

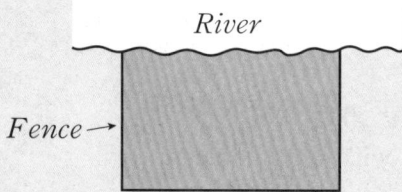

Jack has 121 feet of fences and wants to fence off a rectangular field as shown in the figure above. If the length of the rectangular field is 4 feet less than three times the width, what is the maximum width of the field?

Solution

Let x be the width of the rectangular field. Then the length of the field is $3x-4$. Since Jack has 121 feet of fences, we have the following inequality:

$$2x+(3x-4) \leq 121$$
$$5x-4 \leq 121$$
$$5x \leq 125$$
$$x \leq 25$$

Therefore, the maximum width of the field is 25 feet.

Check Point 2

Solutions_Page 64

The base of the triangle is 8 inches. If the area of the triangle is less than or equal to 40 square inches, what is the maximum height of the triangle?

Example 3

Ashley works part-time at the mall. If she earns $32 a day as well as $0.5 for every product she sells, how many products would she have to sell to earn at least $80 a day?

Solution

Let x be the number of product Ashley sells a day. Then we have the following inequality:

$$32+0.5x \geq 80$$
$$\frac{1}{2}x \geq 48$$
$$x \geq 96$$

Therefore, she has to sell at least 96 or more products.

Check Point 3

Solutions_Page 64

A rental company charges a one-time rental fee of $24 plus $3.50 per hour to rent a lawnmower. If John has only $45 to spend, what is the maximum amount of time in hours he can rent the lawnmower?

Example 4

Jane took a taxi. The taxi charges $3.5 for the first mile and $1.25 for each additional $\frac{1}{2}$ mile. What is the maximum distance in miles she can travel if she has only $41?

Solution

Let x be the number of miles Jane travels after the first 1 mile. Since the taxi charges $1.25 for each additional $\frac{1}{2}$ mile after the first mile, the taxi charges $2.5 for each additional mile. Then we have the following inequality:

$$3.5+2.5x \leq 41$$
$$35+25x \leq 410$$
$$25x \leq 375$$
$$x \leq 15$$

Therefore, the maximum distance she can travel is 16 miles(15 miles+first 1 mile).

Check Point 4

Solutions_Page 64

Olivia sometimes takes a taxi to work. The taxi charges $4.25 for the first mile and $0.5 for each additional quarter of a mile. If the maximum amount that Eugene can pay for the taxi is $26.25, what is the maximum distance she can travel by taxi?

Example 5

A company makes boxes of mechanical pencils. Each box should contain 250 pencils, plus or minus 8 pencils. What are the minimum and maximum numbers of mechanical pencils in each box?

Solution

Let x be the number of mechanical pencils in the box. Then the absolute value inequality that gives the solution x is

$$|x-250| \leq 8$$
$$-8 \leq x-250 \leq 8$$
$$242 \leq x \leq 258.$$

Therefore, the minimum and maximum numbers of mechanical pencils in each box is 242 and 258, respectively.

Check Point 5

Solutions_Page 64

A certain car averages 26 miles per gallon on the highway. The actual mileage varies from the average by at most 4 miles per gallon. What is the range of the gas mileage of this car?

Review Exercise

01 An online download movie club has a one-time registration fee of $14.5 and charges $2.25 for downloading each movie. If David has $100 to join the club and download movies, what is the maximum number of movies he can download?

02 In 2016, Country K had approximately 128 million trees. Starting in 2017, the country has been planting 8 million trees each year. At this rate, in which year will Country K first have more than 300 million trees?

03 Daniel invested $12,000 in the stock, making a 6 percent annual return. He also plans to invest in bonds that pay 5 percent annual return. How much should he invest in bonds if he wants to earn at least $1,500 per year on investment?

04 Lisa has just opened a brand new backpack store. Her monthly expenses for running the store are $1,820. If she makes $32 on every backpack she sells, what is the minimum number of backpacks she needs to sell in a month to make a profit?

Review Exercise

05 David and his two older sisters, Jenny and Ariel, are each two years apart in age. The sum of their ages is greater than the age of their mother, who is 54. What is the youngest age that David can be?

06 Daniel wants to visit the amusement park in Florida. The price of admission to the park is $25, and each ride costs an additional $3.50. If he can spend at most $50.00 at the park, what is the maximum number of rides he can go on?

07 James recently opened a new store selling baseball caps. He spent a one-time fee of $2,000 for interior design and decoration of the store. If he purchases plain caps for $12 each, prints graphics on them, and then sell them for $28 each. What is the minimum number of caps that James would need to sell to make a profit of at least $1,000?

08 Peter is inviting 15 guests to his birthday party. He plans to serve each guest at least two slices of pizza. If each pizza contains 8 slices, what is the minimum number of pizza peter must order?

09 Sophia wants to add water to 200 grams of 15% salt water so that the concentration is less than or equal to 8%. Find out the least amount of water she needs to add.

10 Suppose a car is allowed within 6 miles per hour at a speed limit of 60 miles per hour. If the car does not receive a ticket within this range, what is the maximum speed the car is allowed to run?

Chapter Test — Level 1

01 Which of the following numbers is a solution of the inequality $2(x-4)+x \geq 3(1-2x)+7$?

(A) -2
(B) -1
(C) 0
(D) 1
(E) 2

02 Solve the inequality $\dfrac{x+1}{3} - \dfrac{2x-1}{2} > 4x + \dfrac{1}{6}$.

03 Solve the inequality $x + 6.4 \leq 0.4(2-x)$.

04 If the solution of the inequality $6x-2a-10<2(3-x)-6x$ is $x<2$, what is the value of a?

05 Solve the inequality $\dfrac{kx+5}{2} \geq 4$ in terms of k where $k<0$.

06 Find the least integer that satisfies the inequality $\dfrac{2x-1}{3} - \dfrac{x-7}{4} > 1$.

07 Solve the inequality $-8 \leq 1 - \dfrac{5x+1}{4} \leq 7$.

Chapter Test — Level 1

08 Solve the inequality $\frac{2}{3}-|x-2|<-\frac{4}{3}$

09 Graph the system of inequality $\begin{cases} y \leq -2x+3 \\ y > \frac{3}{2}x-1 \end{cases}$.

10 Jenny has two summer jobs. She works as a math tutor, which pays $15 per hour, and she works as a hostess at a seafood restaurant, which pays $12 per hour. As a math tutor, she only works for 8 hours per week. If she wants to earn at least $200 per week, what is the minimum number of hours she has to work at the seafood restaurant?

11 The interior of Earth is chemically divided into layers. The mantle is the layer of the Earth that is more than 100 kilometers and less than 2900 kilometers below the Earth's surface. Which of the following inequalities describes all possible depth x, in kilometers, below the Earth's surface that are in the mantle?

(A) $|x+100|<2,900$
(B) $|x-100|<2,900$
(C) $|x+100|<1,400$
(D) $|x-1,500|<1,400$
(E) $|x+1,500|<1,400$

Chapter Test — Level 2

01 If two inequalities $\frac{1}{3}(x+2)-x \geq -\frac{3x-2}{5}+2$ and $0.8x-\frac{x-k}{2} \leq 0.2(x-4)$ have the same solutions, what is the value of k?

02 If the solution of the inequality $2ax+5 < -13$ is $x>3$, what is the value of a?

03 Solve the inequality $\frac{k}{3}(x+3)-\frac{1}{2} \geq \frac{1}{6}(3+2x)$ where $k<1$.

04 If $\frac{|4x-2|}{2} \leq 5$ and $k=3-5x$, which of the following is the solution k?

(A) $-12 \leq k \leq 13$
(B) $-13 \leq k \leq 12$
(C) $-13 \leq k \leq -12$
(D) $12 \leq k \leq 13$
(E) $13 \leq k \leq 26$

05 If $3x-2y=6$, find the solution x that satisfies the inequality $-4 \leq 5x-4y < 11$.

06 $\begin{cases} y \leq 3 \\ x \leq 1 \\ 2x+y \geq -2 \end{cases}$

For the system of linear inequalities above, find the area of the solution region.

07 Andrea is considering accepting one of two sales positions. Company A offers a yearly salary of $39,000. Company B offers a yearly salary of $25,000 plus a 4% annual commission on sales. For what amount of sales is the salary at company B greater than the salary at company A?

08 Tom wants to make more than 12% brine by mixing 400g of 6% brine and 15% brine. How many grams of 15% brine does he need to mix?

09 Eugene sometimes takes a taxi to work. The taxi charge $1.25 for the first quarter of a mile and $0.875 for each additional half of a mile. If the maximum amount that Eugene can pay for the taxi is $24, what is the maximum distance he can travel by cab?

memo

Chapter **5**

Manipulating Polynomials

1. Addition and Subtraction of Polynomials
2. Multiplication of Polynomials, Part 1
3. Multiplication of Polynomials, Part 2
4. Chapter Test

1 Addition and Subtraction of Polynomials

01 Definition of Polynomial

A polynomial is an algebraic expression that has one or more terms, which only employs the operations of addition, subtraction, multiplication, and non-negative integer exponents. Polynomial can be classified by number of non-zero terms. Refer to the following table below.

Name	Number of Term(s)	Example
Monomial	1	$2x^2$
Binomial	2	$2x^2 - 4x$
Trinomial	3	$2x^2 - 4x + 5$

The degree of a polynomial is the highest degree for a term. For example, consider the polynomial

$$3x^5 + 2x^3 - 5x^2y^2$$

The first term has a degree of 5, the second term has a degree of 3, and the last term has a degree of 4(the sum of the power of 2 and 2). Therefore, the polynomial has a degree of 5 which is the highest degree of given terms.

02 Polynomials in Standard Form

To write any polynomial in standard from, look at the degree of each term and arrange the terms in order of decreasing degree. For example, the standard form of the polynomial $-4x + 2 + 3x^2$ can be written as $3x^2 - 4x + 2$.

03 Adding and Subtracting Polynomials

Adding and subtracting polynomials is not difficult at all. It is just like adding and subtracting any other type of expression. We simply add or subtract any like terms together. **Likes terms** are terms whose variables and their exponents are the same. For example,

$$3x^2, \; -2x^2, \; \frac{3}{2}x^2, \text{ and } -2.4x^2$$

are all like terms because the variables are all x and their exponents are all 2.

1. Solving Parentheses

    (1) If there is a plus in front of the parentheses, leave the sign in parentheses.
    $$+(A+B-C)=A+B-C$$
    Example: $+(3x^2+2x-1)=3x^2+2x-1$

    (2) If there is a minus in front of the parentheses, reverse the sign in parentheses.
    $$-(A+B-C)=-A-B+C$$
    Example: $-(3x^2+2x-1)=-3x^2-2x+1$

2. Addition and Subtraction of Polynomials

    (1) Solve parentheses.

    (2) Collect like terms.

    (3) Simplify.

Concept Check

$3(x^2+7x-2)-(4x^2+5x+1)$ → Given
$=3x^2+21x-6-4x^2-5x-1$ → Solve the parentheses
$=(3x^2-4x^2)+(21x-5x)+(-6-1)$ → Collect like terms
$=-x^2+16x-7$ → Simplify

Example 1

Simplify the expression.

① $(4x-2)+(3x+1)$　　　　　　　② $2(x^2-2x+3)-(3x^2+x-6)$
③ $(3x^3-4x^2+5x-2)+2(5x^2-7x+1)$　　④ $3(-9x^2+x+12)-2(-x^3-3x^2+6)$

Solution

① $(4x-2)+(3x+1) = 4x-2+3x+1$
$\qquad\qquad\qquad\quad = (4x+3x)+(-2+1)$
$\qquad\qquad\qquad\quad = 7x-1$

② $2(x^2-2x+3)-(3x^2+x-6) = 2x^2-4x+6-3x^2-x+6$
$\qquad\qquad\qquad\qquad\qquad\quad = (2x^2-3x^2)+(-4x-x)+(6+6)$
$\qquad\qquad\qquad\qquad\qquad\quad = -x^2-5x+12$

③ $(3x^3-4x^2+5x-2)+2(5x^2-7x+1) = 3x^3-4x^2+5x-2+10x^2-14x+2$
$\qquad\qquad\qquad\qquad\qquad\qquad\qquad = 3x^3+(-4x^2+10x^2)+(5x-14x)+(-2+2)$
$\qquad\qquad\qquad\qquad\qquad\qquad\qquad = 3x^3+6x^2-9x$

④ $3(-9x^2+x+12)-2(-x^3-3x^2+6) = -27x^2+3x+36+2x^3+6x^2-12$
$\qquad\qquad\qquad\qquad\qquad\qquad\qquad = 2x^3+(-27x^2+6x^2)+3x+(36-12)$
$\qquad\qquad\qquad\qquad\qquad\qquad\qquad = 2x^3-21x^2+3x+24$

Check Point 1

Simplify the expression.

① $(9x+1)+4(-5x+3)$　　　　　　② $(3x-4)-(7x-2)$
③ $4(1-2x+x^2)+2(4x^2-5x+1)$　　④ $3(x^3-3x^2-4x-3)-5(2-5x+6x^2)$

04 Polynomials in Fraction Form

1. Addition and Subtraction of Polynomials in Fraction Form
   (1) Find the common denominator of each term.
   (2) The common denominator should be LCM(Least Common Multiple) of each denominator.

Concept Check

$$\frac{x^2-2x+3}{2} - \frac{2x+1}{3}$$

$$= \frac{x^2-2x+3}{2} \cdot \frac{3}{3} - \frac{2x+1}{3} \cdot \frac{2}{2} \quad \rightarrow \text{LCM of 2 and 3 is } 2 \cdot 3$$

$$= \frac{3(x^2-2x+3) - 2(2x+1)}{6} \quad \rightarrow \text{Keep the denominator the same and then add the numerator}$$

$$= \frac{3x^2-6x+9-4x-2}{6} \quad \rightarrow \text{Solve the parentheses}$$

$$= \frac{3x^2-10x+7}{6} \quad \rightarrow \text{Combine like terms and simplify}$$

Example 2

Simplify the expression.

① $\dfrac{2x-1}{2} - \dfrac{x+3}{4}$ ② $\dfrac{3-x}{4} - \dfrac{3x^2-2}{5}$

③ $2x^2+1 - \dfrac{3x-2}{4}$ ④ $\dfrac{1-3x^2+2x}{2} - \dfrac{x^2+2x-4}{3}$

Solution

① $\dfrac{2x-1}{2} - \dfrac{x+3}{4} = \dfrac{2x-1}{2} \cdot \dfrac{2}{2} - \dfrac{x+3}{4}$

$= \dfrac{2(2x-1)-(x+3)}{4}$

$$= \frac{4x-2-x-3}{4} = \frac{3x-5}{4}$$

② $\dfrac{3-x}{4} - \dfrac{3x^2-2}{5} = \dfrac{3-x}{4} \cdot \dfrac{5}{5} - \dfrac{3x^2-2}{5} \cdot \dfrac{4}{4}$

$$= \frac{5(3-x) - 4(3x^2-2)}{20}$$

$$= \frac{15 - 5x - 12x^2 + 8}{20} = \frac{-12x^2 - 5x + 23}{20}$$

③ $2x^2 + 1 - \dfrac{3x-2}{4} = \dfrac{2x^2+1}{1} \cdot \dfrac{4}{4} - \dfrac{3x-2}{4}$

$$= \frac{4(2x^2+1) - (3x-2)}{4}$$

$$= \frac{8x^2 + 4 - 3x + 2}{4} = \frac{8x^2 - 3x + 6}{4}$$

④ $\dfrac{1-3x^2+2x}{2} - \dfrac{x^2+2x-4}{3} = \dfrac{1-3x^2+2x}{2} \cdot \dfrac{3}{3} - \dfrac{x^2+2x-4}{3} \cdot \dfrac{2}{2}$

$$= \frac{3(1-3x^2+2x) - 2(x^2+2x-4)}{6}$$

$$= \frac{3 - 9x^2 + 6x - 2x^2 - 4x + 8}{6} = \frac{-11x^2 + 2x + 11}{6}$$

Check Point 2

Solutions_Page 70

Simplify the expression.

① $\dfrac{2-4x}{3} + \dfrac{2x-5}{2}$

② $\dfrac{3x-1}{2} + 3 - 4x$

③ $\dfrac{x^2-x}{4} - \dfrac{x-x^2}{2}$

④ $\dfrac{2x^2-x+1}{3} - \dfrac{x-3x^2}{4} + 1$

Review Exercise

01 Simplify the expression.

(1) $(2x-7)+(5-4x)$

(2) $(1-2x+x^2)-(4x^2-5x+1)$

(3) $(4x^2-2+5x)+2(3x^2+3x-7)$

(4) $(2a^3-3a^2-3a+5)$
$\quad\quad\quad +(4a^3-6a^2+5a-1)$

(5) $6(2a^3-a^2+4)-3(4a^3-3a^2-4a+2)$

(6) $(4-y-5y^2+2y^3)$
$\quad\quad\quad -2\left(-\dfrac{1}{2}y^3+y^2-5y-1\right)$

(7) $4(3b^2-b+1)-2(b+3)-\dfrac{1}{2}(4b^2-8)$

(8) $4(a^2-3a-2)+5(a^2-1)$
$\quad\quad\quad -9(a^2-a+2)$

02 Simplify the expression.

(1) $\dfrac{3x-1}{2}+\dfrac{x+2}{3}$

(2) $\dfrac{4x+5}{2}-\dfrac{x-1}{4}$

Review Exercise

(3) $x+3-\dfrac{3(2-x)}{5}$

(4) $\dfrac{x+1}{4}-\dfrac{2(3-x)}{3}+\dfrac{3x-2}{2}$

Challenging

03 Simplify the expression.

(1) $\dfrac{x-y}{2}-\dfrac{y-z}{3}-\dfrac{z-x}{6}$

(2) $\dfrac{a+b+c}{6}-\dfrac{a+b-c}{4}+\dfrac{a-b-c}{8}$

Challenging

04 Write the correct expression in $\boxed{}$.

(1) $4(2x^2+x-3)+\boxed{}=4x^2-3x$

(2) $\dfrac{3x^2-4x}{2}+\boxed{}=\dfrac{x^2+2x+8}{4}$

(3) $\dfrac{a+2b}{3}-\boxed{}-\dfrac{a-2b}{6}=\dfrac{a+b}{6}$

Chapter 5. Manipulating Polynomials

Challenging

05 Simplify the expression.

(1) $3a-[4b-5a-\{4b+2(3b+3a)\}]$

(2) $4x-[2x^2+3x-2\{3x-(5x^2-x)+2\}]$

06 In some expression, a^2-3a-2 should be added to A, but subtracted from A by mistake. If the resulting expression is $4a^2+5a-4$,

(1) Find the expression A.

(2) Find the correct expression.

07 If $\dfrac{x-2y}{3}-\dfrac{3x+2y}{4}=ax+by$, what is the value of $a+b$?

2. Multiplication of Polynomials, Part 1

To multiply two polynomials, distribute each term of the first polynomial to every term of the second polynomial. Then combine like terms if you can.

01 Monomial × Binomial

Expand the expression using distribution law.

$$a(b+c) = (a \times b) + (a \times c) = ab + ac$$

Concept Check

1. $a(3a+2) = (a \times 3a) + (a \times 2) = 3a^2 + 2a$

2. Geometric interpretation

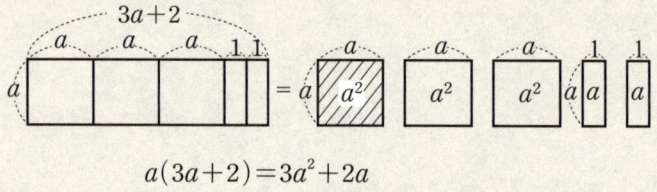

$$a(3a+2) = 3a^2 + 2a$$

Example 1

Multiply the polynomials.

① $4(2a+3)$
② $(y-4)2y$
③ $2x(3x^2 - 1)$
④ $(2a - a^2)5a^3$

178 Chapter 5. Manipulating Polynomials

Solution

① $4(2a+3)=(4\times 2a)+(4\times 3)=8a+12$
② $(y-4)2y=(y\times 2y)+(-4\times 2y)=2y^2-8y$
③ $2x(3x^2-1)=(2x\times 3x^2)+(2x\times(-1))=6x^3-2x$
④ $(2a-a^2)5a^3=(2a\times 5a^3)+(-a^2\times 5a^3)=10a^4-5a^5$

Check Point 1   Solutions_Page 73

Multiply the polynomials.

① $2(4x+1)$ ② $4x(2x^2-5x+3)$

③ $5(3a-1)+4(2-3a)$ ④ $\left(2a-\dfrac{1}{2}\right)(-4)-6\left(-4+\dfrac{a}{3}\right)$

02 Binomial × Binomial

Expand the expression using the technique called FOIL (First, Outer, Inner, Last).

$$(a+b)(c+d)=\underset{\text{First}}{(a\times c)}+\underset{\text{Outer}}{(a\times d)}+\underset{\text{Inner}}{(b\times c)}+\underset{\text{Last}}{(b\times d)}$$
$$=ac+ad+bc+bd$$

Concept Check

1. $(a+2)(a+1)=(a\times a)+(a\times 1)+(2\times a)+(2\times 1)$
$\qquad\qquad\quad =a^2+a+2a+2=a^2+3a+2$

2. Geometric interpretation

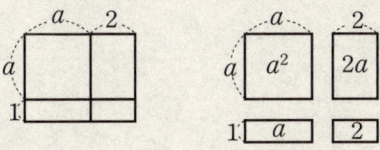

3. Use the law of distribution

$(a+2)(a+1)=a(a+1)+2(a+1)$
$\qquad\qquad\quad =a^2+a+2a+2=a^2+3a+2$

Example 2

Multiply the polynomials.

① $(x+2)(x+3)$
② $(2a+3)(a-4)$
③ $(x-1)(x^2+2)$
④ $(1-4b)(3+2b)$

Solution

① $(x+2)(x+3) = (x \times x) + (x \times 3) + (2 \times x) + (2 \times 3)$
$\qquad\qquad\quad = x^2 + 3x + 2x + 6$
$\qquad\qquad\quad = x^2 + 5x + 6$

② $(2a+3)(a-4) = (2a \times a) + (2a \times -4) + (3 \times a) + (3 \times -4)$
$\qquad\qquad\quad = 2a^2 - 8a + 3a - 12$
$\qquad\qquad\quad = 2a^2 - 5a - 12$

③ $(x-1)(x^2+2) = (x \times x^2) + (x \times 2) + (-1 \times x^2) + (-1 \times 2)$
$\qquad\qquad\quad = x^3 + 2x - x^2 - 2$
$\qquad\qquad\quad = x^3 - x^2 + 2x - 2$

④ $(1-4b)(3+2b) = (1 \times 3) + (1 \times 2b) + (-4b \times 3) + (-4b \times 2b)$
$\qquad\qquad\quad = 3 + 2b - 12b - 8b^2$
$\qquad\qquad\quad = 3 - 10b - 8b^2$
$\qquad\qquad\quad = -8b^2 - 10b + 3$

Solutions_Page 73

Check Point 2

Multiply the polynomials.

① $(4a+1)(a-2)$
② $(3x-1)(x+2)$
③ $(2y+1)(4y^2-3)$
④ $(a^2-2)(4a^2+1)$

03 Binomial × Trinomial

Expand the expression using distributive law.

$$(a+b)(c+d+e) = (a \times c) + (a \times d) + (a \times e) + (b \times c) + (b \times d) + (b \times e)$$
$$= ac + ad + ae + bc + bd + be$$

Concept Check

1. $(a+1)(a^2+a+2) = (a \times a^2) + (a \times a) + (a \times 2) + (1 \times a^2) + (1 \times a) + (1 \times 2)$

$$= a^3 + a^2 + 2a + a^2 + a + 2$$
$$= a^3 + 2a^2 + 3a + 2$$

2. Geometric interpretation

3. Use the law of distribution

$(a+1)(a^2+a+2) = a(a^2+a+2) + 1(a^2+a+2)$
$$= a^3 + a^2 + 2a + a^2 + a + 2$$
$$= a^3 + 2a^2 + 3a + 2$$

4. Trinomial × Binomial

$(a+b+c)(d+e) = (a \times d) + (a \times e) + (b \times d) + (b \times e) + (c \times d) + (c \times e)$
$$= ad + ae + bd + be + cd + ce$$

Chapter 5. Manipulating Polynomials

Example 3

Multiply the polynomials.

① $(a+2)(2a^2-a+4)$ ② $(x+1)(x^2-2x+3)$

Solution

① $(a+2)(2a^2-a+4) = (a \times 2a^2) + (a \times (-a)) + (a \times 4) + (2 \times 2a^2) + (2 \times (-a)) + (2 \times 4)$
$= 2a^3 - a^2 + 4a + 4a^2 - 2a + 8$
$= 2a^3 + 3a^2 + 2a + 8$

② $(x+1)(x^2-2x+3) = (x \times x^2) + (x \times -2x) + (x \times 3) + (1 \times x^2) + (1 \times -2x) + (1 \times 3)$
$= x^3 - 2x^2 + 3x + x^2 - 2x + 3$
$= x^3 - x^2 + x + 3$

Check Point 3

Solutions_Page 73

Multiply the polynomials.

① $(x-3)(x^2-x+1)$ ② $(2x^2-4x+1)(3x+1)$

③ $(2a^2-a+1)(a^2-1)$

Review Exercise

01 Multiply the polynomials.

(1) $3x(x^2-1)$

(2) $\dfrac{2x}{5}\left(25-\dfrac{25}{2}x^2\right)$

(3) $(a+4)(-2a)$

(4) $-4a(3a^2-a+3)$

(5) $2a^2(2a-a^2)$

(6) $(2x^2+3x-1)(-5x)$

02 Multiply the polynomials.

(1) $2(a^2-3)+3(4a-2)$

(2) $\dfrac{1}{3}(6x^2-9x+1)-\dfrac{2x}{5}(10x-15)$

(3) $-2(x^2+2x-5)-2x(x-1)$

(4) $5(x^2-1)+3(x^2+x-1)+4$

Review Exercise

03 Multiply the polynomials.

(1) $(x-1)(2x+3)$

(2) $(3x-1)(2x-4)$

(3) $(-2y+3)(y-1)$

(4) $(1-y)(-1-3y)$

(2) $(a^2-2)(4a+1)$

(3) $(2a+a^2)\left(-5+\dfrac{1}{2}a\right)$

(4) $(1+2m)(2m^2-m)$

05 Multiply the polynomials.

(1) $(2x-1)(x^2+3x-3)$

Challenging

04 Multiply the polynomials.

(1) $(x^2-1)(2x+3)$

(2) $(-a^2+a+4)(3a+2)$

06 Find the value of $a+b$ in the equation given below.

(1) $(x-a)(2x+3)=2x^2+bx-12$

(2) $(x-3)(5x+a)=5x^2-11x+b$

Challenging

07 If $(2x+a)(bx-5)=cx^2-4x-10$, what is the value of $a+b+c$?

08 Find the coefficient of x term in the equation given below.

(1) $(3x+3)(3x-4)$

(2) $(4-2x)(5-2x^2+2x)$

Challenging

09 If the coefficient of y of $(3+2y)(ay^2-3y+b)$ is 8, what is the value of b?

10 A tennis court is shaped like a rectangle. It has a width of $2k+1$ feet and a length of $3+2k-k^2$ feet. Which expression gives the area of the tennis court in square feet?

(A) $2k^3+5k^2+8k+3$

(B) $2k^3-3k^2+4k+3$

(C) $2k^3-3k^2-8k-3$

(D) $-2k^3-5k^2+4k+3$

(E) $-2k^3+3k^2+8k+3$

3. Multiplication of Polynomials, Part 2

01 Expanding $(a+b)^2$ and $(a-b)^2$

1. $(a+b)^2 = a^2 + 2ab + b^2$ → $(\Delta + O)^2 = \Delta^2 + 2\Delta O + O^2$
2. $(a-b)^2 = a^2 - 2ab + b^2$ → $(\Delta - O)^2 = \Delta^2 - 2\Delta O + O^2$

Concept Check

1. Expand $(a+b)^2$ and $(a-b)^2$ by FOIL method.

   (1) $(a+b)^2 = (a+b)(a+b) = (a \times a) + (a \times b) + (b \times a) + (b \times b)$
   $= a^2 + ab + ba + b^2 = a^2 + 2ab + b^2$

   $(a-b)^2 = (a-b)(a-b) = (a \times a) + (a \times -b) + (-b \times a) + (-b \times -b)$
   $= a^2 - ab - ba + b^2 = a^2 - 2ab + b^2$

2. Geometric Interpretation

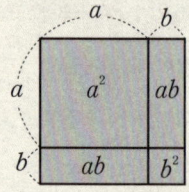 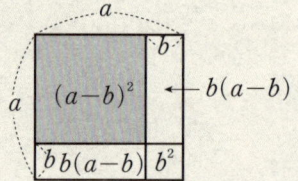

$(a+b)^2 =$ Area of the shaded square
$\quad = a^2 + ab + ab + b^2$
$\quad = a^2 + 2ab + b^2$

$(a-b)^2 =$ Area of the shaded square
$\quad = a^2 - b(a-b) - b(a-b) - b^2$
$\quad = a^2 - ba + b^2 - ba + b^2 - b^2$
$\quad = a^2 - 2ab + b^2$

3. Note the following

   (1) $(-a-b)^2 = (a+b)^2$

   Because $(-a-b)^2 = (-a)^2 + 2(-a)(-b) + (-b)^2 = a^2 + 2ab + b^2 = (a+b)^2$.

(2) $(-a+b)^2 = (a-b)^2$
   Because $(-a+b)^2 = (-a)^2 + 2(-a)b + b^2 = a^2 - 2ab + b^2 = (a-b)^2$.
(3) $(a+b)^2 \neq a^2 + b^2$ and $(a-b)^2 \neq a^2 - b^2$.

Example 1

Multiply the polynomials.

① $(x+4)^2$ ② $(4a-1)^2$ ③ $(x-3y)^2$ ④ $(2a+3b)^2$

Solution

① $(x+4)^2 = x^2 + 2(x)(4) + 4^2 = x^2 + 8x + 16$
② $(4a-1)^2 = (4a)^2 - 2(4a)(1) + 1^2 = 16a^2 - 8a + 1$
③ $(x-3y)^2 = x^2 - 2(x)(3y) + (3y)^2 = x^2 - 6xy + 9y^2$
④ $(2a+3b)^2 = (2a)^2 + 2(2a)(3b) + (3b)^2 = 4a^2 + 12ab + 9b^2$

Check Point 1

Solutions_Page 76

Multiply the polynomials.

① $(x+2)^2$

② $(2x-5)^2$

③ $\left(\dfrac{1}{4} + 3b\right)^2$

④ $\left(-a - \dfrac{2b}{3}\right)^2$

02 Expanding $(a+b)(a-b)$

$(a+b)(a-b) = a^2 - b^2 \rightarrow (\triangle - \bigcirc)(\triangle + \bigcirc) = \triangle^2 - \bigcirc^2$

Concept Check

1. Expand $(a+b)(a-b)$ by FOIL method.

$$(a+b)(a-b) = (a \times a) + (a \times -b) + (b \times a) + (b \times -b)$$
$$= a^2 - ab + ba - b^2 = a^2 - b^2$$

2. Geometric Interpretation

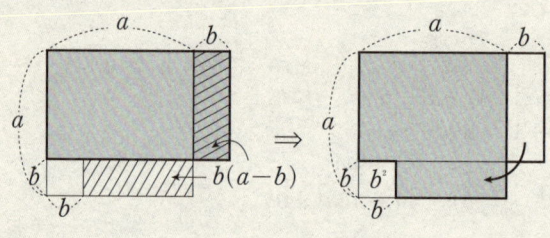

$$(a+b)(a-b) = a^2 - b^2$$

3. Note the following

   (1) $(-a+b)(a+b) = (b-a)(b+a) = b^2 - a^2$

   (2) $(-a-b)(a-b) = -(a+b)(a-b) = -(a^2 - b^2) = b^2 - a^2$

Example 2

Multiply the polynomials.

① $(a+2)(a-2)$ ② $(5x-3)(5x+3)$

③ $(x+4y)(-x+4y)$ ④ $(3a-2b)(3a+2b)$

Solution

① $(a+2)(a-2)=a^2-2^2=a^2-4$
② $(5x-3)(5x+3)=(5x)^2-3^2=25x^2-9$
③ $(x+4y)(-x+4y)=(4y+x)(4y-x)=(4y)^2-x^2=16y^2-x^2$
④ $(3a-2b)(3a+2b)=(3a)^2-(2b)^2=9a^2-4b^2$

Check Point 2   Solutions_Page 76

Multiply the polynomials.

① $(x-5)(x+5)$ ② $(2x-5y)(2x+5y)$

③ $\left(\dfrac{3a}{4}-\dfrac{b}{3}\right)\left(\dfrac{3a}{4}+\dfrac{b}{3}\right)$ ④ $(a-3)(a+3)(a^2+9)$

03 Numerical Calculation using Multiplication Formula

1. Calculation in square form
   $(a+b)^2=a^2+2ab+b^2$
   $(a-b)^2=a^2-2ab+b^2$

2. Calculation of product of two numbers
   $(a+b)(a-b)=a^2-b^2$

Concept Check

1. $104^2=(100+4)^2=100^2+2(100\times 4)+4^2=10{,}000+800+16=10{,}816$
   $99^2=(100-1)^2=100^2-2(100\times 1)+1^2=10{,}000-200+1=9{,}801$

2. $101\times 99=(100+1)(100-1)=100^2-1^2=10{,}000-1=9{,}999$

Example 3

Calculate the following using the multiplication formula.

① 102^2 ② 1003×997

Solution

① Use $(a+b)^2 = a^2 + 2ab + b^2$.
$102^2 = (100+2)^2 = 100^2 + 2(100 \times 2) + 2^2$
$= 10,000 + 400 + 4 = 10,404$

② Use $(a+b)(a-b) = a^2 - b^2$.
$1,003 \times 997 = (1,000+3)(1,000-3)$
$= 1,000^2 - 3^2 = 1,000,000 - 9 = 999,991$

Check Point 3

Solutions_Page 76

Calculate the following using the multiplication formula.

① 98^2 ② 9.8×10.2 ③ 101×103

Review Exercise

01 Multiply the polynomials.

(1) $(x+3)^2$

(2) $(2x-1)^2$

(3) $\left(3a+\dfrac{1}{3}\right)^2$

(4) $\left(\dfrac{a}{4}-6\right)^2$

02 Multiply the polynomials.

(1) $(x+5y)^2$

(2) $\left(\dfrac{2x}{3}-4y\right)^2$

(3) $(-3a+4b)^2$

(4) $\left(-\dfrac{2a}{3}-\dfrac{b}{2}\right)^2$

Review Exercise

03 Multiply the polynomials.

(1) $(x-3)(x+3)$

(2) $\left(x+\dfrac{1}{2}\right)\left(x-\dfrac{1}{2}\right)$

(3) $(2a-3b)(2a+3b)$

(4) $\left(\dfrac{2b}{3}-\dfrac{a}{3}\right)\left(\dfrac{2b}{3}+\dfrac{a}{3}\right)$

04 Find the correct positive integer in ☐.

(1) $(4x+\boxed{})^2$
$=16x^2+16x+\boxed{}$

(2) $(\boxed{}x-4)^2$
$=9x^2-\boxed{}x+16$

05 If $x^2=32$ and $y^2=20$, what is the value of $\left(\dfrac{3x}{4}-\dfrac{5y}{2}\right)\left(\dfrac{3x}{4}+\dfrac{5y}{2}\right)$?

06 Calculate the following using the multiplication formula.

(1) 10.2^2

(2) 299^2

(3) 50.2×49.8

Challenging

07 Simplify each of the following.

(1) $(3-1)(3+1)(3^2+1)(3^4+1)$

(2) $(2^3-1)(2^3+1)(2^6+1)$

Challenging

08 Calculate $2022 \times 2020 - 2021 \times 2019$ using the multiplication formula.

Chapter Test — Level 1

01 Simplify the expression $2(3x^2-x+2)-3(3x+2x^2+1)$.

02 Simplify the expression $\dfrac{2(3x^2-2x)}{5}+\dfrac{x^2-x+3}{4}$.

$$2(3a^2+a+4)-2(a^2-3a+1)-\boxed{}=a^2-3$$

03 Write the correct expression in $\boxed{}$ above.

04 Suppose that $A=x^2-2x+3$, $B=3x^2-2$, and $C=2x^2+x$.
If $3A-(B+2C)+4C=ax^2+bx+c$, what is the value of $a+b+c$?

05 Which of the following is equal to $(4x-3)(4x+3)-4(2x-1)^2$?

(A) $16x-5$ (B) $16x-13$ (C) $8x^2+16x-9$

(D) $8x^2-16x-13$ (E) $8x^2-16x+9$

06 Multiply the polynomial $(x+2)(-2x^2-x+3)$.

Chapter Test — Level 1

07 Which of the following is different from the other four for the values of A to E?

(A) $(x-1)^2 = x^2 - Ax + 1$
(B) $(3x+By)^2 = 9x^2 + 12xy + 4y^2$
(C) $\left(\dfrac{a}{2}+4\right)\left(\dfrac{a}{2}-4\right) = \dfrac{a^2}{C} - 16$
(D) $(a-5)(2a+8) = 2a^2 - Da - 40$
(E) $(x-y)(x-y-4) = x^2 - Exy - 4x + y^2 + 4y$

08 Calculate $\dfrac{2021 \times 2023 + 1}{2022}$ using the multiplication formula.

09 Simplify $(4-1)(4+1)(4^2+1)(4^4+1)$.

10 Suppose $a+b=8$ and $ab=6$. Find the value of each of the following.

(1) a^2+b^2

(2) $\dfrac{1}{a}+\dfrac{1}{b}$

11 The unit of the side of the cube is k. The new cube is formed with each side 4 units longer than the original cube's side. Find the expression expressed as k representing the volume of the new cube.

Chapter Test — Level 2

01 Simplify the expression $\dfrac{3(2a^2+a-1)}{2}+\dfrac{3a-a^2+1}{6}$.

02 Simplify the expression $5-2\left[3x^2-4x+\dfrac{1}{2}\{5x-(4x^2-x)-6\}\right]$.

03 Multiply the polynomial $(a^3-2a+2)(2a-5)$.

04 If $3x+[x-\{2x-(4x-\boxed{})+x^2\}+3x^2]=8x^2+7x$, find the correct expression in $\boxed{}$.

05 If $(x+m)(x+n)=x^2+kx+40$, where m, n, and k are positive integer and $n>m$, which of the following values cannot be k.

(A) 41 (B) 36 (C) 22 (D) 14 (E) 13

06 If $a^2=16$, find the value of $(a-4)(a-2)a^2(a+2)(a+4)$.

07 If $(2+1)(2^2+1)(2^4+1)(2^8+1)=2^a-b$, where $0<b<10$, what is the value of ab?

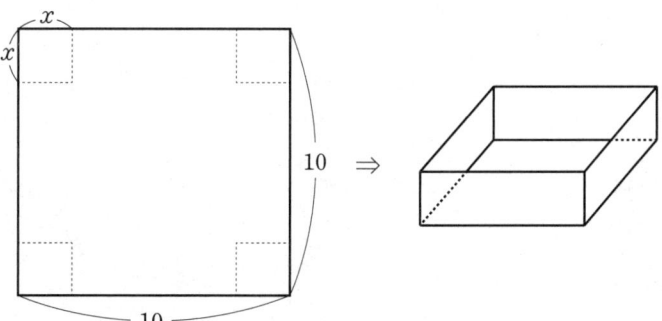

08 Find the volume of the box in x made of a square sheet by removing and folding the four identical corners as shown in the picture above.

memo

Chapter **6**

Factoring

1. Factors and Prime Factorization
2. Factoring Binomials
3. Factoring Trinomials
4. Chapter Test

1 Factors and Prime Factorization

01 Factors

Sometimes a number can be written as the product of two or more numbers. Those numbers are called factors of that number.

Concept Check

$8 = 1 \times 8 = 2 \times 4 \Rightarrow 1, 2, 4,$ and 8 are factors of 8.

The same is true for monomials. Unless they are prime numbers, monomials can be written as the product of two or more numbers or variables. Those numbers and variables are called factors of that monomial.

Concept Check

$5a = 1 \times 5a = 5 \times a \Rightarrow 1, 5, a,$ and $5a$ are factors of $5a$.

Prime numbers are whole numbers greater than 1 that have exactly two factors, the number itself and 1. Whole numbers greater than 1 that have more than two factors are called composite numbers.

Concept Check

$2, 3, 5, 7, 11, 13, 19, \cdots$ are prime numbers.

$4, 6, 8, 9, 10, 12, 14, \cdots$ are composite numbers.

02 Prime Factorization

The prime factorization of a number is all of the prime numbers that multiply to create the original number.

Concept Check

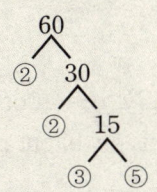

Factor tree of 60

⇒ The prime factorization of 60 can be written as
$60 = 2 \times 2 \times 3 \times 5 = 2^2 \times 3 \times 5$.

⇒ 2, 3, and 5 are prime factors of 60.

A factor tree is a tool that breaks down any number into its prime factors as shown above.

Example 1

Find the prime factorization of 420.

Solution

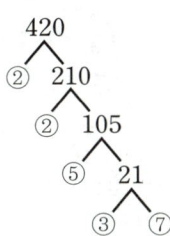

⇒ The prime factorization of 420 can be written as
$420 = 2 \times 2 \times 3 \times 5 \times 7 = 2^2 \times 3 \times 5 \times 7$.

$420 = 2^2 \times 3 \times 5 \times 7$

Solutions_Page 81

Check Point 1

① Find the prime factorization of 450.

② Find the prime factorization of 378.

03 The Greatest Common Factor

The greatest common factor (GCF) of two or more terms is simply the product of all the common factors of each term. Write the smallest exponent on each prime and variable common to the factorization.

Concept Check

(1) Find the GCF of 54 and 72.

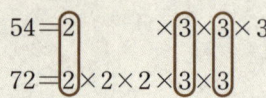

$54 = 2 \times 3 \times 3 \times 3$
$72 = 2 \times 2 \times 2 \times 3 \times 3$

Therefore, the GCF is $2 \times 3 \times 3 = 18$.

(2) Find the GCF of $6x^2$ and $10x^3$.

$6x^2 = 2 \times 3 \times x \times x$
$10x^3 = 2 \times 5 \times x \times x \times x$

Therefore, the GCF is $2 \times x \times x = 2x^2$.

Another method of finding the greatest common factor involves dividing the numbers or variables by common prime factors.

Concept Check

(1) Find the GCF of 54 and 72.

```
2 | 54   72
3 | 27   36
3 |  9   12
     3    4
```

The GCF is $2 \times 3 \times 3 = 18$

(2) Find the GCF of $6x^2$ and $10x^3$

```
x² | 6x²   10x³
 2 |  6    10x
      3     5x
```

The GCF is $x^2 \times 2 \times 3 = 6x^2$

Example 2

Find the greatest common factor of $90x^2$ and $100x$.

Solution

Method 1 :
$$90x^2 = \boxed{2} \times 3 \times 3 \times \boxed{5} \times \boxed{x} \times x$$
$$100x = \boxed{2} \times 2 \times \boxed{5} \times 5 \times \boxed{x}$$

Write the smallest exponent on each prime and variable common to the factorization. Therefore, the GCF is $2 \times 5 \times x = 10x$.

Method 2 :

$$\begin{array}{r|rr} x & 90x^2 & 100x \\ 2 & 90x & 100 \\ 5 & 45x & 50 \\ & 9x & 10 \end{array}$$

Therefore, the GCF is $x \times 2 \times 5 = 10x$.

The greatest common factor is $10x$.

Check Point 2   Solutions_Page 81

Find the greatest common factor.

① 50 and 85
② $30xy^3$ and $18x^2y^2$

04 Factors of Polynomials

When a polynomial can be expressed as the product of two or more numbers, monomials, or polynomials, each of these is called a factor of that polynomial.

Concept Check

The polynomial x^2-2x can be written as $x^2-2x=1\cdot(x^2-2x)$ or $x^2-2x=x(x-2)$. Therefore, the factors of x^2-2x are 1, x, $x-2$, and x^2-2x.

05 Definition of Factoring

Factoring is to decompose a polynomial into a product of two or more polynomials. In other words, it is finding what to multiply together to get the original polynomial expression.

$$x^2-x-12 \underset{\text{expanding}}{\overset{\text{factoring}}{\rightleftarrows}} (x-4)(x+3)$$

To find the factors of a polynomial, start by finding the greatest common factor (GCF) of all the terms.

Concept Check

Factor the polynomial $2x^2+6x$

First, $2x^2=\underline{2x}\times x$ and $6x=\underline{2x}\times 3$. Therefore, $\underline{2x}$ is the GCF of $2x^2$ and $6x$.

Now, use the distributive property to factor the polynomial as shown below.

$$\begin{aligned}2x^2+6x&=\underline{2x}\times x+\underline{2x}\times 3\\&=\underline{2x}(x+3)\end{aligned}$$

Example 3

Factor the polynomial.

① $12a^3+4a^2$ ② $20y^3-12y^2+8y$

Solution

① $12a^3+4a^2$ ⇒ $12a^3=\underline{4a^2}\times 3a$ and $4a^2=\underline{4a^2}\times 1$
The GCF of the polynomial is $4a^2$.
Therefore, $12a^3+4a^2=4a^2(3a+1)$.

$$12a^3+4a^2=4a^2(3a+1)$$

② $20y^3-12y^2+8y$
⇒ $20y^3=\underline{4y}\times 5y^2$, $-12y^2=\underline{4y}\times(-3y)$ and $8y=\underline{4y}\times 2$
The GCF of the polynomial is $4y$.
Therefore, $20y^3-12y^2+8y=4y(5y^2-3y+2)$.

$$20y^3-12y^2+8y=4y(5y^2-3y+2)$$

Check Point 3

Solutions_Page 81

Factor the polynomial.

① $6x-3$ ② $12x^4+8x^2$

③ $4a^3-6a^2+12a$ ④ $18a^2-12a-24$

Review Exercise

01 Find the prime factorization of each number.

(1) 168

(2) 392

(3) 25, 90, and 150

(4) $16x^3y^2$, $28x^2y^3$ and $100x^5y^4$

02 Find the greatest common factor.

(1) 100 and 225

(2) $9x^3y^4$ and $15xy^2$

03 Which of the following is NOT a factor of polynomial $a(a+b)(a-b)$?

(A) a (B) $a-b$
(C) a^2-b^2 (D) a^2+b^2
(E) $a(a+b)$

04 Factor the polynomial.

(1) $16x^3 - 12x^2$

(2) $30xy^2 + 36y$

(3) $xy^2 - x^2 + 2xy$

(4) $8ab^2 + 4ab - 6ab^3$

$2y(x-y)(x-2y)$, $x^2y - 2xy^2$

05 Which of the following is common factor to the two polynomials given above?

(A) $2xy$
(B) $x-y$
(C) $y(x-2y)$
(D) $y(x-y)$
(E) $xy(x-2y)$

2 Factoring Binomials

01 Factoring Binomials

1. If each term in the polynomial has a greatest common factor, the factors are grouped together and factored.
2. Use the rule $a^2-b^2=(a-b)(a+b)$.
3. Sometimes the substitution method is very useful for complicated binomials.

Concept Check

1. $4x^2+20x$

   $=\underline{4x}\cdot x+5\cdot \underline{4x}$ → The GCF is $4x$

   $=\underline{4x}(x+5)$ → Factor the GCF

2. y^2-4

   $=y^2-2^2$

   $=(y-2)(y+2)$ → $a^2-b^2=(a-b)(a+b)$

3. $(x+2)^2+4(x+2)$

   $=A^2+4A$ → Let $x+2=A$

   $=\underline{A}\cdot A+4\underline{A}$ → The GCF is A

   $=\underline{A}(A+4)$ → Factor the GCF

   $=(x+2)(x+2+4)$ → Replace A for $x+2$

   $=(x+2)(x+6)$ → Simplify

Example 1

Factor the polynomial.

① $2x^2 - 4x$

② $9a^3 - 27a$

③ $4a^2 - 25$

④ $6xy^3 - 54xy$

⑤ $3(x+2)^2 + 48(x+2)$

⑥ $x(3a-2b) + 4y(2b-3a)$

Solution

① $2x^2 - 4x = 2x(x-2)$

② $9a^3 - 27a = 9a(a^2 - 3)$

③ $4a^2 - 25 = (2a)^2 - 5^2$
　　　　　$= (2a-5)(2a+5)$ 　　→ $a^2 - b^2 = (a-b)(a+b)$

④ $6xy^3 - 54xy = 6xy(y^2 - 9)$
　　　　　　$= 6xy(y^2 - 3^2)$
　　　　　　$= 6xy(y-3)(y+3)$ 　→ $a^2 - b^2 = (a-b)(a+b)$

⑤ $3(x+2)^2 + 48(x+2) = 3A^2 + 48A$ 　→ Let $x+2 = A$
　　　　　　　　　　$= 3A(A+16) = 3(x+2)(x+2+16)$
　　　　　　　　　　$= 3(x+2)(x+18)$

⑥ $x(3a-2b) + 4y(2b-3a) = x(3a-2b) - 4y(3a-2b)$
　　　　　　　　　　　$= xA - 4yA$ 　　　→ Let $3a-2b = A$
　　　　　　　　　　　$= A(x-4y) = (3a-2b)(x-4y)$

Check Point 1

Solutions_Page 83

Factor the polynomial.

① $24x^3 + 12x$

② $9x^2 - 36$

③ $4x^2 - \dfrac{y^2}{25}$

④ $32a^3b - 8ab^3$

⑤ $(a^2 - 4)^2 - 5(a^2 - 4)$

⑥ $a^4 - b^4$

Review Exercise

01 Factor the polynomial.

(1) x^2-4

(2) $4x^2-100$

(3) $2ay+4ax$

(4) $16x^2-1$

02 Factor the polynomial.

(1) $10ab^2-15a^2b$

(2) $2x^2-8y^2$

(3) $x(a+b)-y(a+b)$

(4) $a(x-y)+b(y-x)$

Challenging

03 Factor the polynomial.

(1) $2x(2a+b^2)-4y(2a+b^2)$

(2) $3a(4x-y)-2b(y-4x)$

Challenging

04 Factor the polynomial.

(1) $4(x^2+6)^2-25(x^2+6)$

(2) $3(9a^2-4)+(9a^2-4)^2$

05 If
$$6ab^2(a-3)+4ab(3-a)=2ab(a-3)(xb+y),$$
what is the value of xy?

Challenging

06 If $9y^2-16x^4=-8$ and $4x^2-3y=2$, what is the value of $3y+4x^2$?

07 If $x+y=4$ and $x-y=-3$, what is the value of $x^2(x-y)+y^2(y-x)$?

3 Factoring Trinomials

01 Factoring Trinomials: Perfect Squares

1. The square of a polynomial is called the perfect square. A perfect square may be multiplied by a constant.

2. $a^2+2ab+b^2=(a+b)^2$
   $a^2-2ab+b^2=(a-b)^2$ ⎬ perfect Squares

3. The middle term $(2ab)$ of the perfect square is twice the product of the square roots of the first and last terms.

Concept Check

1. For instance, $(x+1)^2$, $(y-2)^2$, and $(a+2b)^2$ are perfect squares.
2. $x^2+6x+9=x^2+2(x)(3)+3^2=(x+3)^2$
   $4a^2+20a+25=(2a)^2+2(2a)(5)+5^2=(2a+5)^2$
3. $9a^2-12a+4$ is a perfect square because $9a^2=(3a)^2$, $4=2^2$, and $12a=2\times 3a\times 2$.

Example 1

Factor the polynomial.

① a^2+4a+4
② $2x^2-16x+32$
③ $9a^2-6a+1$
④ $4x^2+20xy+25y^2$

Solution

① $a^2+4a+4=a^2+2(a)(2)+2^2=(a+2)^2$
② $2x^2-16x+32=2(x^2-8x+16)=2(x^2-2(x)(4)+4^2)=2(x-4)^2$
③ $9a^2-6a+1=(3a)^2-2(3a)(1)+1^2=(3a-1)^2$
④ $4x^2+20xy+25y^2=(2x)^2+2(2x)(5y)+(5y)^2=(2x+5y)^2$

Check Point 1
Factor the polynomial.

① $x^2+10x+25$
② $4x^2-12xy+9y^2$
③ $25a^3b^2-20a^2b^3+4ab^4$
④ $a^2+\dfrac{ab}{2}+\dfrac{b^2}{16}$

02 Factoring Trinomial: $x^2+(a+b)x+ab$

$$x^2+(a+b)x+ab=(x+a)(x+b) \quad \rightarrow \text{ The coefficient of } x^2 \text{ is 1.}$$

1. Find a and b such that
   (1) Their product is equal to the constant term ab.
   (2) Their sum is equal to the coefficient of x.

Concept Check

$x^2+x-6 \quad \rightarrow$ Find two integers with a product of -6 and a sum of 1.

Two integers with a product of -6		Sum of two integers
-1	6	5
1	-6	-5
-2	3	1
2	-3	-1

$x^2+x-6=(x-2)(x+3)$

Example 2

Factor the polynomial.

① $x^2-3x-10$
② $x^2+10x+24$
③ $2x^2-26x+84$
④ $4x^2-4xy-8y^2$

Solution

① Two integers whose product is -10 and whose sum is -3 are -5 and 2.
$x^2-3x-10=(x-5)(x+2)$

② Two integers whose product is 24 and whose sum is 10 are 4 and 6.
$x^2+10x+24=(x+4)(x+6)$

③ $2x^2-26x+84=2(x^2-13x+42)$
Two integers whose product is 42 and whose sum is -13 are -7 and -6.
$2(x^2-13x+42)=2(x-7)(x-6)$

④ $4x^2-4xy-8y^2=4(x^2-xy-2y^2)$
Two integers whose product is -2 and whose sum is -1 are -2 and 1.
$4(x^2-xy-2y^2)=4(x-2y)(x+y)$

Check Point 2

Solutions_Page 84

Factor the polynomial.

① x^2-x-12

② $x^2+3x-10$

③ $x^2-xy-30y^2$

④ $3x^2y+24xy^2+36y^3$

03 Factoring Trinomial: $acx^2+(ad+bc)x+bd$

$acx^2+(ad+bc)x+bd$ → The coefficient of x^2 is NOT 1.

$ax \quad b \to \quad bcx$
$cx \quad d \to \quad (+) \, adx$
$\qquad\qquad\qquad\quad \overline{(ad+bc)x}$

$\Rightarrow (ax+b)(cx+d)$

1. If you multiply in the diagonal direction as shown above, the sum of the two terms is the same as the middle term.

2. Another way is,

   (1) Multiply the leading coefficient and the constant.

(2) List all of the factors from step (1) and determine which two factors add up to the coefficient of x.

Concept Check

1. $\underbrace{3x^2-11x-4}_{3\times-4=-12}$ → $-12=-12\times 1 \Rightarrow -12+1=-11$

$$\begin{array}{c} 3x \searrow \nearrow 1 \to \quad x \\ x \nearrow \searrow -4 \to \underline{(+)-12x} \\ \quad\quad\quad\quad\quad -11x \end{array}$$

$3x^2-11x-4=(3x+1)(x-4)$

2. $3x^2-11x-4$

Two integers with a product of -12. ($3\times -4=-12$)		Sum of two integers
-1	12	11
1	-12	-11
-2	6	4
2	-6	-4
-3	4	1
3	-4	-1

$\Rightarrow 3x^2-11x-4=(3x+1)(x-4)$

Example 3

Factor the polynomial.

① $2x^2+3x-2$ ② $6x^2+11x+3$
③ $2x^4-5x^3-7x^2$ ④ $15x^2-7xy-2y^2$

Solution

① $2x^2+3x-2$ ⟶ $-4=-1\times 4 \Rightarrow -1+4=3$
$\quad\underbrace{}_{2\times -2=-4}$

$\begin{array}{cc} 2x & -1 \\ x & 2 \end{array}$ ⟶ $\begin{array}{r} -x \\ (+)\ 4x \\ \hline 3x \end{array}$

$2x^2+3x-2=(2x-1)(x+2)$

② $6x^2+11x+3$ ⟶ $18=9\times 2 \Rightarrow 9+2=11$
$\quad\underbrace{}_{6\times 3=18}$

$\begin{array}{cc} 3x & 1 \\ 2x & 3 \end{array}$ ⟶ $\begin{array}{r} 2x \\ (+)\ 9x \\ \hline 11x \end{array}$

$6x^2+11x+3=(3x+1)(2x+3)$

③ $2x^4-5x^3-7x^2=x^2(2x^2-5x-7)$

$\underbrace{2x^2-5x-7}_{2\times -7=-14}$ ⟶ $-14=-7\times 2 \Rightarrow -7+2=-5$

$\begin{array}{cc} 2x & -7 \\ x & 1 \end{array}$ ⟶ $\begin{array}{r} -7x \\ (+)\ 2x \\ \hline -5x \end{array}$

$2x^4-5x^3-7x^2=x^2(2x-7)(x+1)$

④ $15x^2-7xy-2y^2$ ⟶ $-30=-10\times 3 \Rightarrow -10+3=-7$
$\quad\underbrace{}_{15\times -2=-30}$

$\begin{array}{cc} 5x & y \\ 3x & -2y \end{array}$ ⟶ $\begin{array}{r} 3xy \\ (+)\ -10xy \\ \hline -7xy \end{array}$

$15x^2-7xy-2y^2=(5x+y)(3x-2y)$

Check Point 3

Solutions_Page 84

Factor the polynomial.

① $6x^2-x-2$

② $3x^2-10x+8$

③ $12x^2-13x-35$

④ $10x^2y+9xy^2-9y^3$

Review Exercise

01 Factor the polynomial.

(1) $x^2+8x+16$

(2) $x^2-12x+36$

(3) $4x^2+4x+1$

(4) $25x^2-30xy+9y^2$

Challenging

02 Factor the polynomial.

(1) $9x^2+3x+\dfrac{1}{4}$

(2) $2x^2-12x+18$

(3) $27x^2-36xy+12y^2$

(4) $20x^2+\dfrac{20xy}{3}+\dfrac{5y^2}{9}$

Review Exercise

03 Factor the polynomial.

(1) x^2-8x+7

(2) $x^2+6x-16$

(3) $\dfrac{x^2}{2}+8x+24$

(4) $18+3x-3x^2$

Challenging

04 Factor the polynomial.

(1) $3x^3y-9x^2y-30xy$

(2) $\dfrac{x^2}{4}-\dfrac{5xy}{2}+4y^2$

05 Factor the polynomial.

(1) $3x^2-7x-6$

(2) $4x^2+7xy+3y^2$

(3) $5x^3y+4x^2y-xy$

(4) $6x^3y-13x^2y^2+6xy^3$

Challenging

06 Factor the polynomial.

(1) $2x^2-\dfrac{7xy}{3}-y^2$

(2) $2x^2-\dfrac{16xy}{3}+\dfrac{5y^2}{6}$

07 Find the value of x^2-x-12 if $x=\sqrt{3}+4$.

Challenging

08 If $x-2$ is a factor of $4x^2-5x+a$, what is the value of a?

Challenging

09 If $6x^2+ax-10$ is divisible by $3x-2$, what is the value of a?

Chapter 6. Factoring 221

Review Exercise

Challenging

10 If $x+3$ is common factor to the two polynomial given above, what is the value of $a+b$?
$$4x^2+11x+a,\ 2x^2+bx+3$$

11 Find the value of a, where $a>0$, for the following trinomial to be perfect square.

(1) $(x+5)(x+3)+a$

(2) $5x^2+4x(x-a)+16$

12 Find the value of a, where $a>0$, so that the expression $16x^2+axy^2+\dfrac{9y^4}{4}$ is a perfect square.

13 If $x^4+4x^2y-12y^2=(x^2+ay)(x^2+by)$, what is the value of $a+b$?

Chapter Test — Level 1

01 Which of the following is NOT a factor of $4xy - 12xy^2$?

(A) xy (B) $4xy^2$ (C) $1-3y$

(D) $4x(1-3y)$ (E) $y(1-3y)$

02 Which of the following is NOT correct?

(A) $3x^2y^2 - 6x^2y = 3x^2y(y-2)$

(B) $2x^2 - 5x - 12 = (2x+3)(x-4)$

(C) $9x^2 + 30x + 25 = (3x+5)^2$

(D) $(2x-y)(2x-y-3) - 4 = (2x-y-4)(2x-y+1)$

(E) None of the above

03 Factor the polynomial.

(1) $(x-5)^2 - 9y^4$

(2) $(2x+1)^2 - (3x-2)^2$

Chapter Test — Level 1

04 Find the value of k, where $k>0$, for the following trinomial to be perfect square.

(1) $4(x-1)(x+7)+k$

(2) $4x^2-(4k-1)xy+y^2$

05 Given $x=1-\sqrt{2}$ and $y=1+\sqrt{2}$, evaluate each of the following.

(1) x^2-y^2

(2) $x^2-2xy+y^2$

06 Which of the following is NOT a perfect square?

(A) $x^2-6xy+9y^2$

(B) $4x^2-x+\dfrac{1}{16}$

(C) $1-2a+a^2$

(D) $9a^2+12ab+4b^2$

(E) $25y^2-\dfrac{10}{3}y+\dfrac{4}{9}$

07 If $ax^2+(2b-1)x-12=(3x+4)(5x+c)$, what is the value of $a+b+c$?

08 Calculate the following using factoring.

(1) $98^2 - 4$

(2) $25 \times 77 - 25 \times 75$

09 If $ax^2 - c = (2x+a)(x+b)$, what is the value of $a+b+c$?

$$6x^2y - 8xy - 8y, \ 12x^3y - 4x^2y - 8xy$$

10 Which of the following is common factor to the two polynomial given above?

(A) $y(3x+2)$ (B) $x(3x+2)$ (C) $y(x-2)$

(D) $x(x-2)$ (E) $xy(x-1)$

11 Find the value of $-a^2(2b-a) - 4b^2(a-2b)$ if $a-2b=2$ and $a+2b=5$?

Chapter Test — Level 2

01 Factor the polynomial $2a^4 - 32b^4$.

02 Suppose that $a = \dfrac{\sqrt{5}+2}{\sqrt{5}-2}$ and $b = \dfrac{\sqrt{5}-2}{\sqrt{5}+2}$. Find the value of $a^2 - b^2$.

03 Factor the polynomial.

(1) $4x^3y - 32x^2y^2 + 64xy^3$

(2) $64 - \dfrac{81}{4}x^4$

(3) $(2x^2+3x)^2 - (2x^2+3x+3) - 3$

(4) $2(x-2)^2 - 3(x-2)(x+3) - 20(x+3)^2$

04 If $2x-1$ is a factor of $4x^2+kx-5$, what is the value of k?

05 Given $x=1-\sqrt{2}$ and $y=1+\sqrt{2}$, what is the value of x^2+y^2?

06 If $3x+2$ is the common factor of two polynomials $3x^2-7x+a$ and $6x^2+bx-2$, what is the value of $a+b$?

07 Suppose that $x^2+ax+16=(x+b)(x+c)$. If a, b, and c are all integers, which of the following cannot be the value of a?

(A) -17 (B) -10 (C) 8 (D) 12 (E) 17

08 Calculate $98\times98+98\times101-98\times99-102\times102$ using factoring.

Chapter **7**

Quadratic Equations

1. Solving Basic Quadratic Equations
2. Completing the Square
3. The Quadratic Formula and the Discriminant
4. Chapter Test

1 Solving Basic Quadratic Equations

01 Introduction to Quadratic Equation

A Quadratic equation is a polynomial equation where the highest exponent of the variable is a square. For example,

$$x^2-4x+3=0,\ 2y^2+3y=0,\ \text{and}\ -4x^2+1=0$$

are all quadratic equations. The general form of a quadratic equation is

$$ax^2+bx+c=0 \Rightarrow \begin{cases} ax^2 : \text{Quadratic term} \\ bx : \text{Linear term} \\ c : \text{Constant term} \end{cases}$$

where a, b, and c are real numbers and $a \neq 0$.

Example 1

Which of the following is NOT a quadratic equation?

(A) $2x^2-5x+1=0$
(B) $2(x-1)(x+2)-x^2=1$
(C) $x(3x-2)-3x(x+1)=0$
(D) $3x^2-4x+1=4x(x-2)$
(E) $(1-x)(1+x)+1=0$

Solution

(A) $2x^2-5x+1=0$ → Quadratic equation
(B) $2(x-1)(x+2)-x^2=1$
$\quad\ 2(x^2+x-2)-x^2=1$
$\quad\ 2x^2+2x-4-x^2=1$
$\quad\quad\ x^2+2x-5=0$ → Quadratic equation
(C) $x(3x-2)-3x(x+1)=0$
$\quad\ 3x^2-2x-3x^2-3x=0$
$\quad\quad\quad\quad\quad -5x=0$ → Linear equation
(D) $3x^2-4x+1=4x(x-2)$
$\quad\ 3x^2-4x+1=4x^2-8x$
$\quad\ x^2-4x-1=0$ → Quadratic equation

(E) $(1-x)(1+x)+1=0$
$1-x^2+1=0$
$-x^2+2=0$ → Quadratic equation

The answer is (C).

Check Point 1 Solutions_Page 90

Which of the following is a quadratic equation?

(A) $4(x-2)=3x+1$
(B) $2x^2-3x+1=2(x^2+1)$
(C) $(2x+1)^2-4x^2=0$
(D) $(2x-1)(2x+1)+3=(x-2)(x+2)$
(E) $(x-4)(4+x)+(x+1)(1-x)=-4x$

02 Solving by finding Square Roots

This method can be used in the following two cases:

1. $ax^2=b$, where $\left(\dfrac{b}{a}\geq 0\right)$. The equation has no x term.
   $\Rightarrow x^2=\dfrac{b}{a}$, $x=\pm\sqrt{\dfrac{b}{a}}$

2. $(x+a)^2=b$, where $(b\geq 0)$.
   $\Rightarrow x+a=\pm\sqrt{b}$, $x=-a\pm\sqrt{b}$

✔ Note that every positive number has two square roots: a positive square root and a negative square root.

Concept Check

1. $4x^2-100=0$

   $4x^2=100$ → Add 100 to each side
   $x^2=25$ → Divide both sides by 4
   $x=\pm 5$ → Take the square root

   The solutions are $x=-5$ and $x=5$.

2. $(x-4)^2 - 10 = 0$

$(x-4)^2 = 10$ → Add 10 to each side

$x - 4 = \pm\sqrt{10}$ → Take the square root

$x = 4 \pm \sqrt{10}$ → Add 4 to each side

The solutions are $x = 4 - \sqrt{10}$ and $x = 4 + \sqrt{10}$.

Example 2

Solve the equation by taking square roots.

① $4x^2 - 9 = 0$ ② $2(x+1)^2 + 3 = 15$

Solution

① $4x^2 - 9 = 0$
$4x^2 = 9$
$x^2 = \dfrac{9}{4}$
$x = \pm\sqrt{\dfrac{9}{4}} = \pm\dfrac{3}{2}$

The solutions are $x = -\dfrac{3}{2}$ and $x = \dfrac{3}{2}$.

② $2(x+1)^2 + 3 = 15$
$2(x+1)^2 = 12$
$(x+1)^2 = 6$
$x + 1 = \pm\sqrt{6}$
$x = -1 \pm \sqrt{6}$

The solutions are $x = -1 - \sqrt{6}$ and $x = -1 + \sqrt{6}$.

Check Point 2

Solutions_Page 90

Solve each equation by taking square roots.

① $6x^2 + 5 = 59$ ② $4x^2 - 3 = 2 - x^2$

③ $(2x-1)^2 = 25$ ④ $2(2x-3)^2 - 4 = 10$

03 Solving by Factoring

Follow the instructions below.

1. Write the quadratic equation in standard form. $\Rightarrow ax^2+bx+c=0$
2. Factor the left side of a quadratic equation. $\Rightarrow a(x-\alpha)(x-\beta)=0$
3. Use Zero-Product Property:

$a(x-\alpha)(x-\beta)=0$	$a(x-\alpha)^2=0$
$x-\alpha=0$ or $x-\beta=0$	$x-\alpha=0$
$x=\alpha$ or $x=\beta$	$x=\alpha$

Concept Check

1. $\quad x^2=2x$
   $x^2-2x=0 \quad\quad\quad \rightarrow$ Write in standard form
   $x(x-2)=0 \quad\quad\quad \rightarrow$ Factor
   $\quad x=0$ or $x-2=0 \quad \rightarrow$ Zero product property
   $\quad x=0$ or $x=2 \quad\quad \rightarrow$ Solve for x

   The solutions are $x=0$ and $x=2$.

Be Careful!

You may solve the equation in following way.
$x^2=2x$
$x=2 \quad\quad\quad \rightarrow$ Divide both sides by x

$x=2$ is indeed solution to the equation, but unfortunately it is not the only solution. That "divide both sides by x" doesn't work if $x=0$. Instead of dividing by x, we have to factor the expression.

2. $(x-2)(x+2)-1=4x$
   $\quad\quad x^2-4-1=4x \quad\quad \rightarrow$ Expand left side
   $\quad\quad x^2-4x-5=0 \quad\quad \rightarrow$ Write in standard form
   $\quad (x-5)(x+1)=0 \quad\quad \rightarrow$ Factor
   $\quad\quad x-5=0$ or $x+1=0 \quad \rightarrow$ Zero product property
   $\quad\quad\quad x=5$ or $\quad x=-1 \rightarrow$ Solve for x

   The solutions are $x=5$ and $x=-1$.

Example 3

Solve each equation by factoring.

① $x^2-6x=0$ ② $x^2-x-2=0$

③ $2x^2+18x+36=0$ ④ $x^2+8=2(4-3x)$

Solution

① $x^2-6x=0$
$x(x-6)=0$
$x=0$ or $x-6=0$
$x=0$ or $x=6$

The solutions are $x=0$ and $x=6$.

② $x^2-x-2=0$
$(x-2)(x+1)=0$
$x-2=0$ or $x+1=0$
$x=2$ or $x=-1$

The solutions are $x=2$ and $x=-1$.

③ $2x^2+18x+36=0$, $x^2+9x+18=0$
$(x+3)(x+6)=0$
$x+3=0$ or $x+6=0$
$x=-3$ or $x=-6$

The solutions are $x=-3$ and $x=-6$.

④ $x^2+8=2(4-3x)$, $x^2+8=8-6x$
$x^2+6x=0$, $x(x+6)=0$
$x=0$ or $x+6=0$
$x=0$ or $x=-6$

The solutions are $x=0$ and $x=-6$.

Check Point 3

Solutions_Page 90

Solve each equation by factoring.

① $2x^2+3x-2=0$ ② $3x^2-2x=2x^2+24$

③ $2(x-3)^2=8x$ ④ $(x+2)(x-2)=3x(x-1)-(x+2)$

Review Exercise

01 Solve each equation by taking square roots.

(1) $x^2+4=8$

(2) $x^2-4=32$

(3) $9x^2-12=600$

(4) $10+5x^2=330$

02 Solve each equation by taking square roots.

(1) $8x^2+7=31$

(2) $(2x-5)^2=81$

(3) $4(3x+1)^2=36$

(4) $\dfrac{5x^2}{2}-x^2=216$

Review Exercise

03 Solve each equation by factoring.

(1) $x^2+4x+4=0$

(2) $x^2-15x-100=0$

(3) $8x^2+4x=0$

(4) $3x^2-33x+72=0$

04 Solve each equation by factoring.

(1) $7x^2+35x-42=0$

(2) $6x^2+15x+9=0$

(3) $7x^2+32=7-40x$

(4) $x(x-2)=3(x-2)$

05 If $2x$ is subtracted from x^2, the result is 8. Find all possible values of x.

06 If the quadratic equation
$$4(x+3)(x-4) = \frac{1}{2}(2x+1)(x-2) + \frac{3}{2}x$$
is written as $ax^2+bx+c=0$, what is the value of $a+b+c$?

07 Which of the following quadratic equations has $x=3$ as the solution?

(A) $3x^2-x=0$

(B) $3x^2+8x-3=0$

(C) $(x-3)^2-1=0$

(D) $(x+3)(x-4)+2x=0$

(E) $\frac{(x+1)^2}{2}=2$

[Challenging]

08 Solve the quadratic equation $(x-2)(x+3)=2(x-2)(2x+1)$.

$$\frac{1}{2}x^2+2kx-5=0$$

09 If one of the solutions to the quadratic equation above is $x=4$, what is the value of k?

[Challenging]

10 If the larger of the two solutions of quadratic equation $x^2+5x-14=0$ is also the solution of quadratic equation $5x^2-2x-k=0$, what is the value of k?

[Challenging]

11 What is the sum of the solutions of $(x-4)^2=(2x+3)^2$?

2 Completing the Square

Quadratic equations are best solved by factoring, but not all quadratic equations can be factored. Consider $x^2-x+1=0$, for example. However, we can solve any forms of quadratic equation by transforming

$$ax^2+bx+c=0 \Rightarrow (x-h)^2=d,$$

where h and d are constants. This process is called **completing the square**.

Concept Check

Given quadratic equation, $\qquad ax^2+bx+c=0$

1. Make the coefficient of the squared term 1. $\quad x^2+\dfrac{bx}{a}+\dfrac{c}{a}=0$

2. Isolate the variable terms. $\quad x^2+\dfrac{bx}{a}=-\dfrac{c}{a}$

3. Add square of one-half the coefficient of the linear term to both sides.

$$x^2+\dfrac{bx}{a}+\left(\dfrac{b}{2a}\right)^2=-\dfrac{c}{a}+\left(\dfrac{b}{2a}\right)^2$$

4. Factor the trinomial on the left side. $\quad \left(x+\dfrac{b}{2a}\right)^2=\text{some constant } d$

5. Solve for x. $\quad x=-\dfrac{b}{2a}\pm\sqrt{d}$

Example 1

Solve the equation by completing the square.

① $x^2-4x+2=0$ ② $2x^2+6x-5=0$

Solution

① $\quad x^2-4x+2=0$
$\quad\quad x^2-4x=-2$ $\qquad$ → Move constant term 2 to the right side
$x^2-4x+(2)^2=-2+(2)^2$ $\qquad$ → Add square of half of 4, 2^2, to both sides
$\quad\quad (x-2)^2=2$ $\qquad$ → Change to $(x-h)^2=d$ form

238 Chapter 7. Quadratic Equations

$$x-2=\pm\sqrt{2}$$ → Take square root for both sides
$$x=2\pm\sqrt{2}$$ → Solve for x

The solutions are $x=2+\sqrt{2}$ and $x=2-\sqrt{2}$.

② $$2x^2+6x-5=0$$
$$x^2+3x-\frac{5}{2}=0$$ → Divide all terms by 2
$$x^2+3x=\frac{5}{2}$$ → Move constant term $-\frac{5}{2}$ to the right side
$$x^2+3x+\left(\frac{3}{2}\right)^2=\frac{5}{2}+\left(\frac{3}{2}\right)^2$$ → Add square of half of 3, $\left(\frac{3}{2}\right)^2$, to both sides
$$\left(x+\frac{3}{2}\right)^2=\frac{5}{2}+\frac{9}{4}$$ → Change to $(x-h)^2=d$ form
$$\left(x+\frac{3}{2}\right)^2=\frac{19}{4}$$ → Simplify the right side
$$x+\frac{3}{2}=\pm\sqrt{\frac{19}{4}}$$ → Take square root for both sides
$$x=-\frac{3}{2}\pm\frac{\sqrt{19}}{2}$$ → Solve for x

The solutions are $x=\frac{-3+\sqrt{19}}{2}$ and $x=\frac{-3-\sqrt{19}}{2}$.

Check Point 1
Solutions_Page 93

Solve the equation by completing the square.

① $x^2-8x+6=0$

② $\frac{1}{2}x^2+8x-\frac{3}{2}=0$

③ $4x^2-8=(x+3)(x-2)$

④ $4x^2+12x-5=0$

Review Exercise

01 Solve the equation by completing the square.

(1) $x^2 - 4x - 12 = 0$

(2) $x^2 - 2x - 35 = 0$

(3) $x^2 = -10x + 3$

02 Solve the equation by completing the square.

(1) $9x^2 - 18x + 5 = 0$

(2) $4x^2 + 8x - 12 = 0$

(3) $5x^2 - 2x = 16$

03 Solve the equation by completing the square.

(1) $\frac{1}{3}x^2 - 3x - \frac{1}{2} = 0$

(2) $\frac{1}{2}x^2 - 4x = -3$

Challenging

04 Solve the equation by completing the square.

(1) $(x+2)^2 = 3(x+4)$

(2) $(x-1)(x+1) - 4x = (2x-1)(2x+1)$

05 If the quadratic equation $x^2 - 2x + a = 0$ is solved by completing the square, the solution is $x = 1 \pm \sqrt{7}$. Find the value of a.

Challenging

06 If $2x^2 + \dfrac{1}{4}x + a = 2\left(x + \dfrac{1}{b}\right)^2$, what is the value of ab?

Challenging

07 If the quadratic equation $5x^2 + 4x + 1 = 0$ can be written in the form $(x+h)^2 = k$, what is the value of $\dfrac{h}{k}$?

3 The Quadratic Formula and the Discriminant

01 Quadratic Formula

The quadratic formula is developed through solving a quadratic equation by completing the square. It expresses the solutions to any quadratic equation.

The solutions to the equation $ax^2+bx+c=0$ $(a\neq 0)$ are $x=\dfrac{-b\pm\sqrt{b^2-4ac}}{2a}$.

Concept Check

$$ax^2+bx+c=0\,(a\neq 0)$$

$$x^2+\frac{bx}{a}+\frac{c}{a}=0 \quad \rightarrow \text{Divide all terms by } a$$

$$x^2+\frac{bx}{a}=-\frac{c}{a} \quad \rightarrow \text{Move constant term, } -\frac{c}{a} \text{ to the right side}$$

$$x^2+\frac{bx}{a}+\left(\frac{b}{2a}\right)^2=-\frac{c}{a}+\left(\frac{b}{2a}\right)^2 \quad \rightarrow \text{Add square of half of } \left(\frac{a}{2b}\right)^2, \text{ to both sides}$$

$$\left(x+\frac{b}{2a}\right)^2=\frac{b^2-4ac}{4a^2} \quad \rightarrow \text{Simplify the right side}$$

$$x+\frac{b}{2a}=\pm\sqrt{\frac{b^2-4ac}{4a^2}} \quad \rightarrow \text{Take square root for both sides}$$

$$x=-\frac{b}{2a}\pm\frac{\sqrt{b^2-4ac}}{2a} \quad \rightarrow \text{Solve for } x$$

The solutions to the equation $ax^2+bx+c=0$ $(a\neq 0)$ are

$$x=\frac{-b+\sqrt{b^2-4ac}}{2a} \text{ and } x=\frac{-b-\sqrt{b^2-4ac}}{2a}.$$

Example 1

Solve the equation by using quadratic formula.

① $x^2+3x-1=0$ ② $2x^2-5x=3$

Solution

① $x^2+3x-1=0$

The equation is in appropriate form $ax^2+bx+c=0$. Since the coefficients can be identified as $a=1$, $b=3$, and $c=-1$, substitute these values into the formula $x=\dfrac{-b\pm\sqrt{b^2-4ac}}{2a}$.

$$x=\dfrac{-3\pm\sqrt{(3)^2-4(1)(-1)}}{2(1)}$$

$$=\dfrac{-3\pm\sqrt{9+4}}{2}=\dfrac{-3\pm\sqrt{13}}{2}$$

$$x=\dfrac{-3+\sqrt{13}}{2} \text{ or } x=\dfrac{-3-\sqrt{13}}{2}$$

The solutions are $x=\dfrac{-3+\sqrt{13}}{2}$ and $x=\dfrac{-3-\sqrt{13}}{2}$.

② $2x^2-5x=3$

$2x^2-5x-3=0$ → Write the equation in general form

Since the coefficients can be identified as $a=2$, $b=-5$, and $c=-3$, substitute these values into the formula $x=\dfrac{-b\pm\sqrt{b^2-4ac}}{2a}$.

$$x=\dfrac{-(-5)\pm\sqrt{(-5)^2-4(2)(-3)}}{2(2)}$$

$$=\dfrac{5\pm\sqrt{25+24}}{4}$$

$$=\dfrac{5\pm\sqrt{49}}{4}=\dfrac{5\pm7}{4}$$

$$x=\dfrac{5-7}{4}=\dfrac{-2}{4}=-\dfrac{1}{2} \text{ or } x=\dfrac{5+7}{4}=\dfrac{12}{4}=3$$

The solutions are $x=-\dfrac{1}{2}$ and $x=3$.

Check Point 1 Solutions_Page 96

Solve the equation by using quadratic formula.

① $x^2-4x-5=0$ ② $2x^2-3x-3=0$

③ $0.3x^2+0.5x-0.1=0$

02 Discriminant

Using the quadratic formula, we could find the solutions of the quadratic equation $ax^2+bx+c=0(a\neq 0)$. In quadratic formula $x=\dfrac{-b\pm\sqrt{b^2-4ac}}{2a}$, the part b^2-4ac is called the discriminant D, and this is to determine the nature of the solutions of a quadratic equation.

> Let $ax^2+bx+c=0(a\neq 0)$ be a quadratic equation with real coefficients.
> 1. $D=b^2-4ac>0$ → There are two real solutions.
> 2. $D=b^2-4ac=0$ → There is one real solution.
> 3. $D=b^2-4ac<0$ → There is no real solution.

Concept Check

Without solving the equation, determine the nature of its solution $x^2+3x=-2$.

$x^2+3x=-2$	→ Given
$x^2+3x+2=0$	→ Rewrite in the form of $ax^2+bx+c=0$
$D=b^2-4ac$	→ Formula for discriminant
$D=3^2-4(1)(2)>0$	→ $a=1$, $b=3$, and $c=2$

Since $D>0$, there are two real solutions to the equation $x^2+3x=-2$.

Example 2

Without solving the equation, determine the nature of its solutions.
① $x^2-x-6=0$
② $2x^2=5x-4$
③ $3x^2-2\sqrt{3}x+1=0$

Solution

① $x^2-x-6=0$ → $a=1$, $b=-1$, and $c=-6$
$D=b^2-4ac$
$=(-1)^2-4(1)(-6)$
$=1+24=25>0$

There are two real solutions.

② $2x^2=5x-4$
$2x^2-5x+4=0$ → $a=2$, $b=-5$, and $c=4$
$D=b^2-4ac$
$=(-5)^2-4(2)(4)$
$=25-32=-7<0$

There is no real solution.

③ $3x^2-2\sqrt{3}x+1=0$ → $a=3$, $b=-2\sqrt{3}$, and $c=1$
$D=b^2-4ac$
$=(-2\sqrt{3})^2-4(3)(1)$
$=12-12=0$

There is one real solution.

Check Point 2 Solutions_Page 96

Without solving the equation, determine the nature of its solutions.

① $3x^2+5x-1=0$

② $\dfrac{1}{2}x^2-5x+\dfrac{25}{2}=0$

③ $2x^2-4x+6=0$

④ $(x-4)^2-7=2x(x-4)$

Example 3

Find the values of k for which the equation $x^2-6x+k=0$ has

① Two real solutions

② One real solution

③ No real solution

Chapter 7. Quadratic Equations 245

> **Solution**
>
> $x^2-6x+k=0 \rightarrow a=1,\ b=-6$ and $c=k$
>
> ① $D=(-6)^2-4(1)(k)>0$
> $36-4k>0,\ k<9$
>
> $\hfill k<9$
>
> ② $D=(-6)^2-4(1)(k)=0$
> $36-4k=0,\ k=9$
>
> $\hfill k=9$
>
> ③ $D=(-6)^2-4(1)(k)<0$
> $36-4k<0,\ k>9$
>
> $\hfill k>9$

Check Point 3 $\hfill$ Solutions_Page 96

Find the values of k for which the equation $3x^2-6x-k=0$ has

① Two real solutions

② One real solution

③ Two imaginary solutions

Review Exercise

01 Solve the equation by using quadratic formula.

(1) $x^2-x-12=0$

(2) $x^2+5x-6=0$

(3) $2x^2-x-6=0$

(4) $x^2-3x+1=0$

02 Solve the equation by using quadratic formula.

(1) $-3x^2=8x+5$

(2) $3x^2-5x=-2$

Challenging

03 Solve the equation by using quadratic formula.

(1) $\dfrac{3}{4}x^2-\dfrac{1}{2}x-1=0$

(2) $0.4x^2-x-0.1=0$

Review Exercise

Challenging

04 Solve the equation by using quadratic formula.

(1) $x^2 - \dfrac{1}{3}x = 0.2$

(2) $(0.5x+2)\left(x-\dfrac{1}{2}\right) = x-1$

(3) $4x^2 - 8x + 4 = 0$

(4) $10x^2 + 2x = x(x-2)$

05 Find the discriminant of the quadratic equation and determine the nature of its solutions of the quadratic equation.

(1) $x^2 - x + 3 = 0$

(2) $2x^2 + 3x - 1 = 0$

06 Find the values of k for which each equation has (A) two real solutions, (B) one real solution, and (C) two imaginary solutions.

(1) $x^2 - 4x - 2k = 0$

(2) $k^2 x^2 - 8x + 4 = 0$

Challenging

07 If the quadratic equation $\frac{1}{2}x^2 - x - \frac{1}{4} = 0$ is solved by using quadratic formula, the solution is $x = a \pm \frac{\sqrt{b}}{c}$, where a, b, and c are positive integers. Find the value of abc.

Challenging

09 If the quadratic equation $a(3x+1) + 2x^2 = \frac{1}{8}$ has only one real solution, find all possible values of a?

08 If the quadratic equation $x^2 - 10x + 2m = 5$ has only one real solution, what is the value of m?

Chapter Test Level 1

01 Which of the following is a quadratic equation? (There are 2 answers)

(A) $2x^3-5x^2+1=0$

(B) $(x+1)(x+2)-(x+3)(x+4)=0$

(C) $x(2x^2+x-1)-2x(x^2-x+1)=0$

(D) $4x^2+3x-2=4(1-x)(1+x)$

(E) $(1-2x)(1+2x)+4x^2=x$

02 Which of the following quadratic equations does NOT have $x=-2$ as the solution?

(A) $x^2+4x+4=0$ (B) $x^2+2x=0$ (C) $2x^2+5x+2=0$

(D) $2x^2-5x+2=0$ (E) $3x^2+4x-4=0$

03 Solve the equation.

(1) $(x+6)^2+x^2=3(x+12)$

(2) $\dfrac{(3x+1)(2x-3)}{2}=x^2-3$

04 What quantity should be added to both sides of the equation $x^2+9x=7$ to complete the square?

(A) $-\dfrac{9}{2}$ (B) $\dfrac{9}{2}$ (C) $-\dfrac{9}{4}$ (D) $-\dfrac{81}{4}$ (E) $\dfrac{81}{4}$

$$
\begin{aligned}
2x^2-12x&=5 &&\rightarrow \text{Given}\\
2(x^2-6x)&=5 &&\rightarrow \text{Step 1}\\
2(x^2-6x+3^2)&=5+3^2 &&\rightarrow \text{Step 2}\\
2(x-3)^2&=14 &&\rightarrow \text{Step 3}\\
(x-3)^2&=7 &&\rightarrow \text{Step 4}\\
x-3=\pm\sqrt{7},\ x&=3\pm\sqrt{7} &&\rightarrow \text{Step 5}
\end{aligned}
$$

05 Which is the first incorrect step in the solution shown above?

(A) Step 1 (B) Step 2 (C) Step 3 (D) Step 4 (E) Step 5

06 If $x=3$ is the solution of both $x^2-4x+m=0$ and $2x^2+nx-7=0$, what is the value of $m+n$?

Chapter Test — Level 1

07 If one of the solutions of $x^2+6x-4=0$ is $x=a$, what is the value of $2a^2+12a+7$?

08 If the quadratic equation $2x^2+12x-9=0$ can be written as $(x+h)^2=k$, what is the value of $h+k$?

09 If the solution to the quadratic equation $2x^2+mx-4=0$ is $x=\dfrac{1\pm\sqrt{n}}{2}$, where m and n are integers, what is the value of $m+n$?

10 If $(a+b)(a+b-3)=10$, what is the positive value of $a+b$?

11 The product of two consecutive positive even integers is 6 more than three times their sum. Find the two integers.

12 A rectangle has an area of 36 cm^2 and a perimeter of 30 cm. Find the dimensions of the rectangle.

Chapter Test — Level 2

01 Solve the equation $x^2-5x=\dfrac{3}{4}(x-4)(x+2)$

02 Find the condition of the constant a such that $(x+3)^2+x^2=ax^2-4x+1$ is a quadratic equation.

$$3x^2+4x-\frac{5}{3}=0, \ \left(3x^2+4x-\frac{5}{3}=0\right)\cdot\frac{1}{3}$$

$$x^2+\frac{4}{3}x-\frac{5}{9}=0, \ x^2+\frac{4}{3}x=\frac{5}{9}$$

$$x^2+\frac{4}{3}x+A=\frac{5}{9}+A$$

$$(x+B)^2=C, \ x=D \text{ or } x=E$$

03 The above is the process of solving quadratic equation by completing the square. Find the value of A, B, C, D and E. ($E>D$)

04 Suppose that $x=2$ is one of the solutions of the quadratic equation $(k^2-4)x^2+(k+2)x=0$. Find all possible values of k.

05 If the quadratic equation $k(2x-1)+x^2=-2$, where $k<0$, has only one real solution, what is the value of k?

$$A : 3x^2-4x+\frac{4}{3}=0$$
$$B : 6x^2-kx+2=0$$

06 Suppose the solution of the quadratic equation A is one of the solutions of the quadratic equation B. What is the other solution of the equation B?

Chapter Test — Level 2

07 If one of the solutions to the quadratic equation $2x^2-x+2=0$ is m, what is the value of $2m^2-m+12$?

08 If $6x^2+7xy-3y^2=0$, where $xy>0$, what is the value of $\dfrac{3x^2+y^2}{4xy}$?

09 Two buses A and B leave the same station at right angles at the same time. Bus B travels 1 mile per hour faster than bus A. If they are $2\sqrt{13}$ miles apart after 2 hours, what is the speed of each bus?

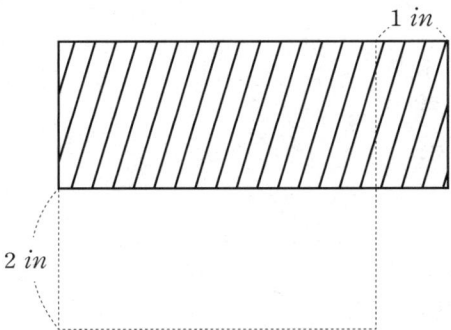

10 Suppose that one side of the square is increased by 1 inch, but the other side is decreased by 2 inches, as shown in Figure above. If the area of the resulting rectangle is 70 square inches, what is the length of one side of the original square?

memo

Chapter 8

Rational Expressions

1. Simplify Rational Expressions
2. Addition and Subtraction
3. Rational Equations
4. Chapter Test

1 Simplifying Rational Expressions

01 Definition of Rational Expression

A rational expression is one that can be expressed as a quotient of polynomials. In rational expression $\frac{A}{B}$, it is the polynomial if B is constant and fractional expression if B has a variable.

Rational Expression:

$$\frac{A}{B}\begin{cases} \text{Polynomial}(B \text{ is a number}): \dfrac{3x}{2},\ \dfrac{2x^2+1}{5},\ \cdots \\ \text{Fractional Expression}(B \text{ contains variables}): \dfrac{1}{x},\ \dfrac{2x^2+1}{3x-5},\ \cdots \end{cases}$$

02 Simplifying Rational Expression

A rational expression is in simplified form when its numerator and denominator have no common factors. To simplify rational expressions, use the following property of fractions:

Let A, B, and C ($B \neq 0$, $C \neq 0$) be nonzero real numbers or variable expressions.

$$\frac{A\cancel{C}}{B\cancel{C}} = \frac{A}{B} \quad \Rightarrow \text{Divide out common factor } C$$

Simplifying a rational expression usually requires following steps.
1. Factor both the numerator and denominator of the fraction.
2. Divide out common factors in the expression.
3. Rewrite any remaining expression in the numerator and denominator.

Concept Check

$$\frac{x^2-x-6}{x^2-4}$$ → Given

$$=\frac{(x-3)(x+2)}{(x-2)(x+2)}$$ → Factor the numerator and the denominator

$$=\frac{(x-3)\cancel{(x+2)}}{(x-2)\cancel{(x+2)}}$$ → Divide out the common factors

$$=\frac{x-3}{x-2}$$ → Rewrite the remaining expression in the numerator and the denominator

Example 1

Simplify the rational expression.

① $\dfrac{4x^2-12x}{16x}$ ② $\dfrac{x^2-x-6}{x^2-3x}$

Solution

① $\dfrac{4x^2-12x}{16x}=\dfrac{4x(x-3)}{16x}=\dfrac{\cancel{4x}(x-3)}{\cancel{4x}\cdot 4}=\dfrac{x-3}{4}$

② $\dfrac{x^2-x-6}{x^2-3x}=\dfrac{(x-3)(x+2)}{x(x-3)}=\dfrac{x+2}{x}$

Check Point 1   Solutions_Page 104

Simplify the rational expression.

① $\dfrac{6x^2-8x}{10x}$ ② $\dfrac{x^2-x-2}{x^2+x-6}$

③ $\dfrac{3x^2+x-4}{5x^2-3x-2}$ ④ $\dfrac{2x^3+11x^2+12x}{3x^2+11x-4}$

03 Multiplication of Rational Expressions

To multiply rational expressions, use the following property of fractions:

Let A, B, C, 0 and $D(B \neq 0, D \neq 0)$ be nonzero real numbers or variable expressions.

$$\frac{A}{B} \times \frac{C}{D} = \frac{AC}{BD} \Rightarrow (\text{Denominator} \times \text{Denominator}) \text{ and } (\text{Numerator} \times \text{Numerator})$$

Multiplying rational expressions usually requires following steps.
1. Factor both numerator and denominator of each expression.
2. Divide out common factors in the expression.
3. Multiply the numerators with each other and the denominators each other.

Concept Check

$\dfrac{3x-12}{2x+2} \times \dfrac{x^2-x-2}{x^2-4x}$ → Given

$= \dfrac{3(x-4)}{2(x+1)} \times \dfrac{(x-2)(x+1)}{x(x-4)}$ → Factor the numerators and denominators.

$= \dfrac{3\cancel{(x-4)}}{2\cancel{(x+1)}} \times \dfrac{(x-2)\cancel{(x+1)}}{x\cancel{(x-4)}}$ → Divide out the common factors.

$= \dfrac{3}{2} \times \dfrac{(x-2)}{x} = \dfrac{3(x-2)}{2x}$ → Multiply the numerators and the denominators

Example 2

Multiply the rational expression.

① $\dfrac{x+1}{2} \times \dfrac{4x}{5x+5}$

② $\dfrac{a^2-a-6}{3a-6} \times \dfrac{a^2-4}{a^2-9}$

Solution

① $\dfrac{x+1}{2} \times \dfrac{2 \cdot 2x}{5x+5} = \dfrac{\cancel{x+1}}{\cancel{2}} \times \dfrac{\cancel{2} \cdot 2x}{5(\cancel{x+1})}$

$= \dfrac{1}{1} \times \dfrac{2x}{5} = \dfrac{2x}{5}$

② $\dfrac{a^2-a-6}{3a-6} \times \dfrac{a^2-4}{a^2-9} = \dfrac{(\cancel{a-3})(a+2)}{3(\cancel{a-2})} \times \dfrac{(\cancel{a-2})(a+2)}{(\cancel{a-3})(a+3)}$

$= \dfrac{a+2}{3} \times \dfrac{a+2}{a+3} = \dfrac{(a+2)^2}{3(a+3)}$

Check Point 2   Solutions_Page 104

Multiply the rational expression.

① $\dfrac{2}{6x^2} \times \dfrac{8x^2}{10}$ ② $\dfrac{x-3}{x-4} \times \dfrac{x^2-16}{5x-15}$

③ $\dfrac{x^2+8x+16}{3x+6} \times \dfrac{x^2-4}{x^2+7x+12}$ ④ $\dfrac{2x^2-2}{2x^2+x-1} \times (4x-2)$

04 Division of Rational Expressions

To divide rational expressions, use the following property of fractions

Let A, B, C, and D ($B \neq 0$, $D \neq 0$) be nonzero real numbers or variable expressions.

$\dfrac{A}{B} \div \dfrac{C}{D} = \dfrac{A}{B} \times \dfrac{D}{C} = \dfrac{AD}{BC}$ ⇒ Convert division to multiplication

Dividing rational expressions usually requires following steps.

1. Multiply the first expression by the reciprocal of the second expression.
2. Factor both numerator and denominator of each expression.
3. Divide out common factors in the expression.
4. Multiply the numerators with each other and the denominators each other.

Concept Check

$$\frac{2x-2}{2x^2-x-3} \div \frac{x^2-1}{6x-9} \quad \rightarrow \text{Given}$$

$$= \frac{2x-2}{2x^2-x-3} \times \frac{6x-9}{x^2-1} \quad \rightarrow \text{Multiply the reciprocal}$$

$$= \frac{2(x-1)}{(2x-3)(x+1)} \times \frac{3(2x-3)}{(x-1)(x+1)} \quad \rightarrow \text{Factor the numerators and the denominators}$$

$$= \frac{2(\cancel{x-1})}{(\cancel{2x-3})(x+1)} \times \frac{3(\cancel{2x-3})}{(\cancel{x-1})(x+1)} \quad \rightarrow \text{Divide out the common factors}$$

$$= \frac{2}{x+1} \times \frac{3}{x+1} = \frac{6}{(x+1)^2} \quad \rightarrow \text{Multiply the numerators and the denominators}$$

Example 3

Divide the rational expression.

① $\dfrac{9x^2}{4} \div \dfrac{27x}{8}$ 　　② $\dfrac{a^2-ab}{4a+4b} \div \dfrac{a^2-b^2}{a^2+2ab+b^2}$

Solution

① $\dfrac{9x^2}{4} \div \dfrac{27x}{8} = \dfrac{9x^2}{4} \times \dfrac{8}{27x}$

$= \dfrac{\cancel{9x} \cdot x}{\cancel{4}} \times \dfrac{\cancel{4} \cdot 2}{\cancel{9x} \cdot 3}$

$= \dfrac{x}{1} \times \dfrac{2}{3} = \dfrac{2x}{3}$

② $\dfrac{a^2-ab}{4a+4b} \div \dfrac{a^2-b^2}{a^2+2ab+b^2} = \dfrac{a^2-ab}{4a+4b} \times \dfrac{a^2+2ab+b^2}{a^2-b^2}$

$= \dfrac{a(\cancel{a-b})}{4(\cancel{a+b})} \times \dfrac{(\cancel{a+b})^2}{(\cancel{a-b})(\cancel{a+b})}$

$= \dfrac{a}{4} \times \dfrac{1}{1} = \dfrac{a}{4}$

✔ Remember that we do NOT need to find a common denominator to multiply or divide rational expressions.

Check Point 3

Divide the rational expression.

① $\dfrac{9x}{x^3} \div \dfrac{18x^2}{x^3}$

② $\dfrac{x^2+6x-7}{3x^2} \div \dfrac{2x+14}{12x}$

③ $\dfrac{2x-12}{x^2-4} \div \dfrac{x^2-5x-6}{3x-6}$

④ $\dfrac{2x^3-10x^2}{x-4} \div \dfrac{x^2+4x}{x^2-16}$

Review Exercise

01 Simplify the rational expression.

(1) $\dfrac{75x^3}{5x^5}$

(2) $\dfrac{27a^4}{3a}$

(3) $\dfrac{6x^2}{3x^2-9x}$

(4) $\dfrac{6y^4-15y}{9y^2}$

02 Simplify the rational expression.

(1) $\dfrac{2x^3+4x^2}{x^2+x-2}$

(2) $\dfrac{(2x-5)^2}{4x^2-25}$

(3) $\dfrac{a^2-5a+6}{a^2-7a+12}$

(4) $\dfrac{6a^2-5a+1}{12a^2+2a-2}$

03 Simplify the rational expression.

(1) $\dfrac{x^3}{3} \times \dfrac{18}{x^2}$

(2) $\dfrac{16}{x^3} \times \dfrac{x^5}{12}$

(3) $\dfrac{4x^2}{5x^2} \times \dfrac{4x}{8}$

(4) $\dfrac{24}{7y^3} \times \dfrac{21y^2}{18y}$

04 Simplify the rational expression.

(1) $\dfrac{3x^2-12}{10x^2} \times \dfrac{5x^2}{2x-4}$

(2) $\dfrac{x^2-9}{x^2+5x+6} \times \dfrac{x-3}{x+2}$

(3) $\dfrac{3x^2-5x-2}{x^2+3x-10} \times \dfrac{2x+8}{x^2+x-12}$

(4) $\dfrac{y^2-7y+12}{2y^2-32} \times (y^2-5y+6)$

Review Exercise

Challenging

05 Simplify the rational expression.

(1) $\dfrac{6a^2-a-2}{2a^2-5a-3} \times \dfrac{2a^2-18}{3a^2+7a-6}$

(2) $\dfrac{a^2b-b^3}{4ab-8b^2} \times \dfrac{a^2-ab-2b^2}{a^4-2a^3b+a^2b^2}$

06 Simplify the rational expression.

(1) $\dfrac{4x+1}{3x} \div \dfrac{8x^2-2x-1}{15}$

(2) $\dfrac{x^2-5x-14}{x^2-3x+2} \div \dfrac{x^2-14x+49}{x^2-4}$

(3) $\dfrac{2a^2-2a-4}{3a-6} \div \dfrac{6a-4}{9a^2-4}$

(4) $\dfrac{5y-25}{2y^2-18} \div \dfrac{y^2-25}{3y+9}$

Challenging

07 Simplify the rational expression.

(1) $\dfrac{a^2-1}{a^2-4} \div \dfrac{2a-1}{a-2} \times \dfrac{a+2}{2a^2+a}$

(2) $\dfrac{4x^2-1}{2x^2-3x-2} \times \dfrac{2x-1}{x^2-4} \div \dfrac{2x-1}{x+2}$

268 Chapter 8. Rational Expressions

2. Addition and Subtraction

01 Addition and Subtraction of Rational Expressions

To add or subtract rational expressions, use the following properties.

1. When the denominator is identical, simply add or subtract numerators.

$$\frac{A}{B}+\frac{C}{B}=\frac{A+C}{B}, \quad \frac{A}{B}-\frac{C}{B}=\frac{A-C}{B}$$

2. When the denominator is NOT identical, find the least common denominator (LCD) and then add or subtract numerators.

$$\frac{A}{B}+\frac{C}{D}=\frac{AD}{BD}+\frac{BC}{BD}=\frac{AD+BC}{BD}, \quad \frac{A}{B}-\frac{C}{D}=\frac{AD}{BD}-\frac{BC}{BD}=\frac{AD-BC}{BD}$$

Concept Check

$$\frac{4}{x}+\frac{3}{x-2}$$

$$=\frac{4(x-2)}{x(x-2)}+\frac{3x}{x(x-2)} \quad \rightarrow \text{LCD of } x \text{ and } x-2 \text{ is } x(x-2)$$

$$=\frac{4x-8}{x(x-2)}+\frac{3x}{x(x-2)} \quad \rightarrow \text{Simplify each numerator}$$

$$=\frac{4x-8+3x}{x(x-2)} \quad \rightarrow \text{Add the numerators}$$

$$=\frac{7x-8}{x(x-2)} \quad \rightarrow \text{Simplify}$$

Example 1

Simplify the rational expression.

① $\dfrac{4}{x} - \dfrac{3}{2x}$ ② $\dfrac{2}{a} + \dfrac{a}{a+1}$

③ $\dfrac{x-1}{x+1} + \dfrac{3}{2x+3}$ ④ $\dfrac{1}{a^2-1} - \dfrac{a}{a^2-a-2}$

Solution

① $\dfrac{4}{x} - \dfrac{3}{2x} = \dfrac{4 \cdot 2}{x \cdot 2} - \dfrac{3}{2x} = \dfrac{8-3}{2x} = \dfrac{5}{2x}$

② $\dfrac{2}{a} + \dfrac{a}{a+1} = \dfrac{2(a+1)}{a(a+1)} + \dfrac{a(a)}{a(a+1)}$

$= \dfrac{2a+2+a^2}{a(a+1)} = \dfrac{a^2+2a+2}{a(a+1)}$

③ $\dfrac{x-1}{x+1} + \dfrac{3}{2x+3} = \dfrac{(x-1)(2x+3)}{(x+1)(2x+3)} + \dfrac{3(x+1)}{(2x+3)(x+1)}$

$= \dfrac{2x^2+x-3+3x+3}{(x+1)(2x+3)}$

$= \dfrac{2x^2+4x}{(x+1)(2x+3)} = \dfrac{2x(x+2)}{(x+1)(2x+3)}$

④ $\dfrac{1}{a^2-1} - \dfrac{a}{a^2-a-2} = \dfrac{1}{(a-1)(a+1)} - \dfrac{a}{(a-2)(a+1)}$

$= \dfrac{1 \cdot (a-2)}{(a-1)(a+1)(a-2)} - \dfrac{a(a-1)}{(a-2)(a+1)(a-1)}$

$= \dfrac{a-2-(a^2-a)}{(a-1)(a+1)(a-2)}$

$= \dfrac{a-2-a^2+a}{(a-1)(a+1)(a-2)}$

$= \dfrac{-a^2+2a-2}{(a-1)(a+1)(a-2)}$

$= -\dfrac{a^2-2a+2}{(a-1)(a+1)(a-2)}$

Check Point 1

Simplify the rational expression.

① $\dfrac{2}{x-2} - \dfrac{x-1}{x}$

② $\dfrac{x-4}{x} + \dfrac{x+3}{x+2}$

③ $\dfrac{2x-4}{x+3} - \dfrac{x+1}{3x-1}$

④ $\dfrac{x+4}{x^2-x-2} - \dfrac{x+2}{x^2-1}$

Review Exercise

01 Simplify the rational expression.

(1) $\dfrac{x+2}{3}+\dfrac{x-4}{6}$

(2) $\dfrac{5}{2x+2}+\dfrac{2x-3}{x+1}$

(3) $2-\dfrac{x-4}{x-1}$

(4) $\dfrac{-1}{2x^2+2x}+\dfrac{1}{2}$

02 Simplify the rational expression.

(1) $\dfrac{3}{x+5}+\dfrac{5x}{2x-1}$

(2) $\dfrac{x}{2x^2+8x}-\dfrac{5}{x+4}$

(3) $\dfrac{3}{x-6}+\dfrac{1}{x+2}$

(4) $\dfrac{1}{(x-1)^2}-\dfrac{1}{x^2-1}$

03 Simplify the rational expression.

(1) $\dfrac{x^2+x}{x^2-2x} - \dfrac{x}{2x^2-8}$

(2) $\dfrac{3x-1}{x^2+4x+4} - \dfrac{2}{x^2-4}$

Challenging

04 Given the equation $\dfrac{12}{x^2-4} = \dfrac{a}{x-2} + \dfrac{b}{x+2}$ where $x \neq \pm 2$, find the value of $a+b$.

Challenging

05 Show that $\dfrac{2}{1-x} + \dfrac{2}{1+x} + \dfrac{4}{1+x^2}$ is equal to $\dfrac{8}{1-x^4}$.

3. Rational Equations

01 Solving Rational Equations

Equations that contain rational expressions are called rational equations. To solve a rational equation, refer to the following steps.

1. Find least common denominator(LCD).
2. Multiply both sides of the equation by LCD.
3. Solve the resulting polynomial equation.
4. Check the solution(s) to make sure there isn't an extraneous solution. In rational equations, the extraneous solution is the value that makes denominator equal to zero.

Concept Check

$$\frac{1}{x-1}+\frac{4}{x+2}=2 \quad \rightarrow \text{Given}$$

$$\left(\frac{1}{x-1}+\frac{4}{x+2}\right)(x-1)(x+2)=2(x-1)(x+2) \quad \rightarrow \text{Multiply by LCD } (x-1)(x+2)$$

$$(x+2)+4(x-1)=2x^2+2x-4 \quad \rightarrow \text{Expand each side}$$

$$5x-2=2x^2+2x-4 \quad \rightarrow \text{Simplify}$$

$$2x^2-3x-2=0 \quad \rightarrow \text{Subtract } 5x-2$$

$$(2x+1)(x-2)=0 \quad \rightarrow \text{Factor}$$

$$2x+1=0 \text{ or } x-2=0 \quad \rightarrow \text{Zero product property}$$

$$x=-\frac{1}{2} \text{ or } x=2 \quad \rightarrow \text{Solve for } x$$

Check the solution $\dfrac{1}{-\frac{1}{2}-1\neq 0}+\dfrac{4}{-\frac{1}{2}+2\neq 0}=2$ and $\dfrac{1}{2-1\neq 0}+\dfrac{1}{2+2\neq 0}=2$

When we substitute the solution back into the original equation, each denominator is not equal to zero. Therefore, both $x=-\frac{1}{2}$ and $x=2$ are solutions to the equation.

Example 1

Solve the rational equation.

① $\dfrac{2}{x} - 1 = \dfrac{1}{2x}$ ② $\dfrac{5}{x-3} - 2 = \dfrac{30}{x^2-9}$

Solution

① $\dfrac{2}{x} - 1 = \dfrac{1}{2x}$

$\left(\dfrac{2}{x} - 1\right) \cdot 2x = \left(\dfrac{1}{2x}\right) \cdot 2x$ → Multiply by LCD

$4 - 2x = 1$ → Expand each side

$-2x = -3,\ x = \dfrac{3}{2}$ → Solve for x

Check the solution $\dfrac{2}{\dfrac{3}{2} \neq 0} - 1 = \dfrac{1}{2\left(\dfrac{3}{2}\right) \neq 0}$. Since $x = \dfrac{3}{2}$ does not make the denominator zero in the original equation, it is the solution to the equation.

The solution is $x = \dfrac{3}{2}$.

② $\dfrac{5}{x-3} - 2 = \dfrac{30}{x^2-9}$

$\dfrac{5}{x-3} - 2 = \dfrac{30}{(x-3)(x+3)}$ → Factor the denominator

$\left(\dfrac{5}{x-3} - 2\right) \cdot (x-3)(x+3) = \dfrac{30}{(x-3)(x+3)} \cdot (x-3)(x+3)$ → Multiply by LCD

$5(x+3) - 2(x-3)(x+3) = 30$ → Expand each side

$2x^2 - 5x - 3 = 0$ → Simplify

$(2x+1)(x-3) = 0,\ x = -\dfrac{1}{2}$ or $x = 3$ → Factor and solve for x

Check the solution $\dfrac{5}{-\dfrac{1}{2} - 3 \neq 0} - 2 = \dfrac{30}{\left(-\dfrac{1}{2}\right)^2 - 9 \neq 0}$, but $\dfrac{5}{3-3=0} - 2 \neq \dfrac{30}{3^2-9=0}$

Since $x = -\dfrac{1}{2}$ does not make the denominator zero in the original equation, it is the solution to the equation. However $\underline{x=3 \text{ is an extraneous solution}}$ because it is the value that makes denominator zero. So the only solution for this equation is $x = -\dfrac{1}{2}$.

The solution is $x = -\dfrac{1}{2}$.

Chapter 8. Rational Expressions

Check Point 1

Solve the equations.

① $2 + \dfrac{12}{5x} = \dfrac{2}{x}$

② $\dfrac{1}{x} + \dfrac{1}{x^2} = \dfrac{1}{2x^2}$

③ $\dfrac{5}{x^2-2x} + \dfrac{2}{x} = \dfrac{5}{x^2-2x}$

④ $\dfrac{30}{x+2} + \dfrac{x}{x-2} = 9$

Review Exercise

Solutions_Page 109

01 Solve the rational equation.

(1) $\dfrac{6}{x^2} = \dfrac{1}{x^2} + \dfrac{1}{x}$

(2) $\dfrac{1}{x} - \dfrac{1}{3x^2} = -\dfrac{1}{6x^2}$

(3) $\dfrac{1}{x} + \dfrac{3x+12}{x^2-5x} = \dfrac{7x-56}{x^2-5x}$

(4) $1 - \dfrac{1}{x^2+2x} = \dfrac{x-1}{x}$

02 Solve the rational equation.

(1) $\dfrac{1}{x-2} + \dfrac{1}{x^2-7x+10} = \dfrac{6}{x-2}$

(2) $\dfrac{4}{x} + \dfrac{1}{x-1} = 3$

(3) $\dfrac{5}{x+3} - \dfrac{1}{x-4} = \dfrac{3}{2}$

(4) $\dfrac{x-6}{3x} - 1 = \dfrac{x^2-5x-24}{3x}$

Chapter 8. Rational Expressions

Review Exercise

03 Solve the rational equation.

(1) $\dfrac{4}{x+5}+\dfrac{1}{x^2}=\dfrac{5}{x^3+5x^2}$

(2) $\dfrac{x}{x-1}-\dfrac{1}{x+2}=\dfrac{3}{x^2+x-2}$

Challenging

04 Given the equation
$$\dfrac{2}{2x^2-7x-4}=\dfrac{a}{x-4}-\dfrac{bx}{(x-4)(2x+1)},$$
find the value of $a+b$.

Chapter Test — Level 1

01 Simplify the rational expression.

(1) $\dfrac{16x^2-1}{8x-2}$

(2) $\dfrac{6x^2-5x-6}{3x^2+14x+8}$

02 Simplify the rational expression.

(1) $\dfrac{4a+8}{a^2+a-2} \times \dfrac{a^2-1}{4a^3+4a^2}$

(2) $\dfrac{x^2+2x+1}{x^2+3x+2} \div \dfrac{1}{x^2+2x}$

03 Simplify the rational expression $\dfrac{x^2-4}{x+11} \times (3x^3+6x^2) \div \dfrac{2x-4}{x^2+11x}$.

Chapter Test — Level 1

04 Simplify the rational expression.

(1) $\dfrac{1-4x}{2x+1}+\dfrac{2x}{x-4}$

(2) $\dfrac{x+2}{x^2-6x+8}-\dfrac{2}{x-2}$

05 Solve the rational equation.

(1) $\dfrac{x-4}{x^2-x-12}+\dfrac{1}{x+3}=1$

(2) $\dfrac{6}{x+3}+\dfrac{2}{x-2}=3$

06 Given the equation $\dfrac{10}{(2x-1)(x+2)}=\dfrac{a}{2x-1}+\dfrac{b}{x+2}$, find the value of $a+b$.

07 A positive integer is 2 more than the other positive integer. When the reciprocal of the larger number is subtracted from the reciprocal of the smaller one, the result is $\frac{1}{4}$. Find the two integers.

08 One day, Andy drove 50 miles from home to work. When he returned home, he increased his average speed 10 miles per hour higher than the speed on the way to work. If this reduced his return time by 10 minutes, what was his average speed going to work?

Chapter Test — Level 2

01 Simplify the rational expression $\dfrac{6a^2-a-2}{2a^2-5a-3} \times \dfrac{2a^2-18}{3a^2+7a-6}$.

02 Simplify the rational expression $(2x-10) \div \dfrac{x^2-9x+20}{4x^2-9} \div \dfrac{6x^3-9x^2}{x^3-4x^2}$.

03 Simplify the rational expression

(1) $\dfrac{1}{4x^2-y^2}+\dfrac{1}{2x^2-3xy+y^2}$

(2) $\dfrac{1}{x-y}+\dfrac{x}{x+y}-\dfrac{y}{x^2-y^2}$

04 Given the equation $\dfrac{10x+1}{x^2-x-2}=\dfrac{ax+b}{x-2}-\dfrac{cx}{x+1}$, find the value of $a+b+c$.

05 Simplify the rational expression $\dfrac{3}{x^2-x-12}-\dfrac{2}{x^2-16}+\dfrac{1}{x+4}$.

$$\dfrac{AB+C}{A}=\dfrac{AB}{A}+\dfrac{C}{A}=B+\dfrac{C}{A}$$

06 Use the above method to simplify the expression $\dfrac{x^2+2x+2}{x+2}-\dfrac{x-2x+2}{x-2}$.

07 The difference between the reciprocals of two consecutive positive odd integers is $\dfrac{2}{15}$. Find the two integers.

08 On the river, a boat traveled 15 miles upstream and then traveled the same 15 miles downstream. If the total time for the trip was 4 hours and the boat traveled 8 miles per hour in still water, what is the speed of the current in the river?

memo

Chapter 9

Radical Expressions

1. Simplifying Radical Expressions
2. Operations with Radical Expressions
3. Radical Equations
4. Chapter Test

1 Simplifying Radical Expressions

01 Simplifying Radicals

In radical expression, the radicand is the number or expression found inside a radical sign as shown below.

$$\sqrt{a}$$

(radical sign, radicand)

In this section, we will focus on the square root. A square root is said to be simplified if there are

1. No perfect square factors other than 1 in the radicand.
2. No fractions in the radicand.
3. No radicals in the denominator of a fraction.

Concept Check

Radicals	Simplified Form
1. $\sqrt{8a^2}$	$2a\sqrt{2}$
2. $\sqrt{\dfrac{2a}{9}}$	$\dfrac{\sqrt{2a}}{3}$
3. $\dfrac{1}{\sqrt{3}}$	$\dfrac{\sqrt{3}}{3}$

02 Multiplication and Division of Radicals, Part 1

Use the multiplication and division property to simplify radicals.

Assume $\sqrt{a}$ and $\sqrt{b}$ are real numbers. Then,
1. $\sqrt{ab} = \sqrt{a} \cdot \sqrt{b}$
2. $\sqrt{\dfrac{a}{b}} = \dfrac{\sqrt{a}}{\sqrt{b}}$

Concept Check

Simplify $\sqrt{12a^3}$ and $\sqrt{\dfrac{18a^2}{25}}$.

1. $\sqrt{12a^3} = \sqrt{4a^2 \cdot 3}$ → $4a^2$ is the greatest perfect square factor of $12a^3$
   $= \sqrt{4a^2} \cdot \sqrt{3}$ → Use the multiplication property of radicals
   $= 2a\sqrt{3}$ → $\sqrt{4a^2} = 2a$ because $(2a)^2 = 4a^2$

2. $\sqrt{\dfrac{18a^2}{25}} = \dfrac{\sqrt{18a^2}}{\sqrt{25}}$ → Division property of radicals
   $= \dfrac{\sqrt{9a^2 \cdot 2}}{\sqrt{25}}$ → $9a^2$ is the greatest perfect square factor of $18a^2$
   $= \dfrac{\sqrt{9a^2} \cdot \sqrt{2}}{\sqrt{25}}$ → Multiplication property radicals
   $= \dfrac{3a\sqrt{2}}{5}$ → $\sqrt{9a^2} = 3a$ and $\sqrt{25} = 5$

Example 1-1

Simplify the radical expression.

① $\sqrt{48}$
② $\sqrt{125a^2}$
③ $\sqrt{20b^3}$
④ $\sqrt{192x^7}$

Solution

① $\sqrt{48} = \sqrt{16} \cdot \sqrt{3} = 4\sqrt{3}$
② $\sqrt{125a^2} = \sqrt{25a^2} \cdot \sqrt{5} = 5a\sqrt{5}$
③ $\sqrt{20b^3} = \sqrt{4b^2} \cdot \sqrt{5b} = 2b\sqrt{5b}$
④ $\sqrt{192x^7} = \sqrt{64x^6} \cdot \sqrt{3x} = 8x^3\sqrt{3x}$

Example 1-2

Simplify the radical expression.

① $\sqrt{\dfrac{49}{4}}$ ② $\sqrt{\dfrac{45a^3}{36}}$

③ $\sqrt{\dfrac{50b^4}{9}}$ ④ $\sqrt{\dfrac{108b^6}{25a^4}}$

Solution

① $\sqrt{\dfrac{49}{4}} = \dfrac{\sqrt{49}}{\sqrt{4}} = \dfrac{7}{2}$

② $\sqrt{\dfrac{45a^3}{36}} = \dfrac{\sqrt{45a^3}}{\sqrt{36}} = \dfrac{\sqrt{9a^2} \cdot \sqrt{5a}}{\sqrt{36}} = \dfrac{3a\sqrt{5a}}{6} = \dfrac{a\sqrt{5a}}{2}$

③ $\sqrt{\dfrac{50b^4}{9}} = \dfrac{\sqrt{50b^4}}{\sqrt{9}} = \dfrac{\sqrt{25b^4} \cdot \sqrt{2}}{\sqrt{9}} = \dfrac{5b^2\sqrt{2}}{3}$

④ $\sqrt{\dfrac{108b^6}{25a^4}} = \dfrac{\sqrt{108b^6}}{\sqrt{25a^4}} = \dfrac{\sqrt{36b^6} \cdot \sqrt{3}}{\sqrt{25a^4}} = \dfrac{6b^3\sqrt{3}}{5a^2}$

Check Point 1

Solutions_Page 115

Simplify the radical expression.

① $\sqrt{54}$ ② $\sqrt{24a}$

③ $\sqrt{160b^3}$ ④ $\sqrt{44x^8}$

⑤ $\sqrt{\dfrac{20}{81}}$ ⑥ $\sqrt{\dfrac{9a^2}{49}}$

⑦ $\sqrt{\dfrac{27b^5}{100}}$ ⑧ $\sqrt{\dfrac{75b}{121a^2}}$

03 Multiplication and Division of Radicals, Part 2

Assume m and k are rational numbers, and $\sqrt{a}$ and $\sqrt{b}$ are real numbers. Then,

1. $\sqrt{a} \cdot \sqrt{b} = \sqrt{ab}$
2. $\dfrac{\sqrt{a}}{\sqrt{b}} = \sqrt{\dfrac{a}{b}}$
3. $m\sqrt{a} \cdot k\sqrt{b} = mk\sqrt{ab}$
4. $\dfrac{m\sqrt{a}}{k\sqrt{b}} = \dfrac{m}{k}\sqrt{\dfrac{a}{b}}$

✔ Be careful that $\sqrt{a+b} \neq \sqrt{a} + \sqrt{b}$ or $\sqrt{a-b} \neq \sqrt{a} - \sqrt{b}$.

Concept Check

Simplify $3\sqrt{3a} \cdot 2\sqrt{6a^3}$ and $\dfrac{6\sqrt{90a^4}}{2\sqrt{8a}}$.

1. $3\sqrt{3a} \cdot 2\sqrt{6a^3} = 6\sqrt{3a \cdot 6a^3}$ → Multiply the rational numbers and use the multiplication property of radicals

   $= 6\sqrt{9a^4} \cdot \sqrt{2}$ → Multiplication property of radicals

   $= 6 \cdot 3a^2\sqrt{2}$ → Simplify $\sqrt{9a^4}$

   $= 18a^2\sqrt{2}$ → Simplify

2. $\dfrac{6\sqrt{90a^4}}{2\sqrt{8a}} = \dfrac{6}{2}\dfrac{\sqrt{45a^3}}{\sqrt{4}}$ → Division property of radicals

   $= 3\dfrac{\sqrt{9a^2} \cdot \sqrt{5a}}{2}$ → Multiplication property of radicals

   $= 3\dfrac{3a \cdot \sqrt{5a}}{2}$ → Simplify $\sqrt{9a^2}$

   $= \dfrac{9a\sqrt{5a}}{2}$ → Simplify

Example 2

Simplify the radical expression.

① $3\sqrt{14a} \cdot 4\sqrt{7a}$

② $5\sqrt{12b^3} \cdot 2\sqrt{10b}$

③ $\dfrac{12\sqrt{72a^5}}{4\sqrt{6a^2}}$

④ $\dfrac{\sqrt{2b^4}}{6\sqrt{18b^6}}$

Solution

① $3\sqrt{14a} \cdot 4\sqrt{7a} = 12\sqrt{14a \cdot 7a}$
$\qquad\qquad\qquad = 12\sqrt{49a^2} \cdot \sqrt{2}$
$\qquad\qquad\qquad = 12 \cdot 7a \cdot \sqrt{2} = 84a\sqrt{2}$

② $5\sqrt{12b^3} \cdot 2\sqrt{10b} = 10\sqrt{12b^3 \cdot 10b}$
$\qquad\qquad\qquad\;\; = 10\sqrt{4b^4} \cdot \sqrt{30}$
$\qquad\qquad\qquad\;\; = 10 \cdot 2b^2 \cdot \sqrt{30} = 20b^2\sqrt{30}$

③ $\dfrac{12\sqrt{72a^5}}{4\sqrt{6a^2}} = 3\sqrt{12a^3}$
$\qquad\qquad = 3\sqrt{4a^2} \cdot \sqrt{3a}$
$\qquad\qquad = 3 \cdot 2a \cdot \sqrt{3a} = 6a\sqrt{3a}$

④ $\dfrac{\sqrt{2b^4}}{6\sqrt{18b^6}} = \dfrac{1}{6}\dfrac{\sqrt{1}}{\sqrt{9b^2}}$
$\qquad\quad = \dfrac{1}{6} \cdot \dfrac{1}{3b} = \dfrac{1}{18b}$

Check Point 2

Simplify the radical expression.

① $2\sqrt{6} \cdot 3\sqrt{2}$

② $4\sqrt{32a^2} \cdot \sqrt{10a}$

③ $\dfrac{6\sqrt{108b}}{2\sqrt{3b^5}}$

④ $\dfrac{2\sqrt{250a^2}}{5\sqrt{5a^4}}$

Solutions_Page 115

Review Exercise

01 Simplify the radical expression.

(1) $\sqrt{32}$

(2) $\sqrt{80}$

(3) $\sqrt{63a^2}$

(4) $\sqrt{96b^7}$

(5) $\sqrt{128x^5}$

(6) $\sqrt{300x^{11}}$

02 Simplify the radical expression.

(1) $\sqrt{\dfrac{40}{49}}$

(2) $\sqrt{\dfrac{162}{8a^2}}$

(3) $\sqrt{\dfrac{147a^5}{27}}$

(4) $\sqrt{\dfrac{225b^7}{36b^3}}$

Review Exercise

03 Simplify the radical expression.

(1) $\sqrt{15} \cdot 2\sqrt{3}$

(2) $4\sqrt{12a^4} \cdot 6\sqrt{6a}$

(3) $3\sqrt{50a^3} \cdot \sqrt{8a^5}$

(4) $\dfrac{15\sqrt{65}}{3\sqrt{208}}$

(5) $\dfrac{3\sqrt{150b}}{6\sqrt{120b^7}}$

(6) $\dfrac{14\sqrt{30b^4}}{21\sqrt{54b}}$

04 If $2\sqrt{5}=\sqrt{a}$ and $\sqrt{150x^2}=bx\sqrt{c}$, what is the value of $a+b+c$?
(c is the smallest positive interger)

Challenging

05 If $\sqrt{2}=a$, $\sqrt{3}=b$, and $\sqrt{5}=c$, write $\sqrt{360}$ in terms of a, b, and c?

06 If $a=2m$ and $b=4m$, where $m>0$, write each of the following in terms of m.

(1) $\sqrt{ab^2}$

Challenging

(2) $\sqrt{ab} \times \sqrt{2a^2b^3}$

07 Find the minimum value of x for $\sqrt{20x}$ to be a positive integer.

Challenging

08 Find the number of positive integer x that satisfy the inequality $4<\sqrt{3x+1}<5$.

2 Operations with Radical Expressions

01 Addition and Subtraction of Rational Expressions

To add or subtract radicals, first convert each radical to its simplest form. Then simply add or subtract like radicals. Two radicals with the same radicand are called **like radicals**.

Assume m, h, and k are rational numbers, and $n\sqrt{a}$ is real number. Then,

1. $m\sqrt{a}+k\sqrt{a}=(m+k)\sqrt{a}$
2. $m\sqrt{a}-k\sqrt{a}=(m-k)\sqrt{a}$
3. $m\sqrt{a}+h\sqrt{a}-k\sqrt{a}=(m+h-k)\sqrt{a}$

Concept Check

1. $3\sqrt{2}+4\sqrt{2}=(3+4)\sqrt{2}$ → Combine like radicals
   $\phantom{3\sqrt{2}+4\sqrt{2}}=7\sqrt{2}$ → Simplify

2. $5\sqrt{7}-\sqrt{28}=5\sqrt{7}-\sqrt{4}\cdot\sqrt{7}$ → 4 is the greatest perfect square factor of 28
   $\phantom{5\sqrt{7}-\sqrt{28}}=5\sqrt{7}-2\sqrt{7}$ → Simplify
   $\phantom{5\sqrt{7}-\sqrt{28}}=(5-2)\sqrt{7}$ → Combine like radicals
   $\phantom{5\sqrt{7}-\sqrt{28}}=3\sqrt{7}$ → Simplify

3. $5\sqrt{2}+2\sqrt{3}+3\sqrt{2}-5\sqrt{3}$
   $=(5+3)\sqrt{2}+(2-5)\sqrt{3}$ → Combine like radicals
   $=8\sqrt{2}-3\sqrt{3}$ → Simplify

Example 1

Simplify the expression.

① $\sqrt{8}+5\sqrt{2}$

② $5\sqrt{3}-\sqrt{27}+\sqrt{12}$

③ $\sqrt{27}+\sqrt{8}-5\sqrt{3}+4\sqrt{2}$

④ $\dfrac{\sqrt{8}}{4}-\dfrac{\sqrt{12}}{2}+\sqrt{18}$

Solution

① $\sqrt{8}+5\sqrt{2}=\sqrt{4}\cdot\sqrt{2}+5\sqrt{2}$
$=2\sqrt{2}+5\sqrt{2}$
$=(2+5)\sqrt{2}=7\sqrt{2}$

② $5\sqrt{3}-\sqrt{27}+\sqrt{12}=5\sqrt{3}-\sqrt{9}\cdot\sqrt{3}+\sqrt{4}\cdot\sqrt{3}$
$=5\sqrt{3}-3\sqrt{3}+2\sqrt{3}$
$=(5-3+2)\sqrt{3}=4\sqrt{3}$

③ $\sqrt{27}+\sqrt{8}-5\sqrt{3}+4\sqrt{2}=\sqrt{9}\cdot\sqrt{3}+\sqrt{4}\cdot\sqrt{2}-5\sqrt{3}+4\sqrt{2}$
$=3\sqrt{3}+2\sqrt{2}-5\sqrt{3}+4\sqrt{2}$
$=(2+4)\sqrt{2}+(3-5)\sqrt{3}$
$=6\sqrt{2}-2\sqrt{3}$

④ $\dfrac{\sqrt{8}}{4}-\dfrac{\sqrt{12}}{2}+\sqrt{18}=\dfrac{\sqrt{4}\cdot\sqrt{2}}{4}-\dfrac{\sqrt{4}\cdot\sqrt{3}}{2}+\sqrt{9}\cdot\sqrt{2}$
$=\dfrac{2\sqrt{2}}{4}-\dfrac{2\sqrt{3}}{2}+3\sqrt{2}$
$=\dfrac{\sqrt{2}}{2}-\sqrt{3}+3\sqrt{2}$
$=\left(\dfrac{1}{2}+3\right)\sqrt{2}-\sqrt{3}=\dfrac{7\sqrt{2}}{2}-\sqrt{3}$

Check Point 1

Simplify the expression.

① $-3\sqrt{5}+5\sqrt{5}$

② $\sqrt{12}-\sqrt{48}-2\sqrt{3}$

③ $3\sqrt{2}+\sqrt{75}-\sqrt{50}$

④ $\sqrt{200}-\sqrt{125}-\sqrt{32}+6\sqrt{5}$

02 Multiplying Radical Expressions

Just like multiplying polynomials, multiply radical expressions using the distributive property or the FOIL method.

Concept Check

1. $\sqrt{15}(\sqrt{6}+\sqrt{5}) = \sqrt{15}\cdot\sqrt{6}+\sqrt{15}\cdot\sqrt{5}$ → Distributive property
   $= \sqrt{90}+\sqrt{75}$ → Multiplication property of radicals
   $= \sqrt{9}\cdot\sqrt{10}+\sqrt{25}\cdot\sqrt{3}$ → The greatest perfect square factor
   $= 3\sqrt{10}+5\sqrt{3}$ → Simplify

2. $(3+\sqrt{2})(\sqrt{6}-2\sqrt{2}) = 3\sqrt{6}-6\sqrt{2}+\sqrt{12}-2\sqrt{4}$ → FOIL
   $= 3\sqrt{6}-6\sqrt{2}+\sqrt{4}\cdot\sqrt{3}-2\cdot 2$ → The greatest perfect square factor
   $= 3\sqrt{6}-6\sqrt{2}+2\sqrt{3}-4$ → Simplify

Example 2

Simplify the expression.

① $\sqrt{10}(\sqrt{2}+\sqrt{5})$

② $(2-\sqrt{5})(3+2\sqrt{5})$

③ $(\sqrt{3}-2\sqrt{2})^2$

④ $(3\sqrt{2}-\sqrt{6})(\sqrt{2}+5\sqrt{6})$

Solution

① $\sqrt{10}(\sqrt{2}+\sqrt{5}) = \sqrt{10}\cdot\sqrt{2}+\sqrt{10}\cdot\sqrt{5}$
$= \sqrt{20}+\sqrt{50}$
$= \sqrt{4}\cdot\sqrt{5}+\sqrt{25}\cdot\sqrt{2}$
$= 2\sqrt{5}+5\sqrt{2}$

② $(2-\sqrt{5})(3+2\sqrt{5}) = 6+4\sqrt{5}-3\sqrt{5}-2\sqrt{25}$
$= 6+4\sqrt{5}-3\sqrt{5}-2(5)$
$= 6+\sqrt{5}-10$
$= -4+\sqrt{5}$

③ $(\sqrt{3}-2\sqrt{2})^2 = 3-4\sqrt{6}+4\sqrt{4}$ → $(a-b)^2 = a^2-2ab+b^2$
$\qquad\qquad\quad = 3-4\sqrt{6}+4(2)$
$\qquad\qquad\quad = 3-4\sqrt{6}+8$
$\qquad\qquad\quad = 11-4\sqrt{6}$

④ $(3\sqrt{2}-\sqrt{6})(\sqrt{2}+5\sqrt{6}) = 3\sqrt{4}+15\sqrt{12}-\sqrt{12}-5\sqrt{36}$
$\qquad\qquad\qquad\qquad\quad = 3\sqrt{4}+14\sqrt{12}-5\sqrt{36}$
$\qquad\qquad\qquad\qquad\quad = 3(2)+14(\sqrt{4}\cdot\sqrt{3})-5(6)$
$\qquad\qquad\qquad\qquad\quad = 6+14(2\sqrt{3})-30$
$\qquad\qquad\qquad\qquad\quad = -24+28\sqrt{3}$

Check Point 2 Solutions_Page 117

Simplify the expression.

① $\sqrt{15}(\sqrt{12}+4\sqrt{5})$ ② $(\sqrt{6}-\sqrt{3})(\sqrt{6}+\sqrt{3})$

③ $(\sqrt{6}+4\sqrt{2})^2$ ④ $(\sqrt{5}+\sqrt{3})(2\sqrt{5}-3\sqrt{3})$

03 Rationalizing the Denominator

This is a process to remove radical in the denominator.

1. $\dfrac{b}{\sqrt{a}} = \dfrac{b}{\sqrt{a}} \cdot \dfrac{\sqrt{a}}{\sqrt{a}} = \dfrac{b\sqrt{a}}{a}$

$\dfrac{b}{c\sqrt{a}} = \dfrac{b}{c\sqrt{a}} \cdot \dfrac{\sqrt{a}}{\sqrt{a}} = \dfrac{b\sqrt{a}}{ac}$

2. $\dfrac{c}{\sqrt{a}-\sqrt{b}} = \dfrac{c}{\sqrt{a}-\sqrt{b}} \cdot \dfrac{\sqrt{a}+\sqrt{b}}{\sqrt{a}+\sqrt{b}} = \dfrac{c(\sqrt{a}+\sqrt{b})}{a-b}$

$\dfrac{c}{\sqrt{a}+\sqrt{b}} = \dfrac{c}{\sqrt{a}+\sqrt{b}} \cdot \dfrac{\sqrt{a}-\sqrt{b}}{\sqrt{a}-\sqrt{b}} = \dfrac{c(\sqrt{a}-\sqrt{b})}{a-b}$

Concept Check

1. $\dfrac{5}{\sqrt{3}} = \dfrac{5}{\sqrt{3}} \cdot \dfrac{\sqrt{3}}{\sqrt{3}}$ → Multiply by $\dfrac{\sqrt{3}}{\sqrt{3}}$

   $= \dfrac{5\sqrt{3}}{3}$ → $\sqrt{3} \cdot \sqrt{3} = \sqrt{9} = 3$

2. $\dfrac{3}{\sqrt{6}-\sqrt{2}} = \dfrac{3}{\sqrt{6}-\sqrt{2}} \cdot \dfrac{\sqrt{6}+\sqrt{2}}{\sqrt{6}+\sqrt{2}}$ → Multiply by $\dfrac{\sqrt{6}+\sqrt{2}}{\sqrt{6}+\sqrt{2}}$

   $= \dfrac{3(\sqrt{6}+\sqrt{2})}{6-2}$ → $(\sqrt{6}-\sqrt{2})(\sqrt{6}+\sqrt{2}) = \sqrt{36}-\sqrt{4} = 6-2$

   $= \dfrac{3(\sqrt{6}+\sqrt{2})}{4}$ → Simplify

Example 3

Rationalize the denominator.

① $\sqrt{\dfrac{6}{5}}$ ② $\dfrac{1}{1+\sqrt{2}}$ ③ $\dfrac{\sqrt{2}}{\sqrt{3}-\sqrt{2}}$

Solution

① $\sqrt{\dfrac{6}{5}} = \dfrac{\sqrt{6}}{\sqrt{5}} = \dfrac{\sqrt{6}}{\sqrt{5}} \cdot \dfrac{\sqrt{5}}{\sqrt{5}} = \dfrac{\sqrt{30}}{5}$

② $\dfrac{1}{1+\sqrt{2}} = \dfrac{1}{1+\sqrt{2}} \cdot \dfrac{1-\sqrt{2}}{1-\sqrt{2}}$

   $= \dfrac{1-\sqrt{2}}{1-2} = -1+\sqrt{2}$

③ $\dfrac{\sqrt{2}}{\sqrt{3}-\sqrt{2}} = \dfrac{\sqrt{2}}{\sqrt{3}-\sqrt{2}} \cdot \dfrac{\sqrt{3}+\sqrt{2}}{\sqrt{3}+\sqrt{2}}$

   $= \dfrac{\sqrt{6}+\sqrt{4}}{3-2} = \dfrac{\sqrt{6}+2}{1} = \sqrt{6}+2$

Check Point 3 Solutions_Page 117

Rationalize the denominator.

① $\sqrt{\dfrac{3}{2}}$ ② $\dfrac{\sqrt{3}}{\sqrt{6}-2}$ ③ $\dfrac{1}{\sqrt{2}+\sqrt{5}}$

Review Exercise

01 Simplify the expression.

(1) $5\sqrt{2}-3\sqrt{2}$

(2) $7\sqrt{7}-2\sqrt{7}+3\sqrt{7}$

(3) $4\sqrt{2}-\sqrt{5}-2\sqrt{2}+6\sqrt{5}$

(4) $\sqrt{45}+\sqrt{27}+\sqrt{12}-\sqrt{20}$

02 Simplify the expression.

(1) $5\sqrt{72}-4\sqrt{50}$

(2) $\sqrt{98}+\sqrt{8}+\sqrt{18}$

(3) $2\sqrt{32}-3\sqrt{5}+\sqrt{80}$

(4) $2\sqrt{60}-4\sqrt{24}+\sqrt{135}-3\sqrt{54}$

Review Exercise

03 Simplify the expression.

(1) $(\sqrt{5}-1)(\sqrt{5}+1)$

(2) $\sqrt{2}(\sqrt{6}-\sqrt{10})$

(3) $(2\sqrt{3}-5)(2\sqrt{3}+5)$

(4) $\sqrt{3}(\sqrt{6}+\sqrt{2})$

04 Simplify the expression.

(1) $(2\sqrt{5}-\sqrt{3})^2$

(2) $(4+3\sqrt{3})(\sqrt{3}-7)$

(3) $(4\sqrt{2}-2\sqrt{7})^2$

(4) $(5\sqrt{2}-1)(2\sqrt{2}+3)$

05 Rationalize the denominator.

(1) $\dfrac{2}{\sqrt{3}}$

(2) $\dfrac{15\sqrt{2}}{\sqrt{5}}$

(3) $\dfrac{1-\sqrt{3}}{1+\sqrt{3}}$

(4) $\dfrac{4+3\sqrt{2}}{3+\sqrt{2}}$

06 If $a=\sqrt{5}+\sqrt{3}$ and $b=\sqrt{5}-\sqrt{3}$, find each of the following.

(1) ab

(2) $a\sqrt{3}+b\sqrt{5}$

(3) $a\sqrt{5}-2b\sqrt{3}$

(4) $ab\sqrt{3}+ab^2$

Review Exercise

Challenging

07 If $\dfrac{\sqrt{2}}{\sqrt{3}}+\dfrac{2}{\sqrt{6}}+\dfrac{\sqrt{3}}{\sqrt{2}}=a\sqrt{b}$, what is the value of ab? (b is the smallest positive integer)

Challenging

09 If $x=\dfrac{2}{\sqrt{6}-2}$, find the value of x^2-4x+4.

Challenging

08 If the result of the expression below is rational number, what is the value of k?

(1) $2k\sqrt{3}-4k+3-4\sqrt{3}$

(2) $(2-5\sqrt{2})(3k+2\sqrt{2})$

3 Radical Equations

A radical equation is an equation that contains the radical with a variable in the radicand. $x-3=\sqrt{2x-1}$ and $\sqrt{2x-1}-4=0$ are radical equations for instance. To solve the radical equations, we need to eliminate the radicals and obtain a polynomial equation.

However, solving the radical equation sometimes yields an extraneous solution. An extraneous solution is a solution that emerges from the process of solving the equation but is not a valid solution to the equation. When solving the radical equation, we always need to check for an extraneous solution.

Concept Check

1. $\sqrt{x}=4$ ✔ Check $x=16$ in the original equation.
   $(\sqrt{x})^2=(4)^2$ $\sqrt{16}=4$
   $x=16$ $4=4$

   $x=16$ is the solution to the equation $\sqrt{x}=4$.

2. $\sqrt{x}=-4$ ✔ Check $x=16$ in the original equation.
   $(\sqrt{x})^2=(-4)^2$ $\sqrt{16}=-4$
   $x=16$ $4\neq-4$

   $x=16$ is the extraneous solution.

   Therefore, the equation $\sqrt{x}=-4$ has no solution.

Example 1

Solve the equation. Check for extraneous solutions.

① $\sqrt{x-1}-3=0$ ② $\sqrt{2x+9}-x=3$

Solution

① $\sqrt{x-1}-3=0$
  $\sqrt{x-1}=3$ → Isolate the radical term
  $(\sqrt{x-1})^2=(3)^2$ → Square both sides to eliminate the radical
  $x-1=9$ → Simplify
  $x=10$ → Solve for x

✔ Check $x=10$ in the original equation.
  $\sqrt{10-1}-3=0$
  $3-3=0$
  $0=0$ → Solution checks

The solution is $x=10$.

② $\sqrt{2x+9}-x=3$
  $\sqrt{2x+9}=x+3$ → Isolate the radical term
  $(\sqrt{2x+9})^2=(x+3)^2$ → Square both sides to eliminate the radical
  $2x+9=x^2+6x+9$ → Expand
  $x^2+4x=0$ → Simplify
  $x(x+4)=0$ → Factor
  $x=0$ or $x=-4$ → Solve for x

✔ Check $x=0$ in the original equation.
  $\sqrt{2 \cdot 0+9}-0=3$
  $\sqrt{9}=3$
  $3=3$ → Solution checks

✔ Check $x=-4$ in the original equation.
  $\sqrt{2(-4)+9}-(-4)=3$
  $\sqrt{1}+4=3$
  $5 \neq 3$ → Extraneous solution

The solution is $x=0$.

Check Point 1   Solutions_Page 119

Solve the equation. Check for extraneous solutions.

① $\sqrt{6x-5}-7=0$ ② $\sqrt{x-3}-x=-5$

Review Exercise

01 Solve the equation.
Check for extraneous solutions.

(1) $\sqrt{3x+1}=7$

(2) $\sqrt{5x-1}+3=1$

(3) $8\sqrt{2x-5}-7=3$

(4) $2\sqrt{-3x+6}+1=5$

02 Solve the equation.
Check for extraneous solutions.

(1) $\sqrt{x-2}+x=4$

(2) $\sqrt{x+12}-x=0$

(3) $\sqrt{x}-\sqrt{x-5}=2$

(4) $\sqrt{3x+10}=4+x$

Challenging

03 Solve the equation.
Check for extraneous solutions.

(1) $\sqrt{3x-2}-\sqrt{10-x}=2$

(2) $\sqrt{x+3}-3=\sqrt{2-x}$

Chapter Test — Level 1

01 Simplify the radical expression.

(1) $\sqrt{99x^3}$

(2) $\sqrt{\dfrac{24x^4}{81}}$

(3) $3\sqrt{18} \cdot 5\sqrt{12}$

(4) $\dfrac{3\sqrt{75a^3}}{24\sqrt{5a}}$

02 Simplify the radical expression.

(1) $\sqrt{50} - \sqrt{32} + \sqrt{18}$

(2) $(3 - 5\sqrt{2})(\sqrt{8} + 1)$

03 Find the number of positive integer x that satisfy the inequality $\sqrt{6} < x < \sqrt{40}$.

04 If $\dfrac{\sqrt{32} - 4}{\sqrt{2}} - \dfrac{\sqrt{12} + \sqrt{48}}{\sqrt{3}} = a + b\sqrt{c}$, what is the value of abc?

(c is the smallest positive integer)

05 Simplify $(1+\sqrt{2}-\sqrt{3})(1-\sqrt{2}+\sqrt{3})$.

06 If the expression $(\sqrt{12}-2)(\sqrt{27}-a+2)$ is rational number, what is the value of a?

07 If $a=\dfrac{\sqrt{3}-\sqrt{2}}{4}$ and $b=\dfrac{\sqrt{3}+\sqrt{2}}{4}$, what is the value of $(a+b)^2(a-b)^2$?

08 If $x=\dfrac{2}{\sqrt{3}-1}$, what is the value of x^3-x^2-2x?

09 Solve the equation. Check for extraneous solutions.

(1) $2\sqrt{-3x+6}+1=5$ 	(2) $\sqrt{x}-\sqrt{x-5}=2$

Chapter Test Level 2

01 Simplify the expression $\dfrac{4\sqrt{12}}{\sqrt{3}}+\sqrt{6}(\sqrt{24}+2\sqrt{3})-\dfrac{4}{\sqrt{2}-1}$.

02 Find the value of $x\sqrt{\dfrac{2y}{x}}-\dfrac{4}{y}\sqrt{\dfrac{y}{2x}}$ if $x>0$, $y>0$ and $xy=2$.

03 If $\dfrac{a}{\sqrt{10}-3}-\dfrac{b}{\sqrt{10}+3}=6+4\sqrt{10}$, what is the value of a^2-b^2?

04 If $a=\dfrac{1+\sqrt{2}}{1-\sqrt{2}}$ and $b=\dfrac{1-\sqrt{2}}{1+\sqrt{2}}$, what is the value of $\dfrac{\sqrt{a}-\sqrt{b}}{\sqrt{a}+\sqrt{b}}$?

05 If $x=\dfrac{4}{3-\sqrt{5}}$ and $y=\dfrac{4}{3+\sqrt{5}}$, what is the value of x^2-y^2?

06 Solve the equation. Check for extraneous solutions.

(1) $2\sqrt{2x+1}+4x=-2$

(2) $\sqrt{2x+9}-x=3$

(3) $\sqrt{x}-\sqrt{x+3}=\sqrt{3}$

memo

memo

ALGEBRA 1

REVIEW AND WORKBOOK

JOSEPH PAK

JM EDU

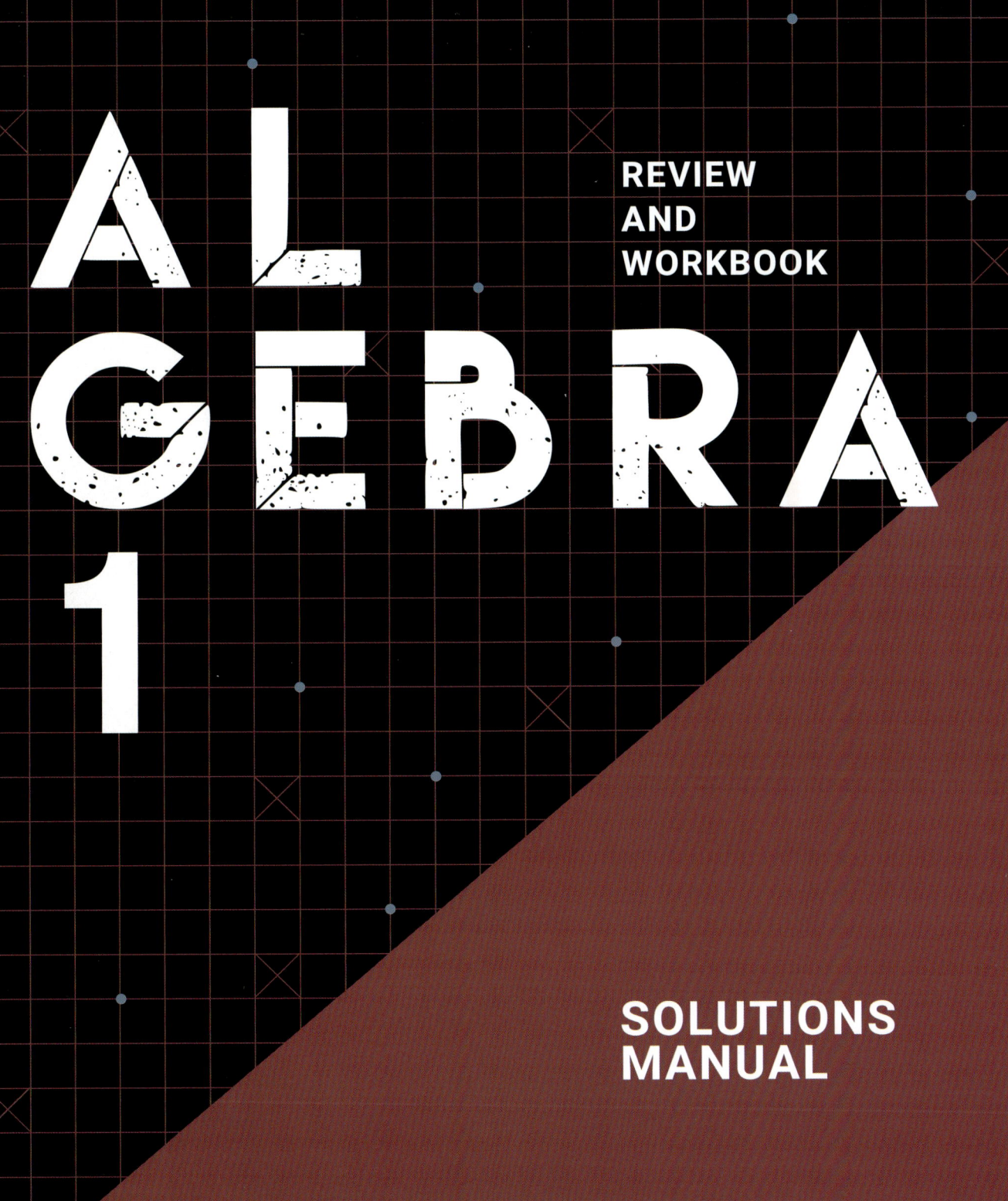

Solutions Manual

Solutions Manual

Chapter **1**

Linear Equations

1. Variable and Expressions

Check Point 1

① $36x \times \left(-\frac{1}{12}\right) = \left(36 \times \left(-\frac{1}{12}\right)\right) \times x = -3x$

② $(-2) \times (-13x) = (-2 \times (-13)) \times x = 26x$

③ $(-25y) \div \frac{5}{3} = (-25y) \times \frac{3}{5}$
$= \left(-25 \times \frac{3}{5}\right) \times y = -15y$

④ $(-28y) \div \left(-\frac{7}{2}\right) = (-28y) \times \left(-\frac{2}{7}\right)$
$= \left(-28 \times \left(-\frac{2}{7}\right)\right) \times y = 8y$

Check Point 2

① $-4\left(-\frac{3}{2}x+8\right) = \left(-4 \times \left(-\frac{3}{2}x\right)\right) + (-4 \times 8)$
$= 6x - 32$

② $\frac{1}{3}(-12x-36) = \left(\frac{1}{3} \times (-12x)\right) + \left(\frac{1}{3} \times (-36)\right)$
$= -4x - 12$

③ $(14y+63) \div \left(-\frac{7}{2}\right) = (14y+63) \times \left(-\frac{2}{7}\right)$
$= \left(14y \times \left(-\frac{2}{7}\right)\right) + \left(63 \times \left(-\frac{2}{7}\right)\right)$
$= -4y - 18$

④ $\left(\frac{15}{4}y-25\right) \div \frac{5}{2} = \left(\frac{15}{4}y-25\right) \times \frac{2}{5}$
$= \left(\frac{15}{4}y \times \frac{2}{5}\right) + \left(-25 \times \frac{2}{5}\right)$

$= \frac{3}{2}y - 10$

Check Point 3

① $-11x+14-6x+3 = -11x-6x+14+3$
$= -17x+17$

② $-3(4x+7)+4(x-3) = -12x-21+4x-12$
$= -12x+4x-21-12$
$= -8x-33$

③ $\frac{5}{6}(12x-24)-7(-2x-3)$
$= 10x-20+14x+21$
$= 10x+14x-20+21$
$= 24x+1$

④ $4x-3(-2x-5)-\frac{3}{2}(6x+10)$
$= 4x+6x+15-9x-15$
$= 4x+6x-9x+15-15$
$= x$

Check Point 4

① $-\frac{2x+1}{5} + \frac{x-2}{3}$

The LCM of 3 and 5 is 15.

$= -\frac{2x+1}{5} \cdot \frac{3}{3} + \frac{x-2}{3} \cdot \frac{5}{5}$

$= \frac{-3(2x+1)+5(x-2)}{15}$

$= \frac{-6x-3+5x-10}{15}$

$= \frac{-x-13}{15} = -\frac{x+13}{15}$

② $\frac{2x-5}{4} - \frac{x+1}{6} + 2$

The LCM of 4 and 6 is 12.

$= \frac{2x-5}{4} \cdot \frac{3}{3} - \frac{x+1}{6} \cdot \frac{2}{2} + \frac{2}{1} \cdot \frac{12}{12}$

$= \frac{3(2x-5)-2(x+1)+2(12)}{12}$

$$= \frac{6x-15-2x-2+24}{12}$$
$$= \frac{4x+7}{12}$$

Review Exercise

01

(A) $24x \times \left(-\frac{3}{4}\right) = \left(24 \times \left(-\frac{3}{4}\right)\right) \times x = -18x$

(B) $\left(-\frac{9}{5}x\right) \div (-6) = \left(-\frac{9}{5}x\right) \times \left(-\frac{1}{6}\right)$
$= \left(-\frac{9}{5} \times \left(-\frac{1}{6}\right)\right) \times x = \frac{3}{10}x$

(C) $\frac{2}{3}(-6x+9) = \left(\frac{2}{3} \times (-6x)\right) + \left(\frac{2}{3} \times 9\right)$
$= -4x+6$

(D) $(12x-15) \div \frac{5}{3} = (12x-15) \times \frac{3}{5}$
$= \left(12x \times \frac{3}{5}\right) + \left(-15 \times \frac{3}{5}\right)$
$= \frac{36}{5}x - 9 \neq \frac{4}{5}x - 9$

The answer is (D)

02

$-4\left(2x-\frac{3}{4}\right) = (-4 \times 2x) + \left(-4 \times \left(-\frac{3}{4}\right)\right)$
$= -8x+3$

(A) $4\left(2x+\frac{3}{4}\right) = (4 \times 2x) + \left(4 \times \frac{3}{4}\right)$
$= 8x+3$

(B) $-2(4x-3) = (-2 \times 4x) + (-2 \times (-3))$
$= -8x+6$

(C) $\left(-2x+\frac{3}{4}\right) \div \frac{1}{4} = \left(-2x+\frac{3}{4}\right) \times 4$
$= (-2x \times 4) + \left(\frac{3}{4} \times 4\right)$
$= -8x+3$

(D) $(4x-3) \div \left(-\frac{1}{2}\right) = (4x-3) \times (-2)$
$= (4x \times (-2)) + (-3 \times (-2))$
$= -8x+6$

The answer is (C)

03

$\left(-\frac{6}{5}x-4\right) \div \left(-\frac{2}{5}\right) = \left(-\frac{6}{5}x-4\right) \times \left(-\frac{5}{2}\right)$
$= \left(-\frac{6}{5}x \times \left(-\frac{5}{2}\right)\right) + \left(-4 \times \left(-\frac{5}{2}\right)\right)$
$= 3x+10$
$\Rightarrow a=3, b=10$

Therefore, $a-b=3-10=-7$.

$a-b=-7$

04

(1) $5(3x-1) - 4(x-2) = 15x-5-4x+8$
$= 11x+3$
$\Rightarrow a=11, b=3$

Therefore, $a+b=11+3=14$.

$a+b=14$

(2) $\frac{1}{2}(6x-10) - 3(x+4) - 5x$
$= 3x-5-3x-12-5x$
$= -5x-17$
$\Rightarrow a=-5, b=-17$

Therefore, $a+b=-5-17=-22$.

$a+b=-22$

05

$2(x-3y) - 5(3x+y) = 2x-6y-15x-5y$
$= 2x-15x-6y-5y$
$= -13x-11y$

$-13x-11y$

06

$4x - 2(ax+3a) + \frac{2}{3}(3x-9)$
$= 4x-2ax-6a+2x-6$
$= (4-2a+2)x + (-6a-6)$
$= (-2a+6)x + (-6a-6)$

Since the coefficient of x is m and the constant is n, $-2a+6=m$ and $-6a-6=n$. Therefore,
$2m-n = 2(-2a+6) - (-6a-6)$
$= -4a+12+6a+6$
$= 2a+18$

$2m-n=2a+18$

Solutions Manual

07

(1) The LCM of 2 and 5 is 10.

$$\frac{5x-4}{2}-\frac{2x+3}{5}=\frac{5x-4}{2}\cdot\frac{5}{5}-\frac{2x+3}{5}\cdot\frac{2}{2}$$
$$=\frac{5(5x-4)-2(2x+3)}{10}$$
$$=\frac{25x-20-4x-6}{10}$$
$$=\frac{21x-26}{10}$$

$\Rightarrow a=21,\ b=-26,\ c=10$

Therefore, $a+b+c=21+(-26)+10=5$.

$$a+b+c=5$$

(2) The LCM of 4, 3, and 2 is 12.

$$\frac{x-5}{4}-\frac{4x-2}{3}+\frac{x+3}{2}$$
$$=\frac{x-5}{4}\cdot\frac{3}{3}-\frac{4x-2}{3}\cdot\frac{4}{4}+\frac{x+3}{2}\cdot\frac{6}{6}$$
$$=\frac{3(x-5)-4(4x-2)+6(x+3)}{12}$$
$$=\frac{3x-15-16x+8+6x+18}{12}$$
$$=\frac{-7x+11}{12}=-\frac{7x-11}{12}$$

$\Rightarrow a=7,\ b=-11,\ c=12$

Therefore, $a+b+c=7+(-11)+12=8$.

$$a+b+c=8$$

08

$$\frac{5}{3}A-\frac{1}{2}(B-5)=\frac{5}{3}(3x-4)-\frac{1}{2}(2x+1-5)$$
$$=\frac{5}{3}(3x-4)-\frac{1}{2}(2x-4)$$
$$=5x-\frac{20}{3}-x+2$$
$$=4x-\frac{14}{3}$$

$$\frac{5}{3}A-\frac{1}{2}(B-5)=4x-\frac{14}{3}$$

09

$3B-2(A-C)$
$=3(5y-3)-2(4x+2-(3x-4y+2))$
$=3(5y-3)-2(4x+2-3x+4y-2)$
$=3(5y-3)-2(x+4y)$
$=15y-9-2x-8y$
$=-2x+7y-9$

$$3B-2(A-C)=-2x+7y-9$$

2. Solving Linear Equations, Part 1

Check Point 1

① $x+13=5$
$x+13-13=5-13$
$x=-8$

$x=-8$

② $x-7=-14$
$x-7+7=-14+7$
$x=-7$

$x=-7$

③ $-\dfrac{x}{7}=15$
$-\dfrac{x}{7}(-7)=15(-7)$
$x=-105$

$x=-105$

④ $-11x=-121$
$\dfrac{-11x}{-11}=\dfrac{-121}{-11}$
$x=11$

$x=11$

Check Point 2

① $5-3x=5x-35$
$5-3x-5x=5x-5x-35$
$5-8x=-35$
$5-5-8x=-35-5$
$-8x=-40$
$\dfrac{-8x}{-8}=\dfrac{-40}{-8}$
$x=5$

$x=5$

② $13-4x-5=7x-5x+2$
$8-4x=2x+2$
$8-4x-2x=2x-2x+2$
$8-6x=2$
$8-8-6x=2-8$

$-6x=-6$
$\dfrac{-6x}{-6}=\dfrac{-6}{-6}$
$x=1$

$x=1$

③ $3x-4+2(1-x)=-8$
$3x-4+2-2x=-8$
$x-2=-8$
$x-2+2=-8+2$
$x=-6$

$x=-6$

④ $4-2x=-4(3-x)-5(x-1)$
$4-2x=-12+4x-5x+5$
$4-2x=-7-x$
$4-2x+x=-7-x+x$
$4-x=-7$
$4-4-x=-7-4$
$-x=-11$
$\dfrac{-x}{-1}=\dfrac{-11}{-1}$
$x=11$

$x=11$

Review Exercise

01

(1) $x+5=-19$
$x+5-5=-19-5$
$x=-24$

$x=-24$

(2) $\dfrac{x-6}{2}=12$
$\dfrac{x-6}{2}\cdot 2=12\cdot 2$
$x-6=24$
$x-6+6=24+6$
$x=30$

$x=30$

(3) $3x-7=14$
$3x-7+7=14+7$

Solutions Manual

$$3x=21$$
$$\frac{3x}{3}=\frac{21}{3}$$
$$x=7$$

(4)
$$x+4=3x-8$$
$$x-3x+4=3x-3x-8$$
$$-2x+4=-8$$
$$-2x+4-4=-8-4$$
$$-2x=-12$$
$$\frac{-2x}{-2}=\frac{-12}{-2}$$
$$x=6$$

02
(1)
$$x-5+6x=4+4x$$
$$7x-5=4+4x$$
$$7x-4x-5=4+4x-4x$$
$$3x-5=4$$
$$3x-5+5=4+5$$
$$3x=9$$
$$\frac{3x}{3}=\frac{9}{3}$$
$$x=3$$

(2)
$$6x-4x+9=7+7x-3$$
$$2x+9=7x+4$$
$$2x-7x+9=7x-7x+4$$
$$-5x+9=4$$
$$-5x+9-9=4-9$$
$$-5x=-5$$
$$\frac{-5x}{-5}=\frac{-5}{-5}$$
$$x=1$$

(3)
$$3x-14=24-16x$$
$$3x+16x-14=24-16x+16x$$
$$19x-14=24$$
$$19x-14+14=24+14$$
$$19x=38$$

$$x=7$$

$$x=6$$

$$x=3$$

$$x=1$$

$$\frac{19x}{19}=\frac{38}{19}$$
$$x=2$$

(4)
$$15x-9-7x=18+6-3x$$
$$8x-9=24-3x$$
$$8x+3x-9=24-3x+3x$$
$$11x-9=24$$
$$11x-9+9=24+9$$
$$11x=33$$
$$\frac{11x}{11}=\frac{33}{11}$$
$$x=3$$

03
(1)
$$4x-4=2(x+3)$$
$$4x-4=2x+6$$
$$4x-2x-4=2x-2x+6$$
$$2x-4=6$$
$$2x-4+4=6+4$$
$$2x=10$$
$$\frac{2x}{2}=\frac{10}{2}$$
$$x=5$$

(2)
$$10-4(x+1)=2(x+5)$$
$$10-4x-4=2x+10$$
$$6-4x=2x+10$$
$$6-4x-2x=2x-2x+10$$
$$6-6x=10$$
$$6-6-6x=10-6$$
$$-6x=4$$
$$\frac{-6x}{-6}=\frac{4}{-6}$$
$$x=-\frac{2}{3}$$

(3)
$$2(2x-7)-x=2-3x$$
$$4x-14-x=2-3x$$
$$3x-14=2-3x$$
$$3x+3x-14=2-3x+3x$$
$$6x-14=2$$

$$x=2$$

$$x=3$$

$$x=5$$

$$x=-\frac{2}{3}$$

$$6x-14+14=2+14$$
$$6x=16$$
$$\frac{6x}{6}=\frac{16}{6}$$
$$x=\frac{8}{3}$$

$$x=\frac{8}{3}$$

(4) $4x-(2-3x)=\frac{1}{2}(2x-5)+\frac{3}{2}$
$$4x-2+3x=x-\frac{5}{2}+\frac{3}{2}$$
$$7x-2=x-1$$
$$7x-x-2=x-x-1$$
$$6x-2=-1$$
$$6x-2+2=-1+2$$
$$6x=1$$
$$\frac{6x}{6}=\frac{1}{6}$$
$$x=\frac{1}{6}$$

$$x=\frac{1}{6}$$

04

First incorrect step is step 1.
$4-6x+10=3x-4\underline{+x}$
It must be $+x$ on the right side, not $-x$.

The answer is (A)

05

$2(x-3k)+1=4k-3(4-x)$
Substitute -3 for x and solve for k.
$$2((-3)-3k)+1=4k-3(4-(-3))$$
$$2(-3-3k)+1=4k-3(4+3)$$
$$-6-6k+1=4k-21$$
$$-6k-5=4k-21$$
$$-10k-5=-21$$
$$-10k=-16$$
$$k=\frac{-16}{-10}=\frac{8}{5}$$

$$k=\frac{8}{5}$$

06

Solve the equation $5x+3=3(x-1)$ first.
$$5x+3=3(x-1)$$
$$5x+3=3x-3$$
$$2x+3=-3$$
$$2x=-6$$
$$x=-3$$

Since $x=-3$ is also the solution of the equation $ax+5=x+a$, substitute -3 for x in the equation and solve for a.
$$ax+5=x+a$$
$$a(-3)+5=-3+a$$
$$-3a+5=-3+a$$
$$-4a+5=-3$$
$$-4a=-8$$
$$a=2$$

$$a=2$$

07

Let $\boxed{}=A$. Then we have
$$7(x+3)-A=4(2x-3)+3x$$
$$7x+21-A=8x-12+3x$$
$$7x+21-A=11x-12$$

Now, leave $-A$ on the left side and move all terms to the right side.
$$7x+21-A=11x-12$$
$$7x-7x+21-A=11x-7x-12$$
$$21-A=4x-12$$
$$21-21-A=4x-12-21$$
$$-A=4x-33$$

Divide each side by -1.
$$\frac{-A}{-1}=\frac{4x}{-1}-\frac{33}{-1}$$
$$A=-4x+33$$

$$\boxed{}=-4x+33$$

08

(1) $\quad A-3(6x-5)=-4x+1$
$$A-18x+15=-4x+1$$
$$A-18x+18x+15=-4x+18x+1$$

$$A+15=14x+1$$
$$A+15-15=14x+1-15$$
$$A=14x-14$$

$$A=14x-14$$

(2) $A+3(6x-5)=(14x-14)+3(6x-5)$
$$=14x-14+18x-15$$
$$=32x-29$$

The correct expression is $32x-29$.

3. Solving Linear Equations, Part 2

Check Point 1

① $\dfrac{x}{8}+\dfrac{1}{2}=\dfrac{3}{8}x-1$

The LCM of 2 and 8 is 8. So, multiply each side by 8.
$$\left(\dfrac{x}{8}+\dfrac{1}{2}\right)\cdot 8=\left(\dfrac{3}{8}x-1\right)\cdot 8$$
$$x+4=3x-8$$
$$-2x+4=-8$$
$$-2x=-12$$
$$x=6$$

$$x=6$$

② $\dfrac{3x-4}{3}+\dfrac{x}{2}=\dfrac{x+2}{2}-\dfrac{1}{3}$

The LCM of 2 and 3 is 6. So, multiply each side by 6.
$$\left(\dfrac{3x-4}{3}+\dfrac{x}{2}\right)\cdot 6=\left(\dfrac{x+2}{2}-\dfrac{1}{3}\right)\cdot 6$$
$$2(3x-4)+3x=3(x+2)-2$$
$$6x-8+3x=3x+6-2$$
$$9x-8=3x+4$$
$$6x-8=4$$
$$6x=12$$
$$x=2$$

$$x=2$$

③ $0.2(2x-7)=0.2-0.4x$

Multiply each side by 10.
$$(0.2(2x-7))\cdot 10=(0.2-0.4x)\cdot 10$$
$$2(2x-7)=2-4x$$
$$4x-14=2-4x$$
$$8x-14=2$$
$$8x=16$$
$$x=2$$

$$x=2$$

④ $0.4(3-x)+0.5x=0.9x-2$

Multiply each side by 10.
$$(0.4(3-x)+0.5x)\cdot 10=(0.9x-2)\cdot 10$$
$$4(3-x)+5x=9x-20$$
$$12-4x+5x=9x-20$$

$$12+x=9x-20$$
$$12-8x=-20$$
$$-8x=-32$$
$$x=4$$

$x=4$

Check Point 2

① $3-\dfrac{5-3x}{4}=\dfrac{7}{8}+\dfrac{3}{4}x$

The LCM of 4, and 8 is 8. So, multiply each side by 8.

$$\left(3-\dfrac{5-3x}{4}\right)\cdot 8=\left(\dfrac{7}{8}+\dfrac{3}{4}x\right)\cdot 8$$
$$24-2(5-3x)=7+6x$$
$$24-10+6x=7+6x$$
$$14+6x=7+6x$$
$$6x-6x=7-14$$
$$(6-6)x=-7$$
$$0\cdot x=-7$$

There is no solution

② $1.8(x-1)+0.5=3.6\left(1+\dfrac{x}{2}\right)-4.9$

Multiply each side by 10.

$$(1.8(x-1)+0.5)\cdot 10=\left(3.6\left(1+\dfrac{x}{2}\right)-4.9\right)\cdot 10$$
$$18(x-1)+5=36\left(1+\dfrac{x}{2}\right)-49$$
$$18x-18+5=36+18x-49$$
$$18x-13=18x-13$$
$$18x-18x=-13+13$$
$$(18-18)x=0$$
$$0\cdot x=0$$

There are infinitely many solutions

Review Exercise

01

(1) $\dfrac{2x-1}{3}-2=\dfrac{x}{3}+6$

Multiply each side by 3.

$$\left(\dfrac{2x-1}{3}-2\right)\cdot 3=\left(\dfrac{x}{3}+6\right)\cdot 3$$
$$2x-1-6=x+18$$
$$2x-7=x+18$$
$$x-7=18$$
$$x=25$$

$x=25$

(2) $\dfrac{3x+1}{2}+\dfrac{2x-1}{3}=3x-4$

The LCM of 2 and 3 is 6. So, multiply each side by 6.

$$\left(\dfrac{3x+1}{2}+\dfrac{2x-1}{3}\right)\cdot 6=(3x-4)\cdot 6$$
$$3(3x+1)+2(2x-1)=18x-24$$
$$9x+3+4x-2=18x-24$$
$$13x+1=18x-24$$
$$-5x+1=-24$$
$$-5x=-25$$
$$x=5$$

$x=5$

02

(1) $1.6x+0.5=0.8x-2.7$

Multiply each side by 10.

$$(1.6x+0.5)\cdot 10=(0.8x-2.7)\cdot 10$$
$$16x+5=8x-27$$
$$8x+5=-27$$
$$8x=-32$$
$$x=-4$$

$x=-4$

(2) $0.25x-0.2=2(0.45-0.05x)+1$

Multiply each side by 100.

$$(0.25x-0.2)\cdot 100=(2(0.45-0.05x)+1)\cdot 100$$
$$25x-20=200(0.45-0.05x)+100$$
$$25x-20=90-10x+100$$
$$25x-20=-10x+190$$
$$35x-20=190$$
$$35x=210$$
$$x=6$$

$x=6$

Solutions Manual

03

$$\frac{x+a}{2}=\frac{3a-x}{4}$$

Substitute 2 for x and solve for a.

$$\frac{2+a}{2}=\frac{3a-2}{4}$$

The LCM of 2 and 4 is 4. So, multiply each side by 4.

$$\left(\frac{2+a}{2}\right)\cdot 4=\left(\frac{3a-2}{4}\right)\cdot 4$$
$$2(2+a)=3a-2$$
$$4+2a=3a-2$$
$$4-a=-2$$
$$-a=-6$$
$$a=6$$

$$a=6$$

04

(A) $0.4x-0.9=0.2x+0.9$

Multiply each side by 10.
$$(0.4x-0.9)\cdot 10=(0.2x+0.9)\cdot 10$$
$$4x-9=2x+9$$
$$2x-9=9$$
$$2x=18,\ x=9$$

(B) $\frac{6x+4}{5}=x+0.2$

Multiply each side by 10.
$$\left(\frac{6x+4}{5}\right)\cdot 10=(x+0.2)\cdot 10$$
$$2(6x+4)=10x+2$$
$$12x+8=10x+2$$
$$2x+8=2$$
$$2x=-6,\ x=-3$$

(C) $\frac{1}{2}(4x+8)=-2(3-x)$
$$2x+4=-6+2x$$
$$2x-2x=-6-4$$
$$(2-2)x=-10$$
$$0\cdot x=-10$$

The equation has no solution.

(D) $2(x+1)-\frac{5}{4}x=\frac{3x+8}{4}$

Multiply each side by 4.
$$\left(2(x+1)-\frac{5}{4}x\right)\cdot 4=\left(\frac{3x+8}{4}\right)\cdot 4$$
$$8(x+1)-5x=3x+8$$
$$8x+8-5x=3x+8$$
$$3x+8=3x+8$$
$$3x-3x=8-8$$
$$(3-3)x=0$$
$$0\cdot x=0$$

The equation has infinitely many solutions.

The answer is (D)

05

$$\frac{ax+5}{2}-\frac{2}{3}=\frac{5}{6}x-\frac{1}{3}b$$

The LCM of 2, 3, and 6 is 6. So, multiply each side by 6.

$$\left(\frac{ax+5}{2}-\frac{2}{3}\right)\cdot 6=\left(\frac{5}{6}x-\frac{1}{3}b\right)\cdot 6$$
$$3(ax+5)-4=5x-2b$$
$$3ax+15-4=5x-2b$$
$$3ax+11=5x-2b$$
$$3ax-5x=-2b-11$$
$$(3a-5)x=-2b-11$$

If the equation is true for all x, then it has infinitely many solutions. Therefore, we must have

$3a-5=0$ and $-2b-11=0$
$3a=5$ $\qquad\qquad -2b=11$
$a=\frac{5}{3}$ $\qquad\qquad b=-\frac{11}{2}$

$$a=\frac{5}{3},\ b=-\frac{11}{2}$$

06

$$2(x-2)=3bx-7$$
$$2x-4=3bx-7$$
$$2x-3bx=-7+4$$
$$(2-3b)x=-3$$

For the equation to have no solution, $2-3b$ must be equal to 0.

$$2-3b=0$$

$-3b=-2,\ b=\dfrac{2}{3}$

$b=\dfrac{2}{3}$

07

$$\dfrac{3x+4}{5}=\dfrac{ax}{2}-2b$$

The LCM of 5 and 2 is 10. So, multiply each side by 10.

$$\left(\dfrac{3x+4}{5}\right)\cdot 10=\left(\dfrac{ax}{2}-2b\right)\cdot 10$$
$$2(3x+4)=5ax-20b$$
$$6x+8=5ax-20b$$
$$6x-5ax=-20b-8$$
$$(6-5a)x=-20b-8$$

For the equation to have infinitely many solutions, $6-5a$ and $-20b-8$ must be equal to 0 respectively.

$6-5a=0$ $-20b-8=0$
$-5a=-6$ and $-20b=8$
$a=\dfrac{6}{5}$ $b=\dfrac{8}{-20}=-\dfrac{2}{5}$

$a=\dfrac{6}{5},\ b=-\dfrac{2}{5}$

08

$$\dfrac{2x-1}{3}-0.9=x-\dfrac{x+2}{4}$$

First, converting 0.9 to a fraction, $0.9=\dfrac{9}{10}$.

Then we have $\dfrac{2x-1}{3}-\dfrac{9}{10}=x-\dfrac{x+2}{4}$

The LCM of 3, 10, and 4 is 60. So, multiply each side by 60.

$$\left(\dfrac{2x-1}{3}-\dfrac{9}{10}\right)\cdot 60=\left(x-\dfrac{x+2}{4}\right)\cdot 60$$
$$20(2x-1)-54=60x-15(x+2)$$
$$40x-20-54=60x-15x-30$$
$$40x-74=45x-30$$
$$-5x-74=-30$$
$$-5x=44,\ x=-\dfrac{44}{5}$$

$x=-\dfrac{44}{5}$

4. Application of Linear Equations

Check Point 1

Let x be the first number. Then, the second number is $21-x$.

$$4x=2(21-x)+6$$
$$4x=42-2x+6$$
$$4x=48-2x$$
$$6x=48,\ x=8$$

Therefore, two numbers are 8 and $21-x=21-8=13$.

8 and 13

Check Point 2

Let x be the least integer. Then, three consecutive integers are x, $x+1$, and $x+2$.

$$x+(x+1)+(x+2)=2x+17$$
$$x+x+1+x+2=2x+17$$
$$3x+3=2x+17$$
$$x+3=17,\ x=14$$

Therefore, the least integer is 14.

14

Check Point 3

Assume that John's father is twice as old as John in x years. After x years later, John is $14+x$ years old and his father is $38+x$ years old.

$$38+x=2(14+x)$$
$$38+x=28+2x$$
$$38-x=28$$
$$-x=-10,\ x=10$$

Therefore, John's father is twice as old as John in 10 years.

10 years

Solutions Manual

Check Point 4

Let x be the number of quarters. Then, the number of nickels is $2x$ and the number of dimes is $x-1$. Since the total value of the coins is $2.15 (215 cents), we have
$$5(2x)+10(x-1)+25x=215$$
$$10x+10x-10+25x=215$$
$$45x-10=215$$
$$45x=225, \ x=5$$
Therefore, there are 5 quarters, $2x=2(5)=10$ nickels, and $x-1=5-1=4$ dimes.

4 dimes, 10 nickels, and 5 quarters

Check Point 5

Let A and B be two cars, and x be the time each car traveled. Then, the distance car A traveled is and the distance car B traveled is, as shown in the figure below.

$$64x+72x=340$$
$$136x=340$$
$$x=\frac{340}{136}=\frac{5}{2} \text{ or } x=2.5$$
Therefore, it takes 2.5 hour(2 hours and 30 minutes) for the two cars to meet.

2.5 hours (2 hours and 30 minutes)

Check Point 6

Let x be the amount a 18% acid-solution.

	18% acid	12% acid	15% acid
Solution	x	8	$x+8$
Acid	$0.18x$	$0.12(8)$	$0.15(x+8)$

$$0.18x+0.12(8)=0.15(x+8)$$
$$(0.18x+0.12(8)) \cdot 100=(0.15(x+8)) \cdot 100$$
$$18x+12(8)=15(x+8)$$
$$18x+96=15x+120$$
$$3x+96=120$$
$$3x=24, \ x=8$$

8 liters of a 18% acid-solution.

Check Point 7

Let x be the number of degrees in second angle. Then, the number of degree in first and third angle is $3x$ and $2x-12$. Since the sum of three angles of a triangle equals 180°, we have
$$3x+x+(2x-12)=180$$
$$3x+x+2x-12=180$$
$$6x-12=180$$
$$6x=192, \ x=32$$
Therefore, the second angle is 32°, the first angle is $3x=3(32)=96°$, and the third angle is $2x-12=2(32)-12=52°$.

The three angles are 96°, 32°, and 52°

Check Point 8

Let x be the amount in dollars invested at Bank Y. Then the amount in dollars invested at Bank X is $x+500$.

	Bank X	Bank Y
The amount invested	$x+500$	x
The interest earned	$0.05(x+500)$	$0.04x$

$$0.05(x+500)+0.04x=133$$
$$(0.05(x+500)+0.04x) \cdot 100=133 \cdot 100$$
$$5(x+500)+4x=13300$$
$$5x+2500+4x=13300$$
$$9x=10800, \ x=1200$$

Therefore, a man invested $1200 in Bank Y and $x+500=1200+500=\$1700$ in Bank X.

$1,700 in Bank X and $1,200 in Bank Y

Review Exercise

01

Let x be the larger number. Then, the smaller number is $x-13$.
$$2x=5(x-13)-1$$
$$2x=5x-65-1$$
$$2x=5x-66$$
$$-3x=-66, \ x=22$$
Therefore, two numbers are 22 and $x-13=22-13=9$.

22 and 9

02

Let x be the smaller integer. Then, the two consecutive even integers are x and $x+2$.
$$\frac{1}{2}(x+2)=x-7$$
$$\frac{x}{2}+1=x-7$$
$$-\frac{x}{2}+1=-7$$
$$-\frac{x}{2}=-8, \ x=16$$
Therefore, the two consecutive integers are $x=16$ and $x+2=16+2=18$.

16 and 18

03

Let Nick be x years old and Ken be $2x$ years old. Five years ago, Nick was $x-5$ years old and Ken was $2x-5$ years old.
$$(x-5)+(2x-5)=26$$
$$x-5+2x-5=26$$
$$3x-10=26$$
$$3x=36, \ x=12$$
Therefore, Nick is $x=12$ years old and Ken is $2x=2(12)=24$ years old.

Nick is 12 years old and Ken is 24 years old.

04

Let Steven be x years old now. Then, Emily is $x+28$ years old now. After 15 years, Steven is $x+15$ years old and Emily is $x+28+15=x+43$ years old. Since Emily is twice as old as Steven 15 years later, we have
$$x+43=2(x+15)$$
$$x+43=2x+30$$
$$-x+43=30$$
$$-x=-13, \ x=13$$
Therefore, Steven is 13 years old now.

13 years old

05

Let x be the number of nickels. Then, the number of dimes is $4x$ and the number of quarters is $4x+1$. Since the total value of the coins is $6.09 (609 cents), we have
$$1(4)+5(x)+10(4x)+25(4x+1)=609$$
$$4+5x+40x+100x+25=609$$
$$145x+29=609$$
$$145x=580$$
$$x=4$$
There are 4 nickels, $4x=4(4)=16$ dimes, and $4x+1=4(4)+1=17$ quarters.

4 nickels, 16 dimes, and 17 quarters

06

Let x be the rate Linda has been driving for the last two hours. Then, the distance she traveled for the first 3 hours is $55 \times 3 = 165$ miles and the distance traveled for the next 2 hours is $x \times 2 = 2x$, as shown in the figure below.

Solutions Manual

$165 + 2x = 275$
$2x = 110, \ x = 55$

Therefore, she drove at a rate of 55 miles per hour.

55 miles per hour

07

Let x be the speed of the bus on the right. Then, the speed of the bus on the left is $2x$. After 3 hours, the bus on the right traveled $x \times 3 = 3x$ miles and the bus on the left traveled $2x \times 3 = 6x$ miles, as shown in the figure below.

$6x = 96 + 3x$
$3x = 96, \ x = 32$

Therefore, the bus on the right is moving at 32 miles per hour and the bus on the left is moving at $2x = 2(32) = 64$ miles per hour.

32 miles per hour and 64 miles per hour

08

First, 1 hour 20 minutes is $1 + \frac{20}{60} = 1 + \frac{1}{3} = \frac{4}{3}$ hours. Let x be the hours Ben walks to work. Then, Ben jogs for $\frac{4}{3} - x$ hours. The distance Ben traveled by walking and jogging is $3x$ and $5\left(\frac{4}{3} - x\right)$, respectively, as shown in the figure below.

$3x + 5\left(\frac{4}{3} - x\right) = 5$
$3x + \frac{20}{3} - 5x = 5$
$-2x + \frac{20}{3} = 5$

$\left(-2x + \frac{20}{3}\right) \cdot 3 = 5 \cdot 3$
$-6x + 20 = 15$
$-6x = -5, \ x = \frac{5}{6}$

Since Ben walked for $x = \frac{5}{6}$ hours, he walked $3 \times \frac{5}{6} = \frac{5}{2}$ miles.

$\frac{5}{2}$ **miles**

09

Let x be the number of students in the laboratory. Since the teacher gave 4 balloons to each of his x students and 1 balloon left, he had a total of $4x + 1$ balloons, which is equal to 65.

$4x + 1 = 65$
$4x = 64, \ x = 16$

Therefore, there are 16 students at the laboratory.

16 students

10

Let x be the amount of water in liters.

	water	25% acid	15% acid
Solution	x	12	$x + 12$
Acid	0	$0.25(12)$	$0.15(x+12)$

$0 + 0.25(12) = 0.15(x + 12)$
$3 = 0.15(x + 12)$
$3 \cdot 100 = (0.15(x + 12)) \cdot 100$
$300 = 15(x + 12)$
$300 = 15x + 180$
$120 = 15x, \ x = 8$

8 liters of water.

11

Let x be the width of the field. Then the length of the field is $3x + 14$. Since the total perimeter of the field 74 feet, we have

$2x + (3x + 14) = 74$

$2x+3x+14=74$
$5x+14=74$
$5x=60, \ x=12$

Therefore, the width is 12 feet and the length is $3x+14=3(12)+14=50$ feet.

> The width is 12 feet and the length is 50 feet.

12

Let x be the amount Samuel invested in stocks. Then, he invested $\$(10,000-x)$ in bonds.

	Stocks	Bonds
The amount invested	x	$10000-x$
The interest earned	$0.05x$	$0.07(10000-x)$

Since he earned \$196 more on bonds than on stocks, we have
$0.07(10000-x)=0.05x+196$
$700-0.07x=0.05x+196$
$700-0.12x=196$
$-0.12x=-504, \ x=4200$

Therefore, he invested \$4200 in stocks and $10000-x=10000-4200=\$5800$ in bonds.

> \$4,200 in stocks and \$5,800 in bonds

13

Let x be the number of adults. Then, $(160-x)$ is the number of students. Since the total revenue was \$4,000, we have
$27x+19(160-x)=4000$
$27x+3040-19x=4000$
$8x+3040=4000$
$8x=960, \ x=120$

Therefore, the number of adult tickets is 120 and the number student tickets is $160-x=160-120=40$.

> 120 adult tickets and 40 students tickets

Chapter 1 Test Level 1

01

$\frac{2}{15}\left(10x-\frac{5}{4}\right)=\frac{4}{3}x-\frac{1}{6}$

(A) $-\frac{2}{15}\left(-10x+\frac{5}{4}\right)=\frac{4}{3}x-\frac{1}{6}$

(B) $\left(10x-\frac{5}{4}\right)\div\frac{15}{2}=\left(10x-\frac{5}{4}\right)\times\frac{2}{15}$
$=\frac{4}{3}x-\frac{1}{6}$

(C) $\left(-\frac{5}{2}x+5\right)\div\left(-\frac{15}{8}\right)$
$=\left(-\frac{5}{2}x+5\right)\times\left(-\frac{8}{15}\right)=\frac{4}{3}x-\frac{8}{3}$

(D) $\frac{2}{3}\left(2x-\frac{1}{4}\right)=\frac{4}{3}x-\frac{1}{6}$

(E) $\left(-\frac{5}{4}x+\frac{5}{32}\right)\div\left(-\frac{15}{16}\right)$
$=\left(-5x+\frac{5}{32}\right)\times\left(-\frac{16}{15}\right)=\frac{4}{3}x-\frac{1}{6}$

> The answer is (C)

02

$-3(2x+1)+(12x-9)\div 3$
$=-3(2x+1)+(12x-9)\times\frac{1}{3}$
$=-6x-3+4x-3$
$=-2x-6$
$\Rightarrow a=-2, \ b=-6$

Therefore, $ab=(-2)(-6)=12$.

> $ab=12$

03

$\frac{1}{4}(ax-8)-\frac{1}{3}(9x+2b)+5$
$=\frac{a}{4}x-2-3x-\frac{2b}{3}+5$
$=\frac{a}{4}x-3x-\frac{2b}{3}+3$
$=\left(\frac{a}{4}-3\right)x-\frac{2b}{3}+3$

Solutions Manual

$$\frac{a}{4}-3=6 \qquad -\frac{2b}{3}+3=4$$
$$\frac{a}{4}=9 \quad \text{and} \quad -\frac{2b}{3}=1$$
$$a=36 \qquad b=-\frac{3}{2}$$

Therefore, $a \div b = 36 \div \left(-\frac{3}{2}\right) = 36 \times \left(-\frac{2}{3}\right) = -24$.

$$a \div b = -24$$

04

$$\frac{3x-4}{6}+\frac{5x-1}{2} = \frac{3x-4}{6}+\frac{5x-1}{2} \cdot \frac{3}{3}$$
$$= \frac{3x-4+3(5x-1)}{6}$$
$$= \frac{3x-4+15x-3}{6}$$
$$= \frac{18x-7}{6}$$
$$\Rightarrow a=18,\ b=-7,\ c=6$$

Therefore, $a+b+c = 18+(-7)+6 = 17$.

$$a+b+c = 17$$

05

$$4\left(A+\frac{5}{2}\right)-3(B-2)$$
$$=4\left(x-\frac{1}{2}+\frac{5}{2}\right)-3(2x+3-2)$$
$$=4(x+2)-3(2x+1)$$
$$=4x+8-6x-3$$
$$=-2x+5$$

$$4\left(A+\frac{5}{2}\right)-3(B-2) = -2x+5$$

06

$$5x+3 = 12x-3(2x-2)$$
$$5x+3 = 12x-6x+6$$
$$5x+3 = 6x+6$$
$$-x=3,\ x=-3 \Rightarrow a=-3$$

$$\left(\frac{x-2}{3}\right)\cdot 6 = \left(\frac{3x-1}{2}-6\right)\cdot 6$$
$$2(x-2) = 3(3x-1)-36$$
$$2x-4 = 9x-3-36$$
$$2x-4 = 9x-39$$

$$-7x = -35,\ x=5 \Rightarrow b=5$$

Therefore, $ab = (-3)(5) = -15$.

$$ab = -15$$

07

$$0.6x-0.08 = 0.2+0.1(2x-4)$$
$$(0.6x-0.08)\cdot 100 = (0.2+0.1(2x-4))\cdot 100$$
$$60x-8 = 20+10(2x-4)$$
$$60x-8 = 20+20x-40$$
$$60x-8 = 20x-20$$
$$40x = -12,\ x = \frac{-12}{40} = -\frac{3}{10}$$
$$x = -\frac{3}{10}$$

08

First, find the solution of the equation
$$\frac{3-(x-6)}{2} = -2(3x-4)+13.$$
$$\left(\frac{3-(x-6)}{2}\right)\cdot 2 = (-2(3x-4)+13)\cdot 2$$
$$3-(x-6) = -4(3x-4)+26$$
$$3-x+6 = -12x+16+26$$
$$-x+9 = -12x+42$$
$$11x = 33,\ x=3$$

$x=3$ is also the solution to the equation $0.4(2x-3k)-1=0.5(-x+4)$. So, substitute 3 for x in this equation.

$$0.4(2(3)-3k)-1 = 0.5(-(3)+4)$$
$$0.4(6-3k)-1 = 0.5$$
$$(0.4(6-3k)-1)\cdot 10 = (0.5)\cdot 10$$
$$4(6-3k)-10 = 5$$
$$24-12k-10 = 5$$
$$14-12k = 5$$
$$-12k = -9,\ k = \frac{-9}{-12} = \frac{3}{4}$$
$$k = \frac{3}{4}$$

09

If the equation is true for all x, then it

has infinitely many solutions.
$$6(3x-2a)+4=-2(bx+5)-8x$$
$$18x-12a+4=-2bx-10-8x$$
$$26x+2bx=-14+12a$$
$$(26+2b)x=-14+12a$$

For the equation to have infinitely many solutions, $26+2b$ and $-14+12a$ must be equal to 0.

$$26+2b=0 \qquad -14+12a=0$$
$$2b=-26 \quad \text{and} \quad 12a=14$$
$$b=-13 \qquad a=\frac{14}{12}=\frac{7}{6}$$

Therefore, $6a-b=6\left(\frac{7}{6}\right)-(-13)=7+13=20$.
$$6a-b=20$$

10

$$\left(4-\frac{1}{6}(4x+5)\right)\cdot 6=(2kx+6)\cdot 6$$
$$24-(4x+5)=12kx+36$$
$$24-4x-5=12kx+36$$
$$-4x+19=12kx+36$$
$$-4x-12kx=17$$
$$(-4-12k)x=17$$

For the equation to have no solution, $-4-12k$ must be equal to 0.
$$-4-12k=0$$
$$-12k=4,\ k=\frac{4}{-12}=-\frac{1}{3}$$
$$k=-\frac{1}{3}$$

11

$$\frac{6x-3m}{2}=4(1+x)-x$$
$$\frac{6x-3m}{2}=4+3x$$
$$\left(\frac{6x-3m}{2}\right)\cdot 2=(4+3x)\cdot 2$$
$$6x-3m=8+6x$$
$$6x-6x=8+3m$$
$$(6-6)x=8+3m$$
$$0\cdot x=8+3m$$

For the equation to have infinitely many solutions, $8+3m$ must be equal to 0.
$$8+3m=0$$
$$3m=-8,\ m=-\frac{8}{3}$$
$$m=-\frac{8}{3}$$

12

Suppose that Chris is twice as old as Helen after x years. Then Chris is $36+x$ years old and Helen is $6+x$ in x years. Now, we have the following equation:
$$36+x=2(6+x)$$
$$36+x=12+2x$$
$$-x=-24,\ x=24$$

Chris is twice as old as Helen after 24 years.

13

Let x be the amount of a 45% saline solution. Then, $20-x$ is the amount of a 20% saline solution.

	45% solution	20% solution	30% solution
	x	$20-x$	20
Salt	$0.45x$	$0.2(20-x)$	$0.3(20)$

$$0.45x+0.2(20-x)=0.3(20)$$
$$0.45x+0.2(20-x)=6$$
$$(0.45x+0.2(20-x))\cdot 100=6\cdot 100$$
$$45x+20(20-x)=600$$
$$45x+400-20x=600$$
$$25x=200,\ x=8$$

8 liters of 45% saline solution and 12 liters of 20% saline solution.

14

Let x be the length of one side of the larger square. Then, $x-3$ is the length of one side of the smaller square. Since the sum of the perimeters of the two squares

is 68 centimeters, we have
$$4(x)+4(x-3)=68$$
$$4x+4x-12=68$$
$$8x-12=68$$
$$8x=80, \ x=10$$

Therefore, the length of one side of the larger square is 10 centimeters.

10 centimeters

Chapter 1 Test Level 2

01

First, write the equation and solve for x.
$$24-3x=2(10)-8$$
$$24-3x=12$$
$$-3x=-12, \ x=4$$

Therefore, $5x=5(4)=20$

$5x=20$

02

$$\frac{2x+3}{6}+\frac{x-2}{8}-\frac{3x-1}{12}=\frac{ax+b}{c}$$

The LCM of 6, 8, and 12 is 24.

$$\frac{2x+3}{6}\cdot\frac{4}{4}+\frac{x-2}{8}\cdot\frac{3}{3}-\frac{3x-1}{12}\cdot\frac{2}{2}$$

$$=\frac{4(2x+3)+3(x-2)-2(3x-1)}{24}$$

$$=\frac{8x+12+3x-6-6x+2}{24}$$

$$=\frac{5x+8}{24}$$

$\Rightarrow a=5, \ b=8, \ c=24$

Therefore, $a+b+c=5+8+24=37$.

$a+b+c=37$

03

$$\tfrac{1}{2}(A+4B)-2(B+C)=\tfrac{1}{2}A+2B-2B-2C$$

$$=\tfrac{1}{2}A-2C$$

$$=\tfrac{1}{2}(3x-1)-2(-2y+2)$$

$$=\tfrac{3}{2}x-\tfrac{1}{2}+4y-4$$

$$=\tfrac{3}{2}x+4y-\tfrac{9}{2}$$

$$\tfrac{1}{2}(A+4B)-2(B+C)=\tfrac{3}{2}x+4y-\tfrac{9}{2}$$

04

$$\frac{3(x-3)+1}{4}=\frac{2(5x+4)}{3}-4x+1$$

The LCM of 4 and 3 is 12. So, multiply each side by 12.

$$\left(\frac{3(x-3)+1}{4}\right)\cdot 12=\left(\frac{2(5x+4)}{3}-4x+1\right)\cdot 12$$

$$9(x-3)+3=8(5x+4)-48x+12$$
$$9x-27+3=40x+32-48x+12$$
$$9x-24=-8x+44$$
$$17x=68,\ x=4 \Rightarrow k=4$$

Substitute 4 for k in the equation $0.4(3k-5)+0.5x=\frac{x+6}{4}$.

$$0.4(3(4)-5)+0.5x=\frac{x+6}{4}$$
$$\frac{4}{10}(7)+\frac{5}{10}x=\frac{x+6}{4}$$
$$\frac{14}{5}+\frac{1}{2}x=\frac{x+6}{4}$$

Since the LCM of 5, 2, and 4 is 20, multiply each side by 20.

$$\left(\frac{14}{5}+\frac{1}{2}x\right)\cdot 20=\left(\frac{x+6}{4}\right)\cdot 20$$
$$56+10x=5(x+6)$$
$$56+10x=5x+30$$
$$5x=-26,\ x=-\frac{26}{5}$$

$$x=-\frac{26}{5}$$

05

$$1.4-(1-x)=\frac{4}{3}(x-3)$$
$$\frac{14}{10}-(1-x)=\frac{4}{3}(x-3)$$

The LCM of 10 and 3 is 30. So, multiply each side by 30.

$$\left(\frac{14}{10}-(1-x)\right)\cdot 30=\left(\frac{4}{3}(x-3)\right)\cdot 30$$
$$42-30(1-x)=40(x-3)$$
$$42-30+30x=40x-120$$
$$12+30x=40x-120$$
$$-10x=-132,\ x=\frac{-132}{-10}=\frac{66}{5}$$

$$x=\frac{66}{5}$$

06

(1)
$$A+\frac{1}{2}(-4x+5)=\frac{3}{2}x-4$$
$$\left(A+\frac{1}{2}(-4x+5)\right)\cdot 2=\left(\frac{3}{2}x-4\right)\cdot 2$$
$$2A-4x+5=3x-8$$
$$2A=7x-13$$
$$A=\frac{7x-13}{2}$$

$$A=\frac{7x-13}{2}$$

(2) $A-\frac{1}{2}(-4x+5)=\frac{7x-13}{2}-\frac{1}{2}(-4x+5)$

$$=\frac{7x-13}{2}+\frac{4x-5}{2}$$
$$=\frac{7x-13+4x-5}{2}$$
$$=\frac{11x-18}{2}$$

$$\frac{11x-18}{2}$$

07

Since $x=5$ is the solution to both equations, substitute 5 for x in each equation.

$$4(5)-2a=-(3(5)+1)+2$$
$$20-2a=-16+2$$
$$20-2a=-14$$
$$-2a=-34,\ a=17$$

$$\frac{1}{3}(b(5)+6)+1=\frac{5-3(5)}{6}$$
$$\frac{5}{3}b+2+1=\frac{(-10)}{6}$$
$$\frac{5}{3}b+3=-\frac{5}{3}$$

Solutions Manual

$$\frac{5}{3}b = -\frac{14}{3}, \ b = -\frac{14}{5}$$

$$a = 17, \ b = -\frac{14}{5}$$

08

$$0.4(-2x-5a) = \frac{bx+3}{6} - \frac{1}{5}$$

$$\frac{4}{10}(-2x-5a) = \frac{bx+3}{6} - \frac{1}{5}$$

$$\frac{2}{5}(-2x-5a) = \frac{bx+3}{6} - \frac{1}{5}$$

The LCM of 5 and 6 is 30. So, multiply each side by 30.

$$\left(\frac{2}{5}(-2x-5a)\right) \cdot 30 = \left(\frac{bx+3}{6} - \frac{1}{5}\right) \cdot 30$$

$$12(-2x-5a) = 5(bx+3) - 6$$

$$-24x - 60a = 5bx + 15 - 6$$

$$-24x - 60a = 5bx + 9$$

$$-24x - 5bx = 60a + 9$$

$$(-24 - 5b)x = 60a + 9$$

For the equation to have infinitely many solutions, $-24-5b$ and $60a+9$ must be equal to 0.

$-24 - 5b = 0$ and $60a + 9 = 0$
$-5b = 24$ $\quad\quad\quad\quad$ $60a = -9$
$b = -\frac{24}{5}$ $\quad\quad\quad\quad$ $a = -\frac{9}{60} = -\frac{3}{20}$

$$a = -\frac{3}{20}, \ b = -\frac{24}{5}$$

09

Let $\boxed{} = A$. Then we have

$$\frac{3x-4}{2} - \frac{A}{3} = \frac{4x+1}{6}.$$

The LCM of 2, 3, and 6 is 6. So, multiply each side by 6.

$$\left(\frac{3x-4}{2} - \frac{A}{3}\right) \cdot 6 = \left(\frac{4x+1}{6}\right) \cdot 6$$

$$3(3x-4) - 2A = 4x + 1$$

$$9x - 12 - 2A = 4x + 1$$

$$-2A = -5x + 13$$

$$A = \frac{-5x+13}{-2} = \frac{5x-13}{2}$$

$$\boxed{} = \frac{5x-13}{2}$$

10

Let x be the largest even integer. Then three consecutive even inters are $x-4$, $x-2$, and x. Since the sum of these consecutive even integers is 144, we have

$$(x-4) + (x-2) + x = 144$$

$$3x - 6 = 144$$

$$3x = 150, \ x = 50$$

The largest even integer is 50.

11

Let x be the distance he traveled to the airport. The fare for x miles at the rate of $1.2 per mile is $1.2x$. There is a basic fare of $6 and Stephen also gave the driver a $10 tip. Therefore, the total amount paid is $1.2x + 6 + 10$. Since the total fare was $70, we have the following equation:

$$1.2x + 6 + 10 = 70$$

$$(1.2x + 16) \cdot 10 = (70) \cdot 10$$

$$12x + 160 = 700$$

$$12x = 540, \ x = 45$$

The distance he traveled to the airport is 45 miles.

12

Let x be the number of male students last year in K high school. Then, the number of female students was $700-x$.

	Male students	Female students
Last year	x	$700-x$
This year	$1.15x$	$0.95(700-x)$

Since the total number of students this year has increased by 41 compared to last year, we have

$$1.15x+0.95(700-x)=700+41$$
$$1.15x+0.95(700-x)=741$$
$$(1.15x+0.95(700-x))\cdot 100=(741)\cdot 100$$
$$115x+95(700-x)=74100$$
$$115x+66500-95x=74100$$
$$20x+66500=74100$$
$$20x=7600,\ x=380$$

Therefore, the number of male students last year in K high school is 380.

380 male students

Solutions Manual

Chapter 2: Graphing Lines

1. Introduction to Graphing Linear Equations

Check Point 1

① $4x - 3y = -12$

The x-intercept: let $y = 0$.
$4x - 3(0) = -12$
$4x = -12$, $x = -3$

The y-intercept: let $x = 0$.
$4(0) - 3y = -12$
$-3y = -12$, $y = 4$

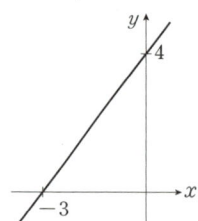

② $2x - \dfrac{y}{4} = 6$

The x-intercept: let $y = 0$.
$2x - \dfrac{(0)}{4} = 6$
$2x = 6$, $x = 3$

The y-intercept: let $x = 0$.
$2(0) - \dfrac{y}{4} = 6$
$-\dfrac{y}{4} = 6$, $y = -24$

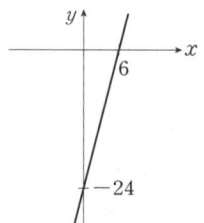

Check Point 2

① $(3, 5)$ and $(0, -1)$

Let $(x_1, y_1) = (3, 5)$ and $(x_2, y_2) = (0, -1)$.

The slope $m = \dfrac{y_2 - y_1}{x_2 - x_1} = \dfrac{-1 - 5}{0 - 3} = 2$.

The slope of the line is 2

② $(-2, 5)$ and $(3, -4)$

Let $(x_1, y_1) = (-2, 5)$ and $(x_2, y_2) = (3, -4)$.

The slope $m = \dfrac{y_2 - y_1}{x_2 - x_1} = \dfrac{-4 - 5}{3 - (-2)} = \dfrac{-9}{5}$.

The slope of the line is $-\dfrac{9}{5}$

Check Point 3

① $x = -4$

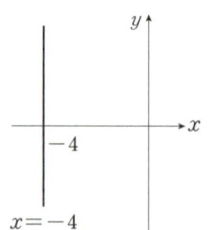

$x = -4$
The slope of the line is undefined

② $y = 2$

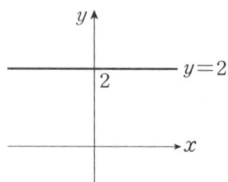

The slope of the line is 0

22 Solutions Manual

Review Exercise

01

To find out if a point (x, y) is on the graph of a line, we substitute in the values and see if we get a true statement.

(A) $4(-2)-5(-1)=-8+5=-3$
$(-2, -1)$ is on the line.
(B) $4(-1)-5(-2)=-4+10=6\neq -3$
$(-1, -2)$ is not on the line.
(C) $4(2)-5(1)=8-5=3\neq -3$
$(2, 1)$ is not on the line.
(D) $4(1)-5(2)=4-10=-6\neq -3$
$(1, 2)$ is not on the line.
(E) $4(2)-5(-1)=8+5=13\neq -3$
$(2, -1)$ is not on the line.

The answer is (A)

02

(1) The x-intercept: let $y=0$.
$6x-4(0)=12$
$6x=12, \ x=2$
The y-intercept: let $x=0$.
$6(0)-4y=12$
$-4y=12, \ y=-3$

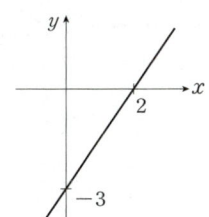

(2) The x-intercept: let $y=0$.
$2x+3(0)=-9$
$2x=-9, \ x=-\dfrac{9}{2}$
The y-intercept: let $x=0$.
$2(0)+3y=-9$
$3y=-9, \ y=-3$

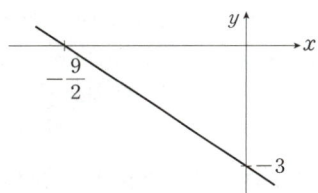

03

(1) $(0, -2)$ and $(4, 6)$
Let $(x_1, y_1)=(0, -2)$ and $(x_2, y_2)=(4, 6)$.
The slope $m=\dfrac{y_2-y_1}{x_2-x_1}=\dfrac{6-(-2)}{4-0}=\dfrac{8}{4}=2$.

The slope of the line is 2

(2) $\left(-\dfrac{3}{2}, 5\right)$ and $(1, -10)$
Let $(x_1, y_1)=\left(-\dfrac{3}{2}, 5\right)$ and $(x_2, y_2)=(1, -10)$.
The slope $m=\dfrac{y_2-y_1}{x_2-x_1}=\dfrac{-10-5}{1-\left(-\dfrac{3}{2}\right)}=\dfrac{-15}{\dfrac{5}{2}}$
$=-6$.

The slope of the line is -6

04

(1) The line passes through two point
$(x_1, y_1)=(0, 0)$ and $(x_2, y_2)=(3, 2)$.
Therefore, the slope is
$$m=\dfrac{y_2-y_1}{x_2-x_1}=\dfrac{2-0}{3-0}=\dfrac{2}{3}$$

$m=\dfrac{2}{3}$

(2) The line passes through two point
$(x_1, y_1)=(-1, 0)$ and $(x_2, y_2)=(0, -2)$.
Therefore, the slope is
$$m=\dfrac{y_2-y_1}{x_2-x_1}=\dfrac{-2-0}{0-(-1)}=-2$$

$m=-2$

(3) The line passes through two point
$(x_1, y_1)=(0, 1)$ and $(x_2, y_2)=(2, 3)$.
Therefore, the slope is
$$m=\dfrac{y_2-y_1}{x_2-x_1}=\dfrac{3-1}{2-0}=\dfrac{2}{2}=1$$

$m=1$

Solutions Manual

(4) Since the line is vertical that passes through the point $(-2, 3)$, the equation of the line is $x=-2$ and its slope is undefined.
$$m=\text{undefined}$$

(5) The line passes through two point $(x_1, y_1)=(-2, 1)$ and $(x_2, y_2)=(2, 0)$. Therefore, the slope is
$$m=\frac{y_2-y_1}{x_2-x_1}=\frac{0-1}{2-(-2)}=-\frac{1}{4}$$
$$m=-\frac{1}{4}$$

(6) Since the line is horizontal that passes through the point $(-2, 3)$, the equation of the line is $y=3$ and its slope is 0.
$$m=0$$

05

(1) Let $(x_1, y_1)=(4, 7)$ and $(x_2, y_2)=(-2, b)$.
$$m=\frac{y_2-y_1}{x_2-x_1}, \quad -\frac{1}{3}=\frac{b-7}{-2-4},$$
$$-\frac{1}{3}=\frac{b-7}{-6}, \quad 2=b-7$$
$$9=b$$
$$b=9$$

(2) Let $(x_1, y_1)=\left(a, \frac{1}{2}\right)$ and $(x_2, y_2)=(3, -8)$.
$$m=\frac{y_2-y_1}{x_2-x_1}, \quad 4=\frac{-8-\frac{1}{2}}{3-a}$$
$$4(3-a)=-\frac{17}{2}, \quad 8(3-a)=-17$$
$$24-8a=-17, \quad -8a=-41, \quad a=\frac{41}{8}$$
$$a=\frac{41}{8}$$

(3) Since the slope $m=0$, the line must be horizontal that passes through $(-2, -7)$ and $(2, -7)$. Therefore, $b=-7$.
$$b=-7$$

(4) Since the slope $m=$undefined, the line must be vertical that passes through $\left(-\frac{1}{2}, \frac{5}{2}\right)$ and $\left(-\frac{1}{2}, \frac{3}{4}\right)$. Therefore, $a=-\frac{1}{2}$.
$$a=-\frac{1}{2}$$

06

Let $(x_1, y_1)=(k+1, 4)$ and $(x_2, y_2)=(2, 3k-1)$.
$$m=\frac{y_2-y_1}{x_2-x_1}, \quad 2=\frac{(3k-1)-4}{2-(k+1)}$$
$$2=\frac{3k-5}{1-k}, \quad 2(1-k)=3k-5$$
$$2-2k=3k-5$$
$$-5k=-7, \quad k=\frac{7}{5}$$
$$k=\frac{7}{5}$$

07

Since all three points lie on the same line, the slope from any two given points must be equal. Let $(x_1, y_1)=(1, 4)$ and $(x_2, y_2)=(2, 2a-3)$. Then
$$m_1=\frac{2a-3-4}{2-1}=2a-7.$$ Let $(x_1, y_1)=(1, 4)$ and $(x_2, y_2)=(-2, 3a+1)$. Then
$$m_2=\frac{3a+1-4}{-2-1}=\frac{3a-3}{-3}.$$ Now since $m_1=m_2$, we have the following equation:
$$2a-7=\frac{3a-3}{-3}$$
$$-3(2a-7)=3a-3$$
$$-6a+21=3a-3$$
$$-9a=-24, \quad a=\frac{24}{9}=\frac{8}{3}$$
$$a=\frac{8}{3}$$

2. Two Forms of the Lines

Check Point 1

$m=3$ and $(x_1,\ y_1)=(-2,\ -5)$
The equation of the line is
$$y-y_1=m(x-x_1)$$
$$y-(-5)=3(x-(-2))$$
$$y+5=3(x+2)$$

$$y+5=3(x+2)$$

Check Point 2

Let $(x_1,\ y_1)=(1,\ 4)$ and $(x_2,\ y_2)=(3,\ -3)$.
Then the slope is
$$m=\frac{y_2-y_1}{x_2-x_1}=\frac{-3-4}{3-1}=-\frac{7}{2}$$
The equation of the line is
$$y-y_1=m(x-x_1)$$
$$y-4=-\frac{7}{2}(x-1)$$

$$y-4=-\frac{7}{2}(x-1)$$

Check Point 3

The equation is in point−slope form,
$y-y_1=m(x-x_1)$. A point
$(x_1,\ y_1)=(-3,-2)$ and the slope is $m=\frac{1}{2}$.

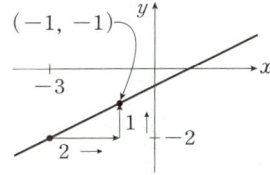

Check Point 4

$y=mx+b \Leftrightarrow y=-4x+6$

The slope is -4 and the y−intercept is 6.

Check Point 5

$m=-\frac{2}{3}$ and $b=3$
The equation of the line is
$$y=mx+b$$
$$y=-\frac{2}{3}x+3$$

$$y=-\frac{2}{3}x+3$$

Check Point 6

The equation is in slope−intercept form, $y=mx+b$. The slope is $m=-2$ and the y−intercept is 3.

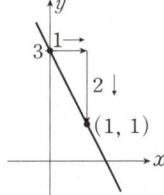

Check Point 7

Let two equations equal to each other.
$$-\frac{1}{2}x+6=3x-22$$
$$-\frac{7}{2}x=-28$$
$$x=8$$
Substitute 8 for x in the equation of either line.
$$y=3x-22$$
$$y=3(8)-22=2$$
Therefore, the intersection point is $(8,\ 2)$.

$(8,\ 2)$

Solutions Manual

Review Exercise

01

(1) $(1, -4)$; $m=-3$

The equation in point-slope form is
$$y-y_1=m(x-x_1)$$
$$y-(-4)=-3(x-1)$$
$$y+4=-3(x-1)$$

The equation in slope-intercept form is
$$y+4=-3x+3$$
$$y=-3x-1$$

$$y+4=-3(x-1),\ y=-3x-1$$

(2) $\left(-\dfrac{3}{2},\ 4\right)$; $m=5$

The equation in point-slope form is
$$y-y_1=m(x-x_1)$$
$$y-4=5\left(x-\left(-\dfrac{3}{2}\right)\right)$$
$$y-4=5\left(x+\dfrac{3}{2}\right)$$

The equation in slope-intercept form is
$$y-4=5x+\dfrac{15}{2}$$
$$y=5x+\dfrac{23}{2}$$

$$y-4=5\left(x+\dfrac{3}{2}\right),\ y=5x+\dfrac{23}{2}$$

02

(1) Let $(x_1,\ y_1)=(-5,\ 3)$ and $(x_2,\ y_2)=(-3,\ -1)$. Then the slope is
$$m=\dfrac{y_2-y_1}{x_2-x_1}=\dfrac{-1-3}{-3-(-5)}=\dfrac{-4}{2}=-2$$

The equation in point-slope form is
$$y-y_1=-2(x-x_1)$$
$$y-3=-2(x-(-5))$$
$$y-3=-2(x+5)$$

The equation in slope-intercept form is
$$y-3=-2x-10$$
$$y=-2x-7$$

$$y-3=-2(x+5),\ y=-2x-7$$

(2) Let $(x_1,\ y_1)=\left(2,\ -\dfrac{1}{2}\right)$ and $(x_2,\ y_2)=\left(-\dfrac{3}{2},\ 3\right)$. Then the slope is

$$m=\dfrac{y_2-y_1}{x_2-x_1}=\dfrac{3-\left(-\dfrac{1}{2}\right)}{-\dfrac{3}{2}-2}=\dfrac{\dfrac{7}{2}}{-\dfrac{7}{2}}=-1$$

The equation in point-slope form is
$$y-y_1=-1(x-x_1)$$
$$y-\left(-\dfrac{1}{2}\right)=-1(x-2)$$
$$y+\dfrac{1}{2}=-(x-2)$$

The equation in slope-intercept form is
$$y+\dfrac{1}{2}=-x+2$$
$$y=-x+\dfrac{3}{2}$$

$$y+\dfrac{1}{2}=-(x-2),\ y=-x+\dfrac{3}{2}$$

03

(1) $y-3=(x-1)$

The equation in point-slope form is $y-y_1=m(x-x_1)$. A point $(x_1,\ y_1)=(1,\ 3)$ and the slope is $m=1$.

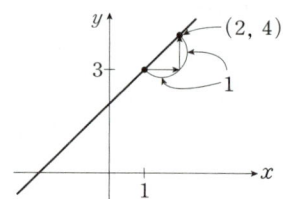

(2) $y-2=-\dfrac{3}{2}(x+2)$

The equation in point-slope form is $y-y_1=m(x-x_1)$. A point $(x_1,\ y_1)=(-2,\ 2)$ and the slope is $m=-\dfrac{3}{2}$.

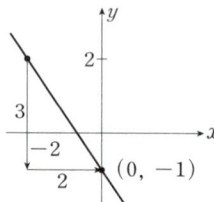

(3) $y=-3x+2$

The equation in slope-intercept form is $y=mx+b$. The slope is $m=-3$ and the y-intercept is 2.

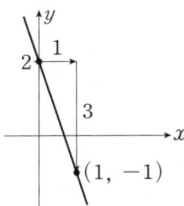

(4) $y = \frac{3}{4}x - 3$

The equation in slope−intercept form is $y = mx + b$. The slope is $m = \frac{3}{4}$ and the y−intercept is -3.

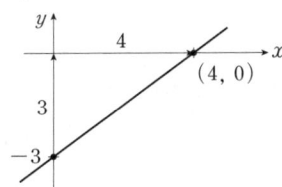

04

(1) $y = -3kx - 8$, $m = 2$

Since $-3k = m$, we have
$$-3k = 2, \quad k = -\frac{2}{3}$$

$$k = -\frac{2}{3}$$

(2) $4x - 3ky = 12$, $m = -\frac{3}{2}$

First, rewrite the equation of the line in slope−intercept form.
$$4x - 3ky = 12$$
$$-3ky = -4x + 12$$
$$y = \frac{4}{3k}x - \frac{4}{k}$$

Since $\frac{4}{3k} = m$, we have
$$\frac{4}{3k} = -\frac{3}{2}$$
$$9k = -8, \quad k = -\frac{8}{9}$$

$$k = -\frac{8}{9}$$

05

Given that $m = -\frac{2}{3}$ and $(x_1, y_1) = (6, 2)$, the equation of the line in point−slope form is
$$y - y_1 = m(x - x_1)$$

$$y - 2 = -\frac{2}{3}(x - 6)$$
$$3(y - 2) = -2(x - 6)$$
$$3y - 6 = -2x + 12$$
$$2x + 3y = 18$$

Now check each given point.

(A) $2(-1) + 3(-6) = -2 - 18 = -20 \neq 18$
→ Not on the line

(B) $2(1) + 3(4) = 2 + 12 = 14 \neq 18$
→ Not on the line

(C) $2(0) + 3(5) = 0 + 15 = 15 \neq 18$
→ Not on the line

(D) $2(3) + 3(-4) = 6 - 12 = -6 \neq 18$
→ Not on the line

(E) $2(-3) + 3(8) = -6 + 24 = 18$
→ On the line

The answer is (E)

06

Since the line has the y−intercept 2, we have $b = 2$. Now, let $(x_1, y_1) = (4, 0)$ and $(x_2, y_2) = (0, 2)$. Then the slope is $m = \frac{2 - 0}{0 - 4} = -\frac{1}{2}$. Therefore,
$$mb = \left(-\frac{1}{2}\right)(2) = -1$$

$$mb = -1$$

07

Since the value of y decreases by 6 units as the value of x increases by 2 units, the slope $m = \frac{\Delta y}{\Delta x} = \frac{-6}{2} = -3$.

$$m = -3$$

08

Since the two graphs are identical, they have the same slope and y−intercept. So $-4 = b$ and $a = -\frac{1}{2}$. Therefore,
$$ab = \left(-\frac{1}{2}\right)(-4) = 2$$

$$ab = 2$$

Solutions Manual

09

First, find the intersection of the two lines.
$$x+1=-\frac{1}{2}x+4$$
$$\frac{3}{2}x=3$$
$$x=2 \Rightarrow y=(2)+1=3$$

Therefore, the area bounded by three lines is shown below.

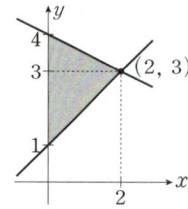

This is the triangle with base 3 and height 2. Therefore, the area of the triangle A is
$$A=\frac{1}{2}(3)(2)=3$$

$$A=3$$

10

Let x be the number of hours it takes to repair and y be the total cost of the repair. Let's find the equation in slope−intercept form $y=mx+b$.

Since a car repair service charges $40 per hour, the slope $m=40$. Also, since a car repair service charges $65 for diagnosis, which is initial fee, the y−intercept is 65. Therefore, the equation is $y=40x+65$.
If a car is repaired for 8 hours, then
$$y=40(8)+65=385$$
will be charged.

$385

11

Let x be the number of days and y be the total cost. Then we can use two points, such as $(x_1, y_1)=(3, 7)$ and $(x_2, y_2)=(5, 13)$ to find the slope

$$m=\frac{y_2-y_1}{x_2-x_1}=\frac{13-7}{5-3}=3.$$

Now, write the equation in point−slope form.
$$y-y_1=m(x-x_1)$$
$$y-7=3(x-3)$$

If a DVD is rented for 10 days, the cost will be
$$y-7=3(10-3)$$
$$y-7=21, \; y=28$$

$28

3. Parallel and Perpendicular Lines

Check Point 1

The slope of the line $-2x+4y=1$ is

$m=-\dfrac{-2}{4}=\dfrac{1}{2}$.

Write an equation of the line that passes through $(-4, 5)$ with slope $\dfrac{1}{2}$.

$$y-y_1=m(x-x_1)$$
$$y-5=\dfrac{1}{2}(x-(-4))$$
$$y-5=\dfrac{1}{2}(x+4)$$
$$y-5=\dfrac{1}{2}x+2$$
$$y=\dfrac{1}{2}x+7$$

$$y=\dfrac{1}{2}x+7$$

Check Point 2

The slope of the line $6x-4y=5$ is

$m=-\dfrac{6}{-4}=\dfrac{3}{2}$.

The opposite reciprocal of $\dfrac{3}{2}$ is $-\dfrac{2}{3}$.

Therefore, the perpendicular line has a slope of $-\dfrac{2}{3}$. Now, write an equation of the line that passes through $(3, 0)$ with slope $-\dfrac{2}{3}$.

$$y-y_1=m(x-x_1)$$
$$y-0=-\dfrac{2}{3}(x-3)$$
$$y=-\dfrac{2}{3}x+2$$

$$y=-\dfrac{2}{3}x+2$$

Review Exercise

01

(1) $(3, -4)$; $y=4x-5$

The slope of the line $y=4x-5$ is $m=4$.
Write an equation of the line that passes through $(3, -4)$ with slope 4.

$$y-y_1=m(x-x_1)$$
$$y-(-4)=4(x-3)$$
$$y+4=4x-12$$
$$y=4x-16$$

$$y=4x-16$$

(2) $\left(-\dfrac{1}{2}, \dfrac{3}{4}\right)$; $4x+2y=3$

The slope of the line $4x+2y=3$ is
$m=-\dfrac{4}{2}=-2$

Write an equation of the line that passes through $\left(-\dfrac{1}{2}, \dfrac{3}{4}\right)$ with slope -2.

$$y-y_1=m(x-x_1)$$
$$y-\dfrac{3}{4}=-2\left(x-\left(-\dfrac{1}{2}\right)\right)$$
$$y-\dfrac{3}{4}=-2x-1$$
$$y=-2x-\dfrac{1}{4}$$

$$y=-2x-\dfrac{1}{4}$$

02

(1) $(-3, -8)$; $y=-x+6$

The slope of the line $y=-x+6$ is $m=-1$.
The opposite reciprocal of -1 is 1.
Therefore, the perpendicular line has a slope of 1. Now, write an equation of the line that passes through $(-3,-8)$ with slope 1.

$$y-y_1=m(x-x_1)$$
$$y-(-8)=1\cdot(x-(-3))$$
$$y+8=x+3$$
$$y=x-5$$

$$y=x-5$$

(2) $\left(5, \dfrac{1}{3}\right)$; $2y-5x=4$

The slope of the line $2y-5x=4$ is

Solutions Manual

$m = -\dfrac{-5}{2} = \dfrac{5}{2}$

The opposite reciprocal of $\dfrac{5}{2}$ is $-\dfrac{2}{5}$.
Therefore, the perpendicular line has a slope of $-\dfrac{2}{5}$. Now, write an equation of the line that passes through $\left(5, \dfrac{1}{3}\right)$ with slope $-\dfrac{2}{5}$.

$y - y_1 = m(x - x_1)$

$y - \dfrac{1}{3} = -\dfrac{2}{5}(x - 5)$

$y - \dfrac{1}{3} = -\dfrac{2}{5}x + 2$

$y = -\dfrac{2}{5}x + \dfrac{7}{3}$

$$y = -\dfrac{2}{5}x + \dfrac{7}{3}$$

03

Since the line $y = -2x + 3$ is $m = -2$, the perpendicular line has a slope of $\dfrac{1}{2}$. The equation of the line that passes through $(2, 5)$ with the slope $\dfrac{1}{2}$ is

$y - y_1 = m(x - x_1)$

$y - 5 = \dfrac{1}{2}(x - 2)$

$2y - 10 = x - 2$

$-8 = x - 2y \Rightarrow x - 2y = -8$

The answer is (A)

04

The parallel lines have the same slope. Since g passes through the two points $(-2, 0)$ and $(0, -3)$, the slope is

$m = \dfrac{-3 - 0}{0 - (-2)} = -\dfrac{3}{2}$

Therefore, the slope of the line h must also be $-\dfrac{3}{2}$. Since h passes through the two points $(1, 0)$ and $(k, 3)$, the slope is

$m = \dfrac{3 - 0}{k - 1}$

$-\dfrac{3}{2} = \dfrac{3}{k - 1}$

$-3(k - 1) = 6$

$k - 1 = -2, \; k = -1$

05

Line k: $3x + 4y = 11$

The slope is $m = -\dfrac{3}{4}$

Line p: $4x - 3y = 9$

The slope is $m = -\dfrac{4}{-3} = \dfrac{4}{3}$

	The line k	The line p
x−int	$3x + 4(0) = 11$ $x = \dfrac{11}{3}$	$4x - 3(0) = 9$ $x = \dfrac{9}{4}$
y−int	$3(0) + 4y = 11$ $y = \dfrac{11}{4}$	$4(0) - 3y = 9$ $y = -3$

Since the product of their slope is $\left(-\dfrac{3}{4}\right)\left(\dfrac{4}{3}\right) = -1$, two lines k and p are perpendicular.

The answer is (D)

06

Since the line l passes through the two points $(-3, -2)$ and $(1, 3)$, the slope is

$m = \dfrac{3 - (-2)}{1 - (-3)} = \dfrac{5}{4}$

The parallel lines have the same slope.

(A) $5x + 4y = 3 \Rightarrow m = -\dfrac{5}{4}$

(B) $4x + 5y = 3 \Rightarrow m = -\dfrac{4}{5}$

(C) $5x - 4y = -3 \Rightarrow m = -\dfrac{5}{-4} = \dfrac{5}{4}$

(D) $-4x + 5y = -3 \Rightarrow m = -\dfrac{-4}{5} = \dfrac{4}{5}$

Therefore, the answer is (C)

07

The opposite reciprocal of $\dfrac{5}{4}$ is $-\dfrac{4}{5}$.
Therefore, the perpendicular line has a slope of $-\dfrac{4}{5}$.

The answer is (B)

Chapter 2 Test Level 1

01

$3x+12y=36$

The x-intercept: let $y=0$.

$3x+12(0)=36$

$3x=36$

$x=12 \Rightarrow a=12$

The y-intercept: let $x=0$.

$3(0)+12y=36$

$12y=36$

$y=3 \Rightarrow b=3$

Therefore, $ab=(12)(3)=36$.

$ab=36$

02

Lines (B), (C), and (E) increase from left to right, so the slopes are all positive. Line (D) is horizontal, so the slope is 0. Line (A) decreases from left to right, so the slope is negative. Therefore, line (A) has the smallest slope.

The answer is (A)

03

Let $(x_1, y_1)=(-2, a+1)$ and $(x_2, y_2)=(2a-3, 6)$.

$m=\dfrac{y_2-y_1}{x_2-x_1}$, $3=\dfrac{6-(a+1)}{2a-3-(-2)}$

$3=\dfrac{5-a}{2a-1}$, $3(2a-1)=5-a$

$6a-3=5-a$, $7a=8$, $a=\dfrac{8}{7}$.

$a=\dfrac{8}{7}$

04

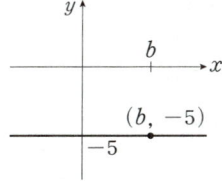

If the line k is horizontal that passes through the point $(b,-5)$, $y=-5$ for all x as shown above. Therefore, the equation of the line is $y=-5$.

$y=-5$

05

Two points A and B are $y-$ and $x-$intercept of the line $7x+5y=21$, respectively.

The x-intercept: let $y=0$.

$7x+5(0)=21$

$7x=21$

$x=3 \Rightarrow B=(3, 0)$

The y-intercept: let $x=0$.

$7(0)+5y=21$

$5y=21$

$y=\dfrac{21}{5} \Rightarrow A=\left(0, \dfrac{21}{5}\right)$

Therefore, the area of $\triangle AOB$ is

$\dfrac{1}{2}(3)\left(\dfrac{21}{5}\right)=\dfrac{63}{10}$.

The area of $\triangle AOB$ is $\dfrac{63}{10}$

06

The slope m of the line that passes two points $(3,-4)$ and $(-1,-9)$ is

$m=\dfrac{-9-(-4)}{-1-3}=\dfrac{5}{4}$

The equation of the line that passes through $(3,-4)$ with the slope $\dfrac{5}{4}$ is

$y-y_1=m(x-x_1)$

$y+4=\dfrac{5}{4}(x-3)$

$y+4=\dfrac{5}{4}x-\dfrac{15}{4}$

$y=\dfrac{5}{4}x-\dfrac{31}{4}$

$y=\dfrac{5}{4}x-\dfrac{31}{4}$

07

The line passes through $(-3, 0)$ and $(4, 3)$. Then the slope m is

Solutions Manual

$$m=\frac{3-0}{4-(-3)}=\frac{3}{7}$$

The equation of the line that passes through $(-3, 0)$ with the slope $\frac{3}{7}$ is

$$y-y_1=m(x-x_1)$$
$$y-0=\frac{3}{7}(x+3)$$
$$y=\frac{3}{7}x+\frac{9}{7}$$

Therefore, $m+b=\frac{3}{7}+\frac{9}{7}=\frac{12}{7}$.

$$m+b=\frac{12}{7}$$

08

Since two graphs are identical, they have same slope and y-intercept. So $4m+n=m$ and $5=-(3n+7)$.

$$5=-3n-7 \qquad 4m+(-4)=m$$
$$12=-3n \qquad \text{and} \qquad 3m=4$$
$$-4=n \qquad m=\frac{4}{3}$$

Therefore, $mn=\left(\frac{4}{3}\right)(-4)=-\frac{16}{3}$.

$$mn=-\frac{16}{3}$$

09

The line that is parallel to the line $y=-\frac{3}{2}x+1$ has the slope $m=-\frac{3}{2}$.
The equation of the line that passes through $(2, 8)$ with the slope $-\frac{3}{2}$ is

$$y-y_1=m(x-x_1)$$
$$y-8=-\frac{3}{2}(x-2)$$
$$y-8=-\frac{3}{2}x+3$$
$$y=-\frac{3}{2}x+11$$

$$y=-\frac{3}{2}x+11$$

10

The slope of the line $3x+4y=10$ is $m=-\frac{3}{4}$. Therefore, the perpendicular line has a slope of $\frac{4}{3}$. The equation of the line that passes through $(-3, 0)$ with the slope $\frac{4}{3}$ is

$$y-y_1=m(x-x_1)$$
$$y-0=\frac{4}{3}(x+3)$$
$$y=\frac{4}{3}x+4$$

$$y=\frac{4}{3}x+4$$

11

Since the line k passes through $(-1, -1)$ and $(3, 1)$, the slope is $m=\frac{1-(-1)}{3-(-1)}=\frac{1}{2}$.
The line l passes through $(-1, -1)$ and $(0, a)$. Since the line l is perpendicular to the line k, the slope of the line l is -2. Therefore, we have.

$$\frac{a-(-1)}{0-(-1)}=-2$$
$$a+1=-2,\ a=-3$$

$$a=-3$$

12

(1) The cost per square yard $\left(\frac{\$}{yd^2}\right)$ represents the slope of the line.

The answer is (C)

(2) The equation of the line in slope-intercept form is $y=mx+b$. The line has the y-intercept at $b=30$ and passes through the points $(0, 30)$ and $(5, 40)$. So the slope m of the line is

$$m=\frac{40-30}{5-0}=\frac{10}{5}=2$$

Therefore, the equation is $y=2x+30$

$$y=2x+30$$

13

Since the total cost was $570, we have the following equation:

$$y=150+70x$$
$$570=150+70x$$
$$420=70x,\ x=6$$

Therefore, the car was rented for 6 days.

14

Let x be the number of hours Andrea works and y be the total amount she charges. Now, let's find the equation in slope−intercept form $y=mx+b$.

Since Andrea charges a $160 fee plus $30 per hour, the y−intercept is $b=160$ and the slope $m=30$. Therefore, the equation is $y=30x+160$. If the project takes 12 hours, she will charge

$$y=30(12)+160=520$$

$520

15

Let x be the number of years since 2016 and y be the total number of trees. Since the city has been planting 50 trees each month, the number of trees planted per year will be $50\times12=600$ tree. Therefore, the equation is $y=600x+16,000$.
In 2025, which is 9 years from 2016, the city will have

$$y=600(9)+16,000=21400 \text{ trees.}$$

21,400 trees.

Chapter 2 Test Level 2

01

$5x-2y=-\dfrac{3}{2}$

The x−intercept: let $y=0$.

$$5x-2(0)=-\dfrac{3}{2}$$
$$5x=-\dfrac{3}{2}$$
$$x=-\dfrac{3}{10} \Rightarrow a=-\dfrac{3}{10}$$

The y−intercept: let $x=0$.

$$5(0)-2y=-\dfrac{3}{2}$$
$$-2y=-\dfrac{3}{2}$$
$$y=\dfrac{3}{4} \Rightarrow b=\dfrac{3}{4}$$

The slope of $5x-2y=-\dfrac{3}{2}$ is

$$m=-\dfrac{5}{-2}=\dfrac{5}{2} \Rightarrow c=\dfrac{5}{2}$$

Therefore, $\dfrac{ac}{b}=\dfrac{\left(-\dfrac{3}{10}\right)\left(\dfrac{5}{2}\right)}{\dfrac{3}{4}}=\dfrac{-\dfrac{3}{4}}{\dfrac{3}{4}}=-1.$

$$\dfrac{ac}{b}=-1$$

02

The slope m of the line k that passes through $(a,0)$ and $(2,4)$ is

$$m=\dfrac{4-0}{2-a}=\dfrac{4}{2-a}$$

The equation of the line k that passes through $(2,4)$ with the slope $\dfrac{4}{2-a}$ is

$$y-y_1=m(x-x_1)$$
$$y-4=\dfrac{4}{2-a}(x-2)$$
$$y-4=\dfrac{4}{2-a}x-\dfrac{8}{2-a}$$
$$y=\dfrac{4}{2-a}x+\left(-\dfrac{8}{2-a}+4\right)$$
$$y=\dfrac{4}{2-a}x+\left(-\dfrac{8}{2-a}+4\right)$$

Solutions Manual

03

The slope m_1 from two points $(0, 0)$ and $(a-3, 4)$ is
$$m_1 = \frac{4-0}{(a-3)-0} = \frac{4}{a-3}$$
The slope m_2 from two points $(0, 0)$ and $(3a+2, -2)$ is
$$m_2 = \frac{y_3 - y_1}{x_3 - x_1} = \frac{-2-0}{(3a+2)-0} = \frac{-2}{3a+2}$$
Since all three points lie on the same line, the slope from any two given points must be equal to each other.
$$m_1 = m_2$$
$$\frac{4}{a-3} = \frac{-2}{3a+2}$$
$$4(3a+2) = -2(a-3)$$
$$12a+8 = -2a+6$$
$$14a = -2, \ a = -\frac{2}{14} = -\frac{1}{7}$$
$$a = -\frac{1}{7}$$

04

$2ax - 5y = b$
Since the slope is 2, we have
$$m = -\frac{2a}{-5}$$
$$2 = \frac{2a}{5}, \ a = 5$$
Since the y-intercept is 6, we also have
$$2a(0) - 5(6) = b$$
$$-30 = b, \ b = -30$$
Therefore, $a+b = 5+(-30) = -25$.
$$a+b = -25$$

05

Since the line increases from left to right, the slope m is positive. Also, the y-intercept b is negative as shown in the graph.
Therefore, we have
$$-\frac{b}{m} = -\frac{-}{+} > 0 \text{ and } -bm = -(-)(+) > 0$$
The line $y = -\frac{b}{m}x - bm$ has a positive slope

and a positive y-intercept, so the line does not pass through quadrant IV as shown below.

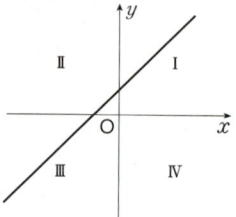

The answer is (D)

06

First, find the intersection of the two lines $y = x+3$ and $4x+3y = 16$. To find the intersection, substitute $x+3$ for y in the equation $4x+3y = 16$.
$$4x + 3(x+3) = 16$$
$$4x + 3x + 9 = 16$$
$$7x = 7, \ x = 1$$
$$\Rightarrow y = (1) + 3 = 4$$
The x-intercept of $y = x+3$ is
$$0 = x+3, \ x = -3$$
The x-intercept of $4x+3y = 16$ is
$$4x + 3(0) = 16$$
$$4x = 16, \ x = 4$$
Therefore, the area bounded by three lines is shown below.

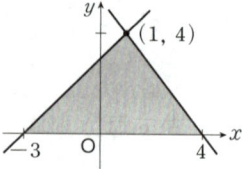

The area of the triangle A is
$$A = \frac{1}{2}(7)(4) = 14.$$
$$A = 14$$

07

The equation of the first line is
$$y - y_1 = m(x - x_1)$$

$y+3=-4(x-1)$
$y+3=-4x+4$
$y=-4x+1$

The second line passes through (2, 10) and $\left(-\frac{1}{2},\ 0\right)$. The slope m of the line is

$m=\dfrac{0-10}{-\frac{1}{2}-2}=\dfrac{-10}{-\frac{5}{2}}=4$

So, the equation is
$y-y_1=m(x-x_1)$
$y-10=4(x-2)$
$y-10=4x-8$
$y=4x+2$

Now, find the intersection of the two lines.
$-4x+1=4x+2$
$-8x=1,\ x=-\dfrac{1}{8}\ \Rightarrow\ m=-\dfrac{1}{8}$
$y=-4\left(-\dfrac{1}{8}\right)+1=\dfrac{3}{2}\ \Rightarrow\ n=\dfrac{3}{2}$

Therefore,
$m\div n=\left(-\dfrac{1}{8}\right)\div\dfrac{3}{2}=-\dfrac{1}{8}\times\dfrac{2}{3}=-\dfrac{1}{12}$

$$m\div n=-\dfrac{1}{12}$$

08

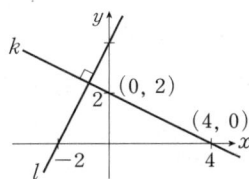

The slope m of the line k is
$m=\dfrac{0-2}{4-0}=-\dfrac{2}{4}=-\dfrac{1}{2}$

Therefore, the perpendicular line l has a slope of 2. The equation of the line l is
$y-y_1=m(x-x_1)$
$y-0=2(x+2)$
$y=2x+4$

$$y=2x+4$$

09

Since the line $y=mx-2$ is parallel to the line $y=-\dfrac{2}{3}x+1$, $m=-\dfrac{2}{3}$. So the line $y=-\dfrac{2}{3}x-2$ and $y=kx+3$ intersects at the $x-$axis as shown below.

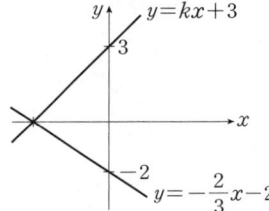

The $x-$intercept of the line $y=-\dfrac{2}{3}x-2$ is
$0=-\dfrac{2}{3}x-2$
$\dfrac{2}{3}x=-2,\ x=-3$

Since the line $y=kx+3$ has the same $x-$intercept, substitute $(-3,\ 0)$ in the equation $y=kx+3$ to find k.
$0=k(-3)+3$
$3k=3,\ k=1$

Therefore, $m+k=-\dfrac{2}{3}+1=\dfrac{1}{3}$.

$$m+k=\dfrac{1}{3}$$

10

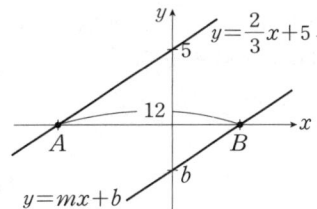

Since the two lines are parallel, the slope $m=\dfrac{2}{3}$. The $x-$intercept of the line $y=\dfrac{2}{3}x+5$ is
$0=\dfrac{2}{3}x+5$
$-\dfrac{2}{3}x=5,\ x=-\dfrac{15}{2}\ \Rightarrow\ A=-\dfrac{15}{2}$

The $x-$intercept of the line $y=\dfrac{2}{3}x+b$ is

Solutions Manual

$$0 = \frac{2}{3}x + b$$
$$-\frac{2}{3}x = b, \quad x = -\frac{3b}{2} \Rightarrow B = -\frac{3b}{2}$$

Since $\overline{AB} = 12$, we have
$$-\frac{3b}{2} - \left(-\frac{15}{2}\right) = 12$$
$$-\frac{3b}{2} + \frac{15}{2} = 12$$
$$-\frac{3b}{2} = \frac{9}{2}, \quad b = -3$$

Therefore, $mb = \left(\frac{2}{3}\right)(-3) = -2$.

$$mb = -2$$

11

The slope of the line $g = 2q + 1$ is 2, so if q increases by 1, then g increases by 2. This means that 2 additional games are played by adding 1 quarter. Therefore, to play 6 additional games, 3 more quarters are needed.

3 quarters

12

Let x be the number of pages of a college essay Mr. Jackson edits and y be the total cost he charges. Then, the equation is $y = 14(x-3) + 30$. If he edits 23 pages, then he will charge
$$y = 14(23-3) + 30$$
$$= 280 + 30 = 310$$

$310

13

Profit is the total revenue minus costs. Since Luke had done 20 car wash services, his total revenue is $9 \times 20 = \$180$. Therefore, Luke's profit is $180 - 80 = \$100$.

$100

Chapter 3

System of Linear Equations

1. Solving System of Linear Equations, Part 1

Check Point 1

Substitute $(-1, -2)$ into the system
$$\begin{cases} 4x - my = 8 \\ nx + 3y = -4 \end{cases}$$

$4(-1) - m(-2) = 8$ and $n(-1) + 3(-2) = -4$
$-4 + 2m = 8$ $\qquad$ $-n - 6 = -4$
$2m = 12$ $\qquad$ $-n = 2$
$m = 6$ $\qquad$ $n = -2$

Therefore, $m - n = 6 - (-2) = 8$.

$$m - n = 8$$

Check Point 2

① $\begin{cases} x - 2y = -6 \\ 2y - 2x = 9 \end{cases}$

Solve the first equation for x.
$x - 2y = -6$
$x = 2y - 6$

Substitute $2y - 6$ for x in the other equation.
$2y - 2(2y - 6) = 9$
$2y - 4y + 12 = 9$
$-2y = -3$, $y = \frac{3}{2}$

Now, substitute $\frac{3}{2}$ for y in the equation $x = 2y - 6$.

$x = 2\left(\frac{3}{2}\right) - 6 = 3 - 6 = -3$

The solution is $\left(-3, \frac{3}{2}\right)$

② $\begin{cases} 3x + y = 4 \\ 2x - 5y = 14 \end{cases}$

Solve the first equation for y.
$3x + y = 4$
$y = -3x + 4$

Substitute $-3x + 4$ for y in the other equation.
$2x - 5(-3x + 4) = 14$
$2x + 15x - 20 = 14$
$17x = 34$, $x = 2$

Now, substitute 2 for x in the equation $y = -3x + 4$.
$y = -3(2) + 4 = -2$

The solution is $(2, -2)$

Check Point 3

① $\begin{cases} x - 2y = 12 \\ 3x - y = -4 \end{cases}$

Multiply $3x - y = -4$ by 2 and then subtract.

$\begin{cases} x - 2y = 12 \\ (3x - y = -4) \cdot 2 \end{cases}$ $\Rightarrow$ $\begin{array}{r} x - 2y = 12 \\ -\underline{6x - 2y = -8} \\ -5x = 20 \\ x = -4 \end{array}$

Substitute -4 for x in the equation $x - 2y = 12$.
$-4 - 2y = 12$
$-2y = 16$, $y = -8$

The solution is $(-4, -8)$

② $\begin{cases} 4x + y = -5 \\ 3x - 2y = -12 \end{cases}$

Multiply $4x + y = -5$ by 2 and then add.

$\begin{cases} (4x + y = -5) \cdot 2 \\ 3x - 2y = -12 \end{cases}$ $\Rightarrow$ $\begin{array}{r} 8x + 2y = -10 \\ +\underline{3x - 2y = -12} \\ 11x = -22 \\ x = -2 \end{array}$

Solutions Manual

Substitute -2 for x in the equation
$4x+y=-5$.
$$4(-2)+y=-5$$
$$y=3$$

The solution is $(-2, 3)$

Check Point 4

Method 1:
$$\begin{cases} 2x-y=3 \\ -6x+3y=-9 \end{cases} \Rightarrow y=2x-3$$

Substitute $2x-3$ for y in the second equation.
$$-6x+3(2x-3)=-9$$
$$-6x+6x-9=-9$$
$$-6x+6x=-9+9$$
$$0 \cdot x = 0$$

Method 2:

From $\begin{cases} 2x-y=3 \\ -6x+3y=-9 \end{cases}$, we have

$$\frac{2}{-6}=\frac{-1}{3}=\frac{3}{-9}.$$

Therefore, the system has infinitely many solutions.

Check Point 5

Method 1:
$$\begin{cases} -x+2y=3 \\ 3x-6y=-8 \end{cases} \Rightarrow x=2y-3$$

Substitute $2y-3$ for x in the second equation.
$$3(2y-3)-6y=-8$$
$$6y-9-6y=-8$$
$$6y-6y=-8+9$$
$$0 \cdot y = 1 \rightarrow 0 \cdot y \neq 0$$

Method 2:

From $\begin{cases} -x+2y=3 \\ 3x-6y=-8 \end{cases}$, we have

$$\frac{-1}{3}=\frac{2}{-6} \neq \frac{3}{-8}.$$

Therefore, the system has no solution.

Review Exercise

01

Since $\left(\dfrac{3}{2}, 12\right)$ is the solution to the system, substitute $\dfrac{3}{2}$ for x and 12 for y.

$$1-\frac{b(12)}{4}=4 \qquad 6a\left(\frac{3}{2}\right)+2(12)=42$$
$$1-3b=4 \qquad \text{and} \qquad 9a+24=42$$
$$-3b=3 \qquad\qquad\qquad 9a=18$$
$$b=-1 \qquad\qquad\qquad a=2$$

Therefore, $ab=2(-1)=-2$

$$ab=-2$$

02

Substitute 4 for x in the equation
$$2x-y=9.$$
$$2(4)-y=9$$
$$-y=1, \ y=-1$$

Now, substitute 4 for x and -1 for y in the equation $3ax+ay=11$.
$$3a(4)+a(-1)=11$$
$$12a-a=11$$
$$11a=11, \ a=1$$

$$a=1$$

03

(1) $\begin{cases} 3x-5y=-1 \\ x+2y=7 \end{cases}$

Solve the second equation for x.
$$x+2y=7$$
$$x=-2y+7$$

Substitute $-2y+7$ for x in the other

equation.
$$3(-2y+7)-5y=-1$$
$$-6y+21-5y=-1$$
$$-11y=-22,\ y=2$$
Now, substitute 2 for y in the equation $x=-2y+7$.
$$x=-2(2)+7=3$$
The solution is (3, 2)

(2) $\begin{cases} x-12y=4 \\ 3x=20y+28 \end{cases}$

Solve the first equation for x.
$$x-12y=4$$
$$x=12y+4$$
Substitute $12y+4$ for x in the other equation.
$$3(12y+4)=20y+28$$
$$36y+12=20y+28$$
$$16y=16,\ y=1$$
Now, substitute 1 for y in the equation $x=12y+4$.
$$x=12(1)+4=16$$
The solution is (16, 1)

(3) $\begin{cases} 6x-4y=-12 \\ 2x-y=-7 \end{cases}$

Solve the second equation for y.
$$2x-y=-7$$
$$-y=-2x-7$$
$$y=2x+7$$
Substitute $2x+7$ for y in the other equation.
$$6x-4(2x+7)=-12$$
$$6x-8x-28=-12$$
$$-2x=16,\ x=-8$$
Now, substitute -8 for x in the equation $y=2x+7$.
$$y=2(-8)+7=-9$$
The solution is $(-8,\ -9)$

(4) $\begin{cases} 5x+4y=2 \\ 3x+y=4 \end{cases}$

Solve the second equation for y.
$$3x+y=4$$

$$y=-3x+4$$
Substitute $-3x+4$ for y in the other equation.
$$5x+4(-3x+4)=2$$
$$5x-12x+16=2$$
$$-7x=-14,\ x=2$$
Now, substitute 2 for x in the equation $y=-3x+4$.
$$y=-3(2)+4=-2$$
The solution is $(2,\ -2)$

04

(1) $\begin{cases} 3x-4y=-9 \\ -3x+5y=6 \end{cases}$

Add two equations.
$$\begin{array}{r} 3x-4y=-9 \\ +\ -3x+5y=6 \\ \hline y=-3 \end{array}$$
Substitute -3 for y in the equation $3x-4y=-9$.
$$3x-4(-3)=-9$$
$$3x+12=-9$$
$$3x=-21,\ x=-7$$
The solution is $(-7,\ -3)$

(2) $\begin{cases} 3x+2y=13 \\ 4x-4y=-1 \end{cases}$

Multiply $3x+2y=13$ by 2 and then add.
$$\begin{cases} (3x+2y=13)\cdot 2 \\ 4x-4y=-1 \end{cases} \Rightarrow \begin{array}{r} 6x+4y=26 \\ +\ 4x-4y=-1 \\ \hline 10x\ \ \ =25 \end{array}$$
$$x=\frac{5}{2}$$
Substitute $\frac{5}{2}$ for x in the equation $3x+2y=13$.
$$3\left(\frac{5}{2}\right)+2y=13$$
$$2y=\frac{11}{2},\ y=\frac{11}{4}$$
The solution is $\left(\frac{5}{2},\ \frac{11}{4}\right)$

(3) $\begin{cases} 4x+6y=12 \\ -2x-3y=-6 \end{cases}$

Solutions Manual

Divide $4x+6y=12$ by 2 and then add.

$$\begin{cases}(4x+6y=12)\cdot\dfrac{1}{2}\\-2x-3y=-6\end{cases} \Rightarrow \begin{array}{r}2x+3y=6\\+\underline{-2x-3y=-6}\\0x+0y=0\end{array}$$

The system has infinitely many solutions.

(4) $\begin{cases}-x-6y=17\\5x-3y=14\end{cases}$

Multiply $5x-3y=14$ by 2 and then subtract.

$$\begin{cases}-x-6y=17\\(5x-3y=14)\cdot 2\end{cases} \Rightarrow \begin{array}{r}-x-6y=17\\-\underline{|10x-6y=28}\\-11x=-11\\x=1\end{array}$$

Substitute 1 for x in the equation $-x-6y=17$.

$-1-6y=17$
$-6y=18,\ y=-3$

The solution is $(1,\ -3)$

05

Substitute 2 for x and -1 for y in the system.

$$\begin{cases}a(2)-b(-1)=5\\b(2)+a(-1)=-2\end{cases} \Rightarrow \begin{cases}2a+b=5\\-a+2b=-2\end{cases}$$

This is a new linear system of equations with two variables a and b. Solve the system using the substitution method.

$\begin{cases}2a+b=5\\-a+2b=-2\end{cases} \Rightarrow b=-2a+5$

Substitute $-2a+5$ for b in the equation $-a+2b=-2$.

$-a+2(-2a+5)=-2$
$-a-4a+10=-2$
$-5a=-12,\ a=\dfrac{12}{5}$

$a=\dfrac{12}{5}$

06

$\begin{cases}x+4y=a\\2x=by+10\end{cases} \Rightarrow \begin{cases}x+4y=a\\2x-by=10\end{cases}$

If the system $\begin{cases}x+4y=a\\2x-by=10\end{cases}$ has infinitely many solutions, we must have

$\dfrac{1}{2}=\dfrac{4}{-b}=\dfrac{a}{10}$.

$\dfrac{1}{2}=\dfrac{4}{-b}$ and $\dfrac{1}{2}=\dfrac{a}{10}$

$-b=8 \Rightarrow b=-8 \qquad 2a=10 \Rightarrow a=5$

Therefore, $a=5$ and $b=-8$

07

$\begin{cases}x=ay+2\\3x-4y=5\end{cases} \Rightarrow \begin{cases}x-ay=2\\3x-4y=5\end{cases}$

If the system has no solution, we must have $\dfrac{1}{3}=\dfrac{-a}{-4}\neq\dfrac{2}{5}$.

$\dfrac{1}{3}=\dfrac{-a}{-4}$

$-3a=-4 \Rightarrow a=\dfrac{4}{3}$

Therefore, $a=\dfrac{4}{3}$

2. Solving System of Linear Equations, Part 2

Check Point 1

① $\begin{cases} x+5=3y \\ 2(x+3y)=4x+10 \end{cases} \Rightarrow \begin{cases} x+5=3y \\ 2x+6y=4x+10 \end{cases}$

$\Rightarrow \begin{cases} x=3y-5 \\ -2x+6y=10 \end{cases}$

Substitute $3y-5$ for x in the second equation.
$$-2(3y-5)+6y=10$$
$$-6y+10+6y=10$$
$$-6y+6y=10-10$$
$$0 \cdot y = 0$$

Therefore, the system has infinitely many solutions

② $\begin{cases} 3(x+y)-y=-6 \\ 5x-4(x+y)=5 \end{cases} \Rightarrow \begin{cases} 3x+3y-y=-6 \\ 5x-4x-4y=5 \end{cases}$

$\Rightarrow \begin{cases} 3x+2y=-6 \\ x=4y+5 \end{cases}$

Substitute $4y+5$ for x in the first equation.
$$3(4y+5)+2y=-6$$
$$12y+15+2y=-6$$
$$14y=-21, \ y=-\frac{3}{2}$$

Substitute $-\frac{3}{2}$ for y in the equation $x=4y+5$.
$$x=4\left(-\frac{3}{2}\right)+5=-6+5=-1$$

The solution is $\left(-1, -\frac{3}{2}\right)$

Check Point 2

① $\begin{cases} x-\dfrac{y}{3}=\dfrac{1}{3} \\ -\dfrac{x}{2}+\dfrac{2y}{5}=1 \end{cases}$

$\begin{cases} \left(x-\dfrac{y}{3}=\dfrac{1}{3}\right) \times 3 \\ \left(-\dfrac{x}{2}+\dfrac{2y}{5}=1\right) \times 10 \end{cases} \Rightarrow \begin{cases} 3x-y=1 \\ -5x+4y=10 \end{cases}$

$\Rightarrow \begin{cases} 3x-1=y \\ -5x+4y=10 \end{cases}$

Substitute $3x-1$ for y in the second equation.
$$-5x+4(3x-1)=10$$
$$-5x+12x-4=10$$
$$7x=14, \ x=2$$

Substitute 2 for x in the equation $y=3x-1$.
$$y=3(2)-1=5$$

The solution is $(2, 5)$

② $\begin{cases} \dfrac{2x}{3}-\dfrac{3y}{2}=5 \\ \dfrac{x}{2}-\dfrac{3y}{4}=3 \end{cases}$

$\begin{cases} \left(\dfrac{2x}{3}-\dfrac{3y}{2}=5\right) \times 6 \\ \left(\dfrac{x}{2}-\dfrac{3y}{4}=3\right) \times 4 \end{cases} \Rightarrow \begin{cases} 4x-9y=30 \\ 2x-3y=12 \end{cases}$

Multiply $2x-3y=12$ by 2 and subtract.

$\begin{cases} 4x-9y=30 \\ (2x-3y=12) \times 2 \end{cases} \Rightarrow \begin{cases} 4x-9y=30 \\ 4x-6y=24 \end{cases}$

$\begin{array}{r} 4x-9y=30 \\ -\underline{4x-6y=24} \\ -3y=6, \ y=-2 \end{array}$

Substitute -2 for y in the equation $4x-9y=30$.
$$4x-9(-2)=30$$
$$4x+18=30$$
$$4x=12, \ x=3$$

The solution is $(3, -2)$

Check Point 3

① $\begin{cases} 1.2x-0.4y=0.3 \\ 4x+y=-\dfrac{4}{3} \end{cases}$

$\begin{cases} (1.2x-0.4y=0.3) \times 10 \\ \left(4x+y=-\dfrac{4}{3}\right) \times 3 \end{cases} \Rightarrow \begin{cases} 12x-4y=3 \\ 12x+3y=-4 \end{cases}$

Subtract the second equation from the first.

Solutions Manual

$\begin{vmatrix} 12x-4y=3 \\ 12x+3y=-4 \end{vmatrix}$
$\overline{-7y=7, \quad y=-1}$

Substitute -1 for y in the equation $12x+3y=-4$.
$$12x+3(-1)=-4$$
$$12x-3=-4$$
$$12x=-1, \quad x=-\frac{1}{12}$$

The solution is $\left(-\frac{1}{12},\ -1\right)$

② $\begin{cases} \dfrac{y}{3}-\dfrac{x+y}{5}=-1 \\ 0.1x+0.2y=1.3 \end{cases}$

$\begin{cases} \left(\dfrac{y}{3}-\dfrac{x+y}{5}=-1\right)\times 15 \\ (0.1x+0.2y=1.3)\times 10 \end{cases}$

$\Rightarrow \begin{cases} 5y-3(x+y)=-15 \\ x+2y=13 \end{cases}$

$\Rightarrow \begin{cases} 5y-3x-3y=-15 \\ x+2y=13 \end{cases} \Rightarrow \begin{cases} -3x+2y=-15 \\ x+2y=13 \end{cases}$

Subtract the second equation from the first.

$\begin{vmatrix} -3x+2y=-15 \\ x+2y=13 \end{vmatrix}$
$\overline{-4x=-28, \quad x=7}$

Substitute 7 for x in the equation $x+2y=13$.
$$7+2y=13$$
$$2y=6, \quad y=3$$

The solution is $(7, 3)$

Check Point 4

$\begin{cases} \dfrac{2}{x}-\dfrac{3}{y}=-\dfrac{1}{2} \\ \dfrac{3}{x}+\dfrac{1}{2y}=\dfrac{11}{12} \end{cases}$

Let $\dfrac{1}{x}=A$ and $\dfrac{1}{y}=B$

$\begin{cases} \left(2A-3B=-\dfrac{1}{2}\right)\times 2 \\ \left(3A+\dfrac{1}{2}B=\dfrac{11}{12}\right)\times 12 \end{cases}$

$\Rightarrow \begin{cases} 4A-6B=-1 \\ 36A+6B=11 \end{cases}$

Add two equations to eliminate B.

$\begin{vmatrix} 4A-6B=-1 \\ 36A+6B=11 \end{vmatrix}$
$\overline{40A=10,}$
$$A=\frac{1}{4} \rightarrow \frac{1}{x}=\frac{1}{4}$$
$$x=4$$

Substitute $\dfrac{1}{4}$ for A in the equation $4A-6B=-1$.
$$4\left(\frac{1}{4}\right)-6B=-1$$
$$-6B=-2$$
$$B=\frac{1}{3}, \quad \frac{1}{y}=\frac{1}{3}$$
$$y=3$$

The solution is $(4, 3)$

Check Point 5

From the equation
$$7x+2y=4x+y=2x-y-4,$$
let the system be
$$\begin{cases} 7x+2y=4x+y \\ 7x+2y=2x-y-4 \end{cases} \Rightarrow \begin{cases} y=-3x \\ 5x+3y=-4 \end{cases}$$

Substitute $-3x$ for y in the second equation $5x+3y=-4$.
$$5x+3(-3x)=-4$$
$$-4x=-4, \quad x=1$$

Substitute 1 for x in the equation $y=-3x$.
$$y=-3(1)=-3$$

The solution is $(1,-3)$

Review Exercise

01

(1) $\begin{cases} 2(3x+y)=4+4y \\ 4x-3(y-1)=4 \end{cases} \Rightarrow \begin{cases} 6x+2y=4+4y \\ 4x-3y+3=4 \end{cases}$

$\Rightarrow \begin{cases} 6x-2y=4 \\ 4x-3y=1 \end{cases}$

Multiply $6x-2y=4$ by 3 and $4x-3y=1$

42 Solutions Manual

by 2, and then subtract.
$\begin{cases}(6x-2y=4)\times 3 \\ (4x-3y=1)\times 2\end{cases} \Rightarrow \begin{cases}18x-6y=12 \\ 8x-6y=2\end{cases}$

$\begin{array}{r}|18x-6y=12 \\ -|\underline{8x-6y=2} \\ 10x\quad=10,\quad x=1\end{array}$

Substitute 1 for x in the second equation $8x-6y=2$.
$8(1)-6y=2$
$-6y=-6,\ y=1$

The solution is $(1,\ 1)$

(2) $\begin{cases}x+\dfrac{y-1}{3}=1 \\ \dfrac{2x+6}{5}-\dfrac{y+2}{2}=2\end{cases}$

$\Rightarrow \begin{cases}\left(x+\dfrac{y-1}{3}=1\right)\times 3 \\ \left(\dfrac{2x+6}{5}-\dfrac{y+2}{2}=2\right)\times 10\end{cases}$

$\Rightarrow \begin{cases}3x+(y-1)=3 \\ 2(2x+6)-5(y+2)=20\end{cases}$

$\Rightarrow \begin{cases}y=-3x+4 \\ 4x-5y=18\end{cases}$

Substitute $-3x+4$ for y in the second equation $4x-5y=18$.
$4x-5(-3x+4)=18$
$4x+15x-20=18$
$19x=38,\ x=2$

Substitute 2 for x in the equation $y=-3x+4$.
$y=-3(2)+4=-2$

The solution is $(2,\ -2)$

02

(1) $\begin{cases}0.2x-0.1y+0.5=1.2 \\ \dfrac{5x}{3}-\dfrac{y}{2}=\dfrac{11}{2}\end{cases}$

$\Rightarrow \begin{cases}(0.2x-0.1y+0.5=1.2)\times 10 \\ \left(\dfrac{5x}{3}-\dfrac{y}{2}=\dfrac{11}{2}\right)\times 6\end{cases}$

$\Rightarrow \begin{cases}2x-y+5=12 \\ 10x-3y=33\end{cases} \Rightarrow \begin{cases}y=2x-7 \\ 10x-3y=33\end{cases}$

Substitute $2x-7$ for y in the second equation $10x-3y=33$.
$10x-3(2x-7)=33$
$10x-6x+21=33$
$4x=12,\ x=3$

Substitute 3 for x in the equation $y=2x-7$.
$y=2(3)-7=-1$

The solution is $(3,\ -1)$

(2) $\begin{cases}3x-5=\dfrac{3(1-y)}{2}+x \\ 0.3y-0.2x=0.1\end{cases}$

$\Rightarrow \begin{cases}\left(3x-5=\dfrac{3(1-y)}{2}+x\right)\times 2 \\ (0.3y-0.2x=0.1)\times 10\end{cases}$

$\Rightarrow \begin{cases}6x-10=3-3y+2x \\ 3y-2x=1\end{cases} \Rightarrow \begin{cases}4x+3y=13 \\ -2x+3y=1\end{cases}$

Subtract the second equation from the first equation to eliminate y.

$\begin{array}{r}|4x+3y=13 \\ -|\underline{-2x+3y=1} \\ 6x\quad=12,\ x=2\end{array}$

Substitute 2 for x in the equation $-2x+3y=1$.
$-2(2)+3y=1$
$3y=5,\ y=\dfrac{5}{3}$

The solution is $\left(2,\ \dfrac{5}{3}\right)$

03

(1) $\begin{cases}\dfrac{6}{x}+\dfrac{5}{y}=7 \\ \dfrac{3}{x}-\dfrac{5}{y}=-4\end{cases}$

Let $\dfrac{1}{x}=A$ and $\dfrac{1}{y}=B$ $\begin{cases}6A+5B=7 \\ 3A-5B=-4\end{cases}$

Add two equations to eliminate B.

$\begin{array}{r}|6A+5B=7 \\ +|\underline{3A-5B=-4} \\ 9A\quad=3\end{array}$

$A=\dfrac{1}{3} \rightarrow \dfrac{1}{x}=\dfrac{1}{3}$

Solutions Manual

$x=3$

Substitute $\frac{1}{3}$ for A in the equation $6A+5B=7$.

$$6\left(\frac{1}{3}\right)+5B=7$$
$$5B=5$$
$$B=1 \rightarrow \frac{1}{y}=1$$
$$y=1$$

The solution is $(3, 1)$

(2) $\begin{cases}\frac{1}{2x}-\frac{1}{3y}=\frac{5}{36}\\ \frac{2}{5x}+\frac{3}{y}=\frac{6}{5}\end{cases}$

Let $\frac{1}{x}=A$ and $\frac{1}{y}=B$

$\begin{cases}\left(\frac{1}{2}A-\frac{1}{3}B=\frac{5}{36}\right)\times 36\\ \left(\frac{2}{5}A+3B=\frac{6}{5}\right)\times 5\end{cases}$

$\Rightarrow \begin{cases}18A-12B=5\\ (2A+15B=6)\times 9\end{cases} \Rightarrow \begin{cases}18A-12B=5\\ 18A+135B=54\end{cases}$

Subtract the second equation from the first equation to eliminate A.

$$\begin{array}{r}18A-12B=5\\ -\underline{18A+135B=54}\\ -147B=-49\end{array}$$

$B=\frac{1}{3} \rightarrow \frac{1}{y}=\frac{1}{3}$
$y=3$

Substitute $\frac{1}{3}$ for B in the equation $18A-12B=5$.

$$18A-12\left(\frac{1}{3}\right)=5$$
$$18A=9$$
$$A=\frac{1}{2} \rightarrow \frac{1}{x}=\frac{1}{2}$$
$$x=2$$

The solution is $(2, 3)$

04

From the equation $\frac{2x+y}{2}=1-2x=\frac{4y-2}{3}$, let the system be

$\begin{cases}\frac{2x+y}{2}=1-2x\\ \frac{4y-2}{3}=1-2x\end{cases} \Rightarrow \begin{cases}\left(\frac{2x+y}{2}=1-2x\right)\times 2\\ \left(\frac{4y-2}{3}=1-2x\right)\times 3\end{cases}$

$\Rightarrow \begin{cases}2x+y=2-4x\\ 4y-2=3-6x\end{cases}$

$\Rightarrow \begin{cases}y=-6x+2\\ 6x+4y=5\end{cases}$

Substitute $-6x+2$ for y in the equation $6x+4y=5$.

$$6x+4(-6x+2)=5$$
$$6x-24x+8=5$$
$$-18x=-3, \ x=\frac{-3}{-18}=\frac{1}{6}$$

Substitute $\frac{1}{6}$ for x in the equation $y=-6x+2$.

$$y=-6\left(\frac{1}{6}\right)+2=1$$

The solution is $\left(\frac{1}{6}, 1\right)$

05

From the equation $2x+y+7=x-3y=4x+5y+9$, let the system be

$\begin{cases}2x+y+7=x-3y\\ 4x+5y+9=x-3y\end{cases} \Rightarrow \begin{cases}x=-4y-7\\ 3x+8y=-9\end{cases}$

Substitute $-4y-7$ for x in the equation $3x+8y=-9$.

$$3(-4y-7)+8y=-9$$
$$-12y-21+8y=-9$$
$$-4y=12, \ y=-3$$

Substitute -3 for y in the equation $x=-4y-7$.

$$x=-4(-3)-7=5$$

Since the solution $(5, -3)$ satisfies the equation $3x-ay=7$, we have

$$3(5)-a(-3)=7$$
$$15+3a=7$$
$$3a=-8, \ a=-\frac{8}{3}$$

$$a=-\frac{8}{3}$$

06

Since two systems above have the same solution, we can find the solution (x, y) using the equation $5x+y=13$ and $2x-3y=-5$.

$$\begin{cases} 5x+y=13 \\ 2x-3y=-5 \end{cases} \rightarrow y=-5x+13$$

Substitute $-5x+13$ for y in the equation $2x-3y=-5$.

$$2x-3(-5x+13)=-5$$
$$2x+15x-39=-5$$
$$17x=34, \ x=2$$

Substitute 2 for x in the equation $y=-5x+13$.

$$y=-5(2)+13=3$$

Therefore, the solution for both systems is $(2, 3)$ and we can substitute this solution to the equation $4x-ay=7$ and $bx-4y=9$ to find a and b.

$$\begin{array}{ll} 4(2)-a(3)=7 & b(2)-4(3)=9 \\ 8-3a=7 & \text{and} \quad 2b-12=9 \\ -3a=-1 & 2b=21 \\ a=\dfrac{1}{3} & b=\dfrac{21}{2} \end{array}$$

$$a=\dfrac{1}{3} \text{ and } b=\dfrac{21}{2}$$

3. Application of Linear Systems

Check Point 1

Let x and y be the larger and smaller number, respectively. Then we have
$$x-y=13 \text{ and } 2x+(3y+1)=62$$

Now, solve the system $\begin{cases} x-y=13 \\ 2x+(3y+1)=62 \end{cases}$

$$\begin{cases} x-y=13 \\ 2x+(3y+1)=62 \end{cases} \Rightarrow \begin{cases} x=y+13 \\ 2x+3y=61 \end{cases}$$

Substitute $y+13$ for x in the second equation.

$$2(y+13)+3y=61$$
$$2y+26+3y=61$$
$$5y=35, \ y=7$$

Now, substitute 7 for y in the equation $x=y+13$.

$$x=(7)+13=20$$

Two numbers are 7 and 20.

Check Point 2

Let x and y be Jason and his daughter's current age, respectively. Then we have
$$x=3y \text{ and } x+7=2(y+7)+4$$

Now, solve the system $\begin{cases} x=3y \\ x+7=2(y+7)+4 \end{cases}$

$$\begin{cases} x=3y \\ x+7=2(y+7)+4 \end{cases} \Rightarrow \begin{cases} x=3y \\ x+7=2y+14+4 \end{cases}$$

$$\Rightarrow \begin{cases} x=3y \\ x=2y+11 \end{cases}$$

Substitute $3y$ for x in the second equation.

$$3y=2y+11$$
$$y=11$$

Then, $x=3(11)=33$.

Jason is now 33 years old and his daughter is now 11 years old.

Solutions Manual

Check Point 3

Let x and y be the number of dimes and quarters, respectively. Since \$3.35 is equal to 335 cents, we have
$x=2y+2$ and $10x+25y=335$.

Now, solve the system $\begin{cases} x=2y+2 \\ 10x+25y=335 \end{cases}$

$\begin{cases} x=2y+2 \\ 10x+25y=335 \end{cases} \Rightarrow \begin{cases} x=2y+2 \\ 2x+5y=67 \end{cases}$

Substitute $2y+2$ for x in the second equation.
$$2(2y+2)+5y=67$$
$$4y+4+5y=67$$
$$9y=63, \ y=7$$

Now, substitute 7 for y in the equation $x=2y+2$.
$$x=2(7)+2=16$$

There are 16 dimes and 7 quarters.

Check Point 4

Let x and y be the speed of the faster and slower car, respectively.

	Speed	Time	Distance
Faster	x	4	$4x$
Slower	y	4	$4y$

Since the difference in the speed of two cars is 5 miles per hour, we have $x-y=5$. Also, since two cars are 500 miles apart after 4 hours, we have $4x+4y=500$. Now, solve the system $\begin{cases} x-y=5 \\ 4x+4y=500 \end{cases}$.

$\begin{cases} x-y=5 \\ 4x+4y=500 \end{cases} \Rightarrow \begin{cases} x-y=5 \\ x+y=125 \end{cases}$

Add two equations to eliminate y and solve for x.

$\begin{array}{r} x-y=5 \\ +\underline{x+y=125} \\ 2x=130, \ x=65 \end{array}$

Substitute 65 for x in the first equation.
$$65-y=5$$
$$y=60$$

Two cars traveled at 65 and 60 miles per hour, respectively.

Check Point 5

Let x and y be the gallons of a 12% and 18% solution of boric acid, respectively.

	12%	18%	16%
Solution	x	y	12
Boric Acid	$0.12x$	$0.18y$	$0.16(x+y)$

We have the system be
$\begin{cases} x+y=12 \\ 0.12x+0.18y=0.16(x+y) \end{cases}$.

Now, solve the system.

$\begin{cases} x+y=12 \\ 0.12x+0.18y=0.16(x+y) \end{cases}$

$\Rightarrow \begin{cases} x+y=12 \\ 12x+18y=16(x+y) \end{cases}$

$\Rightarrow \begin{cases} x+y=12 \\ 12x+18y=16x+16y \end{cases}$

$\Rightarrow \begin{cases} x+y=12 \\ 2y=4x \ \rightarrow \ y=2x \end{cases}$

Substitute $2x$ for y in the first equation.
$$x+(2x)=12$$
$$3x=12, \ x=4$$

Now, substitute 4 for x in the equation $y=2x$.
$$y=2(4)=8$$

4 gallons of a 12% solution and 8 gallons of a 18% solution.

Check Point 6

Let x and y be the width and length of the original rectangle, respectively. Then we have $2x+2y=24$ and $2(3x)+2(2y)=2(24)+10$. Now, solve the system $\begin{cases} 2x+2y=24 \\ 2(3x)+2(2y)=2(24)+10 \end{cases}$.

$\begin{cases} 2x+2y=24 \\ 2(3x)+2(2y)=2(24)+10 \end{cases}$

$\begin{cases} x+y=12 \quad \rightarrow \quad y=-x+12 \\ 6x+4y=58 \end{cases}$

Substitute $-x+12$ for y in the second equation.
$$6x+4(-x+12)=58$$
$$6x-4x+48=58$$
$$2x=10, \; x=5$$

Now, substitute 5 for x in the equation
$$y=-x+12$$
$$y=-(5)+12=7$$

The width and length of the original rectangle is 5 feet and 7 feet, respectively.

Check Point 7

Let x and y be the amount in dollars invested in Bank M and K, respectively. Then we have $x=y+1000$ and $0.03x+0.025y=305$. Now, solve the system $\begin{cases} x=y+1000 \\ 0.03x+0.025y=305 \end{cases}$.

$\begin{cases} x=y+1000 \\ 0.03x+0.025y=305 \end{cases}$

$\Rightarrow \begin{cases} x=y+1000 \\ 30x+25y=305000 \end{cases}$

Substitute $y+1000$ for x in the second equation.
$$30(y+1000)+25y=305000$$
$$30y+30000+25y=305000$$
$$55y=275000, \; y=5000$$

Now, substitute 5000 for y in the equation $x=y+1000$.
$$x=5000+1000=6000$$

Ethan invested $6,000 in Bank M and $5,000 in Bank K.

Review Exercise

01

Let x and y be the larger and smaller integer, respectively. Then we have
$3x=2y+19$ and $x-y=2$.

Now, solve the system $\begin{cases} 3x=2y+19 \\ x-y=2 \end{cases}$.

$\begin{cases} 3x=2y+19 \\ x-y=2 \end{cases} \Rightarrow \begin{cases} 3x=2y+19 \\ x=y+2 \end{cases}$

Substitute $y+2$ for x in the first equation.
$$3(y+2)=2y+19$$
$$3y+6=2y+19$$
$$y=13$$

Now, substitute 13 for y in the equation $x=y+2$.
$$x=(13)+2=15$$

Two integers are 13 and 15

02

Let x and y be the number of dimes and quarters, respectively. Then we have
$x+y=50$ and $10x+25y=1055$.

Now, solve the system $\begin{cases} x+y=50 \\ 10x+25y=1055 \end{cases}$.

$\begin{cases} x+y=50 \\ 10x+25y=1055 \end{cases} \Rightarrow \begin{cases} y=-x+50 \\ 2x+5y=211 \end{cases}$

Substitute $-x+50$ for y in the second equation.
$$2x+5(-x+50)=211$$
$$2x-5x+250=211$$
$$-3x=-39, \; x=13$$

Jonathan has 13 dimes

Solutions Manual

03

Let x and y be the price of the shirt and a pair of pants, respectively. Then we have $x+y=76$ and $1.08x+1.05y=81$.

Now, solve the system $\begin{cases} x+y=76 \\ 1.08x+1.05y=81 \end{cases}$.

$\begin{cases} x+y=76 \\ 1.08x+1.05y=81 \end{cases} \Rightarrow \begin{cases} x=-y+76 \\ 108x+105y=8100 \end{cases}$

Substitute $-y+76$ for x in the second equation.

$108(-y+76)+105y=8100$
$-108y+8208+105y=8100$
$-3y=-108, \ y=36$

Now, Substitute 36 for y in the equation $x=-y+76$.

$x=-(36)+76=40$

The shirt is \$40 and the pair of pants is \$36.

04

Let x and y be the liters of a 20% and 35% saline solution, respectively.

	20%	35%	25%
Solution	x	y	8
Salt	$0.2x$	$0.35y$	$0.25(x+y)$

We have the system
$\begin{cases} x+y=8 \\ 0.2x+0.35y=0.25(x+y) \end{cases}$.

Now, solve the system.

$\begin{cases} x+y=8 \\ 0.2x+0.35y=0.25(x+y) \end{cases}$

$\Rightarrow \begin{cases} x+y=8 \\ 20x+35y=25(x+y) \end{cases}$

$\Rightarrow \begin{cases} x+y=8 \\ 20x+35y=25x+25y \end{cases}$

$\Rightarrow \begin{cases} x+y=8 \\ 10y=5x \ \rightarrow \ 2y=x \end{cases}$

Substitute $2y$ for x in the first equation.

$(2y)+y=8$
$3y=8, \ y=\dfrac{8}{3}$

Now, substitute $\dfrac{8}{3}$ for y in the equation $x=2y$.

$x=2\left(\dfrac{8}{3}\right)=\dfrac{16}{3}$

$\dfrac{16}{3}$ liters of a 20%−saline solution and $\dfrac{8}{3}$ liters of a 35%−saline solution

05

Let x and y be the price of a burger and a soft drink in dollars, respectively. Then we have

$4x+3y=26$ and $3x+6y=27$.

Now, solve the system $\begin{cases} 4x+3y=26 \\ 3x+6y=27 \end{cases}$.

Multiply first equation by 2 and then subtract.

$\begin{cases} (4x+3y=26)\cdot 2 \\ 3x+6y=27 \end{cases} \Rightarrow \begin{cases} 8x+6y=52 \\ 3x+6y=27 \end{cases}$

$\begin{array}{r} 8x+6y=52 \\ -\underline{3x+6y=27} \\ 5x \quad\quad =25, \ x=5 \end{array}$

Substitute 5 for x in the equation $3x+6y=27$.

$3(5)+6y=27$
$6y=12, \ y=2$

The burger is \$5 and the soft drink is \$2

06

Let x and y be the speed of the faster and slower car, respectively.

	Speed	Time	Distance
Faster	x	3	$3x$
Slower	y	3	$3y$

Since the difference in the speed of two cars is 8 miles per hour, we have $x-y=8$. Also, since two cars are 360 miles apart after 3 hours, we have $3x+3y=360$. Now, solve the system $\begin{cases} x-y=8 \\ 3x+3y=360 \end{cases}$

$\begin{cases} x-y=8 \\ 3x+3y=360 \end{cases} \Rightarrow \begin{cases} x-y=8 \\ x+y=120 \end{cases}$

Add two equations to eliminate y and solve for x.

$\begin{array}{r} x-y=8 \\ +\underline{x+y=120} \\ 2x=128, \quad x=64 \end{array}$

Substitute 64 for x in the first equation.
$64-y=8$
$y=56$

Two cars traveled at 64 and 56 miles per hour, respectively.

07

Let x and y be the number of packages with 12 buns and 8 buns, respectively. Then we have
$x+y=20$ and $12x+8y=188$.
Now, solve the system $\begin{cases} x+y=20 \\ 12x+8y=188 \end{cases}$ for y.

$\begin{cases} x+y=20 \\ 12x+8y=188 \end{cases} \Rightarrow \begin{cases} x=-y+20 \\ 3x+2y=47 \end{cases}$

Substitute $-y+20$ for x in the second equation.
$3(-y+20)+2y=47$
$-3y+60+2y=47$
$-y=-13, \quad y=13$

Mike ordered 13 packages of 8 buns

08

Let x and y be the number of tickets for adults and students, respectively. Then we have
$x+y=170$ and $15x+9y=2250$.
Now, solve the system $\begin{cases} x+y=170 \\ 15x+9y=2250 \end{cases}$ for x.

$\begin{cases} x+y=170 \\ 15x+9y=2250 \end{cases} \Rightarrow \begin{cases} y=-x+170 \\ 15x+9y=2250 \end{cases}$

Substitute $-x+170$ for y in the second equation.
$15x+9(-x+170)=2250$
$15x-9x+1530=2250$
$6x=720, \quad x=120$

120 adult tickets were sold

09

Let x and y be the age of Kevin and Paul, respectively. Then we have $x=y+22$. Since Kevin is twice as old as Paul in 7 year, we also have $x+7=2(y+7)$.

Now, solve the system $\begin{cases} x=y+22 \\ x+7=2(y+7) \end{cases}$ for y.

$\begin{cases} x=y+22 \\ x+7=2(y+7) \end{cases} \Rightarrow \begin{cases} x=y+22 \\ x+7=2y+14 \end{cases}$

$\Rightarrow \begin{cases} x=y+22 \\ x=2y+7 \end{cases}$

Substitute $y+22$ for x in the second equation.
$y+22=2y+7$
$-y=-15, \quad y=15$

Paul is 15 years old now

10

Let x and y be the number of dozen pencils and pens, respectively. Then we have
$x+y=8$ and $4.5x+6.5y=42$.
Now, solve the system $\begin{cases} x+y=8 \\ 4.5x+6.5y=42 \end{cases}$ for x.

$\begin{cases} x+y=8 \\ 4.5x+6.5y=42 \end{cases} \Rightarrow \begin{cases} x+y=8 \\ 45x+65y=420 \end{cases}$

$\Rightarrow \begin{cases} y=-x+8 \\ 9x+13y=84 \end{cases}$

Substitute $-x+8$ for y in the second equation.

Solutions Manual

$9x+13(-x+8)=84$
$9x-13x+104=84$
$-4x=-20$, $x=5$

5 dozens of pencils

11

Let x and y be the width and length of the original rectangle, respectively. Then we have $2x+2y=40$ and $2(2x)+2\left(\frac{1}{2}y\right)=\frac{1}{2}(40)+12$. Now, solve the system $\begin{cases} 2x+2y=40 \\ 2(2x)+2\left(\frac{1}{2}y\right)=\frac{1}{2}(40)+12 \end{cases}$.

$\begin{cases} 2x+2y=40 \\ 2(2x)+2\left(\frac{1}{2}y\right)=\frac{1}{2}(40)+12 \end{cases}$
$\Rightarrow \begin{cases} x+y=20 \\ 4x+y=32 \end{cases} \rightarrow y=-4x+32$

Substitute $-4x+32$ for y in the first equation.
$x+y=20$
$x+(-4x+32)=20$
$-3x=-12$, $x=4$

Now, substitute 4 for x in the equation $y=-4x+32$.
$y=-4(4)+32=16$.

Therefore, the area of the original rectangle is $A=xy=(4)(16)=64$.

$A=64$

Chapter 3 Test Level 1

01

(1) $\begin{cases} x=-2y-2 \\ 3x+5y=-3 \end{cases}$

Substitute $-2y-2$ for x in the second equation.
$3(-2y-2)+5y=-3$
$-6y-6+5y=-3$
$-y=3$, $y=-3$

Now, substitute -3 for y in the equation $x=-2y-2$.
$x=-2(-3)-2=4$

The solution is $(4, -3)$

(2) $\begin{cases} 2x-3y=6 \\ -4x+6y=12 \end{cases}$

Multiply $2x-3y=6$ by 2 and then add.
$\begin{cases} (2x-3y=6)\cdot 2 \\ -4x+6y=12 \end{cases} \Rightarrow \begin{array}{r} 4x-6y=12 \\ +\underline{-4x+6y=12} \\ 0x+0y=24 \end{array}$

The system has no solution.

(3) $\begin{cases} 2x-5y=1 \\ 3x-15y=3 \end{cases}$

Multiply $2x-5y=1$ by 3 and then subtract.
$\begin{cases} (2x-5y=1)\cdot 3 \\ 3x-15y=3 \end{cases} \Rightarrow \begin{array}{r} 6x-15y=3 \\ -\underline{3x-15y=3} \\ 3x=0 \\ x=0 \end{array}$

Substitute 0 for x in the equation $2x-5y=1$.
$2(0)-5y=1$
$-5y=1$, $y=-\frac{1}{5}$

The solution is $\left(0, -\frac{1}{5}\right)$

(4) $\begin{cases} 5x-y=5 \\ 6x-4y=-8 \end{cases}$

Solve the first equation for y.
$5x-y=5 \Rightarrow y=5x-5$

Substitute $5x-5$ for y in the second equation.

$$6x-4(5x-5)=-8$$
$$6x-20x+20=-8$$
$$-14x=-28,\ x=2$$

Now, substitute 2 for x in the equation $y=5x-5$.
$$y=5(2)-5=5$$

The solution is $(2, 5)$

02

Since $y=3$ is the solution to the system substitute 3 for y in the equation $5x-2y=-16$.
$$5x-2(3)=-16$$
$$5x=-10,\ x=-2$$

Now, substitute -2 for x and 3 for y in the equation $2kx+3y=1$ to find k.
$$2k(-2)+3(3)=1$$
$$-4k+9=1$$
$$-4k=-8,\ k=2$$

$k=2$

03

$$\begin{cases}(3x+4y=-2)\times 4\\(4x-2y=7)\times 3\end{cases} \Rightarrow \begin{cases}12x+16y=-8\\12x-6y=21\end{cases}$$

Now we can eliminate x by subtracting the second equation from the first. Therefore, we need to do $(1)\times 4-(2)\times 3$.

The answer is (D)

04

$$\begin{cases}x-4y=7\\8y=2x-15\end{cases} \Rightarrow \begin{cases}x-4y=7\\-2x+8y=-15\end{cases}$$

Since we have $\dfrac{1}{-2}=\dfrac{-4}{8}\neq \dfrac{7}{-15}$

from the system above, it has no solution. Therefore, the number of solution is zero.

The answer is (A)

05

If $(2, 1)$ is the solution to the equation, then we have

$$3a(2)-b(1)=a(2)-2b(1)-7=(2)+4(1)+1$$
$$6a-b=2a-2b-7 \qquad =7$$

Now, let the system be
$$\begin{cases}6a-b=7\\2a-2b-7=7\end{cases} \Rightarrow \begin{cases}-b=-6a+7\\2a-2b=14\end{cases}$$
$$\Rightarrow \begin{cases}b=6a-7\\a-b=7\end{cases}$$

Substitute $6a-7$ for b in the second equation $a-b=7$.
$$a-(6a-7)=7$$
$$a-6a+7=7$$
$$-5a=0,\ a=0$$

Substitute 0 for a in the equation $b=6a-7$.
$$b=6(0)-7=-7$$

Therefore, $a+b=0+(-7)=-7$

$a+b=-7$

06

If the system $\begin{cases}ax+2y=6\\8x-by=-12\end{cases}$ has infinitely many solutions, we must have
$$\dfrac{a}{8}=\dfrac{2}{-b}=\dfrac{6}{-12}.$$

$$\dfrac{a}{8}=\dfrac{6}{-12} \qquad \dfrac{2}{-b}=\dfrac{6}{-12}$$
$$-12a=48 \quad \text{and} \quad -24=-6b$$
$$a=-4 \qquad\qquad 4=b$$

$a=-4,\ b=4$

07

If the system $\begin{cases}kx+5y=12\\3x-2y=4\end{cases}$ has no solution, we must have $\dfrac{k}{3}=\dfrac{5}{-2}\neq \dfrac{12}{4}$.

$$\dfrac{k}{3}=\dfrac{5}{-2}$$
$$-2k=15,\ k=-\dfrac{15}{2}$$

$k=-\dfrac{15}{2}$

Solutions Manual

08

$\begin{cases} my - 12x = -21 \\ 4x - 3y = n \end{cases} \Rightarrow \begin{cases} -12x + my = -21 \\ 4x - 3y = n \end{cases}$

If the system has infinitely many solutions, we must have $\dfrac{-12}{4} = \dfrac{m}{-3} = \dfrac{-21}{n}$.

$\dfrac{-12}{4} = \dfrac{m}{-3}$ $\dfrac{-12}{4} = \dfrac{-21}{n}$

$36 = 4m$ and $-12n = -84$

$9 = m$ $n = \dfrac{-84}{-12} = 7$

$n = 7, \ m = 9$

09

Let x and y be the number of $5 bills and $10 bills, respectively. Then we have $x + y = 22$ and $5x + 10y = 155$.

Now, solve the system $\begin{cases} x + y = 22 \\ 5x + 10y = 155 \end{cases}$.

$\begin{cases} x + y = 22 \\ 5x + 10y = 155 \end{cases} \Rightarrow \begin{cases} x = -y + 22 \\ x + 2y = 31 \end{cases}$

Substitute $-y + 22$ for x in the second equation.

$(-y + 22) + 2y = 31$
$-y + 22 + 2y = 31$
$y = 9$

Now, substitute 9 for y in the equation $x = -y + 22$.

$x = -(9) + 22 = 13$

The number of $5 and $10 bills are 13 and 9.

10

1.5−liter is equal to 1500 milliliters. Let x and y be the liters of a 20% and 60% orange juice, respectively.

	20%	60%	35%
Juice	x	y	1500
Orange	$0.2x$	$0.6y$	$0.35(x+y)$

We have the system
$\begin{cases} x + y = 1500 \\ 0.2x + 0.6y = 0.35(x+y) \end{cases}$.

Now, solve the system.

$\begin{cases} x + y = 1500 \\ 0.2x + 0.6y = 0.35(x+y) \end{cases}$

$\Rightarrow \begin{cases} x + y = 1500 \\ 20x + 60y = 35(x+y) \end{cases}$

$\Rightarrow \begin{cases} x + y = 1500 \\ 20x + 60y = 35x + 35y \end{cases}$

$\Rightarrow \begin{cases} x + y = 1500 \\ 25y = 15x \end{cases} \Rightarrow \begin{cases} y = -x + 1500 \\ 5y = 3x \end{cases}$

Substitute $-y + 1500$ for x in the second equation.

$5y = 3(-y + 1500)$
$5y = -3y + 4500$
$8y = 4500, \ y = 562.5$

562.5 milliliters of a 60% orange juice.

011

Since the Celsius temperature is equal to 20% of the Fahrenheit temperature, we have $C = 0.2F$. Now, solve the system

$\begin{cases} F = \dfrac{9}{5}C + 32 \\ C = 0.2F \end{cases} \Rightarrow \begin{cases} F = \dfrac{9}{5}C + 32 \\ C = \dfrac{1}{5}F \end{cases}$

Substitute $\dfrac{1}{5}F$ for C in the first equation.

$F = \dfrac{9}{5}\left(\dfrac{1}{5}F\right) + 32$

$F = \dfrac{9}{25}F + 32$

$25F = 9F + 800$

$16F = 800, \ F = 50$

$F = 50$

Chapter 3 Test Level 2

01

$\begin{cases} 1.3x+y=0.7 \\ -0.02x-0.1y=0.04 \end{cases}$

$\begin{cases} (1.3x+y=0.7)\cdot 10 \\ (-0.02x-0.1y=0.04)\cdot 100 \end{cases}$

$\Rightarrow \begin{cases} 13x+10y=7 \\ -2x-10y=4 \end{cases}$

Add two equations to eliminate y.

$\begin{array}{r} 13x+10y=7 \\ +\underline{-2x-10y=4} \\ 11x=11, \quad x=1 \end{array}$

Now, substitute 1 for x in the equation $13x+10y=7$.

$13(1)+10y=7$

$10y=-6, \quad y=\dfrac{-6}{10}=-\dfrac{3}{5}$

Therefore, $x+y=1+\left(-\dfrac{3}{5}\right)=\dfrac{2}{5}$.

$$x+y=\dfrac{2}{5}$$

02

Substitute 1 for x and 2 for y in the system $\begin{cases} x+ay=-3 \\ 3x+by=5 \end{cases}$.

$\begin{cases} (1)+a(2)=-3 \\ 3(1)+b(2)=5 \end{cases} \Rightarrow \begin{cases} 1+2a=-3 \\ 3+2b=5 \end{cases}$

$\Rightarrow \begin{cases} 2a=-4 \\ 2b=2 \end{cases} \Rightarrow \begin{cases} a=-2 \\ b=1 \end{cases}$

Therefore, $a=-2b$.

The answer is (D)

03

$x=2y+1$

Substitute $2y+1$ for x in the second equation of the system $2x+6y=-8$.

$2(2y+1)+6y=-8$

$4y+2+6y=-8$

$10y=-10, \quad y=-1$

$\Rightarrow x=2y+1=2(-1)+1=-1$

Now, substitute -1 for x and y in the equation $4x-5y=c$ to find c.

$4(-1)-5(-1)=c$

$-4+5=c, \quad c=1$

$$c=1$$

04

In the system $\begin{cases} x+2y=k+2 \\ 2x-y=k \end{cases}$, substitute $2x-y$ for k in the first equation $x+2y=k+2$.

$x+2y=2x-y+2$

$3y=x+2$

Since $x+y=10 \Rightarrow x=-y+10$, substitute $-y+10$ for x in the equation $3y=x+2$.

$3y=-y+10+2$

$4y=12, \quad y=3$

$\Rightarrow x=-y+10=-(3)+10=7$

Now, substitute 7 for x and 3 for y in the equation $2x-y=k$.

$2(7)-(3)=k$

$11=k$

$$k=11$$

05

If the solution of $\begin{cases} kx+0.5y=13 \\ \dfrac{5}{6}x+\dfrac{3}{2}y=8 \end{cases}$ satisfies the equation $x-2y=2$, we can solve the system $\begin{cases} x-2y=2 \\ \dfrac{5}{6}x+\dfrac{3}{2}y=8 \end{cases}$.

$\begin{cases} x-2y=2 \\ \left(\dfrac{5}{6}x+\dfrac{3}{2}y=8\right)\cdot 6 \end{cases} \Rightarrow \begin{cases} x=2y+2 \\ 5x+9y=48 \end{cases}$

Substitute $2y+2$ for x in the equation $5x+9y=48$.

$5(2y+2)+9y=48$

$10y+10+9y=48$

$19y=38, \quad y=2$

$\Rightarrow x=2y+2=2(2)+2=6$

Now, substitute 6 for x and 2 for y in the equation $kx+0.5y=13$.

Solutions Manual

$$k(6)+0.5(2)=13$$
$$6k+1=13$$
$$6k=12,\ k=2$$

$$k=2$$

06

Both expressions are equal to 123, so set them equal to each other.
$$15x-28y=13x-27y$$
$$2x=y$$

Now, substitute $2x$ for y in the equation $15x-28y=123$.
$$15x-28(2x)=123$$
$$15x-56x=123$$
$$-41x=123,\ x=-3$$
$$\Rightarrow y=2x=2(-3)=-6$$

The solution is $(-3,-6)$

07

Since two systems have the same solution, we can find the solution (x, y) using the equation $3x-y=11$ and $2x-y=7$.
Subtract $2x-y=7$ from $3x-y=11$.

$$\begin{array}{r} 3x-y=11 \\ -\underline{2x-y=7} \\ x=4 \end{array}$$

Substitute 4 for x in the equation $3x-y=11$.
$$3(4)-y=11$$
$$-y=-1,\ y=1$$

Now, substitute 4 for x and 1 for y in the equation $\frac{a}{2}x-by=1$ and $ax-\frac{5b}{3}y=3$, and solve the system.

$$\begin{cases} a(4)-\frac{5b}{3}(1)=3 \\ \frac{a}{2}(4)-b(1)=1 \end{cases} \Rightarrow \begin{cases} 4a-\frac{5b}{3}=3 \\ 2a-b=1 \to b=2a-1 \end{cases}$$

Substitute $2a-1$ for b in the equation $4a-\frac{5b}{3}=3$.
$$4a-\frac{5(2a-1)}{3}=3$$

$$12a-5(2a-1)=9$$
$$12a-10a+5=9$$
$$2a=4,\ a=2$$
$$\Rightarrow b=2a-1=2(2)-1=3$$
Therefore, $a+b=2+3=5$.

$$a+b=5$$

08

If the system $\begin{cases} 2x+6y=a \\ 3x-by=6 \end{cases}$ has no solution, we must have $\frac{2}{3}=\frac{6}{-b}\neq\frac{a}{6}$.

$$\frac{2}{3}=\frac{6}{-b} \qquad \frac{2}{3}\neq\frac{a}{6}$$
$$-2b=18 \quad \text{and} \quad 12\neq 3a$$
$$b=-9 \qquad 4\neq a$$

The answer is (A)

09

Let $\sqrt{x}=A$ and $\sqrt{y}=B$. Then we have
$$\begin{cases} A+2B=12 \\ 4A-3B=4 \end{cases} \Rightarrow \begin{cases} A=-2B+12 \\ 4A-3B=4 \end{cases}$$

Substitute $-2B+12$ for A in the equation $4A-3B=4$.
$$4(-2B+12)-3B=4$$
$$-8B+48-3B=4$$
$$-11B=-44$$
$$B=4 \Rightarrow \sqrt{y}=4,\ y=16$$

Now, substitute 4 for B in the equation $A=-2B+12$.
$$A=-2(4)+12=4$$
$$\Rightarrow \sqrt{x}=4,\ x=16$$

$$x=16,\ y=16$$

10

Create a table as shown below.

	10-inch	8-inch	Total
Black	90	b	150
White	a	x	50
Total	0.6(200)	0.4(200)	200

$90+b=150$, $b=60$

$b+x=0.4(200)$

$60+x=80$, $x=20$

Therefore, there are 20 of 8-inch white tablet PCs.

11

Let x and y be the amount in pounds of pork and salmon, respectively. Then we have $x=2y$. Also, let p and s be the price of pork and salmon per pound respectively. Then we have $s=1.5p$. The total price John spend on park is px and on salmon is sy. Since he spend a $8.4 for pork and salmon, we have

$px+sy=8.4$

Now, substitute $1.5p$ for s and $0.5x$ for y.

$px+(1.5p)(0.5x)=8.4$

$(px+(1.5p)(0.5x)=8.4)\cdot 100$

$100px+75px=840$

$175px=840$

$px=\dfrac{840}{175}=\dfrac{24}{5}=4.8$

Therefore, John spent $4.8 on pork.

Solutions Manual

Chapter 4: Linear Inequalities

1. Solving Linear Inequalities, Part 1

Check Point 1

① $3x-2 \geq 16$
$3x \geq 18$
$x \geq 6 \qquad \Rightarrow [6, \infty)$

② $x-3 < -15+4x$
$-3x-3 < -15$
$-3x < -12$
$x > 4 \qquad \Rightarrow (4, \infty)$

③ $4x-1 \leq 9-x$
$5x-1 \leq 9$
$5x \leq 10$
$x \leq 2 \qquad \Rightarrow (-\infty, 2]$

④ $\frac{1}{3}x - \frac{1}{2} < -\frac{4}{3}x + 7$
$\frac{5}{3}x - \frac{1}{2} < 7$
$\frac{5}{3}x < \frac{15}{2}$
$x < \frac{9}{2} \qquad \Rightarrow \left(-\infty, \frac{9}{2}\right)$

Check Point 2

① $4-12x \geq 2(x+6)$
$4-12x \geq 2x+12$
$4-14x \geq 12$
$-14x \geq 8$
$x \leq -\frac{4}{7} \qquad \Rightarrow \left(-\infty, -\frac{4}{7}\right]$

② $3(x-2) > 4x-3(2x+1)$
$3x-6 > 4x-6x-3$
$3x-6 > -2x-3$
$5x-6 > -3$
$5x > 3$
$x > \frac{3}{5} \qquad \Rightarrow \left(\frac{3}{5}, \infty\right)$

③ $\frac{2x-4}{3}+2 \leq 3x-11$
$\left(\frac{2x-4}{3}+2\right) \cdot 3 \leq (3x-11) \cdot 3$
$2x-4+6 \leq 9x-33$
$2x+2 \leq 9x-33$
$-7x+2 \leq -33$
$-7x \leq -35$
$x \geq 5 \qquad \Rightarrow [5, \infty)$

④ $1.2x-4.8 < -0.6x+2.4$
$(1.2x-4.8) \cdot 10 < (-0.6x+2.4) \cdot 10$
$12x-48 < -6x+24$
$18x-48 < 24$
$18x < 72$
$x < 4 \qquad \Rightarrow (\infty, 4)$

Review Exercise

01

(1) $5x < 3x-12$
$2x < -12$
$x < -6 \qquad \Rightarrow (-\infty, -6)$

(2) $3x+4 > 2x-8$
$x+4 > -8$
$x > -12 \qquad \Rightarrow (-12, \infty)$

(3) $-8-4x \geq x-23$
$-8-5x \geq -23$
$-5x \geq -15$
$x \leq 3 \qquad \Rightarrow (-\infty, 3]$

(4) $13x-8 \leq 32-7x$
$20x-8 \leq 32$
$20x \leq 40$
$x \leq 2 \qquad \Rightarrow (-\infty, 2]$

02

(1) $2(x-4) < -3x+7$
$2x-8 < -3x+7$
$5x-8 < 7$
$5x < 15$
$x < 3 \quad \Rightarrow (-\infty, 3)$

(2) $-3x+5 > 4(x-3)+7$
$-3x+5 > 4x-12+7$
$-3x+5 > 4x-5$
$-7x+5 > -5$
$-7x > -10$
$x < \dfrac{10}{7} \quad \Rightarrow \left(-\infty, \dfrac{10}{7}\right)$

(3) $5(3x-1)+4 < 4(5x+1)$
$15x-5+4 < 20x+4$
$15x-1 < 20x+4$
$-5x-1 < 4$
$-5x < 5$
$x > -1 \quad \Rightarrow (-1, \infty)$

(4) $2x-6(3-x) \geq 3(x+2)$
$2x-18+6x \geq 3x+6$
$8x-18 \geq 3x+6$
$5x-18 \geq 6$
$5x \geq 24$
$x \geq \dfrac{24}{5} \quad \Rightarrow \left[\dfrac{24}{5}, \infty\right)$

03

(1) $3 - \dfrac{x-2}{4} > 3x+1$
$\left(3 - \dfrac{x-2}{4}\right) \cdot 4 > (3x+1) \cdot 4$
$12 - (x-2) > 12x+4$
$14 - x > 12x+4$
$14 - 13x > 4$
$-13x > -10$
$x < \dfrac{10}{13} \quad \Rightarrow \left(-\infty, \dfrac{10}{13}\right)$

(2) $\dfrac{x+1}{2} + \dfrac{x-1}{3} \leq \dfrac{2x+1}{6}$
$\left(\dfrac{x+1}{2} + \dfrac{x-1}{3}\right) \cdot 6 \leq \dfrac{2x+1}{6} \cdot 6$
$3(x+1) + 2(x-1) \leq 2x+1$
$3x+3+2x-2 \leq 2x+1$
$5x+1 \leq 2x+1$
$3x+1 \leq 1$
$3x \leq 0$
$x \leq 0 \quad \Rightarrow (-\infty, 0]$

(3) $2 + \dfrac{x-2}{2} \geq \dfrac{x+2}{10} - \dfrac{3}{5}$
$\left(2 + \dfrac{x-2}{2}\right) \cdot 10 \geq \left(\dfrac{x+2}{10} - \dfrac{3}{5}\right) \cdot 10$
$20 + 5(x-2) \geq (x+2) - 6$
$20 + 5x - 10 \geq x + 2 - 6$
$5x + 10 \geq x - 4$
$4x + 10 \geq -4$
$4x \geq -14$
$x \geq -\dfrac{7}{2} \quad \Rightarrow \left[-\dfrac{7}{2}, \infty\right)$

(4) $\dfrac{2}{3}x - \dfrac{5}{2} > \dfrac{7}{3} - \dfrac{1}{4}x$
$\left(\dfrac{2}{3}x - \dfrac{5}{2}\right) \cdot 12 > \left(\dfrac{7}{3} - \dfrac{1}{4}x\right) \cdot 12$
$8x - 30 > 28 - 3x$
$11x - 30 > 28$
$11x > 58$
$x > \dfrac{58}{11} \quad \Rightarrow \left(\dfrac{58}{11}, \infty\right)$

04

(1) $0.4x + 0.6 > 0.8x - 1$
$(0.4x + 0.6) \cdot 10 > (0.8x - 1) \cdot 10$
$4x + 6 > 8x - 10$
$-4x + 6 > -10$
$-4x > -16$
$x < 4 \quad \Rightarrow (-\infty, 4)$

(2) $0.5(3x-1) \geq \dfrac{x-4}{5} + 0.4$
$(0.5(3x-1)) \cdot 10 \geq \left(\dfrac{x-4}{5} + 0.4\right) \cdot 10$
$5(3x-1) \geq 2(x-4) + 4$
$15x - 5 \geq 2x - 8 + 4$
$15x - 5 \geq 2x - 4$
$13x - 5 \geq -4$
$13x \geq 1$
$x \geq \dfrac{1}{13} \quad \Rightarrow \left[\dfrac{1}{13}, \infty\right)$

Solutions Manual

05

$3x-5 \geq -2(4-x)+1$
$3x-5 \geq -8+2x+1$
$3x-5 \geq 2x-7$
$x-5 \geq -7$
$x \geq -2 \quad \Rightarrow [-2, \infty)$

$\longleftrightarrow$ -5 -4 -3 -2 -1 0 1 2 3 4 5

Therefore, the answer is (A).

06

$ax-2a < 5$
$ax < 2a+5$

Since $a<0$, dividing both sides by a changes the direction of the inequality sign. Therefore, we have $x > \frac{2a+5}{a}$.

$$x > \frac{2a+5}{a}$$

07

$4(2-y) \leq 3y - \frac{1}{3}(y+6)$
$8-4y \leq 3y - \frac{1}{3}y - 2$
$8-4y \leq \frac{8}{3}y - 2$
$8 - \frac{20}{3}y \leq -2$
$-\frac{20}{3}y \leq -10$
$y \geq \frac{3}{2} \quad \Rightarrow \left[\frac{3}{2}, \infty\right)$

The smallest possible value of $2y+1$ is when $y=\frac{3}{2}$. Therefore, the answer is

$2y+1 = 2\left(\frac{3}{2}\right)+1 = 3+1 = 4.$

$$2y+1 = 4$$

2. Solving Linear Inequalities, Part 2

Check Point 1

① $-4 < 3x-6 < 9$
$2 < 3x < 15$
$\frac{2}{3} < x < 5$

$\frac{2}{3} < x < 5 \Rightarrow \left(\frac{2}{3}, 5\right)$

② $3 \leq \frac{1}{2} - \frac{3}{2}x \leq 8$
$(3)\cdot 2 \leq \left(\frac{1}{2} - \frac{3}{2}x\right)\cdot 2 \leq (8)\cdot 2$
$6 \leq 1-3x \leq 16$
$5 \leq -3x \leq 15$
$-\frac{5}{3} \geq x \geq -5$

$-5 \leq x \leq -\frac{5}{3} \Rightarrow \left[-5, -\frac{5}{3}\right]$

③ $\frac{2-x}{3} > 2 \quad$ or $\quad 2x-5 > 9$

$\left(\frac{2-x}{3}\right)\cdot 3 > (2)\cdot 3$
$2-x > 6 \quad$ or $\quad 2x > 14$
$-x > 4 \qquad\qquad\quad x > 7$
$x < -4$

$x < -4$ or $x > 7 \Rightarrow (-\infty, -4) \cup (7, \infty)$

④ $\frac{3}{5}x+2 \leq x - \frac{5}{2} \quad$ or $\quad -7-2x \geq 2$
$\left(\frac{3}{5}x+2\right)\cdot 10 \leq \left(x - \frac{5}{2}\right)\cdot 10$
$6x+20 \leq 10x-25$
$-4x+20 \leq -25 \qquad\quad -7-2x \geq 2$
$-4x \leq -45 \qquad\qquad\quad\; -2x \geq 9$
$x \geq \frac{45}{4} \qquad\qquad\qquad\quad x \leq -\frac{9}{2}$

$x \leq -\frac{9}{2}$ or $x \geq \frac{45}{4}$

$\Rightarrow \left(-\infty, -\frac{9}{2}\right] \cup \left[\frac{45}{4}, \infty\right)$

Check Point 2

① $|2x+5| \leq 13$
$-13 \leq 2x+5 \leq 13$

$$-18 \leq 2x \leq 8$$
$$-9 \leq x \leq 4$$
$$-9 \leq x \leq 4 \Rightarrow [-9, 4]$$

② $|4-3x| \geq 11$

$$4-3x \leq -11 \quad\quad 4-3x \geq 11$$
$$-3x \leq -15 \text{ or } \quad -3x \geq 7$$
$$x \geq 5 \text{ or } \quad\quad x \leq -\frac{7}{3}$$

$$x \leq -\frac{7}{3} \text{ or } x \geq 5 \Rightarrow \left(-\infty, -\frac{7}{3}\right] \cup [5, \infty)$$

③ $\left|\frac{1}{2}x-1\right| - 4 < 4$

$$\left|\frac{1}{2}x-1\right| < 8$$
$$-8 < \frac{1}{2}x-1 < 8$$
$$(-8) \cdot 2 < \left(\frac{1}{2}x-1\right) \cdot 2 < (8) \cdot 2$$
$$-16 < x-2 < 16$$
$$-14 < x < 18$$

$$-14 < x < 18 \Rightarrow (-14, 18)$$

④ $6 + \frac{1}{4}|3x+2| \geq 31$

$$\frac{1}{4}|3x+2| \geq 25$$
$$|3x+2| \geq 100$$

$$3x+2 \leq -100 \quad\quad 3x+2 \geq 100$$
$$3x \leq -102 \quad \text{or} \quad 3x \geq 98$$
$$x \leq -34 \quad\quad\quad x \geq \frac{98}{3}$$

$$x \leq -34 \text{ or } x \geq \frac{98}{3}$$
$$\Rightarrow (-\infty, -34] \cup \left[\frac{98}{3}, \infty\right)$$

Review Exercise

01

(1) $8 < 2x - 4 < 14$
$$12 < 2x < 18$$
$$6 < x < 9$$
$$6 < x < 9 \Rightarrow (6, 9)$$

(2) $-8 \leq 6 - x \leq -4$
$$-14 \leq -x \leq -10$$
$$14 \geq x \geq 10$$
$$10 \leq x \leq 14 \Rightarrow [10, 14]$$

(3) $-4 \leq \frac{4x-2}{3} \leq 1$
$$-12 \leq 4x-2 \leq 3$$
$$-10 \leq 4x \leq 5$$
$$-\frac{5}{2} \leq x \leq \frac{5}{4}$$
$$-\frac{5}{2} \leq x \leq \frac{5}{4} \Rightarrow \left[-\frac{5}{2}, \frac{5}{4}\right]$$

(4) $-4 \leq 2(3-x) < 10$
$$-4 \leq 6-2x < 10$$
$$-10 \leq -2x < 4$$
$$5 \geq x > -2$$
$$-2 < x \leq 5 \Rightarrow (-2, 5]$$

02

(1) $x - 3 > 9$ or $2x + 5 < -3$
$$\quad\quad\quad\quad\quad 2x < -8$$
$$x > 12 \text{ or } \quad x < -4$$
$$(-\infty, -4) \cup (12, \infty)$$

(2) $4x - 9 \geq -1$ or $\frac{1}{2}x - 3 \leq -3$
$$4x \geq 8 \quad\quad\quad \frac{1}{2}x \leq 0$$
$$\quad\quad\text{ or }$$
$$x \geq 2 \quad\quad\quad\quad x \leq 0$$
$$x \leq 0 \text{ or } x \geq 2 \Rightarrow (-\infty, 0] \cup [2, \infty)$$

(3) $4 - x < \frac{1}{3}$ or $\frac{3-x}{2} - \frac{5}{3} \geq \frac{4}{3}$

$$(4-x) \cdot 3 < \left(\frac{1}{3}\right) \cdot 3 \quad\quad \left(\frac{3-x}{2} - \frac{5}{3}\right) \cdot 6 \geq \left(\frac{4}{3}\right) \cdot 6$$
$$12 - 3x < 1 \quad\quad\quad\quad 3(3-x) - 10 \geq 8$$
$$\quad\quad\quad\quad\quad \text{or} \quad\quad 9 - 3x - 10 \geq 8$$
$$-3x < -11 \quad\quad\quad\quad -3x - 1 \geq 8$$
$$x > \frac{11}{3} \quad\quad\quad\quad\quad\quad -3x \geq 9$$
$$\quad\quad\quad\quad\quad\quad\quad\quad\quad\quad x \leq -3$$

$$x \leq -3 \text{ or } x > \frac{11}{3} \Rightarrow (-\infty, -3] \cup \left(\frac{11}{3}, \infty\right)$$

(4) $\frac{x-3}{6} + 1 \geq x$ or $\frac{x-6}{3} - x \geq 4$

$$\left(\frac{x-3}{6} + 1\right) \cdot 6 \geq (x) \cdot 6 \quad\quad \left(\frac{x-6}{3} - x\right) \cdot 3 \geq (4) \cdot 3$$
$$x - 3 + 6 \geq 6x \quad\quad\quad\quad x - 6 - 3x \geq 12$$
$$x + 3 \geq 6x \quad\quad \text{or} \quad\quad -6 - 2x \geq 12$$

Solutions Manual

$$3 \geq 5x \qquad\qquad -2x \geq 18$$
$$\frac{3}{5} \geq x \qquad\qquad x \leq -9$$

$$x \leq \frac{3}{5} \Rightarrow \left(-\infty, \frac{3}{5}\right]$$

03

(1) $\quad -3 < \dfrac{3x+4}{3} - \dfrac{x-3}{2} \leq 2$

$\quad (-3)\cdot 6 < \left(\dfrac{3x+4}{3} - \dfrac{x-3}{2}\right)\cdot 6 \leq (2)\cdot 6$

$\quad -18 < 2(3x+4) - 3(x-3) \leq 12$
$\quad -18 < \quad 6x+8-3x+9 \quad \leq 12$
$\quad -18 < \qquad 3x+17 \qquad \leq 12$
$\quad -35 < \qquad 3x \qquad\qquad \leq -5$
$\quad -\dfrac{35}{3} < \qquad x \qquad\qquad \leq -\dfrac{5}{3}$

$\quad -\dfrac{35}{3} < x \leq -\dfrac{5}{3} \Rightarrow \left(-\dfrac{35}{3}, -\dfrac{5}{3}\right]$

(2) $-2 < x-4 < 3$ or $-5 \leq 5x-8 \leq 12$
$\quad 2 < x < 7 \qquad\qquad 3 \leq 5x \leq 20$
$\qquad\qquad\qquad\qquad\quad \dfrac{3}{5} \leq x \leq 4$

$\dfrac{3}{5} \leq x < 7 \Rightarrow \left[\dfrac{3}{5}, 7\right)$

04

(1) $|2x-5| > 8$
$\quad 2x-5 < -8$ or $2x-5 > 8$
$\quad 2x < -3 \qquad\quad 2x > 13$
$\quad x < -\dfrac{3}{2} \qquad\quad x > \dfrac{13}{2}$

$\qquad x < -\dfrac{3}{2}$ or $x > \dfrac{13}{2}$
$\Rightarrow \left(-\infty, -\dfrac{3}{2}\right) \cup \left(\dfrac{13}{2}, \infty\right)$

(2) $|4x+1| - 1 \leq 2$
$\quad |4x+1| \leq 3$
$\quad -3 \leq 4x+1 \leq 3$
$\quad -4 \leq 4x \leq 2$

$\quad -1 \leq x \leq \dfrac{1}{2}$

$-1 \leq x \leq \dfrac{1}{2} \Rightarrow \left[-1, \dfrac{1}{2}\right]$

(3) $\dfrac{|x-2|}{2} + 2 < 8$

$\quad \dfrac{|x-2|}{2} < 6$

$\quad |x-2| < 12$
$\quad -12 < x-2 < 12$
$\quad -10 < \quad x \quad < 14$

$\qquad\qquad -10 < x < 14 \Rightarrow (-10, 14)$

(4) $\dfrac{3|5x+1|}{2} - 2 \geq 7$

$\quad \dfrac{3|5x+1|}{2} \geq 9$

$\quad 3|5x+1| \geq 18$
$\quad |5x+1| \geq 6$
$\quad 5x+1 \leq -6 \qquad\qquad 5x+1 \geq 6$
$\quad 5x \leq -7 \quad$ or $\quad 5x \geq 5$
$\quad x \leq -\dfrac{7}{5} \qquad\qquad\quad x \geq 1$

$x \leq -\dfrac{7}{5}$ or $x \geq 1 \Rightarrow \left(-\infty, -\dfrac{7}{5}\right] \cup [1, \infty)$

05

$1 < |x| < 6 \rightarrow 1 < |x|$ and $|x| < 6$
$1 < |x| \rightarrow x > 1$ or $x < -1$
$\qquad \Rightarrow (-\infty, -1) \cup (1, \infty)$
$|x| < 6 \rightarrow -6 < x < 6$
$\qquad \Rightarrow (-6, 6)$

Therefore, the solution for $1 < |x|$ and $|x| < 6$ is the intersection of two solutions as shown below.

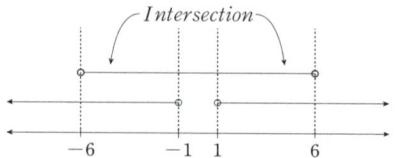

The solution is $-6 < x < -1$ or $1 < x < 6$.
$\Rightarrow (-6, -1) \cup (1, 6)$

06

$|2x-1|+2=1$
$|2x-1|=-1$

Since $|2x-1|\geq 0$, there is no x value such that $|2x-1|=-1$.

The answer is (E)

07

$2x-1<7$ $2-3x<11$
$2x<8$ and $-3x<9$
$x<4$ $x>-3$

The solution to the inequality is $-3<x<4$. Therefore, the number of integer values of x is 6 ($-2, -1, 0, 1, 2, 3$).

6 integer values of x

3. Graphing Linear Inequality

Check Point 1

① $y>\frac{1}{2}x-2$

Graph $y=\frac{1}{2}x-2$ as a dotted line and then shade the area above the line.

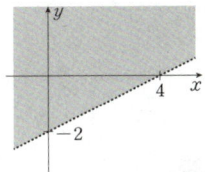

② $2x+4y\leq 6$

First, rearrange the equation for y.
$2x+4y\leq 6$
$4y\leq -2x+6$
$y\leq -\frac{1}{2}x+\frac{3}{2}$

Now, graph $y=-\frac{1}{2}x+\frac{3}{2}$ as a solid line and then shade the area below the line.

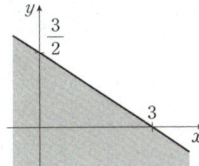

Check Point 2

The solution to the system is the region where the shadings from each inequality overlap one another.

① $\begin{cases} y<\frac{6}{5}x+3 \\ y\geq -3x-6 \end{cases}$

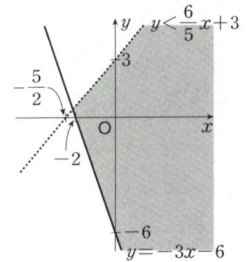

Solutions Manual

② $\begin{cases} y < \frac{1}{2}x+2 \\ y \geq x-1 \end{cases}$

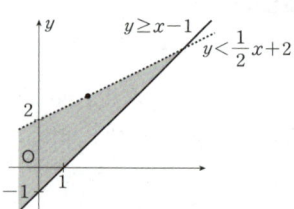

Review Exercise

01

(1) $y \geq -2x+1$

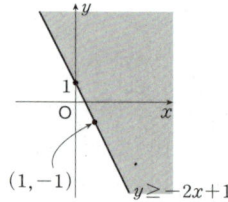

(2) $y < \frac{1}{2}x-1$

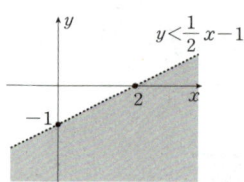

(3) $3x+2y \leq 4$
$2y \leq -3x+4$
$y \leq -\frac{3}{2}x+2$

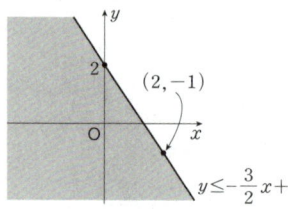

(4) $2x-3y < 6$
$-3y < -2x+6$
$y > \frac{2}{3}x-2$

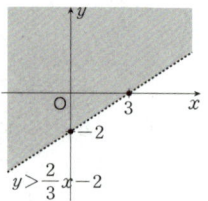

02

(1) The equation of the line is $y=2$.
Since the region of the solution is above the solid line, $y \geq 2$.

$$y \geq 2$$

(2) The line passes through two points, $(1, 0)$ and $(0, -3)$. So the equation of the line is $y=3x-3$. Since the region of the solution is below the solid line, $y \leq 3x-3$.

$$y \leq 3x-3$$

03

(1) $\begin{cases} y < -x+2 \\ y \geq \frac{1}{3}x-2 \end{cases}$

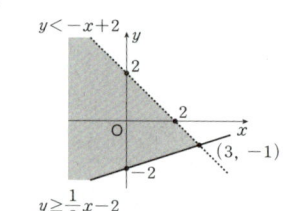

(2) $\begin{cases} 2x-y \leq 3 \\ x+3y \geq -2 \end{cases} \Rightarrow \begin{cases} -y \leq -2x+3 \\ 3y \geq -x-2 \end{cases}$

$\Rightarrow \begin{cases} y \geq 2x-3 \\ y \geq -\frac{1}{3}x - \frac{2}{3} \end{cases}$

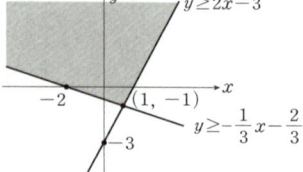

62 Solutions Manual

04

(1) The equation of the solid vertical line is $x=-1$. Since the right side of the region is shaded, $x \geq -1$. The other line passes through two points, $(-1, -2)$ and $(0, 0)$. So the equation is $y=2x$. Since the shaded region is above the solid line, $y \geq 2x$. Therefore,

the system of inequalities is $\begin{cases} x \geq -1 \\ y \geq 2x \end{cases}$.

$$\begin{cases} x \geq -1 \\ y \geq 2x \end{cases}$$

(2) Since the dotted line on the left passes through the points $(-2, 2)$ and $(0, -1)$, the equation is $y=\frac{-3}{2}x-1$. Also, since the dotted line on the right passes through the points $(1, 0)$ and $(0, -1)$, the equation is $y=x-1$. To have a solution region shown on the graph, the system of inequalities must be $\begin{cases} y<\frac{-3}{2}x-1 \\ y<x-1 \end{cases}$.

$$\begin{cases} y<\frac{-3}{2}x-1 \\ y<x-1 \end{cases}$$

05

If the point is in the solution region of the system of inequalities, the assigned point satisfies the system.

(A) $\begin{cases} 2(1)-3(2)>-1 \\ -(1)+5(2) \leq 3 \end{cases} \Rightarrow \begin{cases} -4 \not> -1 \\ 9 \not\leq 3 \end{cases}$

(B) $\begin{cases} 2(1)-3(-2)>-1 \\ -(1)+5(-2) \leq 3 \end{cases} \Rightarrow \begin{cases} 8>-1 \\ -11 \leq 3 \end{cases}$

(C) $\begin{cases} 2(-1)-3(-2)>-1 \\ -(-1)+5(-2) \leq 3 \end{cases} \Rightarrow \begin{cases} 4>-1 \\ -9 \leq 3 \end{cases}$

(D) $\begin{cases} 2(2)-3(1)>-1 \\ -(2)+5(1) \leq 3 \end{cases} \Rightarrow \begin{cases} 1>-1 \\ 3 \leq 3 \end{cases}$

(E) $\begin{cases} 2(2)-3(-1)>-1 \\ -(2)+5(-1) \leq 3 \end{cases} \Rightarrow \begin{cases} 7>-1 \\ -7 \leq 3 \end{cases}$

The answer is (A)

06

$\begin{cases} y \geq -2 \\ x \geq 1 \\ 2x+y \leq 6 \end{cases} \Rightarrow \begin{cases} y \geq -2 \\ x \geq 1 \\ y \leq -2x+6 \end{cases}$

The intersection of $y=-2$ and $y=-2x+6$ is

$-2x+6=-2$
$-2x=-8, \quad x=4$
$\Rightarrow (4, -2)$

The intersection of $x=1$ and $y=-2x+6$ is
$y=-2(1)+6=4$
$\Rightarrow (1, 4)$

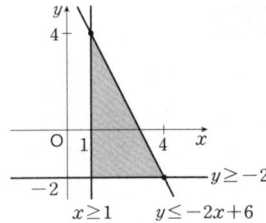

Therefore, the solution region is a right triangle. So the area A is

$A=\frac{1}{2}(4-1)(4-(-2))$
$=\frac{1}{2}(3)(6)=9$

The area is $A=9$

4. Application of Linear Inequality

Check Point 1

Let x be the fourth exam score. The sum of the scores of these three exams is $88 \times 3 = 264$. Since his average including fourth exam must be at least 90, we have the following inequality:
$$\frac{264+x}{4} \geq 90$$
$$264+x \geq 360$$
$$x \geq 96$$

Therefore, the minimum score Jeffery must receive on the fourth test is 96.

Check Point 2

Let x be the height of the triangle. Since the area is less than or equal to 40 square inches, we have the following inequality:
$$\frac{1}{2}(8)x \leq 40$$
$$4x \leq 40$$
$$x \leq 10$$

Therefore, the maximum height of the triangle is 10

Check Point 3

Let x be the number of hours John rents the lawnmower. Then we have the following inequality:
$$24+3.5x \leq 45$$
$$\frac{7}{2}x \leq 21$$
$$x \leq 6$$

Therefore, the maximum amount of hours is 6

Check Point 4

Let x be the number of miles Olivia travels after first 1 mile. Since the taxi charges $0.5 for each additional quarter of a mile after the first mile, then the taxi charges $2 for each additional mile. Then we have the following inequality:
$$4.25+2x \leq 26.25$$
$$2x \leq 22$$
$$x \leq 11$$

Therefore, the maximum distance she can travel is 12 miles(11 miles + first 1 mile).

Check Point 5

Let x be the gas mileage of the car. Then the absolute value inequality that gives the solution x is
$$|x-26| \leq 4$$
$$-4 \leq x-26 \leq 4$$
$$22 \leq x \leq 30$$

Therefore, the range of the gas mileage is $22 \leq x \leq 30$

Review Exercise

01

Let x be the number of movies David downloads. Then we have the following inequality:
$$14.5+2.25x \leq 100$$
$$1450+225x \leq 10000$$
$$225x \leq 8550$$
$$x \leq 38$$

Therefore, the maximum number of movies he can download is 38

02

Let x be the number of years after 2016. Then we have the following inequality:
$$128+8x>300$$
$$8x>172$$
$$x>21.5$$
In 22 years, there will be more than 300 million trees in country K. That year is 2016 + 22 = 2038.

Year 2038

03

Let x be the amount in dollars Daniel invests in bonds. Then we have the following inequality:
$$0.06(12000)+0.05x\geq 1500$$
$$720+0.05x\geq 1500$$
$$0.05x\geq 780$$
$$x\geq 15600$$
Therefore, Daniel has to invest $15,600 or more.

04

Let x be the number of backpacks Lisa sells in a month. Since the profit is the revenue minus the expenses, we have the following inequality:
$$32x-1820>0$$
$$32x>1820$$
$$x>56.875$$
Therefore, Lisa has to sell at least 57 backpacks to make a profit.

05

Let x be David's age. Then we have the following inequality:
$$x+(x+2)+(x+4)>54$$
$$3x+6>54$$
$$3x>48$$
$$x>16$$

Therefore, the youngest age is 17 years old.

06

Let x be the number of rides Daniel can go on. Then we have the following inequality:
$$25+3.5x\leq 50$$
$$3.5x\leq 25$$
$$x\leq 7.14$$
Therefore, the maximum number of rides is 7.

07

Let x be the number of caps James sells. Since the profit is the revenue minus the expenses, we have the following inequality:
$$28x-(12x+2000)\geq 1000$$
$$28x-12x-2000\geq 1000$$
$$16x\geq 3000$$
$$x\geq 187.5$$
Therefore, the minimum number of caps he has to sell is 188.

08

Let x be the number of pizzas. Then we have the following inequality:
$$8x\geq 2(15)$$
$$8x\geq 30$$
$$x\geq 3.75$$
Therefore, the minimum number of pizza peter has to order is 4.

09

Let x be the amount of water in grams. The amount of salt contained in 200 grams of 15% salt water is $0.15(200)=30$ grams. If x grams of water is added, we must have the following inequality:
$$\frac{30}{200+x}\leq \frac{8}{100}$$
$$3000\leq 8(200+x)$$

Solutions Manual

$$3000 \leq 1600 + 8x$$
$$1400 \leq 8x$$
$$175 \leq x$$

Therefore, the least amount of water added is 175 grams

10

Let x be the speed of the car in miles per hour. Then the absolute value inequality that gives the solution x is

$$|x-60| \leq 6$$
$$-6 \leq x - 60 \leq 6$$
$$54 \leq \ x\ \leq 66.$$

Therefore, the maximum speed is 66 miles per hour

Chapter 4 Test Level 1

01

$$2(x-4)+x \geq 3(1-2x)+7$$
$$2x-8+x \geq 3-6x+7$$
$$3x-8 \geq -6x+10$$
$$9x \geq 18$$
$$x \geq 2$$

The answer is (E)

02

$$\frac{x+1}{3} - \frac{2x-1}{2} > 4x + \frac{1}{6}$$
$$\left(\frac{x+1}{3} - \frac{2x-1}{2}\right) \cdot 6 > \left(4x + \frac{1}{6}\right) \cdot 6$$
$$2(x+1) - 3(2x-1) > 24x+1$$
$$2x+2-6x+3 > 24x+1$$
$$-4x+5 > 24x+1$$
$$-28x > -4$$
$$x < \frac{1}{7}$$

$$x < \frac{1}{7} \Rightarrow \left(-\infty, \frac{1}{7}\right)$$

03

$$x+6.4 \leq 0.4(2-x)$$
$$(x+6.4) \cdot 10 \leq (0.4(2-x)) \cdot 10$$
$$10x+64 \leq 4(2-x)$$
$$10x+64 \leq 8-4x$$
$$14x \leq -56$$
$$x \leq -4$$

$$x \leq -4 \Rightarrow (-\infty, -4]$$

04

$$6x-2a-10 < 2(3-x)-6x$$
$$6x-2a-10 < 6-2x-6x$$
$$6x-2a-10 < 6-8x$$
$$14x < 16+2a$$
$$x < \frac{16+2a}{14}$$

Since $x < 2$, we must have $\frac{16+2a}{14} = 2$

$$16+2a = 28$$
$$2a = 12,\ a = 6$$

$$a = 6$$

05

$$\frac{kx+5}{2} \geq 4$$
$$kx+5 \geq 8$$
$$kx \geq 3$$

Since $k<0$, we have $x \leq \frac{3}{k}$.

$$x \leq \frac{3}{k}$$

06

$$\frac{2x-1}{3} - \frac{x-7}{4} > 1$$
$$\left(\frac{2x-1}{3} - \frac{x-7}{4}\right) \cdot 12 > 1 \cdot 12$$
$$4(2x-1) - 3(x-7) > 12$$
$$8x - 4 - 3x + 21 > 12$$
$$5x + 17 > 12$$
$$5x > -5$$
$$x > -1$$

The least integer that satisfies $x>-1$ is zero.

07

$$-8 \leq 1 - \frac{5x+1}{4} \leq 7$$
$$-9 \leq -\frac{5x+1}{4} \leq 6$$
$$-36 \leq -(5x+1) \leq 24$$
$$36 \geq 5x+1 \geq -24$$
$$35 \geq 5x \geq -25$$
$$7 \geq x \geq -5$$

08

$$\frac{2}{3} - |x-2| < -\frac{4}{3}$$
$$\left(\frac{2}{3} - |x-2|\right) \cdot 3 < \left(-\frac{4}{3}\right) \cdot 3$$
$$2 - 3|x-2| < -4$$
$$-3|x-2| < -6$$
$$|x-2| > 2$$

$x-2 < -2$ or $x-2 > 2$
$x < 0$ $x > 4$

$$x < 0 \text{ or } x > 4$$

09

$$\begin{cases} y \leq -2x+3 \\ y > \frac{3}{2}x-1 \end{cases}$$

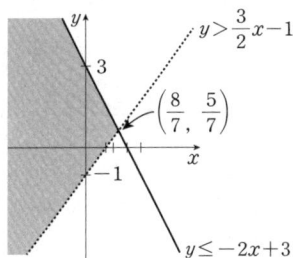

10

Let x be the number of hours Jenny works as a hostess. Then we have the following inequality:

$$15(8) + 12x \geq 200$$
$$120 + 12x \geq 200$$
$$12x \geq 80$$
$$x \geq \frac{20}{3} = 6\frac{2}{3}$$

Therefore, Jenny has to work at least 7 hours

11

We must have following inequality as shown below.

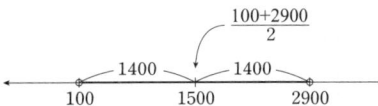

The absolute value inequality that gives the solution above is $|x-1,500| < 1,400$.
Because

$$|x-1,500| < 1,400$$
$$-1,400 < x-1,500 < 1,400$$
$$100 < x < 2,900$$

The answer is (D)

Solutions Manual

Chapter 4 Test Level 2

01

Solve each inequality first.

$$\frac{1}{3}(x+2)-x \geq -\frac{3x-2}{5}+2$$

$$\left(\frac{1}{3}(x+2)-x\right)\cdot 15 \geq \left(-\frac{3x-2}{5}+2\right)\cdot 15$$

$$5(x+2)-15x \geq -3(3x-2)+30$$

$$5x+10-15x \geq -9x+6+30$$

$$10-10x \geq -9x+36$$

$$-x \geq 26$$

$$x \leq -26$$

$$0.8x-\frac{x-k}{2} \leq 0.2(x-4)$$

$$\left(0.8x-\frac{x-k}{2}\right)\cdot 10 \leq (0.2(x-4))\cdot 10$$

$$8x-5(x-k) \leq 2(x-4)$$

$$8x-5x+5k \leq 2x-8$$

$$3x+5k \leq 2x-8$$

$$x \leq -8-5k$$

Since two inequalities have the same solutions, we have

$$-8-5k = -26$$

$$-5k = -18, \quad k = \frac{18}{5}$$

$$k = \frac{18}{5}$$

02

$$2ax+5 < -13$$

$$2ax < -18$$

$$ax < -9$$

Since the solution is $x > 3$, a must be negative so that $x > \frac{-9}{a}$ and $\frac{-9}{a} = 3$, $a = -3$.

$$a = -3$$

03

$$\frac{k}{3}(x+3)-\frac{1}{2} \geq \frac{1}{6}(3+2x)$$

$$\left(\frac{k}{3}(x+3)-\frac{1}{2}\right)\cdot 6 \geq \left(\frac{1}{6}(3+2x)\right)\cdot 6$$

$$2k(x+3)-3 \geq 3+2x$$

$$2kx+6k-3 \geq 3+2x$$

$$2kx-2x \geq 6-6k$$

By the distributive property,
$2kx-2x = 2x(k-1)$ and $6-6k = -6(k-1)$.
Now we have,

$$2kx-2x \geq 6-6k$$

$$2x(k-1) \geq -6(k-1)$$

Since $k<1$, $k-1<0$ and dividing both sides by $k-1$ changes the direction of the inequality sign. Therefore, $x \leq -3$.

$$x \leq -3$$

04

$$\frac{|4x-2|}{2} \leq 5$$

$$|4x-2| \leq 10$$

$$-10 \leq 4x-2 \leq 10$$

$$-8 \leq 4x \leq 12$$

$$-2 \leq x \leq 3$$

Now, multiply each side by -5 and then add 3.

$$10 \geq -5x \geq -15$$

$$13 \geq 3-5x \geq -12$$

$$13 \geq k \geq -12$$

Therefore, $-12 \leq k \leq 13$.

The answer is (A)

05

$$3x-2y=6$$

$$-2y=-3x+6$$

$$y=\frac{3}{2}x-3$$

Substitute $\frac{3}{2}x-3$ for y in the equality

$$-4 \leq 5x-4y < 11.$$

$$-4 \leq 5x-4\left(\frac{3}{2}x-3\right) < 11$$

$$-4 \leq 5x-6x+12 < 11$$

$$-4 \leq -x+12 < 11$$

$$-16 \leq -x < -1$$

$$16 \geq x > 1$$

$$1 < x \leq 16$$

06

$\begin{cases} y \leq 3 \\ x \leq 1 \\ 2x+y \geq -2 \end{cases} \Rightarrow \begin{cases} y \leq 3 \\ x \leq 1 \\ y \geq -2x-2 \end{cases}$

The intersection of $y=3$ and $y=-2x-2$ is

$-2x-2=3$

$-2x=5,\ x=-\frac{5}{2}$

$\Rightarrow \left(-\frac{5}{2},\ 3\right)$

The intersection of $x=1$ and $y=-2x-2$ is

$y=-2(1)-2=-4$

$\Rightarrow (1,-4)$

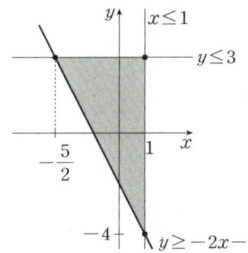

Therefore, the solution region is a right triangle. So the area A is

$A = \frac{1}{2}(3-(-4))\left(1-\left(-\frac{5}{2}\right)\right)$

$= \frac{1}{2}(7)\left(\frac{7}{2}\right) = \frac{49}{4}$

The area is $A = \frac{49}{4}$

07

Let x be company B's amount of sales in dollars. Then we have the following inequality:

$39000 < 25000 + 0.04x$

$14000 < 0.04x$

$350000 < x$

When the amount of sales is over $350,000, company B's salary is greater than company A's salary.

08

Let x be the amount of 15% brine in grams. Create a table as shown below.

	6% brine	15% brine	12% brine
Grams	400	x	$x+400$
Salt	0.06(400)	0.15x	0.12($x+400$)

$0.06(400) + 0.15x > 0.12(x+400)$

$6(400) + 15x > 12(x+400)$

$2400 + 15x > 12x + 4800$

$3x > 2400$

$x > 800$

Tom needs to mix more than 800 grams of 15% brine

09

Let x be the number of miles Eugene travels after the first quarter of a mile. Since the taxi charges $0.875 for each additional half of a mile, they charge $0.875 \times 2 = \$1.75$ for each additional mile. So we have the following inequality:

$1.25 + 1.75x \leq 24$

$1.75x \leq 22.75$

$x \leq 13$

Therefore, the maximum distance he can travel is 13.25 miles (13 miles + the first quarter of a mile)

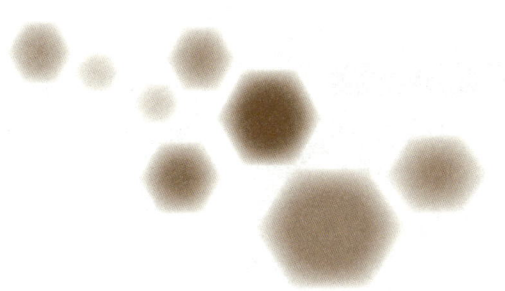

Solutions Manual

Chapter 5
Manipulating Polynomials

1. Addition and Subtraction of Polynomials

Check Point 1

① $(9x+1)+4(-5x+3)=9x+1-20x+12$
$\qquad =(9x-20x)+(1+12)$
$\qquad =-11x+13$

② $(3x-4)-(7x-2)=3x-4-7x+2$
$\qquad =(3x-7x)+(-4+2)$
$\qquad =-4x-2$

③ $4(1-2x+x^2)+2(4x^2-5x+1)$
$=4-8x+4x^2+8x^2-10x+2$
$=(4x^2+8x^2)+(-8x-10x)+(4+2)$
$=12x^2-18x+6$

④ $3(x^3-3x^2-4x-3)-5(2-5x+6x^2)$
$=3x^3-9x^2-12x-9-10+25x-30x^2$
$=3x^3+(-9x^2-30x^2)+(-12x+25x)$
$\qquad\qquad\qquad\qquad +(-9-10)$
$=3x^3-39x^2+13x-19$

Check Point 2

① $\dfrac{2-4x}{3}+\dfrac{2x-5}{2}=\dfrac{2-4x}{3}\cdot\dfrac{2}{2}+\dfrac{2x-5}{2}\cdot\dfrac{3}{3}$
$\qquad =\dfrac{2(2-4x)+3(2x-5)}{6}$
$\qquad =\dfrac{4-8x+6x-15}{6}$
$\qquad =\dfrac{-2x-11}{6}=-\dfrac{2x+11}{6}$

② $\dfrac{3x-1}{2}+3-4x=\dfrac{3x-1}{2}+\dfrac{3-4x}{1}\cdot\dfrac{2}{2}$
$\qquad =\dfrac{3x-1+2(3-4x)}{2}$
$\qquad =\dfrac{3x-1+6-8x}{2}$
$\qquad =\dfrac{-5x+5}{2}$

③ $\dfrac{x^2-x}{4}-\dfrac{x-x^2}{2}=\dfrac{x^2-x}{4}-\dfrac{x-x^2}{2}\cdot\dfrac{2}{2}$
$\qquad =\dfrac{(x^2-x)-2(x-x^2)}{4}$
$\qquad =\dfrac{x^2-x-2x+2x^2}{4}$
$\qquad =\dfrac{3x^2-3x}{4}$

④ $\dfrac{2x^2-x+1}{3}-\dfrac{x-3x^2}{4}+1$
$=\dfrac{2x^2-x+1}{3}\cdot\dfrac{4}{4}-\dfrac{x-3x^2}{4}\cdot\dfrac{3}{3}+\dfrac{1}{1}\cdot\dfrac{12}{12}$
$=\dfrac{4(2x^2-x+1)-3(x-3x^2)+12}{12}$
$=\dfrac{8x^2-4x+4-3x+9x^2+12}{12}$
$=\dfrac{17x^2-7x+16}{12}$

Review Exercise

01

(1) $(2x-7)+(5-4x)=2x-7+5-4x$
$\qquad =(2x-4x)+(-7+5)$
$\qquad =-2x-2$

(2) $(1-2x+x^2)-(4x^2-5x+1)$
$=1-2x+x^2-4x^2+5x-1$
$=(x^2-4x^2)+(-2x+5x)+(1-1)$
$=-3x^2+3x$

(3) $(4x^2-2+5x)+2(3x^2+3x-7)$
$=4x^2-2+5x+6x^2+6x-14$
$=(4x^2+6x^2)+(5x+6x)+(-2-14)$
$=10x^2+11x-16$

70 Solutions Manual

(4) $(2a^3-3a^2-3a+5)+(4a^3-6a^2+5a-1)$
$=2a^3-3a^2-3a+5+4a^3-6a^2+5a-1$
$=(2a^3+4a^3)+(-3a^2-6a^2)$
$\quad+(-3a+5a)+(5-1)$
$=6a^3-9a^2+2a+4$

(5) $6(2a^3-a^2+4)-3(4a^3-3a^2-4a+2)$
$=12a^3-6a^2+24-12a^3+9a^2+12a-6$
$=(12a^3-12a^3)+(-6a^2+9a^2)+12a+(24-6)$
$=3a^2+12a+18$

(6) $(4-y-5y^2+2y^3)-2\left(-\dfrac{1}{2}y^3+y^2-5y-1\right)$
$=4-y-5y^2+2y^3+y^3-2y^2+10y+2$
$=(2y^3+y^3)+(-5y^2-2y^2)$
$\quad+(-y+10y)+(4+2)$
$=3y^3-7y^2+9y+6$

(7) $4(3b^2-b+1)-2(b+3)-\dfrac{1}{2}(4b^2-8)$
$=12b^2-4b+4-2b-6-2b^2+4$
$=(12b^2-2b^2)+(-4b-2b)+(4-6+4)$
$=10b^2-6b+2$

(8) $4(a^2-3a-2)+5(a^2-1)-9(a^2-a+2)$
$=4a^2-12a-8+5a^2-5-9a^2+9a-18$
$=(4a^2+5a^2-9a^2)+(-12a+9a)+(-8-5-18)$
$=-3a-31$

02

(1) $\dfrac{3x-1}{2}+\dfrac{x+2}{3}=\dfrac{3x-1}{2}\cdot\dfrac{3}{3}+\dfrac{x+2}{3}\cdot\dfrac{2}{2}$
$=\dfrac{3(3x-1)+2(x+2)}{6}$
$=\dfrac{9x-3+2x+4}{6}$
$=\dfrac{11x+1}{6}$

(2) $\dfrac{4x+5}{2}-\dfrac{x-1}{4}=\dfrac{4x+5}{2}\cdot\dfrac{2}{2}-\dfrac{x-1}{4}$
$=\dfrac{2(4x+5)-(x-1)}{4}$
$=\dfrac{8x+10-x+1}{4}$
$=\dfrac{7x+11}{4}$

(3) $x+3-\dfrac{3(2-x)}{5}=\dfrac{x+3}{1}\cdot\dfrac{5}{5}-\dfrac{3(2-x)}{5}$
$=\dfrac{5(x+3)-3(2-x)}{5}$
$=\dfrac{5x+15-6+3x}{5}$
$=\dfrac{8x+9}{5}$

(4) $\dfrac{x+1}{4}-\dfrac{2(3-x)}{3}+\dfrac{3x-2}{2}$
$=\dfrac{x+1}{4}\cdot\dfrac{3}{3}-\dfrac{2(3-x)}{3}\cdot\dfrac{4}{4}+\dfrac{3x-2}{2}\cdot\dfrac{6}{6}$
$=\dfrac{3(x+1)-8(3-x)+6(3x-2)}{12}$
$=\dfrac{3x+3-24+8x+18x-12}{12}$
$=\dfrac{29x-33}{12}$

03

(1) $\dfrac{x-y}{2}-\dfrac{y-z}{3}-\dfrac{z-x}{6}$
$=\dfrac{x-y}{2}\cdot\dfrac{3}{3}-\dfrac{y-z}{3}\cdot\dfrac{2}{2}-\dfrac{z-x}{6}$
$=\dfrac{3(x-y)-2(y-z)-(z-x)}{6}$
$=\dfrac{3x-3y-2y+2z-z+x}{6}$
$=\dfrac{4x-5y+z}{6}$

(2) $\dfrac{a+b+c}{6}-\dfrac{a+b-c}{4}+\dfrac{a-b-c}{8}$
$=\dfrac{a+b+c}{6}\cdot\dfrac{4}{4}-\dfrac{a+b-c}{4}\cdot\dfrac{6}{6}+\dfrac{a-b-c}{8}\cdot\dfrac{3}{3}$
$=\dfrac{4(a+b+c)-6(a+b-c)+3(a-b-c)}{24}$
$=\dfrac{4a+4b+4c-6a-6b+6c+3a-3b-3c}{24}$
$=\dfrac{a-5b+7c}{24}$

04

(1) $4(2x^2+x-3)+\boxed{}=4x^2-3x$
$\boxed{}=(4x^2-3x)-4(2x^2+x-3)$
$=4x^2-3x-8x^2-4x+12$
$=-4x^2-7x+12$

(2) $\dfrac{3x^2-4x}{2}+\boxed{}=\dfrac{x^2+2x+8}{4}$

Solutions Manual

$\boxed{} = \dfrac{x^2+2x+8}{4} - \dfrac{3x^2-4x}{2}$

$= \dfrac{x^2+2x+8}{4} - \dfrac{3x^2-4x}{2} \cdot \dfrac{2}{2}$

$= \dfrac{(x^2+2x+8) - 2(3x^2-4x)}{4}$

$= \dfrac{x^2+2x+8-6x^2+8x}{4}$

$= \dfrac{-5x^2+10x+8}{4}$

(3) $\dfrac{a+2b}{3} - \boxed{} - \dfrac{a-2b}{6} = \dfrac{a+b}{6}$

$\boxed{} = \dfrac{a+2b}{3} - \dfrac{a-2b}{6} - \dfrac{a+b}{6}$

$= \dfrac{a+2b}{3} \cdot \dfrac{2}{2} - \dfrac{a-2b}{6} - \dfrac{a+b}{6}$

$= \dfrac{2a+4b-(a-2b)-(a+b)}{6}$

$= \dfrac{2a+4b-a+2b-a-b}{6} = \dfrac{5b}{6}$

05

Simplify in order from ( ) → { } → [ ]

(1) $3a - [4b - 5a - \{4b + 2(3b + 3a)\}]$
$= 3a - [4b - 5a - \{4b + 6b + 6a\}]$
$= 3a - [4b - 5a - \{6a + 10b\}]$
$= 3a - [4b - 5a - 6a - 10b]$
$= 3a - [-11a - 6b]$
$= 3a + 11a + 6b$
$= 14a + 6b$

(2) $4x - [2x^2 + 3x - 2\{3x - (5x^2 - x) + 2\}]$
$= 4x - [2x^2 + 3x - 2\{3x - 5x^2 + x + 2\}]$
$= 4x - [2x^2 + 3x - 2\{-5x^2 + 4x + 2\}]$
$= 4x - [2x^2 + 3x + 10x^2 - 8x - 4]$
$= 4x - [12x^2 - 5x - 4]$
$= 4x - 12x^2 + 5x + 4$
$= -12x^2 + 9x + 4$

06

(1) $A - (a^2 - 3a - 2) = 4a^2 + 5a - 4$
$A = 4a^2 + 5a - 4 + (a^2 - 3a - 2)$
$= 4a^2 + 5a - 4 + a^2 - 3a - 2$
$= 5a^2 + 2a - 6$

(2) If we simplify correctly, the expression is
$A + (a^2 - 3a - 2) = 5a^2 + 2a - 6 + a^2 - 3a - 2$
$= 6a^2 - a - 8$

07

$\dfrac{x-2y}{3} - \dfrac{3x+2y}{4} = \dfrac{x-2y}{3} \cdot \dfrac{4}{4} - \dfrac{3x+2y}{4} \cdot \dfrac{3}{3}$

$= \dfrac{4(x-2y) - 3(3x+2y)}{12}$

$= \dfrac{4x - 8y - 9x - 6y}{12}$

$= \dfrac{-5x - 14y}{12} = -\dfrac{5}{12}x - \dfrac{14}{12}y$

Since $-\dfrac{5}{12}x - \dfrac{14}{12}y = ax + by$, $a = -\dfrac{5}{12}$ and $b = -\dfrac{14}{12}$, $a + b = -\dfrac{5}{12} + \left(-\dfrac{14}{12}\right) = -\dfrac{19}{12}$

2. Multiplication of Polynomials, Part 1

Check Point 1

① $2(4x+1)=(2\times 4x)+(2\times 1)$
$\qquad = 8x+2$

② $4x(2x^2-5x+3)$
$=(4x\times 2x^2)+(4x\times -5x)+(4x\times 3)$
$=8x^3-20x^2+12x$

③ $5(3a-1)+4(2-3a)$
$=(5\times 3a)+(5\times -1)+(4\times 2)+(4\times(-3a))$
$=15a-5+8-12a$
$=3a+3$

④ $\left(2a-\dfrac{1}{2}\right)(-4)-6\left(-4+\dfrac{a}{3}\right)$
$=(2a\times(-4))+\left(-\dfrac{1}{2}\times(-4)\right)$
$\quad +(-6\times(-4))+\left(-6\times\dfrac{a}{3}\right)$
$=-8a+2+24-2a$
$=-10a+26$

Check Point 2

① $(4a+1)(a-2)$
$=(4a\times a)+(4a\times(-2))+(1\times a)+(1\times(-2))$
$=4a^2-8a+a-2$
$=4a^2-7a-2$

② $(3x-1)(x+2)$
$=(3x\times x)+(3x\times 2)+(-1\times x)+(-1\times 2)$
$=3x^2+6x-x-2$
$=3x^2+5x-2$

③ $(2y+1)(4y^2-3)$
$=(2y\times 4y^2)+(2y\times(-3))$
$\quad +(1\times 4y^2)+(1\times(-3))$
$=8y^3-6y+4y^2-3$
$=8y^3+4y^2-6y-3$

④ $(a^2-2)(4a^2+1)$
$=(a^2\times 4a^2)+(a^2\times 1)+(-2\times 4a^2)+(-2\times 1)$
$=4a^4+a^2-8a^2-2$
$=4a^4-7a^2-2$

Check Point 3

① $(x-3)(x^2-x+1)$
$=(x\times x^2)+(x\times(-x))+(x\times 1)$
$\quad +(-3\times x^2)+(-3\times(-x))+(-3\times 1)$
$=x^3-x^2+x-3x^2+3x-3$
$=x^3-4x^2+4x-3$

② $(2x^2-4x+1)(3x+1)$
$=(2x^2\times 3x)+(2x^2\times 1)+(-4x\times 3x)$
$\quad +(-4x\times 1)+(1\times 3x)+(1\times 1)$
$=6x^3+2x^2-12x^2-4x+3x+1$
$=6x^3-10x^2-x+1$

③ $(2a^2-a+1)(a^2-1)$
$=(2a^2\times a^2)+(2a^2\times(-1))+(-a\times a^2)$
$\quad +(-a\times(-1))+(1\times a^2)+(1\times(-1))$
$=2a^4-2a^2-a^3+a+a^2-1$
$=2a^4-a^3-a^2+a-1$

Review Exercise

01

(1) $3x(x^2-1)=(3x\times x^2)+(3x\times(-1))$
$\qquad\qquad\quad =3x^3-3x$

(2) $\dfrac{2x}{5}\left(25-\dfrac{25}{2}x^2\right)=\left(\dfrac{2x}{5}\times 25\right)+\left(\dfrac{2x}{5}\times\left(-\dfrac{25}{2}x^2\right)\right)$
$\qquad\qquad\qquad\qquad =10x-5x^3$
$\qquad\qquad\qquad\qquad =-5x^3+10x$

(3) $(a+4)(-2a)=(a\times(-2a))+(4\times(-2a))$
$\qquad\qquad\qquad =-2a^2-8a$

(4) $-4a(3a^2-a+3)$
$=(-4a\times 3a^2)+(-4a\times(-a))+(-4a\times 3)$
$=-12a^3+4a^2-12a$

(5) $2a^2(2a-a^2)=(2a^2\times 2a)+(2a^2\times(-a^2))$
$\qquad\qquad\qquad =4a^3-2a^4$
$\qquad\qquad\qquad =-2a^4+4a^3$

(6) $(2x^2+3x-1)(-5x)$
$=(2x^2\times(-5x))+(3x\times(-5x))$
$\quad +(-1\times(-5x))$
$=-10x^3-15x^2+5x$

Solutions Manual

02

(1) $2(a^2-3)+3(4a-2)$
$=(2\times a^2)+(2\times(-3))+(3\times 4a)+(3\times(-2))$
$=2a^2-6+12a-6$
$=2a^2+12a-12$

(2) $\frac{1}{3}(6x^2-9x+1)-\frac{2x}{5}(10x-15)$
$=\left(\frac{1}{3}\times 6x^2\right)+\left(\frac{1}{3}\times(-9x)\right)+\left(\frac{1}{3}\times 1\right)$
$\quad+\left(-\frac{2x}{5}\times 10x\right)+\left(-\frac{2x}{5}\times(-15)\right)$
$=2x^2-3x+\frac{1}{3}-4x^2+6x$
$=-2x^2+3x+\frac{1}{3}$

(3) $-2(x^2+2x-5)-2x(x-1)$
$=(-2\times x^2)+(-2\times 2x)+(-2\times(-5))$
$\quad+(-2x\times x)+(-2x\times(-1))$
$=-2x^2-4x+10-2x^2+2x$
$=-4x^2-2x+10$

(4) $5(x^2-1)+3(x^2+x-1)+4$
$=(5\times x^2)+(5\times(-1))+(3\times x^2)$
$\quad+(3\times x)+(3\times(-1))+4$
$=5x^2-5+3x^2+3x-3+4$
$=8x^2+3x-4$

03

(1) $(x-1)(2x+3)$
$=(x\times 2x)+(x\times 3)+(-1\times 2x)+(-1\times 3)$
$=2x^2+3x-2x-3$
$=2x^2+x-3$

(2) $(3x-1)(2x-4)$
$=(3x\times 2x)+(3x\times(-4))$
$\quad+(-1\times 2x)+(-1\times(-4))$
$=6x^2-12x-2x+4$
$=6x^2-14x+4$

(3) $(-2y+3)(y-1)$
$=(-2y\times y)+(-2y\times(-1))$
$\quad+(3\times y)+(3\times(-1))$
$=-2y^2+2y+3y-3$
$=-2y^2+5y-3$

(4) $(1-y)(-1-3y)$
$=(1\times(-1))+(1\times(-3y))$
$\quad+(-y\times(-1))+(-y\times(-3y))$
$=-1-3y+y+3y^2$
$=3y^2-2y-1$

04

(1) $(x^2-1)(2x+3)$
$=(x^2\times 2x)+(x^2\times 3)+(-1\times 2x)+(-1\times 3)$
$=2x^3+3x^2-2x-3$

(2) $(a^2-2)(4a+1)$
$=(a^2\times 4a)+(a^2\times 1)+((-2)\times 4a)+((-2)\times 1)$
$=4a^3+a^2-8a-2$

(3) $(2a+a^2)\left(-5+\frac{1}{2}a\right)$
$=(2a\times(-5))+\left(2a\times\frac{1}{2}a\right)$
$\quad+(a^2\times(-5))+\left(a^2\times\frac{1}{2}a\right)$
$=-10a+a^2-5a^2+\frac{1}{2}a^3$
$=\frac{1}{2}a^3-4a^2-10a$

(4) $(1+2m)(2m^2-m)$
$=(1\times 2m^2)+(1\times(-m))$
$\quad+(2m\times 2m^2)+(2m\times(-m))$
$=2m^2-m+4m^3-2m^2$
$=4m^3-m$

05

(1) $(2x-1)(x^2+3x-3)$
$=(2x\times x^2)+(2x\times 3x)+(2x\times(-3))$
$\quad+(-1\times x^2)+(-1\times 3x)+(-1\times(-3))$
$=2x^3+6x^2-6x-x^2-3x+3$
$=2x^3+5x^2-9x+3$

(2) $(-a^2+a+4)(3a+2)$
$=(-a^2\times 3a)+(-a^2\times 2)+(a\times 3a)$
$\quad+(a\times 2)+(4\times 3a)+(4\times 2)$
$=-3a^3-2a^2+3a^2+2a+12a+8$
$=-3a^3+a^2+14a+8$

06

(1) $(x-a)(2x+3)=2x^2+3x-2ax-3a$
$\qquad\qquad\qquad\quad=2x^2+(3-2a)x-3a$

Since $2x^2+(3-2a)x-3a=2x^2+bx-12$,
$\quad 3a=12 \Rightarrow a=4$
$\quad 3-2a=b$
$\quad 3-2(4)=b \Rightarrow b=-5$

Therefore, $a+b=4+(-5)=-1$.
$$a+b=-1$$

(2) $(x-3)(5x+a)=5x^2+ax-15x-3a$
$\qquad\qquad\qquad\quad=5x^2+(a-15)x-3a$

Since $5x^2+(a-15)x-3a=5x^2-11x+b$,
$\quad a-15=-11 \Rightarrow a=4$
$\quad -3a=b$
$\quad -3(4)=b \Rightarrow b=-12$

Therefore, $a+b=4+(-12)=-8$.
$$a+b=-8$$

07

$(2x+a)(bx-5)=2bx^2-10x+abx-5a$
$\qquad\qquad\qquad=2bx^2+(-10+ab)x-5a$

Since
$2bx^2+(-10+ab)x-5a=cx^2-4x-10$,
$\quad 5a=10 \Rightarrow a=2$
$\quad -10+ab=-4$,
$\quad -10+(2)b=-4 \Rightarrow b=3$
$\quad 2b=c$
$\quad 2(3)=c \Rightarrow c=6$

Therefore, $a+b+c=2+3+6=11$.
$$a+b+c=11$$

08

Expand only the part of the x term.

(1) $(3x+3)(3x-4)$
$\quad \Rightarrow (3x \times -4)+(3 \times 3x)$
$\quad =-12x+9x=-3x$

Therefore, the coefficient of x term is -3.
$$-3$$

(2) $(4-2x)(5-2x^2+2x)$
$\quad \Rightarrow (4 \times 2x)+(-2x \times 5)$
$\quad =8x-10x=-2x$

Therefore, the coefficient of x term is -2.
$$-2$$

09

Expand only the part of the y terms.
$\quad (3+2y)(ay^2-3y+b)$
$\quad \Rightarrow (3 \times (-3y))+(2y \times b)$
$\quad =-9y+2by$
$\quad =(-9+2b)y$

Since the coefficient of y term is 8,
$\quad -9+2b=8$
$\quad 2b=17 \Rightarrow b=\dfrac{17}{2}$
$$b=\dfrac{17}{2}$$

10

Let w and l be the width and the length respectively. Then the area A of the rectangle is
$\quad A=wl$
$\quad\quad =(2k+1)(3+2k-k^2)$
$\quad\quad =6k+4k^2-2k^3+3+2k-k^2$
$\quad\quad =-2k^3+3k^2+8k+3$

The answer is (E)

Solutions Manual

3. Multiplication of Polynomials, Part 2

Check Point 1

① $(x+2)^2 = x^2 + 2(x)(2) + 2^2$
$\qquad = x^2 + 4x + 4$

② $(2x-5)^2 = (2x)^2 + 2(2x)(-5) + (-5)^2$
$\qquad = 4x^2 - 20x + 25$

③ $\left(\dfrac{1}{4} + 3b\right)^2 = \left(\dfrac{1}{4}\right)^2 + 2\left(\dfrac{1}{4}\right)(3b) + (3b)^2$
$\qquad = \dfrac{1}{16} + \dfrac{3b}{2} + 9b^2$

④ $\left(-a - \dfrac{2b}{3}\right)^2 = \left(a + \dfrac{2b}{3}\right)^2$
$\qquad = a^2 + 2(a)\left(\dfrac{2b}{3}\right) + \left(\dfrac{2b}{3}\right)^2$
$\qquad = a^2 + \dfrac{4ab}{3} + \dfrac{4b^2}{9}$

Check Point 2

① $(x-5)(x+5) = x^2 - 5^2$
$\qquad = x^2 - 25$

② $(2x-5y)(2x+5y) = (2x)^2 - (5y)^2$
$\qquad = 4x^2 - 25y^2$

③ $\left(\dfrac{3a}{4} - \dfrac{b}{3}\right)\left(\dfrac{3a}{4} + \dfrac{b}{3}\right) = \left(\dfrac{3a}{4}\right)^2 - \left(\dfrac{b}{3}\right)^2$
$\qquad = \dfrac{9a^2}{16} - \dfrac{b^2}{9}$

④ $(a-3)(a+3)(a^2+9) = (a^2 - 3^2)(a^2+9)$
$\qquad = (a^2 - 9)(a^2 + 9)$
$\qquad = (a^2)^2 - 9^2$
$\qquad = a^4 - 81$

Check Point 3

① $98^2 = (100-2)^2 = 100^2 - 2(100 \times 2) + 2^2$
$\qquad = 1{,}000 - 400 + 4 = 9{,}604$

② $9.8 \times 10.2 = (10 - 0.2)(10 + 0.2)$
$\qquad = 10^2 - 0.2^2 = 100 - 0.04 = 99.96$

③ $101 \times 103 = (100+1)(100+3)$
$\qquad = 100^2 + 300 + 100 + 3 = 10{,}403$

Review Exercise

01

(1) $(x+3)^2 = x^2 + 2(3)x + 3^2$
$\qquad = x^2 + 6x + 9$

(2) $(2x-1)^2 = (2x)^2 - 2(2x)(1) + 1^2$
$\qquad = 4x^2 - 4x + 1$

(3) $\left(3a + \dfrac{1}{3}\right)^2 = (3a)^2 + 2(3a)\left(\dfrac{1}{3}\right) + \left(\dfrac{1}{3}\right)^2$
$\qquad = 9a^2 + 2a + \dfrac{1}{9}$

(4) $\left(\dfrac{a}{4} - 6\right)^2 = \left(\dfrac{a}{4}\right)^2 - 2\left(\dfrac{a}{4}\right)(6) + 6^2$
$\qquad = \dfrac{a^2}{16} - 3a + 36$

02

(1) $(x+5y)^2 = x^2 + 2x(5y) + (5y)^2$
$\qquad = x^2 + 10xy + 25y^2$

(2) $\left(\dfrac{2x}{3} - 4y\right)^2 = \left(\dfrac{2x}{3}\right)^2 - 2\left(\dfrac{2x}{3}\right)(4y) + (4y)^2$
$\qquad = \dfrac{4x^2}{9} - \dfrac{16xy}{3} + 16y^2$

(3) $(-3a+4b)^2 = (3a-4b)^2$
$\qquad = (3a)^2 - 2(3a)(4b) + (4b)^2$
$\qquad = 9a^2 - 24ab + 16b^2$

(4) $\left(-\dfrac{2a}{3} - \dfrac{b}{2}\right)^2 = \left(\dfrac{2a}{3} + \dfrac{b}{2}\right)^2$
$\qquad = \left(\dfrac{2a}{3}\right)^2 + 2\left(\dfrac{2a}{3}\right)\left(\dfrac{b}{2}\right) + \left(\dfrac{b}{2}\right)^2$
$\qquad = \dfrac{4a^2}{9} + \dfrac{2ab}{3} + \dfrac{b^2}{4}$

03

(1) $(x-3)(x+3) = x^2 - 3^2$
$\qquad = x^2 - 9$

(2) $\left(x+\dfrac{1}{2}\right)\left(x-\dfrac{1}{2}\right) = x^2 - \left(\dfrac{1}{2}\right)^2$
$\qquad = x^2 - \dfrac{1}{4}$

(3) $(2a-3b)(2a+3b) = (2a)^2 - (3b)^2$
$\qquad = 4a^2 - 9b^2$

(4) $\left(\dfrac{2b}{3} - \dfrac{a}{3}\right)\left(\dfrac{2b}{3} + \dfrac{a}{3}\right) = \left(\dfrac{2b}{3}\right)^2 - \left(\dfrac{a}{3}\right)^2$

$$= \frac{4b^2}{9} - \frac{a^2}{9}$$
$$= \frac{4b^2 - a^2}{9}$$

04

(1) $\qquad (4x + \boxed{A})^2 = 16x^2 + 16x + \boxed{B}$
$(4x)^2 + 2(4x)A + A^2 = 16x^2 + 16x + B$
$16x^2 + 8Ax + A^2 = 16x^2 + 16x + B$
$8A = 16 \Rightarrow A = 2$
$A^2 = B$
$2^2 = B \Rightarrow B = 4$
$\qquad\qquad\qquad\qquad A = 2$ and $B = 4$

(2) $\qquad (\boxed{A}x - 4)^2 = 9x^2 - \boxed{B}x + 16$
$(Ax)^2 - 2(Ax)(4) + 4^2 = 9x^2 - Bx + 16$
$A^2x^2 - 8Ax + 16 = 9x^2 - Bx + 16$
$A^2 = 9 \Rightarrow A = \pm 3$.
But, since $A > 0$, $A = 3$.
$8A = B$
$8(3) = B \Rightarrow B = 24$
$\qquad\qquad\qquad\qquad A = 3$ and $B = 24$

05

$\left(\dfrac{3x}{4} - \dfrac{5y}{2}\right)\left(\dfrac{3x}{4} + \dfrac{5y}{2}\right) = \left(\dfrac{3x}{4}\right)^2 - \left(\dfrac{5y}{2}\right)^2$
$\qquad\qquad\qquad\qquad = \dfrac{9x^2}{16} - \dfrac{25y^2}{4}$
$\qquad\qquad\qquad\qquad = \dfrac{9(32)}{16} - \dfrac{25(20)}{4}$
$\qquad\qquad\qquad\qquad = 18 - 125 = -107$

06

(1) $10.2^2 = (10 + 0.2)^2$
$\qquad = 10^2 + 2(10)(0.2) + (0.2)^2$
$\qquad = 100 + 4 + 0.04 = 104.04$

(2) $299^2 = (300 - 1)^2$
$\qquad = 300^2 - 2(300)(1) + 1^2$
$\qquad = 90000 - 600 + 1 = 89,401$

(3) $50.2 \times 49.8 = (50 + 0.2)(50 - 0.2)$
$\qquad = 50^2 - 0.2^2$
$\qquad = 2500 - 0.04 = 2,499.96$

07

(1) $(3-1)(3+1)(3^2+1)(3^4+1)$
$= (3^2 - 1)(3^2 + 1)(3^4 + 1)$
$= ((3^2)^2 - 1)(3^4 + 1)$
$= (3^4 - 1)(3^4 + 1)$
$= (3^4)^2 - 1$
$= 3^8 - 1$

(2) $(2^3 - 1)(2^3 + 1)(2^6 + 1)$
$= ((2^3)^2 - 1)(2^6 + 1)$
$= (2^6 - 1)(2^6 + 1)$
$= ((2^6)^2 - 1)$
$= 2^{12} - 1$

08

Let $A = 2021$ and $B = 2020$.
$2022 \times 2020 - 2021 \times 2019$
$= (A+1)(A-1) - (B+1)(B-1)$
$= (A^2 - 1) - (B^2 - 1)$
$= A^2 - B^2$
$= (A - B)(A + B)$
$= (2021 - 2020)(2021 + 2020)$
$= 1 \cdot 4041 = 4041$

Solutions Manual

Chapter 5 Test Level 1

01

$2(3x^2-x+2)-3(3x+2x^2+1)$
$=6x^2-2x+4-9x-6x^2-3$
$=-11x+1$

02

$\dfrac{2(3x^2-2x)}{5}+\dfrac{x^2-x+3}{4}$
$=\dfrac{2(3x^2-2x)}{5}\cdot\dfrac{4}{4}+\dfrac{x^2-x+3}{4}\cdot\dfrac{5}{5}$
$=\dfrac{8(3x^2-2x)+5(x^2-x+3)}{20}$
$=\dfrac{24x^2-16x+5x^2-5x+15}{20}$
$=\dfrac{29x^2-21x+15}{20}$

03

$2(3a^2+a+4)-2(a^2-3a+1)-\boxed{}=a^2-3$
$\boxed{}=2(3a^2+a+4)-2(a^2-3a+1)$
$\qquad\qquad-(a^2-3)$
$=6a^2+2a+8-2a^2+6a-2-a^2+3$
$=3a^2+8a+9$
$\boxed{}=3a^2+8a+9$

04

$3A-(B+2C)+4C$
$=3A-B-2C+4C=3A-B+2C$
$=3(x^2-2x+3)-(3x^2-2)+2(2x^2+x)$
$=3x^2-6x+9-3x^2+2+4x^2+2x$
$=4x^2-4x+11$
Therefore, $a+b+c=4+(-4)+11=11$.
$\qquad\qquad\qquad a+b+c=11$

05

$(4x-3)(4x+3)-4(2x-1)^2$
$=(4x)^2-3^2-4(4x^2-4x+1)$
$=16x^2-9-16x^2+16x-4$
$=16x-13$

The answer is (B)

06

$(x+2)(-2x^2-x+3)$
$=-2x^3-x^2+3x-4x^2-2x+6$
$=-2x^3-5x^2+x+6$

07

(A) $(x-1)^2=x^2-2x+1 \Rightarrow A=2$
(B) $(3x+By)^2=9x^2+6Bxy+B^2y^2$
$\qquad \Rightarrow 6B=12,\ B=2$
(C) $\left(\dfrac{a}{2}+4\right)\left(\dfrac{a}{2}-4\right)=\left(\dfrac{a}{2}\right)^2-4^2=\dfrac{a^2}{4}-16$
$\qquad \Rightarrow C=4$
(D) $(a-5)(2a+8)=2a^2+8a-10a-40$
$\qquad\qquad\qquad\qquad =2a^2-2a-40 \Rightarrow D=2$
(E) $(x-y)(x-y-4) \rightarrow$ Let $x-y=X$
$\quad (X)(X-4)=X^2-4X$
$\qquad\qquad\qquad =(x-y)^2-4(x-y)$
$\qquad\qquad\qquad =x^2-2xy+y^2-4x+4y$
$\qquad\qquad\qquad =x^2-2xy-4x+y^2+4y \Rightarrow E=2$

Therefore, the answer is (C)

08

$\dfrac{2021\times 2023+1}{2022}=\dfrac{(2022-1)\times(2022+1)+1}{2022}$
$=\dfrac{2022^2-1+1}{2022}$
$=\dfrac{2022^2}{2022}=2022$

$\dfrac{2021\times 2023+1}{2022}=2022$

09

$(4-1)(4+1)(4^2+1)(4^4+1)$
$=(4^2-1)(4^2+1)(4^4+1)$
$=(4^4-1)(4^4+1)$
$=4^8-1$

$$(4-1)(4+1)(4^2+1)(4^4+1)=4^8-1$$

10

(1) $(a+b)^2=a^2+2ab+b^2$
$a^2+b^2=(a+b)^2-2ab$
$=8^2-2(6)$
$=64-12=52$

$$a^2+b^2=52$$

(2) $\dfrac{1}{a}+\dfrac{1}{b}=\dfrac{1}{a}\cdot\dfrac{b}{b}+\dfrac{1}{b}\cdot\dfrac{a}{a}=\dfrac{b+a}{ab}$
$=\dfrac{8}{6}=\dfrac{4}{3}$

$$\dfrac{1}{a}+\dfrac{1}{b}=\dfrac{4}{3}$$

11

Each side of the new cube is $k+4$. Then the volume V of the cube is
$V=(k+4)^3$
$=(k+4)^2(k+4)$
$=(k^2+2k(4)+4^2)(k+4)$
$=(k^2+8k+16)(k+4)$
$=k^3+4k^2+8k^2+32k+16k+64$
$=k^3+12k^2+48k+64$

$$V=k^3+12k^2+48k+64$$

Chapter 5 Test Level 2

01

$\dfrac{3(2a^2+a-1)}{2}+\dfrac{3a-a^2+1}{6}$
$=\dfrac{3(2a^2+a-1)}{2}\cdot\dfrac{3}{3}+\dfrac{3a-a^2+1}{6}$
$=\dfrac{9(2a^2+a-1)+(3a-a^2+1)}{6}$
$=\dfrac{18a^2+9a-9+3a-a^2+1}{6}$
$=\dfrac{17a^2+12a-8}{6}$

02

$5-2\left[3x^2-4x+\dfrac{1}{2}\{5x-(4x^2-x)-6\}\right]$
$=5-2\left[3x^2-4x+\dfrac{1}{2}\{5x-4x^2+x-6\}\right]$
$=5-2\left[3x^2-4x+\dfrac{1}{2}\{-4x^2+6x-6\}\right]$
$=5-2\left[3x^2-4x-2x^2+3x-3\right]$
$=5-2[x^2-x-3]$
$=5-2x^2+2x+6$
$=-2x^2+2x+11$

03

$(a^3-2a+2)(2a-5)$
$=2a^4-5a^3-4a^2+10a+4a-10$
$=2a^4-5a^3-4a^2+14a-10$

04

$3x+[x-\{2x-(4x-\boxed{})+x^2\}+3x^2]$
$=3x+[x-\{2x-4x+\boxed{}+x^2\}+3x^2]$
$=3x+[x-\{-2x+\boxed{}+x^2\}+3x^2]$
$=3x+[x+2x-\boxed{}-x^2+3x^2]$
$=3x+[3x-\boxed{}+2x^2]$
$=3x+3x-\boxed{}+2x^2$
$=6x-\boxed{}+2x^2$
Since $6x-\boxed{}+2x^2=8x^2+7x$,
$\boxed{}=6x+2x^2-8x^2-7x=-6x^2-x$

$$\boxed{} = -6x^2 - x$$

05

$(x+m)(x+n) = x^2 + nx + mx + mn$
$ = x^2 + (n+m)x + mn$
$ = x^2 + kx + 40$

$n + m = k$ and $mn = 40$

Possible positive integers for m and n that satisfies $mn = 40$ are

m	n	$n+m=k$
1	40	41
2	20	22
4	10	14
5	8	13

Therefore, the answer is (B)

06

$(a-4)(a-2)a^2(a+2)(a+4)$
$= a^2(a-2)(a+2)(a-4)(a+4)$
$= a^2(a^2-4)(a^2-16)$
$= 16(16-4)(16-16)$
$= 16(12)(0) = 0$
$$(a-4)(a-2)a^2(a+2)(a+4) = 0$$

07

Multiply both sides by $(2-1)$. The we have
$\underline{(2-1)}(2+1)(2^2+1)(2^4+1)(2^8+1)$
$= \underline{(2-1)}(2^a - b)$

Then, we have
$(2^2-1)(2^2+1)(2^4+1)(2^8+1) = 2^a - b$
$(2^4-1)(2^4+1)(2^8+1) = 2^a - b$
$(2^8-1)(2^8+1) = 2^a - b$
$2^{16} - 1 = 2^a - b$
$\Rightarrow a = 16$ and $b = 1$

Therefore, $ab = (16)(1) = 16$
$$ab = 16$$

08

The side of the square base is $10 - 2x$ and the height is x. Therefore, the volume V of the box is

$V = (10 - 2x)^2 \cdot x$
$ = (10^2 - 2(10)(2x) + (2x^2)) \cdot x$
$ = (100 - 40x + 4x^2) \cdot x$
$ = 4x^3 - 40x^2 + 100x$
$$V = 4x^3 - 40x^2 + 100x$$

Chapter 6

Factoring

1. Factors and Prime Factorization

Check Point 1

① 450

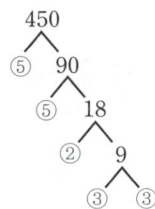

$450 = 2 \times 3^2 \times 5^2$

② 378

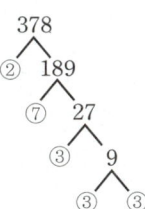

$378 = 2 \times 3^3 \times 7$

Check Point 2

① 50 and 85

Method 1:
$50 = 2 \times \boxed{5} \times 5$
$85 = \boxed{5} \times 17$

Method 2:

$\boxed{5} \begin{array}{|cc} 50 & 85 \\ \hline 10 & 17 \end{array}$

Therefore, the GCF is 5.

② $210xy^3$ and $198x^2y^2$

Method 1:

Method 2:

$\begin{array}{c|cc} \boxed{xy^2} & 30xy^3 & 18x^2y^2 \\ 3 & 30y & 18x \\ 2 & 10y & 6x \\ \hline & 5y & 3x \end{array}$

Therefore, the GCF is $2 \cdot 3xy^2 = 6xy^2$.

Check Point 3

① $6x - 3$

$\Rightarrow 6x = \underline{3} \times 2x$ and $-3 = \underline{3} \times (-1)$

The GCF of the polynomial is 3.

Therefore, $6x - 3 = 3(2x - 1)$.

② $12x^4 + 8x^2$

$\Rightarrow 12x^4 = \underline{4x^2} \times 3x^2$ and $8x^2 = \underline{4x^2} \times 2$

The GCF of the polynomial is $4x^2$.

Therefore, $12x^4 + 8x^2 = 4x^2 \ (3x^2 + 2)$

③ $4a^3 - 6a^2 + 12a$

$\Rightarrow 4a^3 = \underline{2a} \times 2a^2$, $-6a^2 = \underline{2a} \times (-3a)$, and $12a = \underline{2a} \times 6$

The GCF of the polynomial is $2a$.

Therefore, $4a^3 - 6a^2 + 12a = 2a(2a^2 - 3a + 6)$

④ $18a^2 - 12a - 24$

$\Rightarrow 18a^2 = \underline{6} \times 3a^2$, $-12a = \underline{6} \times (-2a)$, and $-24 = \underline{6} \times (-4)$

The GCF of the polynomial is 6.

Therefore, $18a^2 - 12a - 24 = 6(3a^2 - 2a - 4)$

Solutions Manual

Review Exercise

01

(1) 168

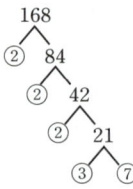

$168 = 2^3 \times 3 \times 7$

(2) 392

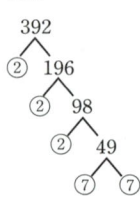

$392 = 2^3 \times 7^2$

02

(1) 100 and 225

```
5 | 100   225
5 |  20    45
       4     9
```

Therefore, the GCF is $5 \times 5 = 25$

(2) $9x^3y^4$ and $15xy^2$

```
xy² | 9x³y⁴   15xy²
  3 | 9x²y²    15
      3x²y²     5
```

Therefore, the GCF is $xy^2 \times 3 = 3xy^2$

(3) 25, 90 and 150

```
5 | 25   90   150
      5   18    30
```

Therefore, the GCF is 5

(4) $16x^3y^2$, $28x^2y^3$ and $100x^5y^4$

```
x²y² | 16x³y²   28x²y³   100x⁵y⁴
   2 | 16x       28y      100x³y²
   2 |  8x       14y       50x³y²
         4x        7y       25x³y²
```

Therefore, the GCF is $x^2y^2 \times 2 \times 2 = 4x^2y^2$

03

$a(a+b)(a-b) = a \times (a+b) \times (a-b)$

The factors are

1, a, $(a+b)$, $(a-b)$, $a(a+b)$, $a(a-b)$,

$(a+b)(a-b)$, and $a(a+b)(a-b)$

Since $(a+b)(a-b) = a^2 - b^2$,

The only expression that is not a factor is $a^2 + b^2$.

The answer is (D)

04

(1) $16x^3 - 12x^2$

$16x^3 = \underline{4x^2} \times 4x$ and $-12x^2 = \underline{4x^2} \times (-3)$

The GCF of the polynomial is $4x^2$.

$$16x^3 - 12x^2 = 4x^2(4x-3)$$

(2) $30xy^2 + 36y$

$30xy^2 = \underline{6y} \times 5xy$ and $36y = \underline{6y} \times 6$

The GCF of the polynomial is $6y$.

$$30xy^2 + 36y = 6y(5xy + 6)$$

(3) $xy^2 - x^2 + 2xy$

$xy^2 = \underline{x} \times y^2$, $-x^2 = \underline{x} \times (-x)$, and $2xy = \underline{x} \times 2y$

The GCF of the polynomial is x.

$$xy^2 - x^2 + 2xy = x(y^2 - x + 2y)$$

(4) $8ab^2 + 4ab - 6ab^3$

$8ab^2 = \underline{2ab} \times 4b$, $4ab = \underline{2ab} \times 2$ and $-6ab^3 = \underline{2ab} \times (-3b^2)$

The GCF of the polynomial is $2ab$.

$$8ab^2 + 4ab - 6ab^3 = 2ab(4b + 2 - 3b^2)$$

05

$2y(x-y)(x-2y)$

$x^2y - 2xy^2 = xy(x-2y)$

In answer choices, $y(x-2y)$ is the only common factor

The answer is (C)

2. Factoring Binomials

Check Point 1

① $24x^3+12x=12x(2x^2+1)$
② $9x^2-36=9(x^2-4)=9(x^2-2^2)$
$\qquad =9(x-2)(x+2)$
③ $4x^2-\dfrac{y^2}{25}=(2x)^2-\left(\dfrac{y}{5}\right)^2$
$\qquad =\left(2x-\dfrac{y}{5}\right)\left(2x+\dfrac{y}{5}\right)$
④ $32a^3b-8ab^3=8ab(4a^2-b^2)$
$\qquad =8ab((2a)^2-b^2)$
$\qquad =8ab(2a-b)(2a+b)$
⑤ $(a^2-4)^2-5(a^2-4)$ → Let $a^2-4=A$
$=A^2-5A=A(A-5)$
$=(a^2-4)(a^2-4-5)$
$=(a^2-4)(a^2-9)$
$=(a^2-2^2)(a^2-3^2)$
$=(a-2)(a+2)(a-3)(a+3)$
⑥ $a^4-b^4=(a^2)^2-(b^2)^2$
$\qquad =(a^2-b^2)(a^2+b^2)$
$\qquad =(a-b)(a+b)(a^2+b^2)$

Review Exercise

01
(1) $x^2-4=x^2-2^2=(x-2)(x+2)$
(2) $4x^2-100=4(x^2-25)=4(x^2-5^2)$
$\qquad =4(x-5)(x+5)$
(3) $2ay+4ax=2a(y+2x)$
(4) $16x^2-1=(4x)^2-1^2=(4x-1)(4x+1)$

02
(1) $10ab^2-15a^2b=5ab(2b-3a)$
(2) $2x^2-8y^2=2(x^2-4y^2)$
$\qquad =2(x^2-(2y)^2)$
$\qquad =2(x-2y)(x+2y)$
(3) $x(a+b)-y(a+b)$ → Let $a+b=A$
$=xA-yA=A(x-y)$
$=(a+b)(x-y)$
(4) $a(x-y)+b(y-x)$
$=a(x-y)-b(x-y)$ → Let $x-y=A$
$=aA-bA=A(a-b)$
$=(x-y)(a-b)$

03
(1) $2x(2a+b^2)-4y(2a+b^2)$ → Let $2a+b^2=A$
$=2xA-4yA=A(2x-4y)$
$=(2a+b^2)(2x-4y)$
(2) $3a(4x-y)-2b(y-4x)$
$=3a(4x-y)+2b(4x-y)$ → Let $4x-y=A$
$=3aA+2bA=A(3a+2b)$
$=(4x-y)(3a+2b)$

04
(1) $4(x^2+6)^2-25(x^2+6)$ → Let $x^2+6=A$
$=4A^2-25A=A(4A-25)$
$=(x^2+6)(4(x^2+6)-25)$
$=(x^2+6)(4x^2-1)$
$=(x^2+6)((2x)^2-1^2)$
$=(x^2+6)(2x-1)(2x+1)$
(2) $3(9a^2-4)+(9a^2-4)^2$ → Let $9a^2-4=A$
$=3A+A^2=A(3+A)$
$=(9a^2-4)(3+(9a^2-4))$
$=(9a^2-4)(9a^2-1)$
$=((3a)^2-2^2)((3a)^2-1^2)$
$=(3a-2)(3a+2)(3a-1)(3a+1)$

05

$6ab^2(a-3)+4ab(3-a)$
$=6ab^2(a-3)-4ab(a-3)$
$=(a-3)(6ab^2-4ab)$
$=2ab(a-3)(3b-2)$
$=2ab(a-3)(xb+y)$
$\Rightarrow x=3,\ y=-2$
So, $xy=(3)(-2)=-6$

$\qquad\qquad\qquad\qquad xy=6$

06

$9y^2-16x^4=(3y)^2-(4x^2)^2$

Solutions Manual

$= (3y-4x^2)(3y+4x^2)$
Since $3y-4x^2=-(4x^2-3y)=-2$,
$9y^2-16x^4=(3y-4x^2)(3y+4x^2)$
$-8=(-2)(3y+4x^2), \ 3y+4x^2=4$
$$3y+4x^2=4$$

07

$x^2(x-y)+y^2(y-x)=x^2(x-y)-y^2(x-y)$
$= (x-y)(x^2-y^2)$
$= (x-y)(x-y)(x+y)$
$= (x-y)^2(x+y)$
$= (-3)^2(4)=36$

3. Factoring Trinomials

Check Point 1

① $x^2+10x+25=x^2+2(x)(5)+5^2=(x+5)^2$
② $4x^2-12xy+9y^2$
$=(2x)^2-2(2x)(3y)+(3y)^2=(2x-3y)^2$
③ $25a^3b^2-20a^2b^3+4ab^4$
$=ab^2(25a^2-20ab+4b^2)$
$=ab^2((5a)^2-2(5a)(2b)+(2b)^2)$
$=ab^2(5a-2b)^2$
④ $a^2+\dfrac{ab}{2}+\dfrac{b^2}{16}=a^2+2(a)\left(\dfrac{b}{4}\right)+\left(\dfrac{b}{4}\right)^2=\left(a+\dfrac{b}{4}\right)^2$

Check Point 2

① x^2-x-12
Since $-4\times 3=-12$ and $-4+3=-1$,
$x^2-x-12=(x-4)(x+3)$
② $x^2+3x-10$
Since $-2\times 5=-10$ and $-2+5=3$,
$x^2+3x-10=(x-2)(x+5)$
③ $x^2-xy-30y^2$
Since $-6\times 5=-30$ and $-6+5=-1$,
$x^2-xy-30y^2=(x-6y)(x+5y)$

④ $3x^2y+24xy^2+36y^3=3y(x^2+8xy+12y^2)$
Since $2\times 6=12$ and $2+6=8$,
$3y(x^2+8xy+12y^2)=3y(x+2y)(x+6y)$

Check Point 3

① $\underbrace{6x^2-x-2}_{6\times-2=-12} \rightarrow -12=-4\times 3 \Rightarrow -4+3=-1$

$\begin{array}{c} 3x \\ 2x \end{array} \times \begin{array}{c} -2 \\ 1 \end{array} \rightarrow \begin{array}{c} -4x \\ (+) \ 3x \\ \hline -x \end{array}$

$6x^2-x-2=(3x-2)(2x+1)$

② $\underbrace{3x^2-10x+8}_{3\times 8=24}$

$\rightarrow 24=-4\times-6 \Rightarrow -4+(-6)=-10$

$\begin{array}{c} 3x \\ x \end{array} \times \begin{array}{c} -4 \\ -2 \end{array} \rightarrow \begin{array}{c} -4x \\ (+) \ -6x \\ \hline -10x \end{array}$

$3x^2-10x+8=(3x-4)(x-2)$

③ $\underbrace{12x^2-13x-35}_{12\times-35=-420}$

$\rightarrow -420=15\times-28 \Rightarrow 15+(-28)=-13$

$\begin{array}{c} 4x \\ 3x \end{array} \times \begin{array}{c} 5 \\ -7 \end{array} \rightarrow \begin{array}{c} 15x \\ (+) \ -28x \\ \hline -13x \end{array}$

$12x^2-13x-35=(4x+5)(3x-7)$

④ $10x^2y+9xy^2-9y^3=y(10x^2+9xy-9y^2)$
$\underbrace{10x^2+9xy-9y^2}_{10\times-9=-90}$

$\rightarrow -90=15\times-6 \Rightarrow 15+(-6)=9$

$\begin{array}{c} 5x \\ 2x \end{array} \times \begin{array}{c} -3y \\ 3y \end{array} \rightarrow \begin{array}{c} -6xy \\ (+) \ 15xy \\ \hline 9xy \end{array}$

$10x^2y+9xy^2-9y^3=y(5x-3y)(2x+3y)$

Review Exercise

01

(1) $x^2+8x+16=x^2+2(x)(4)+4^2=(x+4)^2$
(2) $x^2-12x+36=x^2-2(x)(6)+6^2=(x-6)^2$

(3) $4x^2+4x+1=(2x)^2+2(2x)(1)+1^2$
$=(2x+1)^2$
(4) $25x^2-30xy+9y^2$
$=(5x)^2-2(5x)(3y)+(3y)^2=(5x-3y)^2$

02

(1) $9x^2+3x+\dfrac{1}{4}=(3x)^2+2(3x)\left(\dfrac{1}{2}\right)+\left(\dfrac{1}{2}\right)^2$
$=\left(3x+\dfrac{1}{2}\right)^2$
(2) $2x^2-12x+18=2(x^2-6x+9)$
$=2(x^2-2(x)(3)+3^2)$
$=2(x-3)^2$
(3) $27x^2-36xy+12y^2=3(9x^2-12xy+4y^2)$
$=3((3x)^2-2(3x)(2y)+(2y)^2)$
$=3(3x-2y)^2$
(4) $20x^2+\dfrac{20xy}{3}+\dfrac{5y^2}{9}=5\left(4x^2+\dfrac{4}{3}xy+\dfrac{1}{9}y^2\right)$
$=5\left((2x)^2+2(2x)\left(\dfrac{1}{3}y\right)+\left(\dfrac{1}{3}y\right)^2\right)$
$=5\left(2x+\dfrac{1}{3}y\right)^2$

03

(1) x^2-8x+7
Since $-7\times-1=7$ and $-7+(-1)=-8$,
$x^2-8x+7=(x-1)(x-7)$
(2) $x^2+6x-16$
Since $-2\times 8=-16$ and $-2+8=6$,
$x^2+6x-16=(x-2)(x+8)$
(3) $\dfrac{x^2}{2}+8x+24=\dfrac{1}{2}(x^2+16x+48)$
Since $4\times 12=48$ and $4+12=16$,
$\dfrac{1}{2}(x^2+16x+48)=\dfrac{1}{2}(x+4)(x+12)$
(4) $18+3x-3x^2=-3(x^2-x-6)$
Since $-3\times 2=-6$ and $-3+2=-1$,
$-3(x^2-x-6)=-3(x-3)(x+2)$

04

(1) $3x^3y-9x^2y-30xy=3xy(x^2-3x-10)$
Since $-5\times 2=-10$ and $-5+2=-3$,
$3xy(x^2-3x-10)=3xy(x-5)(x+2)$

(2) $\dfrac{x^2}{4}-\dfrac{5xy}{2}+4y^2=\dfrac{1}{4}(x^2-10xy+16y^2)$
Since $-8\times-2=16$ and $-8+(-2)=-10$,
$\dfrac{1}{4}(x^2-10xy+16y^2)=\dfrac{1}{4}(x-8y)(x-2y)$

05

(1) $\underbrace{3x^2-7x-6}_{3\times -6=-18} \rightarrow -18=-9\times 2 \Rightarrow -9+2=-7$

$\begin{array}{rcr} 3x & \searrow \quad 2 \rightarrow & 2x \\ x & \nearrow \quad -3 \rightarrow & (+)\ -9x \\ & & \overline{-7x} \end{array}$

$3x^2-7x-6=(3x+2)(x-3)$

(2) $\underbrace{4x^2+7xy+3y^2}_{4\times 3=12} \rightarrow 12=3\times 4 \Rightarrow 3+4=7$

$\begin{array}{rcr} 4x & \searrow \quad 3y \rightarrow & 3xy \\ x & \nearrow \quad y \rightarrow & (+)\ 4xy \\ & & \overline{7xy} \end{array}$

$4x^2+7xy+3y^2=(4x+3y)(x+y)$

(3) $5x^3y+4x^2y-xy=xy(5x^2+4x-1)$
$\underbrace{5x^2+4x-1}_{5\times -1=-5} \rightarrow 5=-1\times 5 \Rightarrow -1+5=4$

$\begin{array}{rcr} 5x & \searrow \quad -1 \rightarrow & -x \\ x & \nearrow \quad 1 \rightarrow & (+)\ 5x \\ & & \overline{4x} \end{array}$

$xy(5x^2+4x-1)=xy(5x-1)(x+1)$

(4) $6x^3y-13x^2y^2+6xy^3=xy(6x^2-13xy+6y^2)$
$\underbrace{6x^2-13xy+6y^2}_{6\times 6=36}$

$\rightarrow 36=-9\times -4 \Rightarrow -9+(-4)=-13$

$\begin{array}{rcr} 3x & \searrow \quad -2y \rightarrow & -4xy \\ 2x & \nearrow \quad -3y \rightarrow & (+)\ -9xy \\ & & \overline{-13xy} \end{array}$

$xy(6x^2-13xy+6y^2)=xy(3x-2y)(2x-3y)$

06

(1) $2x^2-\dfrac{7xy}{3}-y^2=\dfrac{1}{3}(6x^2-7xy-3y^2)$
$\underbrace{6x^2-7xy-3y^2}_{6\times -3=-18}$

$\rightarrow -18=-9\times 2 \Rightarrow -9+2=-7$

Solutions Manual

$$\begin{array}{l} 3x \searrow \nearrow y \to 2xy \\ 2x \nearrow \searrow -3y \to (+) \ -9xy \\ \hline -7xy \end{array}$$

$$\frac{1}{3}(6x^2-7xy-3y^2)=\frac{1}{3}(3x+y)(2x-3y)$$

(2) $2x^2-\frac{16xy}{3}+\frac{5y^2}{6}=\frac{1}{6}(12x^2-32xy+5y^2)$

$\underbrace{12x^2-32xy+5y^2}_{12\times 5=60}$

$\to 60=-30\times -2 \Rightarrow -30+(-2)=-32$

$$\begin{array}{l} 6x \searrow \nearrow -y \to -2xy \\ 2x \nearrow \searrow -5y \to (+) \ -30xy \\ \hline -32xy \end{array}$$

$$\frac{1}{6}(12x^2-32xy+5y^2)=\frac{1}{6}(6x-y)(2x-5y)$$

07

$x^2-x-12=(x-4)(x+3)$
$=(\sqrt{3}+4-4)(\sqrt{3}+4+3)$
$=\sqrt{3}\ (\sqrt{3}+7)=3+7\sqrt{3}$

08

Let $4x^2-5x+a=(x-2)(4x+k)$. Then,
$4x^2-5x+a=4x^2+kx-8x-2k$
$=4x^2+(k-8)x-2k$
$-5x=(k-8)x,\ k=3$
$a=-2k=-2(3)=-6$

$a=-6$

09

Let $\dfrac{6x^2+ax-10}{3x-2}=A$.

$\Rightarrow 6x^2+ax-10=(3x-2)A$
$=(3x-2)(2x+k)$
$=6x^2+3kx-4x-2k$
$=6x^2+(3k-4)x-2k$
$-10=-2k,\ k=5$
$ax=(3k-4)x$
$a=3k-4=3(5)-4=11$

$a=11$

10

Let $4x^2+11x+a=(x+3)(4x+m)$. Then,
$11x=mx+12x,\ 11x=(m+12)x,\ m=-1$
$a=3m=3(-1)=-3$
Also, let $2x^2+bx+3=(x+3)(2x+n)$. Then,
$3=3n,\ n=1$
$bx=nx+6x,\ bx=(n+6)x$
$bx=(1+6)x,\ b=7$
So, $a+b=-3+7=4$

$a+b=4$

11

(1) $(x+5)(x+3)+a=x^2+3x+5x+15+a$
$=x^2+8x+(15+a)$
Since $8x$ is equal to $2(x)(4)$,
$15+a=4^2,\ a=1$

$a=1$

(2) $5x^2+4x(x-a)+16=5x^2+4x^2-4ax+16$
$=9x^2-4ax+16$
$=(3x)^2-4ax+4^2$
Since $4ax$ must be equal to $2(3x)(4)$,
$4ax=2(3x)(4),\ 4ax=24x,\ a=6$

$a=6$

12

$16x^2+axy^2+\dfrac{9y^4}{4}=(4x)^2+axy^2+\left(\dfrac{3y^2}{2}\right)^2$

$axy^2=2(4x)\left(\dfrac{3y^2}{2}\right),\ axy^2=12xy^2,\ a=12$

$a=12$

13

$x^4+4x^2y-12y^2=(x^2+ay)(x^2+by)$
$4x^2y=bx^2y+ax^2y,\ 4x^2y=(b+a)x^2y$
$4=b+a \Rightarrow a+b=4$

$a+b=4$

Chapter 6 Test Level 1

01

$4xy - 12xy^2 = 4xy(1-3y)$

$4xy^2$ is not a factor.

Therefore, the answer is (B)

02

(A)~(C) are all correct.

(D) $(2x-y)(2x-y-3)-4 \to$ Let $2x-y=A$
$= A(A-3)-4 = A^2-3A-4$
$= (A-4)(A+1)$
$= (2x-y-4)(2x-y+1)$

Therefore, the answer is (E)

03

(1) $(x-5)^2 - 9y^4$
$= (x-5)^2 - (3y^2)^2$
$= ((x-5)-3y^2)((x-5)+3y^2)$
$= -(3y^2-x+5)(3y^2+x-5)$

(2) $(2x+1)^2 - (3x-2)^2$
$\to$ Let $2x+1=A$ and $3x-2=B$
$= A^2 - B^2$
$= (A-B)(A+B)$
$= ((2x+1)-(3x-2))((2x+1)+(3x-2))$
$= (3-x)(5x-1) = -(x-3)(5x-1)$

04

(1) $4(x-1)(x+7)+k$
$= 4(x^2+7x-x-7)+k = 4(x^2+6x-7)+k$
$= 4x^2+24x-28+k$
$= (2x)^2 + 24x + (-28+k)$

Since $24x$ is equal to $2(2x)(6)$,
$-28+k=6^2$, $k=36+28=64$

$k=64$

(2) $4x^2 - (4k-1)xy + y^2$
$= (2x)^2 - (4k-1)xy + y^2$

Since $(4k-1)xy$ must be equal to $2(2x)y$,
$(4k-1)xy = 2(2x)y$
$4k-1=4$, $k=\dfrac{5}{4}$

$k=\dfrac{5}{4}$

05

$x+y = (1-\sqrt{2})+(1+\sqrt{2}) = 2$
$x-y = (1-\sqrt{2})-(1+\sqrt{2}) = -2\sqrt{2}$

(1) $x^2-y^2 = (x-y)(x+y) = -2\sqrt{2} \times 2 = -4\sqrt{2}$

$x^2-y^2 = -4\sqrt{2}$

(2) $x^2-2xy+y^2 = (x-y)^2 = (-2\sqrt{2})^2 = 8$

$x^2-2xy+y^2 = 8$

06

(A) $x^2-6xy+9y^2 = x^2-2(3x)y+(3y)^2$
$= (x-3y)^2$

(B) $4x^2 - x + \dfrac{1}{16} = (2x)^2 - 2(2x)\left(\dfrac{1}{4}\right)+\left(\dfrac{1}{4}\right)^2$
$= \left(2x - \dfrac{1}{4}\right)^2$

(C) $1-2a+a^2 = 1^2 - 2(1)(a)+a^2 = (1-a)^2$

(D) $9a^2+12ab+4b^2 = (3a)^2+2(3a)(2b)+(2b)^2$
$= (3a+2b)^2$

(E) $25y^2 - \dfrac{10}{3}y + \dfrac{4}{9} \neq (5y)^2 - 2(5y)\left(\dfrac{2}{3}\right)+\left(\dfrac{2}{3}\right)^2$

Therefore, the answer is (E)

07

$ax^2 + (2b-1)x - 12 = (3x+4)(5x+c)$
$= 15x^2 + 3cx + 20x + 4c$
$= 15x^2 + (3c+20)x + 4c$

$\Rightarrow a=15$
$-12 = 4c$, $c=-3$
$2b-1 = 3c+20$
$2b-1 = 3(-3)+20$
$2b-1 = 11$, $2b=12$, $b=6$

Therefore, $a+b+c = 15+6+(-3) = 18$

$a+b+c = 18$

08

(1) $98^2 - 4 = 98^2 - 2^2$
$= (98-2)(98+2)$
$= 96 \times 100 = 9{,}600$

(2) $25 \times 77 - 25 \times 75 = 25(77-75)$
$= 25 \times 2 = 50$

09

$ax^2 - c = (2x+a)(x+b)$
$\quad = 2x^2 + 2bx + ax + ab$
$\quad = 2x^2 + (2b+a)x + ab$
$\Rightarrow a = 2$
$\quad 0 = 2b+a, \ 0 = 2b+2, \ b = -1$
$\quad -c = ab = (2)(-1), \ c = 2$
Therefore, $a+b+c = 2+(-1)+2 = 3$
$$a+b+c = 3$$

10

$6x^2y - 8xy - 8y = 2y(3x^2 - 4x - 4)$
$\qquad\qquad\qquad\quad = 2y(3x+2)(x-2)$
$12x^3y - 4x^2y - 8xy = 4xy(3x^2 - x - 2)$
$\qquad\qquad\qquad\qquad = 4xy(3x+2)(x-1)$

In answer choices, $y(3x+2)$ is one of the common factors.

$$\text{The answer is (A)}$$

11

$-a^2(2b-a) - 4b^2(a-2b)$
$= a^2(a-2b) - 4b^2(a-2b)$
$= (a-2b)(a^2 - 4b^2)$
$= (a-2b)(a^2 - (2b)^2)$
$= (a-2b)(a-2b)(a+2b)$
$= (a-2b)^2(a+2b) = 2^2 \times 5 = 20$
$$-a^2(2b-a) - 4b^2(a-2b) = 20$$

Chapter 6 Test Level 2

01

$2a^4 - 32b^4 = 2(a^4 - 16b^4)$
$\qquad\qquad = 2((a^2)^2 - (4b^2)^2)$
$\qquad\qquad = 2(a^2 - 4b^2)(a^2 + 4b^2)$
$\qquad\qquad = 2(a^2 - (2b)^2)(a^2 + 4b^2)$
$\qquad\qquad = 2(a-2b)(a+2b)(a^2 + 4b^2)$

02

First, rationalize a and b.
$a = \dfrac{\sqrt{5}+2}{\sqrt{5}-2} \cdot \dfrac{\sqrt{5}+2}{\sqrt{5}+2} = \dfrac{(\sqrt{5}+2)^2}{(\sqrt{5})^2 - (2)^2}$
$\quad = \dfrac{5+4\sqrt{5}+4}{5-4} = 9+4\sqrt{5}$
$b = \dfrac{\sqrt{5}-2}{\sqrt{5}+2} \cdot \dfrac{\sqrt{5}-2}{\sqrt{5}-2} = \dfrac{(\sqrt{5}-2)^2}{(\sqrt{5})^2 - (2)^2}$
$\quad = \dfrac{5-4\sqrt{5}+4}{5-4} = 9-4\sqrt{5}$
$a^2 - b^2 = (a-b)(a+b)$
$\qquad = ((9+4\sqrt{5}) - (9-4\sqrt{5}))((9+4\sqrt{5}) + (9-4\sqrt{5}))$
$\qquad = (8\sqrt{5})(18) = 144\sqrt{5}$
$$a^2 - b^2 = 144\sqrt{5}$$

03

(1) $4x^3y - 32x^2y^2 + 64xy^3$
$\quad = 4xy(x^2 - 8xy + 16y^2)$
$\quad = 4xy(x^2 - 2(x)(4y) + (4y)^2)$
$\quad = 4xy(x-4y)^2$

(2) $64 - \dfrac{81}{4}x^4 = \dfrac{1}{4}(256 - 81x^4)$
$\qquad\qquad\quad = \dfrac{1}{4}(16^2 - (9x^2)^2)$
$\qquad\qquad\quad = \dfrac{1}{4}(16 - 9x^2)(16 + 9x^2)$
$\qquad\qquad\quad = \dfrac{1}{4}(4^2 - (3x)^2)(16 + 9x^2)$
$\qquad\qquad\quad = \dfrac{1}{4}(4-3x)(4+3x)(16 + 9x^2)$

(3) $(2x^2+3x)^2 - (2x^2+3x+3) - 3$
$\qquad\qquad\qquad\qquad\qquad \rightarrow \text{Let } 2x^2+3x = A$
$= A^2 - (A+3) - 3$
$= A^2 - A - 6$
$= (A-3)(A+2)$

$\quad =(2x^2+3x-3)(2x^2+3x+2)$
(4) $2(x-2)^2-3(x-2)(x+3)-20(x+3)^2$
$\qquad\qquad\qquad\rightarrow$ Let $x-2=A$ and $x+3=B$
$=2A^2-3AB-20B^2$
$=(2A+5B)(A-4B)$
$=(2(x-2)+5(x+3))((x-2)-4(x+3))$
$=(7x+11)(-3x-14)$
$=-(7x+11)(3x+14)$

04

Let $4x^2+kx-5=(2x-1)(2x+a)$. Then,
$\quad 4x^2+kx-5=4x^2+2ax-2x-a$
$\qquad\qquad\quad =4x^2+(2a-2)x-a$
$\Rightarrow a=5$
$\quad k=2a-2=2(5)-2=8$
$\hfill k=8$

05

$x+y=(1-\sqrt{2})+(1+\sqrt{2})=2$
$xy=(1-\sqrt{2})(1+\sqrt{2})=1^2-(\sqrt{2})^2=-1$
Since $(x+y)^2=x^2+2xy+y^2$,
$\quad x^2+y^2=(x+y)^2-2xy$
$\qquad\quad =2^2-2(-1)=6$
$\hfill x^2+y^2=6$

06

Let $3x^2-7x+a=(3x+2)(x+m)$. Then,
$\quad -7x=3mx+2x$,
$\quad -7x=(3m+2)x,\ m=-3$
$\quad a=2m=2(-3)=-6$
Let $6x^2+bx-2=(3x+2)(2x+n)$. Then,
$-2=2n,\ n=-1$
$bx=3nx+4x,\ bx=(3n+4)x$,
$bx=(3(-1)+4)x,\ b=1$
Threrefore, $a+b=(-6)+1=-5$
$\hfill a+b=-5$

07

$x^2+ax+16=(x+b)(x+c)$
$\qquad\qquad\quad =x^2+(b+c)x+bc$

Find two integers b and c whose product is $bc=16$.

b	c	$a=b+c$
1	16	17
-1	-16	-17
2	8	10
-2	-8	-10
4	4	8
-4	-4	-8

So the answer is (D)

08

$98\times 98+98\times 101-98\times 99-102\times 102$
$=98^2-102^2+98\times 101-98\times 99$
$=(98-102)(98+102)+98(101-99)$
$=(-4)(200)+98(2)$
$=-800+196=-604$

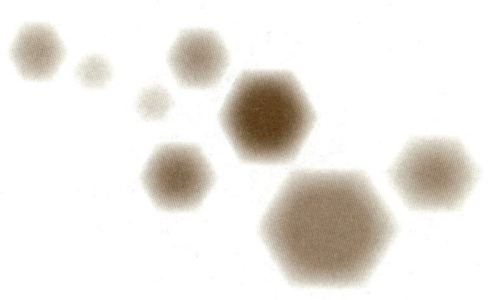

Solutions Manual

Chapter 7: Quadratic Equations

1. Solving Basic Quadratic Equations

Check Point 1

(A) $4(x-2)=3x+1$
$4x-8=3x+1$
$x-9=0$ → Linear equation

(B) $2x^2-3x+1=2(x^2+1)$
$2x^2-3x+1=2x^2+2$
$-3x-1=0$ → Linear equation

(C) $(2x+1)^2-4x^2=0$
$4x^2+4x+1-4x^2=0$
$4x+1=0$ → Linear equation

(D) $(2x-1)(2x+1)+3=(x-2)(x+2)$
$4x^2-1+3=x^2-4$
$4x^2+2=x^2-4$
$3x^2+6=0$
   → Quadratic equation

(E) $(x-4)(4+x)+(x+1)(1-x)=-4x$
$(x-4)(x+4)+(1+x)(1-x)=-4x$
$x^2-16+(1-x^2)=-4x$
$x^2-16+1-x^2=-4x$
$-15=-4x$
$4x-15=0$
   → Linear equation

   The answer is (D)

Check Point 2

① $6x^2+5=59$
$6x^2=54$
$x^2=9$
$x=\pm\sqrt{9}=\pm 3$
   The solutions are $x=-3$ and $x=3$

② $4x^2-3=2-x^2$
$5x^2=5$
$x^2=1$
$x=\pm\sqrt{1}=\pm 1$
   The solutions are $x=-1$ and $x=1$

③ $(2x-1)^2=25$
$2x-1=\pm\sqrt{25}$
$2x-1=\pm 5$
$2x=6$ or $2x=-4$
$x=3$ or $x=-2$
   The solutions are $x=-2$ and $x=3$

④ $2(2x-3)^2-4=10$
$2(2x-3)^2=14$
$(2x-3)^2=7$
$2x-3=\pm\sqrt{7}$
$2x=3\pm\sqrt{7}$, $x=\dfrac{3\pm\sqrt{7}}{2}$

The solutions are $x=\dfrac{3-\sqrt{7}}{2}$ and $x=\dfrac{3+\sqrt{7}}{2}$

Check Point 3

① $2x^2+3x-2=0$
$(2x-1)(x+2)=0$
$2x-1=0$ or $x+2=0$
$x=\dfrac{1}{2}$ or $x=-2$
   The solutions are $x=-2$ and $x=\dfrac{1}{2}$

② $3x^2-2x=2x^2+24$
$x^2-2x-24=0$
$(x-6)(x+4)=0$
$x-6=0$ or $x+4=0$
$x=6$ or $x=-4$
   The solutions are $x=-4$ and $x=6$

③ $\quad 2(x-3)^2=8x$
$\quad\quad (x-3)^2=4x$
$\quad\quad x^2-6x+9=4x$
$\quad\quad x^2-10x+9=0$
$\quad (x-1)(x-9)=0$
$\quad x-1=0$ or $x-9=0$
$\quad x=1$ or $\quad x=9$
$\quad\quad\quad$ The solutions are $x=1$ and $x=9$

④ $(x+2)(x-2)=3x(x-1)-(x+2)$
$\quad\quad x^2-4=3x^2-3x-x-2$
$\quad -2x^2+4x-2=0$
$\quad\quad x^2-2x+1=0$
$\quad\quad (x-1)^2=0$
$\quad\quad x-1=0,\ x=1$
$\quad\quad\quad$ The solution is $x=1$

Review Exercise

01

(1) $x^2+4=8$
$\quad x^2=4,\ x=\pm 2$
$\quad\quad$ The solutions are $x=-2$ and $x=2$

(2) $x^2-4=32$
$\quad x^2=36, x=\pm 6$
$\quad\quad$ The solutions are $x=-6$ and $x=6$

(3) $9x^2-12=600$
$\quad\quad 9x^2=612$
$\quad\quad x^2=68,\ x=\pm 2\sqrt{17}$
$\quad$ The solutions are $x=-2\sqrt{17}$ and $x=2\sqrt{17}$

(4) $10+5x^2=330$
$\quad\quad 5x^2=320$
$\quad\quad x^2=64, x=\pm 8$
$\quad\quad$ The solutions are $x=-8$ and $x=8$

02

(1) $8x^2+7=31$
$\quad\quad 8x^2=24$
$\quad\quad x^2=3,\ x=\pm\sqrt{3}$
$\quad\quad$ The solutions are $x=-\sqrt{3}$ and $x=\sqrt{3}$

(2) $(2x-5)^2=81$
$\quad 2x-5=9$ or $2x-5=-9$
$\quad\quad x=7$ or $x=-2$
$\quad\quad$ The solutions are $x=-2$ and $x=7$

(3) $4(3x+1)^2=36$
$\quad\quad (3x+1)^2=9$
$\quad 3x+1=3$ or $3x+1=-3$
$\quad\quad x=\dfrac{2}{3}$ or $\quad x=-\dfrac{4}{3}$
$\quad\quad$ The solutions are $x=-\dfrac{4}{3}$ and $x=\dfrac{2}{3}$

(4) $\dfrac{5x^2}{2}-x^2=216$
$\quad\quad \dfrac{3x^2}{2}=216$
$\quad\quad x^2=144,\ x=\pm 12$
$\quad\quad$ The solutions are $x=-12$ and $x=12$

03

(1) $x^2+4x+4=0$
$\quad (x+2)^2=0$
$\quad x+2=0,\ x=-2$
$\quad\quad$ The solution is $x=-2$

(2) $x^2-15x-100=0$
$\quad (x-20)(x+5)=0$
$\quad x-20=0$ or $x+5=0$
$\quad\quad x=20$ or $\quad x=-5$
$\quad\quad$ The solutions are $x=-5$ and $x=20$

(3) $8x^2+4x=0$
$\quad 4x(2x+1)=0$
$\quad 4x=0$ or $2x+1=0$
$\quad\quad x=0$ or $\quad x=-\dfrac{1}{2}$
$\quad\quad$ The solutions are $x=-\dfrac{1}{2}$ and $x=0$

(4) $3x^2-33x+72=0$
$\quad x^2-11x+24=0$
$\quad (x-8)(x-3)=0$
$\quad x-8=0$ or $x-3=0$
$\quad\quad x=8$ or $\quad x=3$
$\quad\quad$ The solutions are $x=3$ and $x=8$

Solutions Manual

04

(1) $7x^2+35x-42=0$
$x^2+5x-6=0$
$(x-1)(x+6)=0$
$x-1=0$ or $x+6=0$
$x=1$ or $x=-6$
 The solutions are $x=-6$ and $x=1$

(2) $6x^2+15x+9=0$
$2x^2+5x+3=0$
$(x+1)(2x+3)=0$
$x+1=0$ or $2x+3=0$
$x=-1$ or $x=-\dfrac{3}{2}$
 The solutions are $x=-\dfrac{3}{2}$ and $x=-1$

(3) $7x^2+32=7-40x$
$7x^2+40x+25=0$
$(x+5)(7x+5)=0$
$x+5=0$ or $7x+5=0$
$x=-5$ or $x=-\dfrac{5}{7}$
 The solutions are $x=-5$ and $x=-\dfrac{5}{7}$

(4) $x(x-2)=3(x-2)$
$x^2-2x=3x-6$
$x^2-5x+6=0$
$(x-3)(x-2)=0$
$x-3=0$ or $x-2$
$x=3$ or $x=2$
 The solutions are $x=2$ and $x=3$

05

$x^2-2x=8$
$x^2-2x-8=0$
$(x+2)(x-4)=0$
$x+2=0$ or $x-4=0$
$x=-2$ or $x=4$
 The possible values of x are $x=-2$ and $x=4$

06

$4(x+3)(x-4)=\dfrac{1}{2}(2x+1)(x-2)+\dfrac{3}{2}x$
$4(x^2-x-12)=\dfrac{1}{2}(2x^2-3x-2)+\dfrac{3}{2}x$
$4x^2-4x-48=x^2-\dfrac{3}{2}x-1+\dfrac{3}{2}x$
$3x^2-4x-47=0$
$\Rightarrow a=3,\ b=-4,\ c=-47$
Therefore,
$a+b+c=3+(-4)+(-47)=-48$
$a+b+c=-48$

07

(A) $3x^2-x=0$
$x(3x-1)=0,\ x=0$ or $x=\dfrac{1}{3}$

(B) $3x^2+8x-3=0$
$(3x-1)(x+3)=0,\ x=\dfrac{1}{3}$ or $x=-3$

(C) $(x-3)^2-1=0$
$(x-3)^2=1$
$x-3=\pm 1,\ x=4$ or $x=2$

(D) $(x+3)(x-4)+2x=0$
$x^2-x-12+2x=0$
$x^2+x-12=0$
$(x+4)(x-3)=0,\ x=-4$ or $x=3$

(E) $\dfrac{(x+1)^2}{2}=2$
$(x+1)^2=4$
$x+1=\pm 2,\ x=-3$ or $x=1$
 The answer is (D)

08

$(x-2)(x+3)=2(x-2)(2x+1)$
$x^2+x-6=2(2x^2-3x-2)$
$x^2+x-6=4x^2-6x-4$
$3x^2-7x+2=0$
$(3x-1)(x-2)=0,\ x=\dfrac{1}{3}$ or $x=2$
 The solutions are $x=\dfrac{1}{3}$ and $x=2$

09

Substitute the solution $x=4$ into the equation.

$$\tfrac{1}{2}(4)^2+2k(4)-5=0$$
$$8+8k-5=0$$
$$8k+3=0$$
$$8k=-3,\ k=-\tfrac{3}{8}$$

$$k=-\tfrac{3}{8}$$

10

$$x^2+5x-14=0$$
$$(x+7)(x-2)=0,\ x=-7\ \text{or}\ x=2$$

Therefore, $x=2$ is the solution to the equation $5x^2-2x-k=0$. Now, substitute $x=2$ into the equation $5x^2-2x-k=0$.

$$5(2)^2-2(2)-k=0$$
$$20-4-k=0$$
$$16-k=0,\ k=16$$

$$k=16$$

11

If $a^2=b^2$, then $|a|=|b|$ ($a=\pm b$ or $\pm a=b$). So we have

$$(x-4)^2=(2x+3)^2$$
$$x-4=2x+3\ \text{or}\ x-4=-(2x+3)$$

(1) $x-4=2x+3,\ x=-7$

(2) $x-4=-(2x+3)$
$$x-4=-2x-3$$
$$3x=1,\ x=\tfrac{1}{3}$$

The solutions are $x=\tfrac{1}{3}$ and $x=-7$

2. Completing the Square

Check Point 1

① $\quad x^2-8x+6=0$
$$x^2-8x=-6$$
$$x^2-8x+(4)^2=-6+(4)^2$$
$$(x-4)^2=10$$
$$x-4=\pm\sqrt{10},\ x=4\pm\sqrt{10}$$

The solutions are $x=4+\sqrt{10}$ and $x=4-\sqrt{10}$

② $\quad \tfrac{1}{2}x^2+8x-\tfrac{3}{2}=0$

$\rightarrow$ Multiply both sides by 2

$$x^2+16x-3=0$$
$$x^2+16x=3$$
$$x^2+16x+(8)^2=3+(8)^2$$
$$(x+8)^2=67$$
$$x+8=\pm\sqrt{67}, x=-8\pm\sqrt{67}$$

The solutions are $x=-8+\sqrt{67}$ and $x=-8-\sqrt{67}$

③ $\quad 4x^2-8=(x+3)(x-2)$
$$4x^2-8=x^2+x-6$$
$$3x^2-x=2\ \rightarrow\ \text{Divide both sides by 3}$$
$$x^2-\tfrac{1}{3}x=\tfrac{2}{3}$$
$$x^2-\tfrac{1}{3}x+\left(\tfrac{1}{6}\right)^2=\tfrac{2}{3}+\left(\tfrac{1}{6}\right)^2$$
$$\left(x-\tfrac{1}{6}\right)^2=\tfrac{25}{36}$$
$$x-\tfrac{1}{6}=\pm\sqrt{\tfrac{25}{36}}$$
$$x=\tfrac{1}{6}\pm\tfrac{5}{6},\ x=1\ \text{or}\ x=-\tfrac{2}{3}$$

The solutions are $x=-\tfrac{2}{3}$ and $x=1$

④ $\quad 4x^2+12x-5=0$

$\rightarrow$ Divide both sides by 4

$$x^2+3x-\tfrac{5}{4}=0$$
$$x^2+3x=\tfrac{5}{4}$$
$$x^2+3x+\left(\tfrac{3}{2}\right)^2=\tfrac{5}{4}+\left(\tfrac{3}{2}\right)^2$$
$$\left(x+\tfrac{3}{2}\right)^2=\tfrac{14}{4}$$

Solutions Manual

$$x+\frac{3}{2}=\pm\sqrt{\frac{14}{4}}$$

$$x=-\frac{3}{2}\pm\frac{\sqrt{14}}{2}$$

The solutions are $x=-\frac{3}{2}+\frac{\sqrt{14}}{2}$ and $x=-\frac{3}{2}-\frac{\sqrt{14}}{2}$

Review Exercise

01

(1) $x^2-4x-12=0$
$x^2-4x+(2)^2=12+(2)^2$
$(x-2)^2=16$
$x-2=\pm 4$, $x=6$ or $x=-2$
The solutions are $x=-2$ and $x=6$

(2) $x^2-2x-35=0$
$x^2-2x+(1)^2=35+(1)^2$
$(x-1)^2=36$
$x-1=\pm 6$, $x=7$ or $x=-5$
The solutions are $x=-5$ and $x=7$

(3) $x^2=-10x+3$
$x^2+10x+(5)^2=3+(5)^2$
$(x+5)^2=28$
$x+5=\pm 2\sqrt{7}$, $x=-5\pm 2\sqrt{7}$
The solutions are $x=-5-2\sqrt{7}$ and $x=-5+2\sqrt{7}$

02

(1) $9x^2-18x+5=0$ → Divide both sides by 9
$x^2-2x+\frac{5}{9}=0$
$x^2-2x=-\frac{5}{9}$
$x^2-2x+(1)^2=-\frac{5}{9}+(1)^2$
$(x-1)^2=\frac{4}{9}$
$x-1=\pm\frac{2}{3}$, $x=\frac{5}{3}$ or $x=\frac{1}{3}$
The solutions are $x=\frac{1}{3}$ and $x=\frac{5}{3}$

(2) $4x^2+8x-12=0$ → Divide both sides by 4
$x^2+2x-3=0$

$x^2+2x=3$
$x^2+2x+(1)^2=3+(1)^2$
$(x+1)^2=4$
$x+1=\pm 2$, $x=-3$ or $x=1$
The solutions are $x=-3$ and $x=1$

(3) $5x^2-2x=16$
→ Divide both sides by 5
$x^2-\frac{2}{5}x=\frac{16}{5}$
$x^2-\frac{2}{5}x+\left(\frac{1}{5}\right)^2=\frac{16}{5}+\left(\frac{1}{5}\right)^2$
$\left(x-\frac{1}{5}\right)^2=\frac{81}{25}$
$x-\frac{1}{5}=\pm\frac{9}{5}$, $x=2$ or $x=-\frac{8}{5}$
The solutions are $x=-\frac{8}{5}$ and $x=2$

03

(1) $\frac{1}{3}x^2-3x-\frac{1}{2}=0$
$\frac{1}{3}x^2-3x=\frac{1}{2}$
→ Multiply both sides by 3
$x^2-9x=\frac{3}{2}$
$x^2-9x+\left(\frac{9}{2}\right)^2=\frac{3}{2}+\left(\frac{9}{2}\right)^2$
$\left(x-\frac{9}{2}\right)^2=\frac{87}{4}$
$\left(x-\frac{9}{2}\right)=\pm\frac{\sqrt{87}}{2}$, $x=\frac{9}{2}\pm\frac{\sqrt{87}}{2}$
The solutions are $x=\frac{9}{2}-\frac{\sqrt{87}}{2}$ and $x=\frac{9}{2}+\frac{\sqrt{87}}{2}$

(2) $\frac{1}{2}x^2-4x=-3$
→ Multiply both sides by 2
$x^2-8x=-6$
$x^2-8x+(4)^2=-6+(4)^2$
$(x-4)^2=10$
$x-4=\pm\sqrt{10}$, $x=4\pm\sqrt{10}$
The solutions are $x=4+\sqrt{10}$ and $x=4-\sqrt{10}$

04

(1) $(x+2)^2=3(x+4)$
$x^2+4x+4=3x+12$
$x^2+x=8$
$x^2+x+\left(\frac{1}{2}\right)^2=8+\left(\frac{1}{2}\right)^2$
$\left(x+\frac{1}{2}\right)^2=\frac{33}{4}$
$x+\frac{1}{2}=\pm\frac{\sqrt{33}}{2}, \ x=-\frac{1}{2}\pm\frac{\sqrt{33}}{2}$

The solutions are $x=-\frac{1}{2}+\frac{\sqrt{33}}{2}$ and $x=-\frac{1}{2}-\frac{\sqrt{33}}{2}$

(2) $(x-1)(x+1)-4x=(2x-1)(2x+1)$
$x^2-1-4x=4x^2-1$
$-3x^2-4x=0$
$\rightarrow$ Divide both sides by -3
$x^2+\frac{4}{3}x=0$
$x^2+\frac{4}{3}x+\left(\frac{2}{3}\right)^2=\left(\frac{2}{3}\right)^2$
$\left(x+\frac{2}{3}\right)^2=\left(\frac{2}{3}\right)^2$
$x+\frac{2}{3}=\pm\frac{2}{3}, \ x=0 \text{ or } x=-\frac{4}{3}$

The solutions are $x=-\frac{4}{3}$ and $x=0$

05

$x^2-2x+a=0$
$x^2-2x=-a$
$x^2-2x+1^2=-a+1^2$
$(x-1)^2=1-a$
$x-1=\pm\sqrt{1-a}$
$x=1\pm\sqrt{1-a}$
$\Rightarrow 1-a=7, \ a=-6$

$a=-6$

06

Expand $\left(x+\frac{1}{b}\right)^2$ on the right side of the equation.

$2x^2+\frac{1}{4}x+a=2\left(x+\frac{1}{b}\right)^2$
$2x^2+\frac{1}{4}x+a=2\left(x^2+\frac{2}{b}x+\frac{1}{b^2}\right)$
$2x^2+\frac{1}{4}x+a=2x^2+\frac{4}{b}x+\frac{2}{b^2}$

Each like term on both sides must be the same, so

$\frac{1}{4}=\frac{4}{b}, \ b=16$ and $a=\frac{2}{b^2}=\frac{2}{16^2}$.

Therefore, $ab=\frac{2}{16^2}\times 16=\frac{1}{8}$.

$ab=\frac{1}{8}$

07

$5x^2+4x+1=0$
$\rightarrow$ Divide both sides by 5
$x^2+\frac{4}{5}x+\frac{1}{5}=0$
$x^2+\frac{4}{5}x=-\frac{1}{5}$
$x^2+\frac{4}{5}x+\left(\frac{2}{5}\right)^2=-\frac{1}{5}+\left(\frac{2}{5}\right)^2$
$\left(x+\frac{2}{5}\right)^2=-\frac{1}{25}$

Since $(x+h)^2=k$, $h=\frac{2}{5}$ and $k=-\frac{1}{25}$.

Therefore, $\frac{h}{k}=\frac{\frac{2}{5}}{-\frac{1}{25}}=-10$.

$\frac{h}{k}=-10$

Solutions Manual

3. The Quadratic Formula and the Discriminant

Check Point 1

① $x^2-4x-5=0 \to a=1, b=-4, c=-5$

$$x=\frac{-(-4)\pm\sqrt{(-4)^2-4(1)(-5)}}{2(1)}$$

$$=\frac{4\pm\sqrt{16+20}}{2}$$

$$=\frac{4\pm\sqrt{36}}{2}=\frac{4\pm 6}{2}$$

$x=\frac{4+6}{2}=5$ or $x=\frac{4-6}{2}=-1$

The solutions are $x=-1$ and $x=5$

② $2x^2-3x-3=0 \to a=2, b=-3, c=-3$

$$x=\frac{-(-3)\pm\sqrt{(-3)^2-4(2)(-3)}}{2(2)}$$

$$=\frac{3\pm\sqrt{9+24}}{4}=\frac{3\pm\sqrt{33}}{4}$$

The solutions are $x=\frac{3-\sqrt{33}}{4}$ and $x=\frac{3+\sqrt{33}}{4}$

③ $0.3x^2+0.5x-0.1=0$

$\to$ Multiply both sides by 10

$3x^2+5x-1=0 \to a=3, b=5, c=-1$

$$x=\frac{-5\pm\sqrt{(5)^2-4(3)(-1)}}{2(3)}$$

$$=\frac{-5\pm\sqrt{25+12}}{6}=\frac{-5\pm\sqrt{37}}{6}$$

The solutions are $x=\frac{-5-\sqrt{37}}{6}$ and $x=\frac{-5+\sqrt{37}}{6}$

Check Point 2

① $3x^2+5x-1=0 \to a=3, b=5, c=-1$

$D=b^2-4ac$

$=5^2-4(3)(-1)$

$=37>0$

There are two real solutions

② $\frac{1}{2}x^2-5x+\frac{25}{2}=0 \to a=\frac{1}{2}, b=-5, c=\frac{25}{2}$

$D=b^2-4ac$

$=(-5)^2-4\left(\frac{1}{2}\right)\left(\frac{25}{2}\right)=0$

There is one real solution

③ $2x^2-4x+6=0 \to a=2, b=-4, c=6$

$D=b^2-4ac$

$=(-4)^2-4(2)(6)$

$=-32<0$

There is no real solution.

④ $(x-4)^2-7=2x(x-4)$

$x^2-8x+16-7=2x^2-8x$

$x^2-9=0$

$\to a=1, b=0, c=-9$

$D=b^2-4ac$

$=0^2-4(1)(-9)$

$=36>0$

There are two real solutions

Check Point 3

$3x^2-6x-k=0 \to a=3, b=-6,$ and $c=-k$

① $D=(-6)^2-4(3)(-k)>0$

$36+12k>0 \to k>-3$

$k>-3$

② $D=(-6)^2-4(3)(-k)=0$

$36+12k=0 \to k=-3$

$k=-3$

③ $D=(-6)^2-4(3)(-k)<0$

$36+12k<0 \to k<-3$

$k<-3$

Review Exercise

01

(1) $x^2-x-12=0 \to a=1, b=-1, c=-12$

$$x=\frac{-(-1)\pm\sqrt{(-1)^2-4(1)(-12)}}{2(1)}$$

$$=\frac{1\pm\sqrt{1+48}}{2}$$

$$=\frac{1\pm\sqrt{49}}{2}=\frac{1\pm 7}{2}$$
$x=-3$ or $x=4$

　　The solutions are $x=-3$ and $x=4$

(2) $x^2+5x-6=0 \rightarrow a=1,\ b=5,\ c=-6$
$$x=\frac{-(5)\pm\sqrt{(5)^2-4(1)(-6)}}{2(1)}$$
$$=\frac{-5\pm\sqrt{25+24}}{2}$$
$$=\frac{-5\pm\sqrt{49}}{2}=\frac{-5\pm 7}{2}$$
$x=-6$ or $x=1$

　　The solutions are $x=-6$ and $x=1$

(3) $2x^2-x-6=0 \rightarrow a=2,\ b=-1,\ c=-6$
$$x=\frac{-(-1)\pm\sqrt{(-1)^2-4(2)(-6)}}{2(2)}$$
$$=\frac{1\pm\sqrt{1+48}}{4}$$
$$=\frac{1\pm\sqrt{49}}{4}=\frac{1\pm 7}{4}$$
$x=-\frac{3}{2}$ or $x=2$

　　The solutions are $x=-\frac{3}{2}$ and $x=2$

(4) $x^2-3x+1=0 \rightarrow a=1,\ b=-3,\ c=1$
$$x=\frac{-(-3)\pm\sqrt{(-3)^2-4(1)(1)}}{2(1)}$$
$$=\frac{3\pm\sqrt{9-4}}{2}=\frac{3\pm\sqrt{5}}{2}$$

　　The solutions are $x=\frac{3-\sqrt{5}}{2}$ and $x=\frac{3+\sqrt{5}}{2}$

02

(1) $-3x^2=8x+5$
$3x^2+8x+5=0 \rightarrow a=3,\ b=8,\ c=5$
$$x=\frac{-(8)\pm\sqrt{(8)^2-4(3)(5)}}{2(3)}$$
$$=\frac{-8\pm\sqrt{64-60}}{6}$$
$$=\frac{-8\pm\sqrt{4}}{6}=\frac{-8\pm 2}{6}$$
$x=-\frac{5}{3}$ or $x=-1$

　　The solutions are $x=-\frac{5}{3}$ and $x=-1$

(2) $3x^2-5x=-2$
$3x^2-5x+2=0 \rightarrow a=3,\ b=-5,\ c=2$
$$x=\frac{-(-5)\pm\sqrt{(-5)^2-4(3)(2)}}{2(3)}$$
$$=\frac{5\pm\sqrt{25-24}}{6}$$
$$=\frac{5\pm\sqrt{1}}{6}=\frac{5\pm 1}{6}$$
$x=\frac{2}{3}$ or $x=1$

　　The solutions are $x=\frac{2}{3}$ and $x=1$

03

(1) $\frac{3}{4}x^2-\frac{1}{2}x-1=0$
　　　　　　$\rightarrow$ Multiply both sides by 4
$3x^2-2x-4=0 \rightarrow a=3,\ b=-2,\ c=-4$
$$x=\frac{-(-2)\pm\sqrt{(-2)^2-4(3)(-4)}}{2(3)}$$
$$=\frac{2\pm\sqrt{4+48}}{6}=\frac{2\pm\sqrt{52}}{6}$$
$$=\frac{2\pm 2\sqrt{13}}{6}=\frac{1\pm\sqrt{13}}{3}$$

　　The solutions are $x=\frac{1-\sqrt{13}}{3}$ and
　　$x=\frac{1+\sqrt{13}}{3}$

(2) $0.4x^2-x-0.1=0$
　　　　　　$\rightarrow$ Multiply both sides by 10
$4x^2-10x-1=0 \rightarrow a=4,\ b=-10,\ c=-1$
$$x=\frac{-(-10)\pm\sqrt{(-10)^2-4(4)(-1)}}{2(4)}$$
$$=\frac{10\pm\sqrt{100+16}}{8}=\frac{10\pm\sqrt{116}}{8}$$
$$=\frac{10\pm 2\sqrt{29}}{8}=\frac{5\pm\sqrt{29}}{4}$$

　　The solutions are $x=\frac{5-\sqrt{29}}{4}$ and
　　$x=\frac{5+\sqrt{29}}{4}$

04

(1) $x^2-\frac{1}{3}x=0.2$
$x^2-\frac{1}{3}x-0.2=0,\ x^2-\frac{1}{3}x-\frac{1}{5}=0$

Solutions Manual

$15x^2-5x-3=0$ → Multiply both sides by 15
→ $a=15$, $b=-5$, $c=-3$

$$x=\frac{-(-5)\pm\sqrt{(-5)^2-4(15)(-3)}}{2(15)}$$

$$=\frac{5\pm\sqrt{25+180}}{30}=\frac{5\pm\sqrt{205}}{30}$$

The solutions are $x=\frac{5\pm\sqrt{205}}{30}$ and $x=\frac{5\pm\sqrt{205}}{30}$

(2) $(0.5x+2)\left(x-\frac{1}{2}\right)=x-1$

$0.5x^2+\frac{7}{4}x-1=x-1$

$\frac{1}{2}x^2+\frac{3}{4}x=0$

→ Multiply both sides by 4

$2x^2+3x=0$ → $a=2$, $b=3$, $c=0$

$$x=\frac{-(3)\pm\sqrt{(3)^2-4(2)(0)}}{2(2)}$$

$$=\frac{-3\pm\sqrt{9-0}}{4}=\frac{-3\pm 3}{4}$$

$x=-\frac{3}{2}$ or $x=0$

The solutions are $x=-\frac{3}{2}$ and $x=0$

05

(1) $x^2-x+3=0$ → $a=1$, $b=-1$, and $c=3$
$D=(-1)^2-4(1)(3)=1-12=-11<0$
There is no real solution, but two imaginary solutions.

(2) $2x^2+3x-1=0$ → $a=2$, $b=3$, and $c=-1$
$D=(3)^2-4(2)(-1)=9+8=17>0$
There are two real solutions

(3) $4x^2-8x+4=0$ → $a=4$, $b=-8$, and $c=4$
$D=(-8)^2-4(4)(4)=64-64=0$
There is one real solution

(4) $10x^2+2x=x(x-2)$
$10x^2+2x=x^2-2x$
$9x^2+4x=0$ → $a=9$, $b=4$, and $c=0$
$D=(16)^2-4(9)(0)=16^2>0$
There are two real solutions

06

(1) $x^2-4x-2k=0$ → $a=1$, $b=-4$, and $c=-2k$

(A) $D=(-4)^2-4(1)(-2k)>0$
$16+8k>0$ → $k>-2$

(B) $D=(-4)^2-4(1)(-2k)=0$
$16+8k=0$ → $k=-2$

(C) $D=(-4)^2-4(1)(-2k)<0$
$16+8k<0$ → $k<-2$

(2) $k^2x^2-8x+4=0$ → $a=k^2$, $b=-8$, and $c=4$

(A) $D=(-8)^2-4(k^2)(4)>0$
$64-16k^2>0$
$k^2<4$ → $-2<k<2$

(B) $D=(-8)^2-4(k^2)(4)=0$
$64-16k^2=0$
$k^2=4$ → $k=\pm 2$

(C) $D=(-8)^2-4(k^2)(4)<0$
$64-16k^2<0$
$k^2>4$ → $k>2$ or $k<-2$

07

$\frac{1}{2}x^2-x-\frac{1}{4}=0$

→ Multiply both sides by 4

$2x^2-4x-1=0$ → $a=2$, $b=-4$, $c=-1$

$$x=\frac{-(-4)\pm\sqrt{(-4)^2-4(2)(-1)}}{2(2)}$$

$$=\frac{4\pm\sqrt{24}}{4}=\frac{4\pm 2\sqrt{6}}{4}$$

$$=1\pm\frac{\sqrt{6}}{2}$$

Since $x=a\pm\frac{\sqrt{b}}{c}$, $a=1$, $b=6$, and $c=2$.

Therefore, $abc=(1)(6)(2)=12$.

$abc=12$

08

$x^2-10x+2m=5$
$x^2-10x+2m-5=0$
→ $a=1$, $b=-10$, $c=2m-5$

Using the discriminant $D=b^2-4ac=0$,
$(-10)^2-4(1)(2m-5)=0$
$100-8m+20=0$

$$120-8m=0$$
$$-8m=-120, \ m=15$$
$$m=15$$

09
$$a(3x+1)+2x^2=-\frac{1}{8}$$
$$3ax+a+2x^2=-\frac{1}{8}$$
$$2x^2+3ax+a+\frac{1}{8}=0$$
$$\rightarrow a=2, \ b=3a, \ c=a+\frac{1}{8}$$

Using the discriminant $D=b^2-4ac=0$,
$$(3a)^2-4(2)\left(a+\frac{1}{8}\right)=0$$
$$9a^2-8\left(a+\frac{1}{8}\right)=0$$
$$9a^2-8a-1=0$$
$$(9a+1)(a-1)=0, \ a=-\frac{1}{9} \text{ or } a=1$$
$$a=-\frac{1}{9} \text{ or } a=1$$

Chapter 7 Test Level 1

01
(A) $2x^3-5x^2+1=0$ → Cubic equation
(B) $(x+1)(x+2)-(x+3)(x+4)=0$
$$x^2+3x+2-(x^2+7x+12)=0$$
$$-4x-10=0$$
→ Linear equation
(C) $x(2x^2+x-1)-2x(x^2-x+1)=0$
$$2x^3+x^2-x-2x^3+2x^2-2x=0$$
$$3x^2-3x=0$$
→ Quadratic equation
(D) $4x^2+3x-2=4(1-x)(1+x)$
$$4x^2+3x-2=4(1-x^2)$$
$$4x^2+3x-2=4-4x^2$$
$$8x^2+3x-6=0$$
→ Quadratic equation
(E) $(1-2x)(1+2x)+4x^2=x$
$$1-4x^2+4x^2=x$$
$$x-1=0$$
→ Linear equation

The answer is (C) and (D).

02
(A) $x^2+4x+4=0$
$$(x+2)^2=0, \ x=-2$$
(B) $x^2+2x=0$
$$x(x+2)=0, \ x=0 \text{ or } x=-2$$
(C) $2x^2+5x+2=0$
$$(2x+1)(x+2)=0, \ x=-\frac{1}{2} \text{ or } x=-2$$
(D) $2x^2-5x+2=0$
$$(2x-1)(x-2)=0, \ x=\frac{1}{2} \text{ or } x=2$$
(E) $3x^2+4x-4=0$
$$(3x-2)(x+2)=0, \ x=\frac{2}{3} \text{ or } x=-2$$

Only (D) does NOT have $x=-2$ as the solution.

The answer is (D).

Solutions Manual

03

(1) $(x+6)^2+x^2=3(x+12)$
$x^2+12x+36+x^2=3x+36$
$2x^2+9x=0$
$x(2x+9)=0$
$x=0$ or $2x+9=0$
$x=0$ or $x=-\frac{9}{2}$

The solutions are $x=0$ and $x=-\frac{9}{2}$

(2) $\frac{(3x+1)(2x-3)}{2}=x^2-3$
$(3x+1)(2x-3)=2x^2-6$
$6x^2-7x-3=2x^2-6$
$4x^2-7x+3=0$
$(x-1)(4x-3)=0$
$x-1=0$ or $4x-3=0$
$x=1$ or $x=\frac{3}{4}$

The solutions are $x=1$ and $x=\frac{3}{4}$

04

$x^2+9x=7$

We should add square of one−half the coefficient of the linear term.

$\left(\frac{9}{2}\right)^2=\frac{81}{4}$

The answer is (E)

05

The first step is to divide both sides by 2 to make the coefficient of the square term equal to 1.

$2x^2-12x=5 \Rightarrow x^2-6x=\frac{5}{2}$

Therefore, the answer is (A)

06

Substitute $x=3$ into two equations
$x^2-4x+m=0$ and $2x^2+nx-7=0$.

$3^2-4(3)+m=0$, $m=3$
$2(3)^2+n(3)-7=0$
$3n=-11$, $n=-\frac{11}{3}$

Therefore, $m+n=3+\left(-\frac{11}{3}\right)=-\frac{2}{3}$

$$m+n=-\frac{2}{3}$$

07

Substitute $x=a$ into $x^2+6x-4=0$.
$a^2+6a-4=0$, $a^2+6a=4$
Therefore,
$2a^2+12a+7=2(a^2+6a)+7$
$=2(4)+7=15$

$$2a^2+12a+7=15$$

08

Solve the equation $2x^2+12x-9=0$ by completing the square.

$(2x^2+12x-9=0)\cdot\frac{1}{2}$
$x^2+6x-\frac{9}{2}=0$
$x^2+6x=\frac{9}{2}$
$x^2+6x+(3)^2=\frac{9}{2}+(3)^2$
$(x+3)^2=\frac{27}{2} \Rightarrow h=3$ and $k=\frac{27}{2}$

Therefore, $h+k=3+\frac{27}{2}=\frac{33}{2}$

$$h+k=\frac{33}{2}$$

09

Solve the equation $2x^2+mx-4=0$ by using quadratic formula.

$x=\frac{-m\pm\sqrt{m^2-4(2)(-4)}}{2(2)}=\frac{-m\pm\sqrt{m^2+32}}{4}$

Since $x=\frac{1\pm\sqrt{n}}{2}\cdot\frac{2}{2}=\frac{2\pm 2\sqrt{n}}{4}$,

$-m=2$, $m=-2$
$2\sqrt{n}=\sqrt{m^2+32}$

$$\sqrt{4n}=\sqrt{m^2+32}$$
$$4n=m^2+32,$$
$$4n=(-2)^2+32=36$$
$$n=9$$
Therefore, $m+n=-2+9=7$.
$$m+n=7$$

10

$(a+b)(a+b-3)=10$
Substitute k for $a+b$.
$$k(k-3)=10$$
$$k^2-3k-10=0$$
$$(k-5)(k+2)=0$$
$k=5$ or $k=-2 \Rightarrow a+b=5$ or $a+b=-2$
Since $a+b>0$, $a+b=5$.
$$a+b=5$$

11

Let x be the first odd integer. Then next odd integer is $x+2$ and we have the following equation.
$$x(x+2)=3(x+(x+2))+6$$
$$x^2+2x=3(2x+2)+6$$
$$x^2+2x=6x+12$$
$$x^2-4x-12=0$$
$(x+2)(x-6)=0$, $x=-2$ or $x=6$
Since we are looking for a positive integer, $x=6$.

Therefore, two consecutive even integers are 6 and 8

12

Let x and y be the width and the length of the rectangle, respectively. The area is $xy=36$ and the perimeter is $2x+2y=30 \rightarrow y=15-x$. Now substitute $15-x$ for y in the equation $xy=36$. Then

we have
$$x(15-x)=36$$
$$15x-x^2=36$$
$$x^2-15x+36=0$$
$(x-12)(x-3)=0$, $x=12$ or $x=3$
Since the length is longer side of the rectangle while width is the shorter side, $x=3$ and
$$xy=36$$
$$(3)y=36, \ y=12$$

Therefore, the dimensions of the rectangle are 3 cm by 12 cm.

Chapter 7 Test Level 2

01

$$x^2-5x=\frac{3}{4}(x-4)(x+2)$$
$$4(x^2-5x)=3(x-4)(x+2)$$
$$4x^2-20x=3x^2-6x-24$$
$$x^2-14x+24=0$$
$$(x-2)(x-12)=0$$
$$x-2=0 \text{ or } x-12=0$$
$$x=2 \text{ or } x=12$$
The solutions are $x=2$ and $x=12$

02

$$(x+3)^2+x^2=ax^2-4x+1$$
$$x^2+6x+9+x^2=ax^2-4x+1$$
$$ax^2-2x^2-10x-8=0$$
$$(a-2)x^2-10x-8=0$$
Since the coefficient of the quadratic term cannot be zero,
$$a-2\neq 0, \ a\neq 2$$
$$a\neq 2$$

Solutions Manual 101

Solutions Manual

03

$$x^2 + \frac{4}{3}x = \frac{5}{9}$$

$$x^2 + \frac{4}{3}x + \left(\frac{2}{3}\right)^2 = \frac{5}{9} + \left(\frac{2}{3}\right)^2$$

$$\left(x + \frac{2}{3}\right)^2 = 1$$

$$x + \frac{2}{3} = \pm 1$$

$$x = -\frac{2}{3} \pm 1, \quad x = -\frac{5}{3} \text{ or } x = \frac{1}{3}$$

$$\Rightarrow A = \left(\frac{2}{3}\right)^2 = \frac{4}{9}, \quad B = \frac{2}{3}, \quad C = 1,$$

$$D = -\frac{5}{3}, \text{ and } E = \frac{1}{3}$$

$$A = \frac{4}{9}, \quad B = \frac{2}{3}, \quad C = 1, \quad D = -\frac{5}{3}, \text{ and } E = \frac{1}{3}$$

04

Since $x=2$ is the solution of the equation $(k^2-4)x^2+(k+2)x=0$, substitute $x=2$ into the equation.

$$(k^2-4) \cdot 2^2 + (k+2) \cdot 2 = 0$$
$$4k^2 - 16 + 2k + 4 = 0$$
$$4k^2 + 2k - 12 = 0$$
$$2k^2 + k - 6 = 0$$
$$(k+2)(2k-3) = 0, \quad k=-2 \text{ or } k=\frac{3}{2}$$

$$k=-2 \text{ or } k=\frac{3}{2}$$

05

$$k(2x-1) + x^2 = -2$$
$$x^2 + 2kx + (-k+2) = 0$$

Using the discriminant,
$$D = b^2 - 4ac$$
$$= (2k)^2 - 4(1)(-k+2) = 0$$
$$4k^2 + 4k - 8 = 0$$
$$k^2 + k - 2 = 0$$
$$(k+2)(k-1) = 0, \quad k=-2 \text{ or } k=1$$

Since $k<0$, $k=-2$.

$$k=-2$$

06

$A: 3x^2 - 4x + \frac{4}{3} = 0$

$$\frac{1}{3}(9x^2 - 12x + 4) = 0$$

$$\frac{1}{3}(3x-2)^2 = 0, \quad x = \frac{2}{3}$$

Substitute $x=\frac{2}{3}$ into the equation B.

$$6\left(\frac{2}{3}\right)^2 - k\left(\frac{2}{3}\right) + 2 = 0$$

$$\frac{8}{3} - \frac{2}{3}k + 2 = 0, \quad k=7$$

So the equation of B is $6x^2 - 7x + 2 = 0$.

$$6x^2 - 7x + 2 = 0$$
$$(2x-1)(3x-2) = 0, \quad x=\frac{1}{2} \text{ or } x=\frac{2}{3}$$

The other solution is $x=\frac{1}{2}$

07

Substitute the solution $x=m$ into the equation. Then, we have $2m^2 - m + 2 = 0$.

Since $2m^2 - m = -2$,
$$2m^2 - m + 12 = -2 + 12 = 10$$

$$2m^2 - m + 12 = 10$$

08

$$6x^2 + 7xy - 3y^2 = 0$$
$$(3x-y)(2x+3y) = 0, \quad x=\frac{y}{3} \text{ or } x=-\frac{3y}{2}$$

Since $xy>0$, $x=\frac{y}{3}$. Therefore,

$$\frac{3x^2+y^2}{4xy} = \frac{3\left(\frac{y}{3}\right)^2 + y^2}{4\left(\frac{y}{3}\right)y} = \frac{\frac{y^2}{3}+y^2}{\frac{4y^2}{3}} \cdot \frac{3}{3}$$

$$= \frac{y^2+3y^2}{4y^2} = \frac{4y^2}{4y^2} = 1$$

$$\frac{3x^2+y^2}{4xy} = 1$$

09

Let x be the speed of the bus A. Then, the speed of the bus B is $x+1$.

	Bus A	Bus B
Speed	x	$x+1$
Time	2	2
Distance	$2x$	$2(x+1)$

By the Pythagorean Theorem, we have
$$(2x)^2+(2(x+1))^2=(2\sqrt{13})^2$$
$$4x^2+4x^2+8x+4=52$$
$$8x^2+8x-48=0$$
$$x^2+x-6=0$$
$$(x+3)(x-2)=0,\ x=-3 \text{ or } x=2$$
Since $x>0$, $x=2$.

Therefore, the speed of the bus A and B is 2 miles per hour and 3 miles per hour, respectively.

10

Let x be the length of one side of the original square. Then we have
$$(x+1)(x-2)=70$$
$$x^2-x-2=70$$
$$x^2-x-72=0$$
$$(x+8)(x-9)=0,\ x=-8 \text{ or } x=9$$
Since $x>0$, $x=9$.

Therefore, the length of one side of the original square is 9 inches

Solutions Manual

Chapter 8: Rational Expressions

1. Simplifying Rational Expressions

Check Point 1

① $\dfrac{6x^2-8x}{10x} = \dfrac{2x(3x-4)}{2x \cdot 5}$

$\quad = \dfrac{3x-4}{5}$

② $\dfrac{x^2-x-2}{x^2+x-6} = \dfrac{(x-2)(x+1)}{(x-2)(x+3)}$

$\quad = \dfrac{x+1}{x+3}$

③ $\dfrac{3x^2+x-4}{5x^2-3x-2} = \dfrac{(3x+4)(x-1)}{(5x+2)(x-1)}$

$\quad = \dfrac{3x+4}{5x+2}$

④ $\dfrac{2x^3+11x^2+12x}{3x^2+11x-4} = \dfrac{x(2x^2+11x+12)}{3x^2+11x-4}$

$\quad = \dfrac{x(2x+3)(x+4)}{(3x-1)(x+4)}$

$\quad = \dfrac{x(2x+3)}{3x-1}$

Check Point 2

① $\dfrac{2}{6x^2} \times \dfrac{8x^2}{10} = \dfrac{2}{2x^2 \cdot 3} \times \dfrac{2x^2 \cdot 4}{2 \cdot 5}$

$\quad = \dfrac{1 \times 4}{3 \times 5} = \dfrac{4}{15}$

② $\dfrac{x-3}{x-4} \times \dfrac{x^2-16}{5x-15} = \dfrac{x-3}{x-4} \times \dfrac{(x-4)(x+4)}{5(x-3)}$

$\quad = \dfrac{1}{1} \times \dfrac{x+4}{5} = \dfrac{x+4}{5}$

③ $\dfrac{x^2+8x+16}{3x+6} \times \dfrac{x^2-4}{x^2+7x+12}$

$\quad = \dfrac{(x+4)^2}{3(x+2)} \times \dfrac{(x-2)(x+2)}{(x+3)(x+4)}$

$\quad = \dfrac{x+4}{3} \times \dfrac{x-2}{x+3}$

$\quad = \dfrac{(x+4)(x-2)}{3(x+3)}$

④ $\dfrac{2x^2-2}{2x^2+x-1} \times (4x-2)$

$\quad = \dfrac{2(x^2-1)}{2x^2+x-1} \times \dfrac{4x-2}{1}$

$\quad = \dfrac{2(x-1)(x+1)}{(2x-1)(x+1)} \times \dfrac{2(2x-1)}{1}$

$\quad = \dfrac{2(x-1)}{1} \times \dfrac{2}{1}$

$\quad = \dfrac{4(x-1)}{1} = 4(x-1)$

Check Point 3

① $\dfrac{9x}{x^3} \div \dfrac{18x^2}{x^3} = \dfrac{9x}{x^3} \times \dfrac{x^3}{18x^2}$

$\quad = \dfrac{9x}{x^3} \times \dfrac{x^3}{9x \cdot 2x}$

$\quad = \dfrac{1}{1} \times \dfrac{1}{2x} = \dfrac{1}{2x}$

② $\dfrac{x^2+6x-7}{3x^2} \div \dfrac{2x+14}{12x} = \dfrac{x^2+6x-7}{3x^2} \times \dfrac{12x}{2x+14}$

$\quad = \dfrac{(x-1)(x+7)}{3x \cdot x} \times \dfrac{3x \cdot 2 \cdot 2}{2(x+7)}$

$\quad = \dfrac{x-1}{x} \times \dfrac{2}{1} = \dfrac{2(x-1)}{x}$

③ $\dfrac{2x-12}{x^2-4} \div \dfrac{x^2-5x-6}{3x-6} = \dfrac{2x-12}{x^2-4} \times \dfrac{3x-6}{x^2-5x-6}$

$\quad = \dfrac{2(x-6)}{(x-2)(x+2)} \times \dfrac{3(x-2)}{(x-6)(x+1)}$

$\quad = \dfrac{2}{x+2} \times \dfrac{3}{x+1} = \dfrac{6}{(x+2)(x+1)}$

(4) $\dfrac{2x^3-10x^2}{x-4} \div \dfrac{x^2+4x}{x^2-16} = \dfrac{2x^3-10x^2}{x-4} \times \dfrac{x^2-16}{x^2+4x}$

$= \dfrac{2x^2(x-5)}{x-4} \times \dfrac{(x-4)(x+4)}{x(x+4)}$

$= \dfrac{2x(x-5)}{1} \times \dfrac{1}{1} = 2x(x-5)$

Review Exercise

01

(1) $\dfrac{75x^3}{5x^5} = \dfrac{5x^3 \cdot 15}{5x^3 \cdot x^2} = \dfrac{15}{x^2}$

(2) $\dfrac{27a^4}{3a} = \dfrac{3a \cdot 9a^3}{3a} = 9a^3$

(3) $\dfrac{6x^2}{3x^2-9x} = \dfrac{3x \cdot 2x}{3x(x-3)} = \dfrac{2x}{x-3}$

(4) $\dfrac{6y^4-15y}{9y^2} = \dfrac{3y(2y^3-5)}{3y \cdot 3y} = \dfrac{2y^3-5}{3y}$

02

(1) $\dfrac{2x^3+4x^2}{x^2+x-2} = \dfrac{2x^2(x+2)}{(x-1)(x+2)} = \dfrac{2x^2}{x-1}$

(2) $\dfrac{(2x-5)^2}{4x^2-25} = \dfrac{(2x-5)^2}{(2x)^2-5^2} = \dfrac{(2x-5)^2}{(2x-5)(2x+5)}$

$= \dfrac{2x-5}{2x+5}$

(3) $\dfrac{a^2-5a+6}{a^2-7a+12} = \dfrac{(a-3)(a-2)}{(a-3)(a-4)} = \dfrac{a-2}{a-4}$

(4) $\dfrac{6a^2-5a+1}{12a^2+2a-2} = \dfrac{6a^2-5a+1}{2(6a^2+a-1)}$

$= \dfrac{(2a-1)(3a-1)}{2(2a+1)(3a-1)}$

$= \dfrac{2a-1}{2(2a+1)}$

03

(1) $\dfrac{x^3}{3} \times \dfrac{18}{x^2} = \dfrac{x^2 \cdot x}{3} \times \dfrac{3 \cdot 6}{x^2} = \dfrac{x}{1} \times \dfrac{6}{1} = 6x$

(2) $\dfrac{16}{x^3} \times \dfrac{x^5}{12} = \dfrac{4 \cdot 4}{x^3} \times \dfrac{x^3 \cdot x^2}{4 \cdot 3} = \dfrac{4}{1} \times \dfrac{x^2}{3} = \dfrac{4x^2}{3}$

(3) $\dfrac{4x^2}{5x^2} \times \dfrac{4x}{8} = \dfrac{4 \cdot x^2}{5 \cdot x^2} \times \dfrac{2 \cdot 2x}{4 \cdot 2} = \dfrac{1}{5} \times \dfrac{2x}{1} = \dfrac{2x}{5}$

(4) $\dfrac{24}{7y^3} \times \dfrac{21y^2}{18y} = \dfrac{6 \cdot 4}{7y^2 \cdot y} \times \dfrac{3 \cdot 7y^2}{6 \cdot 3 \cdot y} = \dfrac{4}{y} \times \dfrac{1}{y} = \dfrac{4}{y^2}$

04

(1) $\dfrac{3x^2-12}{10x^2} \times \dfrac{5x^2}{2x-4} = \dfrac{3(x^2-4)}{2 \cdot 5x^2} \times \dfrac{5x^2}{2(x-2)}$

$= \dfrac{3(x-2)(x+2)}{2 \cdot 5x^2} \times \dfrac{5x^2}{2(x-2)}$

$= \dfrac{3(x+2)}{2} \times \dfrac{1}{2}$

$= \dfrac{3(x+2)}{4}$

(2) $\dfrac{x^2-9}{x^2+5x+6} \times \dfrac{x-3}{x+2} = \dfrac{(x-3)(x+3)}{(x+2)(x+3)} \times \dfrac{x-3}{x+2}$

$= \dfrac{x-3}{x+2} \times \dfrac{x-3}{x+2}$

$= \dfrac{(x-3)^2}{(x+2)^2}$

(3) $\dfrac{3x^2-5x-2}{x^2+3x-10} \times \dfrac{2x+8}{x^2+x-12}$

$= \dfrac{(3x+1)(x-2)}{(x+5)(x-2)} \times \dfrac{2(x+4)}{(x-3)(x+4)}$

$= \dfrac{3x+1}{x+5} \times \dfrac{2}{x-3}$

$= \dfrac{2(3x+1)}{(x+5)(x-3)}$

(4) $\dfrac{y^2-7y+12}{2y^2-32} \times (y^2-5y+6)$

$= \dfrac{(y-3)(y-4)}{2(y^2-16)} \times \dfrac{(y-2)(y-3)}{1}$

$= \dfrac{(y-3)(y-4)}{2(y-4)(y+4)} \times \dfrac{(y-2)(y-3)}{1}$

$= \dfrac{y-3}{2(y+4)} \times \dfrac{(y-2)(y-3)}{1}$

$= \dfrac{(y-2)(y-3)^2}{2(y+4)}$

05

(1) $\dfrac{6a^2-a-2}{2a^2-5a-3} \times \dfrac{2a^2-18}{3a^2+7a-6}$

$= \dfrac{(2a+1)(3a-2)}{(a-3)(2a+1)} \times \dfrac{2(a^2-9)}{(a+3)(3a-2)}$

$= \dfrac{(2a+1)(3a-2)}{(a-3)(2a+1)} \times \dfrac{2(a-3)(a+3)}{(a+3)(3a-2)}$

$=\dfrac{1}{1}\times\dfrac{2}{1}=2$

(2) $\dfrac{a^2b-b^3}{4ab-8b^2}\times\dfrac{a^2-ab-2b^2}{a^4-2a^3b+a^2b^2}$

$=\dfrac{b(a^2-b^2)}{4b(a-2b)}\times\dfrac{(a+b)(a-2b)}{a^2(a^2-2ab+b^2)}$

$=\dfrac{(a-b)(a+b)}{4(a-2b)}\times\dfrac{(a+b)(a-2b)}{a^2(a-b)^2}$

$=\dfrac{a+b}{4}\times\dfrac{(a+b)}{a^2(a-b)}$

$=\dfrac{(a+b)^2}{4a^2(a-b)}$

06

(1) $\dfrac{4x+1}{3x}\div\dfrac{8x^2-2x-1}{15}=\dfrac{4x+1}{3x}\times\dfrac{15}{8x^2-2x-1}$

$=\dfrac{4x+1}{3x}\times\dfrac{3\cdot 5}{(4x+1)(2x-1)}$

$=\dfrac{1}{x}\times\dfrac{5}{2x-1}=\dfrac{5}{x(2x-1)}$

(2) $\dfrac{x^2-5x-14}{x^2-3x+2}\div\dfrac{x^2-14x+49}{x^2-4}$

$=\dfrac{x^2-5x-14}{x^2-3x+2}\times\dfrac{x^2-4}{x^2-14x+49}$

$=\dfrac{(x-7)(x+2)}{(x-1)(x-2)}\times\dfrac{(x-2)(x+2)}{(x-7)^2}$

$=\dfrac{x+2}{x-1}\times\dfrac{x+2}{x-7}$

$=\dfrac{(x+2)^2}{(x-1)(x-7)}$

(3) $\dfrac{2a^2-2a-4}{3a-6}\div\dfrac{6a-4}{9a^2-4}$

$=\dfrac{2a^2-2a-4}{3a-6}\times\dfrac{9a^2-4}{6a-4}$

$=\dfrac{2(a^2-a-2)}{3(a-2)}\times\dfrac{(3a-2)(3a+2)}{2(3a-2)}$

$=\dfrac{(a-2)(a+1)}{3(a-2)}\times\dfrac{3a+2}{1}$

$=\dfrac{(a+1)}{3}\times\dfrac{3a+2}{1}$

$=\dfrac{(a+1)(3a+2)}{3}$

(4) $\dfrac{5y-25}{2y^2-18}\div\dfrac{y^2-25}{3y+9}$

$=\dfrac{5y-25}{2y^2-18}\times\dfrac{3y+9}{y^2-25}$

$=\dfrac{5(y-5)}{2(y^2-9)}\times\dfrac{3(y+3)}{(y-5)(y+5)}$

$=\dfrac{5}{2(y-3)(y+3)}\times\dfrac{3(y+3)}{(y+5)}$

$=\dfrac{5}{2(y-3)}\times\dfrac{3}{y+5}$

$=\dfrac{15}{2(y-3)(y+5)}$

07

(1) $\dfrac{a^2-1}{a^2-4}\div\dfrac{2a-1}{a-2}\times\dfrac{a+2}{2a^2+a}$

$=\dfrac{a^2-1}{a^2-4}\times\dfrac{a-2}{2a-1}\times\dfrac{a+2}{2a^2+a}$

$=\dfrac{(a-1)(a+1)}{(a-2)(a+2)}\times\dfrac{a-2}{2a-1}\times\dfrac{a+2}{a(2a+1)}$

$=\dfrac{(a-1)(a+1)}{1}\times\dfrac{1}{2a-1}\times\dfrac{1}{a(2a+1)}$

$=\dfrac{(a-1)(a+1)}{a(2a-1)(2a+1)}$

(2) $\dfrac{4x^2-1}{2x^2-3x-2}\times\dfrac{2x-1}{x^2-4}\div\dfrac{2x-1}{x+2}$

$=\dfrac{4x^2-1}{2x^2-3x-2}\times\dfrac{2x-1}{x^2-4}\times\dfrac{x+2}{2x-1}$

$=\dfrac{(2x-1)(2x+1)}{(2x+1)(x-2)}\times\dfrac{2x-1}{(x-2)(x+2)}\times\dfrac{x+2}{2x-1}$

$=\dfrac{2x-1}{x-2}\times\dfrac{1}{x-2}\times\dfrac{1}{1}$

$=\dfrac{2x-1}{(x-2)^2}$

2. Addition and Subtraction

Check Point 1

① $\dfrac{2}{x-2} - \dfrac{x-1}{x} = \dfrac{2x}{(x-2)x} - \dfrac{(x-1)(x-2)}{x(x-2)}$

$= \dfrac{2x - (x^2 - 3x + 2)}{x(x-2)}$

$= \dfrac{2x - x^2 + 3x - 2}{x(x-2)}$

$= \dfrac{-x^2 + 5x - 2}{x(x-2)} = -\dfrac{x^2 - 5x + 2}{x(x-2)}$

② $\dfrac{x-4}{x} + \dfrac{x+3}{x+2} = \dfrac{(x-4)(x+2)}{x(x+2)} + \dfrac{(x+3)x}{(x+2)x}$

$= \dfrac{x^2 - 2x - 8 + x^2 + 3x}{x(x+2)}$

$= \dfrac{2x^2 + x - 8}{x(x+2)}$

③ $\dfrac{2x-4}{x+3} - \dfrac{x+1}{3x-1}$

$= \dfrac{(2x-4)(3x-1)}{(x+3)(3x-1)} - \dfrac{(x+1)(x+3)}{(3x-1)(x+3)}$

$= \dfrac{6x^2 - 14x + 4 - (x^2 + 4x + 3)}{(x+3)(3x-1)}$

$= \dfrac{6x^2 - 14x + 4 - x^2 - 4x - 3}{(x+3)(3x-1)}$

$= \dfrac{5x^2 - 18x + 1}{(x+3)(3x-1)}$

④ $\dfrac{x+4}{x^2 - x - 2} - \dfrac{x+2}{x^2 - 1}$

$= \dfrac{x+4}{(x+1)(x-2)} - \dfrac{x+2}{(x-1)(x+1)}$

$= \dfrac{(x+4)(x-1)}{(x+1)(x-2)(x-1)} - \dfrac{(x+2)(x-2)}{(x-1)(x+1)(x-2)}$

$= \dfrac{x^2 + 3x - 4 - (x^2 - 4)}{(x-1)(x+1)(x-2)}$

$= \dfrac{x^2 + 3x - 4 - x^2 + 4}{(x-1)(x+1)(x-2)}$

$= \dfrac{3x}{(x-1)(x+1)(x-2)}$

Review Exercise

01

(1) $\dfrac{x+2}{3} + \dfrac{x-4}{6} = \dfrac{(x+2)(2)}{3(2)} + \dfrac{x-4}{6}$

$= \dfrac{2x + 4 + x - 4}{6}$

$= \dfrac{3x}{6} = \dfrac{x}{2}$

(2) $\dfrac{5}{2x+2} + \dfrac{2x-3}{x+1} = \dfrac{5}{2(x+1)} + \dfrac{(2x-3)(2)}{(x+1)(2)}$

$= \dfrac{5 + 4x - 6}{2(x+1)}$

$= \dfrac{4x - 1}{2(x+1)}$

(3) $2 - \dfrac{x-4}{x-1} = \dfrac{2(x-1)}{x-1} - \dfrac{x-4}{x-1}$

$= \dfrac{2x - 2 - (x-4)}{x-1} = \dfrac{x+2}{x-1}$

(4) $\dfrac{-1}{2x^2 + 2x} + \dfrac{1}{2} = \dfrac{-1}{2x(x+1)} + \dfrac{x(x+1)}{2x(x+1)}$

$= \dfrac{-1 + x^2 + x}{2x(x+1)}$

$= \dfrac{x^2 + x - 1}{2x(x+1)}$

02

(1) $\dfrac{3}{x+5} + \dfrac{5x}{2x-1}$

$= \dfrac{3(2x-1)}{(x+5)(2x-1)} + \dfrac{5x(x+5)}{(2x-1)(x+5)}$

$= \dfrac{6x - 3 + 5x^2 + 25x}{(x+5)(2x-1)}$

$= \dfrac{5x^2 + 31x - 3}{(2x-1)(x+5)}$

(2) $\dfrac{x}{2x^2 + 8x} - \dfrac{5}{x+4} = \dfrac{x}{2x(x+4)} - \dfrac{2x \cdot 5}{2x(x+4)}$

$= \dfrac{x - 10x}{2x(x+4)}$

$= \dfrac{-9x}{2x(x+4)}$

$= -\dfrac{9}{2(x+4)}$

(3) $\dfrac{3}{x-6}+\dfrac{1}{x+2}$

$=\dfrac{3(x+2)}{(x-6)(x+2)}+\dfrac{(x-6)}{(x+2)(x-6)}$

$=\dfrac{4x}{(x-6)(x+2)}$

(4) $\dfrac{1}{(x-1)^2}-\dfrac{1}{x^2-1}$

$=\dfrac{1}{(x-1)^2}-\dfrac{1}{(x-1)(x+1)}$

$=\dfrac{x+1}{(x-1)^2(x+1)}-\dfrac{x-1}{(x-1)(x+1)(x-1)}$

$=\dfrac{x+1-(x-1)}{(x-1)^2(x+1)}$

$=\dfrac{2}{(x-1)^2(x+1)}$

03

(1) $\dfrac{x^2+x}{x^2-2x}-\dfrac{x}{2x^2-8}$

$=\dfrac{x(x+1)}{x(x-2)}-\dfrac{x}{2(x^2-4)}$

$=\dfrac{x+1}{x-2}-\dfrac{x}{2(x-2)(x+2)}$

$=\dfrac{(x+1)\cdot 2(x+2)}{(x-2)\cdot 2(x+2)}-\dfrac{x}{2(x-2)(x+2)}$

$=\dfrac{2(x^2+2x+x+2)-x}{2(x-2)(x+2)}$

$=\dfrac{2x^2+6x+4-x}{2(x-2)(x+2)}$

$=\dfrac{2x^2+5x+4}{2(x-2)(x+2)}$

(2) $\dfrac{3x-1}{x^2+4x+4}-\dfrac{2}{x^2-4}$

$=\dfrac{3x-1}{(x+2)^2}-\dfrac{2}{(x+2)(x-2)}$

$=\dfrac{(3x-1)(x-2)}{(x+2)^2(x-2)}-\dfrac{2(x+2)}{(x+2)(x-2)(x+2)}$

$=\dfrac{3x^2-7x+2-(2x+4)}{(x+2)^2(x-2)}$

$=\dfrac{3x^2-9x-2}{(x+2)^2(x-2)}$

04

Simplify the right side of a given equation.

$\dfrac{a}{x-2}+\dfrac{b}{x+2}=\dfrac{a(x+2)}{(x-2)(x+2)}+\dfrac{b(x-2)}{(x+2)(x-2)}$

$=\dfrac{a(x+2)+b(x-2)}{(x-2)(x+2)}$

$=\dfrac{ax+2a+bx-2b}{(x-2)(x+2)}$

$=\dfrac{(a+b)x+(2a-2b)}{x^2-4}$

Therefore, the equation is

$\dfrac{12}{x^2-4}=\dfrac{(a+b)x+(2a-2b)}{x^2-4}$

$12=(a+b)x+(2a-2b)$

$\Rightarrow a+b=0$ and $2a-2b=12 \rightarrow a-b=6$

Solving the system of equations, we have $a=3$ and $b=-3$.

Therefore, $a+b=3+(-3)=0$.

$a+b=0$

05

$\dfrac{2}{1-x}+\dfrac{2}{1+x}+\dfrac{4}{1+x^2}$

$=\dfrac{2(1+x)}{(1-x)(1+x)}+\dfrac{2(1-x)}{(1+x)(1-x)}+\dfrac{4}{1+x^2}$

$=\dfrac{2+2x+2-2x}{(1-x)(1+x)}+\dfrac{4}{1+x^2}$

$=\dfrac{4}{1-x^2}+\dfrac{4}{1+x^2}$

$=\dfrac{4(1+x^2)}{(1-x^2)(1+x^2)}+\dfrac{4(1-x^2)}{(1+x^2)(1-x^2)}$

$=\dfrac{4+4x^2+4-4x^2}{(1-x^2)(1+x^2)}$

$=\dfrac{8}{1-x^4}$

3. Rational Equation

Check Point 1

① $2 + \dfrac{12}{5x} = \dfrac{2}{x}$

$\left(2 + \dfrac{12}{5x}\right) \cdot 5x = \left(\dfrac{2}{x}\right) \cdot 5x$

$10x + 12 = 10$

$10x = -2, \ x = -\dfrac{1}{5}$

Check the solution: $2 + \dfrac{12}{5\left(-\dfrac{1}{5}\right) \neq 0} = \dfrac{2}{-\dfrac{1}{5} \neq 0}$

$$x = -\dfrac{1}{5}$$

② $\dfrac{1}{x} + \dfrac{1}{x^2} = \dfrac{1}{2x^2}$

$\left(\dfrac{1}{x} + \dfrac{1}{x^2}\right) \cdot 2x^2 = \left(\dfrac{1}{2x^2}\right) \cdot 2x^2$

$2x + 2 = 1$

$2x = -1, \ x = -\dfrac{1}{2}$

Check the solution:

$\dfrac{1}{-\dfrac{1}{2} \neq 0} + \dfrac{1}{\left(-\dfrac{1}{2}\right)^2 \neq 0} = \dfrac{1}{2\left(-\dfrac{1}{2}\right)^2 \neq 0}$

$$x = -\dfrac{1}{2}$$

③ $\dfrac{5}{x^2 - 2x} + \dfrac{2}{x} = \dfrac{5}{x^2 - 2x}$

$\left(\dfrac{5}{x(x-2)} + \dfrac{2}{x}\right) x(x-2) = \left(\dfrac{5}{x(x-2)}\right) x(x-2)$

$5 + 2(x-2) = 5$

$5 + 2x - 4 = 5$

$2x = 4, \ x = 2$

Check the solution:

$\dfrac{5}{2^2 - 2(2) = 0} + \dfrac{2}{2 \neq 0} = \dfrac{5}{2(2) - 4 = 0}$

$x = 2$ is the extraneous solution. There is NO solution to the equation.

No Solution

④ $\dfrac{30}{x+2} + \dfrac{x}{x-2} = 9$

$\left(\dfrac{30}{x+2} + \dfrac{x}{x-2}\right)(x+2)(x-2) = 9(x+2)(x-2)$

$30(x-2) + x(x+2) = 9(x-2)(x+2)$

$30x - 60 + x^2 + 2x = 9x^2 - 36$

$8x^2 - 32x + 24 = 0$

$x^2 - 4x + 3 = 0$

$(x-3)(x-1) = 0$

$x = 3$ or $x = 1$

Check the solution:

$\dfrac{30}{3+2 \neq 0} + \dfrac{3}{3-2 \neq 0} = 9$ and

$\dfrac{30}{1+2 \neq 0} + \dfrac{1}{1-2 \neq 0} = 9$

$$x = 3 \text{ or } x = 1$$

Review Exercise

01

(1) $\dfrac{6}{x^2} = \dfrac{1}{x^2} + \dfrac{1}{x}$

$\dfrac{6}{x^2} \cdot x^2 = \left(\dfrac{1}{x^2} + \dfrac{1}{x}\right) \cdot x^2$

$6 = 1 + x, \ x = 5$

Check the solution:

$\dfrac{6}{5^2 \neq 0} = \dfrac{1}{5^2 \neq 0} + \dfrac{1}{5^2 \neq 0}$

The solution is $x = 5$

(2) $\dfrac{1}{x} - \dfrac{1}{3x^2} = -\dfrac{1}{6x^2}$

$\left(\dfrac{1}{x} - \dfrac{1}{3x^2}\right) \cdot 6x^2 = -\dfrac{1}{6x^2} \cdot 6x^2$

$6x - 2 = -1, \ x = \dfrac{1}{6}$

Check the solution:

$\dfrac{1}{\dfrac{1}{6} \neq 0} - \dfrac{1}{3\left(\dfrac{1}{6}\right)^2 \neq 0} = -\dfrac{1}{6\left(\dfrac{1}{6}\right)^2 \neq 0}$

The solution is $x = \dfrac{1}{6}$

(3) $\dfrac{1}{x} + \dfrac{3x+12}{x^2 - 5x} = \dfrac{7x-56}{x^2 - 5x}$

$\left(\dfrac{1}{x} + \dfrac{3x+12}{x(x-5)}\right) x(x-5) = \left(\dfrac{7x-56}{x(x-5)}\right) x(x-5)$

$(x-5) + (3x+12) = 7x - 56$

$4x + 7 = 7x - 56, \ x = 21$

Solutions Manual 109

Solutions Manual

Check the solution:
$$\frac{1}{21\neq 0}+\frac{3\cdot 21+12}{21^2-5\cdot 21\neq 0}=\frac{7\cdot 21-56}{21^2-5\cdot 21\neq 0}$$

The solution is $x=21$

(4) $\quad 1-\dfrac{1}{x^2+2x}=\dfrac{x-1}{x}$

$\left(1-\dfrac{1}{x(x+2)}\right)x(x+2)=\dfrac{x-1}{x}\cdot x(x+2)$

$x(x+2)-1=(x-1)(x+2)$

$x^2+2x-1=x^2+x-2,\ x=-1$

Check the solution:
$$1-\frac{1}{(-1)^2+2(-1)\neq 0}=\frac{-1-1}{-1\neq 0}$$

The solution is $x=-1$

02

(1) $\quad \dfrac{1}{x-2}+\dfrac{1}{x^2-7x+10}=\dfrac{6}{x-2}$

$\dfrac{1}{x-2}+\dfrac{1}{(x-2)(x-5)}=\dfrac{6}{x-2}$

$\left(\dfrac{1}{x-2}+\dfrac{1}{(x-2)(x-5)}\right)(x-2)(x-5)$

$=\dfrac{6}{x-2}\cdot (x-2)(x-5)$

$(x-5)+1=6(x-5)$

$x-4=6x-30,\ x=\dfrac{26}{5}$

Check the solution:
$$\frac{1}{\frac{26}{5}-2\neq 0}-\frac{1}{\left(\frac{26}{5}\right)^2-7\left(\frac{26}{5}\right)+10\neq 0}=\frac{6}{\frac{26}{5}-2\neq 0}$$

The solution is $x=\dfrac{26}{5}$

(2) $\quad \dfrac{4}{x}+\dfrac{1}{x-1}=3$

$\left(\dfrac{4}{x}+\dfrac{1}{x-1}\right)x(x-1)=3\cdot x(x-1)$

$4(x-1)+x=3x^2-3x$

$5x-4=3x^2-3x$

$3x^2-8x+4=0$

$(3x-2)(x-2)=0$

$x=\dfrac{2}{3}$ or $x=2$

Check the solution:

$$\frac{4}{\frac{2}{3}\neq 0}+\frac{1}{\frac{2}{3}-1\neq 0}=3 \text{ and } \frac{4}{2\neq 0}+\frac{1}{2-1\neq 0}=3$$

The solutions are $x=\dfrac{2}{3}$ and $x=2$

(3) $\quad \dfrac{5}{x+3}-\dfrac{1}{x-4}=\dfrac{3}{2}$

$\left(\dfrac{5}{x+3}-\dfrac{1}{x-4}\right)2(x+3)(x-4)$

$=\dfrac{3}{2}\cdot 2(x+3)(x-4)$

$10(x-4)-2(x+3)=3(x^2-x-12)$

$10x-40-2x-6=3x^2-3x-36$

$3x^2-11x+10=0$

$(3x-5)(x-2)=0$

$x=\dfrac{5}{3}$ or $x=2$

Check the solution:
$$\frac{5}{\frac{5}{3}+3\neq 0}-\frac{1}{\frac{5}{3}-4\neq 0}=\frac{3}{2} \text{ and}$$
$$\frac{5}{2+3\neq 0}-\frac{1}{2-4\neq 0}=\frac{3}{2}$$

The solutions are $x=\dfrac{5}{3}$ and $x=2$

(4) $\quad \dfrac{x-6}{3x}-1=\dfrac{x^2-5x-24}{3x}$

$\left(\dfrac{x-6}{3x}-1\right)\cdot 3x=\dfrac{x^2-5x-24}{3x}\cdot 3x$

$(x-6)-3x=x^2-5x-24$

$x^2-3x-18=0$

$(x+3)(x-6)=0$

$x=-3$ or $x=6$

Check the solution:
$$\frac{-3-6}{3(-3)\neq 0}-1=\frac{(-3)^2-5(-3)-24}{3(-3)\neq 0} \text{ and}$$
$$\frac{6-6}{3\cdot 6\neq 0}-1=\frac{6^2-5\cdot 6-24}{3\cdot 6\neq 0}$$

The solutions are $x=-3$ and $x=6$

03

(1) $\quad \dfrac{4}{x+5}+\dfrac{1}{x^2}=\dfrac{5}{x^3+5x^2}$

$\dfrac{4}{x+5}+\dfrac{1}{x^2}=\dfrac{5}{x^2(x+5)}$

$\left(\dfrac{4}{x+5}+\dfrac{1}{x^2}\right)x^2(x+5)=\dfrac{5}{x^2(x+5)}\cdot x^2(x+5)$

$\qquad 4x^2+(x+5)=5$

$\qquad\qquad 4x^2+x=0$

$\qquad\qquad x(4x+1)=0$

$\quad x=0$ or $x=-\dfrac{1}{4}$

Check the solution:

$\dfrac{4}{0+5\neq 0}+\dfrac{1}{0^2=0}\neq \dfrac{5}{0^3+5\cdot 0^2=0} \to x=0$

is an <u>extraneous solution</u>.

$\dfrac{4}{-\dfrac{1}{4}+5\neq 0}+\dfrac{1}{\left(-\dfrac{1}{4}\right)^2\neq 0}=\dfrac{5}{\left(-\dfrac{1}{4}\right)^3+5\left(-\dfrac{1}{4}\right)^2\neq 0}$

$\qquad\qquad$ The solution is $x=-\dfrac{1}{4}$

(2) $\dfrac{x}{x-1}-\dfrac{1}{x+2}=\dfrac{3}{x^2+x-2}$

$\quad \dfrac{x}{x-1}-\dfrac{1}{x+2}=\dfrac{3}{(x-1)(x+2)}$

$\quad \left(\dfrac{x}{x-1}-\dfrac{1}{x+2}\right)(x-1)(x+2)$

$\qquad\qquad =\dfrac{3}{(x-1)(x+2)}\cdot(x-1)(x+2)$

$\quad x(x+2)-(x-1)=3$

$\qquad\qquad x^2+x-2=0$

$\qquad (x+2)(x-1)=0$

$\quad x=-2$ or $x=1$

Check the solution:

$\dfrac{-2}{-2-1\neq 0}+\dfrac{1}{-2+2=0}\neq \dfrac{3}{(-2)^2+-2-2=0}$

$\to x=-2$ is an <u>extraneous solution</u>.

$\dfrac{1}{1-1=0}+\dfrac{1}{1+2\neq 0}\neq \dfrac{3}{1^2+1-2=0}$

$\to x=1$ is also an <u>extraneous solution</u>.

$\qquad\qquad$ There is no solution

04

$\dfrac{2}{2x^2-7x-4}=\dfrac{a}{x-4}-\dfrac{bx}{(x-4)(2x+1)}$

$\dfrac{2}{(x-4)(2x+1)}\cdot(x-4)(2x+1)$

$\quad =\left(\dfrac{a}{x-4}-\dfrac{bx}{(x-4)(2x+1)}\right)(x-4)(2x+1)$

$\quad 2=a(2x+1)-bx$

$2=2ax-bx+a$

$2=(2a-b)x+a$

$\Rightarrow\ 2=a$

$2a-b=0$

$2(2)-b=0\ \Rightarrow\ b=4$

Therefore, $a+b=2+4=6$

$\qquad\qquad a+b=6$

Solutions Manual

Chapter 8 Test Level 1

01

(1) $\dfrac{16x^2-1}{8x-2} = \dfrac{(4x-1)(4x+1)}{2(4x-1)} = \dfrac{4x+1}{2}$

(2) $\dfrac{6x^2-5x-6}{3x^2+14x+8} = \dfrac{(2x-3)(3x+2)}{(x+4)(3x+2)} = \dfrac{2x-3}{x+4}$

02

(1) $\dfrac{4a+8}{a^2+a-2} \times \dfrac{a^2-1}{4a^3+4a^2}$

$= \dfrac{4(a+2)}{(a-1)(a+2)} \times \dfrac{(a-1)(a+1)}{4a^2(a+1)} = \dfrac{1}{a^2}$

(2) $\dfrac{x^2+2x+1}{x^2+3x+2} \div \dfrac{1}{x^2+2x}$

$= \dfrac{x^2+2x+1}{x^2+3x+2} \times (x^2+2x)$

$= \dfrac{(x+1)^2}{(x+1)(x+2)} \times x(x+2)$

$= x(x+1)$

03

$\dfrac{x^2-4}{x+11} \times (3x^3+6x^2) \div \dfrac{2x-4}{x^2+11x}$

$= \dfrac{x^2-4}{x+11} \times \dfrac{3x^3+6x^2}{1} \times \dfrac{x^2+11x}{2x-4}$

$= \dfrac{(x-2)(x+2)}{x+11} \times \dfrac{3x^2(x+2)}{1} \times \dfrac{x(x+11)}{2(x-2)}$

$= \dfrac{3x^2(x+2)^2}{2}$

04

(1) $\dfrac{1-4x}{2x+1} + \dfrac{2x}{x-4} = \dfrac{(1-4x)(x-4)+2x(2x+1)}{(2x+1)(x-4)}$

$= \dfrac{-4x^2+17x-4+4x^2+2x}{(2x+1)(x-4)}$

$= \dfrac{19x-4}{(2x+1)(x-4)}$

(2) $\dfrac{x+2}{x^2-6x+8} - \dfrac{2}{x-2} = \dfrac{x+2}{(x-2)(x-4)} - \dfrac{2}{x-2}$

$= \dfrac{x+2-2(x-4)}{(x-2)(x-4)}$

$= \dfrac{-x+10}{(x-2)(x-4)}$

05

(1) $\dfrac{x-4}{x^2-x-12} + \dfrac{1}{x+3} = 1$

$\dfrac{x-4}{(x-4)(x+3)} + \dfrac{1}{x+3} = 1$

$\dfrac{1}{x+3} + \dfrac{1}{x+3} = 1$

$\dfrac{2}{x+3} = 1$

$2 = x+3, \ x = -1$

Check the solution:

$\dfrac{-1-4}{(-1)^2-(-1)-12 \ne 0} + \dfrac{1}{-1+3 \ne 0} = 1$

The solution is $x=-1$

(2) $\dfrac{6}{x+3} + \dfrac{2}{x-2} = 3$

$\left(\dfrac{6}{x+3} + \dfrac{2}{x-2}\right)(x+3)(x-2) = 3(x+3)(x-2)$

$6(x-2) + 2(x+3) = 3(x+3)(x-2)$

$8x-6 = 3x^2+3x-18$

$3x^2-5x-12 = 0$

$(3x+4)(x-3) = 0, \ x = -\dfrac{4}{3} \text{ or } x = 3$

Check the solution:

$\dfrac{6}{-4/3+3 \ne 0} + \dfrac{2}{-4/3-2 \ne 0} = 3$ and

$\dfrac{6}{3+3 \ne 0} + \dfrac{2}{3-2 \ne 0} = 3$

The solutions are $x = -\dfrac{4}{3}$ and $x=3$

06

$\dfrac{a}{2x-1} + \dfrac{b}{x+2} = \dfrac{a(x+2)+b(2x-1)}{(2x-1)(x+2)}$

$= \dfrac{(a+2b)x+2a-b}{(2x-1)(x+2)}$

So the equation is

$\dfrac{10}{(2x-1)(x+2)} = \dfrac{(a+2b)x+2a-b}{(2x-1)(x+2)}$

$10 = (a+2b)x + 2a-b$

$\Rightarrow a+2b = 0, \ 2a-b = 10$

Solving the system of equations, we have $a=4$ and $b=-2$. Therefore,

$a+b=4+(-2)=2$

$a+b=2$

07

Let two positive integers be x and y, and $x>y$. Then we have $\begin{cases} x=y+2 \\ \dfrac{1}{y}-\dfrac{1}{x}=\dfrac{1}{4} \end{cases}$. Solving by substituting the first expression into the second expression, we have

$$\frac{1}{y}-\frac{1}{y+2}=\frac{1}{4}$$
$$\left(\frac{1}{y}-\frac{1}{y+2}\right)\cdot 4y(y+2)=\frac{1}{4}\cdot 4y(y+2)$$
$$4(y+2)-4y=y(y+2)$$
$$4y+8-4y=y^2+2y$$
$$y^2+2y-8=0$$
$$(y+4)(y-2)=0,\ y=-4\ \text{or}\ y=2$$

Since y is a positive integer, $y=2$ and $x=y+2=2+2=4$.

Two positive integers are 2 and 4

08

Let x be the speed of the car from home to work. Since 10 minutes is equal to $\dfrac{1}{6}$ hour, we have

	Going	Returning
Speed	x	$x+10$
Distance	50	50
Time	$\dfrac{50}{x}$	$\dfrac{50}{x+10}$

$$\frac{50}{x}-\frac{50}{x+10}=\frac{1}{6}$$
$$\left(\frac{50}{x}-\frac{50}{x+10}\right)\cdot 6x(x+10)=\frac{1}{6}\cdot 6x(x+10)$$
$$300(x+10)-300x=x^2+10x$$
$$3000=x^2+10x$$
$$x^2+10x-3000=0$$
$$(x-50)(x+60)=0$$
$$x=50\ \text{or}\ x=-60$$

Since the speed of the car is positive, $x=50$.

Andy drove at 50 miles per hour from home to work.

Chapter 8 Test Level 2

01

$$\frac{6a^2-a-2}{2a^2-5a-3}\times\frac{2a^2-18}{3a^2+7a-6}$$
$$=\frac{(2a+1)(3a-2)}{(a-3)(2a+1)}\times\frac{2(a^2-9)}{(a+3)(3a-2)}$$
$$=\frac{(2a+1)(3a-2)}{(a-3)(2a+1)}\times\frac{2(a-3)(a+3)}{(a+3)(3a-2)}$$
$$=2$$

02

$$(2x-10)\div\frac{x^2-9x+20}{4x^2-9}\div\frac{6x^3-9x^2}{x^3-4x^2}$$
$$=\frac{2x-10}{1}\times\frac{4x^2-9}{x^2-9x+20}\times\frac{x^3-4x^2}{6x^3-9x^2}$$
$$=\frac{2(x-5)}{1}\times\frac{(2x-3)(2x+3)}{(x-5)(x-4)}\times\frac{x^2(x-4)}{3x^2(2x-3)}$$
$$=\frac{2(2x+3)}{3}$$

03

(1) $\dfrac{1}{4x^2-y^2}+\dfrac{1}{2x^2-3xy+y^2}$

$$=\frac{1}{(2x-y)(2x+y)}+\frac{1}{(x-y)(2x-y)}$$
$$=\frac{x-y}{(2x-y)(2x+y)(x-y)}$$
$$\quad +\frac{2x+y}{(x-y)(2x-y)(2x+y)}$$
$$=\frac{3x}{(2x-y)(2x+y)(x-y)}$$

(2) $\dfrac{1}{x-y}+\dfrac{x}{x+y}-\dfrac{y}{x^2-y^2}$

$$=\frac{x+y}{(x-y)(x+y)}+\frac{x(x-y)}{(x+y)(x-y)}$$
$$\quad -\frac{y}{(x+y)(x-y)}$$

Solutions Manual

$$=\frac{x+y+x^2-xy-y}{(x-y)(x+y)}=\frac{x^2-xy+x}{(x-y)(x+y)}$$

04

$$\frac{10x+1}{x^2-x-2}=\frac{ax+b}{x-2}-\frac{cx}{x+1}$$

$$\frac{10x+1}{(x+1)(x-2)}=\frac{ax+b}{x-2}-\frac{cx}{x+1}$$

$$\frac{10x+1}{(x+1)(x-2)}\cdot(x+1)(x-2)$$

$$=\left(\frac{ax+b}{x-2}-\frac{cx}{x+1}\right)(x+1)(x-2)$$

$$10x+1=(ax+b)(x+1)-cx(x-2)$$
$$10x+1=ax^2+ax+bx+b-cx^2+2cx$$
$$10x+1=(a-c)x^2+(a+b+2c)x+b$$
$$\Rightarrow b=1$$
$$a+1+2c=10, a+2c=9 \quad\to (1)$$
$$a-c=0 \quad\to (2)$$

Solving the system of equations (1) and (2), we have $a=3$ and $c=3$. Therefore, $a+b+c=3+1+3=7$

$$a+b+c=7$$

05

$$\frac{3}{x^2-x-12}-\frac{2}{x^2-16}+\frac{1}{x+4}$$

$$=\frac{3}{(x-4)(x+3)}-\frac{2}{(x-4)(x+4)}+\frac{1}{x+4}$$

$$=\frac{3(x+4)-2(x+3)+(x-4)(x+3)}{(x-4)(x+3)(x+4)}$$

$$=\frac{3x+12-2x-6+x^2-x-12}{(x-4)(x+3)(x+4)}$$

$$=\frac{x^2-6}{(x-4)(x+3)(x+4)}$$

06

$$\frac{x^2+2x+2}{x+2}-\frac{x^2-2x+2}{x-2}$$

$$=\frac{x(x+2)+2}{x+2}-\frac{x(x-2)+2}{x-2}$$

$$=x+\frac{2}{x+2}-\left(x+\frac{2}{x-2}\right)$$

$$=\frac{2}{x+2}-\frac{2}{x-2}=\frac{2(x-2)-2(x+2)}{(x+2)(x-2)}$$

$$=-\frac{8}{(x+2)(x-2)}$$

07

Let two consecutive positive odd integers be x and $x+2$. Then, we have

$$\frac{1}{x}-\frac{1}{x+2}=\frac{2}{15}$$

$$\left(\frac{1}{x}-\frac{1}{x+2}\right)\cdot 15x(x+2)=\frac{2}{15}\cdot 15x(x+2)$$

$$15(x+2)-15x=2x(x+2)$$
$$15x+30-15x=2x^2+4x$$
$$2x^2+4x-30=0$$
$$x^2+2x-15=0$$
$$(x-3)(x+5)=0, \; x=3 \text{ or } x=-5$$

Since x is a positive odd integer, $x=3$.

Two consecutive positive odd integers are 3 and 5

08

Let x be the speed of the current.

	Upstream	Downstream
Speed	$8-x$	$8+x$
Distance	15	15
Time	$\dfrac{15}{8-x}$	$\dfrac{15}{8+x}$

Since the total time for the trip was 4 hours, we have

$$\frac{15}{8-x}+\frac{15}{8+x}=4$$

$$\left(\frac{15}{8-x}+\frac{15}{8+x}\right)(8-x)(8+x)=4(8-x)(8+x)$$

$$15(8+x)+15(8-x)=4(64-x^2)$$
$$120+15x+120-15x=256-4x^2$$
$$4x^2=16, \; x=\pm 2$$

Since the speed of the current is positive, $x=2$.

The speed of the current is 2 miles per hour

Chapter 9

Radical Expressions

1. Simplifying Radical Expressions

Check Point 1

① $\sqrt{54} = \sqrt{9} \cdot \sqrt{6} = 3\sqrt{6}$
② $\sqrt{24a} = \sqrt{4} \cdot \sqrt{6a} = 2\sqrt{6a}$
③ $\sqrt{160b^3} = \sqrt{16b^2} \cdot \sqrt{10b} = 4b\sqrt{10b}$
④ $\sqrt{44x^8} = \sqrt{4x^8} \cdot \sqrt{11} = 2x^4\sqrt{11}$
⑤ $\sqrt{\dfrac{20}{81}} = \dfrac{\sqrt{20}}{\sqrt{81}} = \dfrac{\sqrt{4} \cdot \sqrt{5}}{\sqrt{81}} = \dfrac{2\sqrt{5}}{9}$
⑥ $\sqrt{\dfrac{9a^2}{49}} = \dfrac{\sqrt{9a^2}}{\sqrt{49}} = \dfrac{3a}{7}$
⑦ $\sqrt{\dfrac{27b^5}{100}} = \dfrac{\sqrt{27b^5}}{\sqrt{100}} = \dfrac{\sqrt{9b^4} \cdot \sqrt{3b}}{\sqrt{100}} = \dfrac{3b^2\sqrt{3b}}{10}$
⑧ $\sqrt{\dfrac{75b}{121a^2}} = \dfrac{\sqrt{75b}}{\sqrt{121a^2}} = \dfrac{\sqrt{25} \cdot \sqrt{3b}}{\sqrt{121a^2}} = \dfrac{5\sqrt{3b}}{11a}$

Check Point 2

① $2\sqrt{6} \cdot 3\sqrt{2} = 6\sqrt{6 \cdot 2}$
$= 6\sqrt{4} \cdot \sqrt{3}$
$= 6 \cdot 2 \cdot \sqrt{3} = 12\sqrt{3}$
② $4\sqrt{32a^2} \cdot \sqrt{10a} = 4\sqrt{32a^2 \cdot 10a}$
$= 4\sqrt{64a^2} \cdot \sqrt{5a}$
$= 4 \cdot 8a \cdot \sqrt{5a} = 32a\sqrt{5a}$

③ $\dfrac{6\sqrt{108b}}{2\sqrt{3b^5}} = \dfrac{3\sqrt{36}}{\sqrt{b^4}}$
$= 3 \cdot \dfrac{6}{b^2} = \dfrac{18}{b^2}$
④ $\dfrac{2\sqrt{250a^2}}{5\sqrt{5a^4}} = \dfrac{2}{5} \dfrac{\sqrt{50}}{\sqrt{a^2}}$
$= \dfrac{2}{5} \dfrac{\sqrt{25} \cdot \sqrt{2}}{a}$
$= \dfrac{2}{5} \cdot \dfrac{5 \cdot \sqrt{2}}{a} = \dfrac{2\sqrt{2}}{a}$

Review Exercise

01

(1) $\sqrt{32} = \sqrt{16} \cdot \sqrt{2} = 4\sqrt{2}$
(2) $\sqrt{80} = \sqrt{16} \cdot \sqrt{5} = 4\sqrt{5}$
(3) $\sqrt{63a^2} = \sqrt{9a^2} \cdot \sqrt{7} = 3a\sqrt{7}$
(4) $\sqrt{96b^7} = \sqrt{16b^6} \cdot \sqrt{6b} = 4b^3\sqrt{6b}$
(5) $\sqrt{128x^5} = \sqrt{64x^4} \cdot \sqrt{2x} = 8x^2\sqrt{2x}$
(6) $\sqrt{300x^{11}} = \sqrt{100x^{10}} \cdot \sqrt{3x} = 10x^5\sqrt{3x}$

02

(1) $\sqrt{\dfrac{40}{49}} = \dfrac{\sqrt{40}}{\sqrt{49}} = \dfrac{\sqrt{4} \cdot \sqrt{10}}{\sqrt{49}} = \dfrac{2\sqrt{10}}{7}$
(2) $\sqrt{\dfrac{162}{8a^2}} = \sqrt{\dfrac{81}{4a^2}} = \dfrac{\sqrt{81}}{\sqrt{4a^2}} = \dfrac{9}{2a}$
(3) $\sqrt{\dfrac{147a^5}{27}} = \sqrt{\dfrac{49a^5}{9}} = \dfrac{\sqrt{49a^5}}{\sqrt{9}}$
$= \dfrac{\sqrt{49a^4} \cdot \sqrt{a}}{\sqrt{9}} = \dfrac{7a^2\sqrt{a}}{3}$
(4) $\sqrt{\dfrac{225b^7}{36b^3}} = \sqrt{\dfrac{25b^4}{4}} = \dfrac{\sqrt{25b^4}}{\sqrt{4}} = \dfrac{5b^2}{2}$

Solutions Manual

03

(1) $\sqrt{15} \cdot 2\sqrt{3} = 2\sqrt{15 \cdot 3}$
$= 2\sqrt{9} \cdot \sqrt{5}$
$= 2 \cdot 3 \cdot \sqrt{5} = 6\sqrt{5}$

(2) $4\sqrt{12a^4} \cdot 6\sqrt{6a} = 24\sqrt{12a^4 \cdot 6a}$
$= 24\sqrt{36a^4} \cdot \sqrt{2a}$
$= 24 \cdot 6a^2 \cdot \sqrt{2a}$
$= 144a^2\sqrt{2a}$

(3) $3\sqrt{50a^3} \cdot \sqrt{8a^5} = 3\sqrt{50a^3 \cdot 8a^5}$
$= 3\sqrt{400a^8}$
$= 3 \cdot 20a^4 = 60a^4$

(4) $\dfrac{15\sqrt{65}}{3\sqrt{208}} = 5\dfrac{\sqrt{5}}{\sqrt{16}} = \dfrac{5\sqrt{5}}{4}$

(5) $\dfrac{3\sqrt{150b}}{6\sqrt{120b^7}} = \dfrac{1}{2}\dfrac{\sqrt{5}}{\sqrt{4b^6}} = \dfrac{1}{2} \cdot \dfrac{\sqrt{5}}{2b^3} = \dfrac{\sqrt{5}}{4b^3}$

(6) $\dfrac{14\sqrt{30b^4}}{21\sqrt{54b}} = \dfrac{2}{3}\dfrac{\sqrt{5b^3}}{\sqrt{9}}$
$= \dfrac{2}{3}\dfrac{\sqrt{b^2} \cdot \sqrt{5b}}{\sqrt{9}}$
$= \dfrac{2}{3} \cdot \dfrac{b\sqrt{5b}}{3} = \dfrac{2b\sqrt{5b}}{9}$

04

$2\sqrt{5} = \sqrt{2^2 \cdot 5} = \sqrt{20} \Rightarrow a = 20$
$\sqrt{150x^2} = \sqrt{25x^2} \cdot \sqrt{6}$
$= 5x\sqrt{6} \Rightarrow b = 5$ and $c = 6$
Therefore, $a + b + c = 20 + 5 + 6 = 31$.

$$a + b + c = 31$$

05

$\sqrt{360} = \sqrt{2^3 \cdot 3^2 \cdot 5} = \sqrt{2^3} \cdot \sqrt{3^2} \cdot \sqrt{5}$
$= (\sqrt{2})^3 \cdot (\sqrt{3})^2 \cdot \sqrt{5}$
$= a^3 \cdot b^2 \cdot c = a^3 b^2 c$
Therefore, $\sqrt{360} = a^3 b^2 c$

$$\sqrt{360} = a^3 b^2 c$$

06

(1) $\sqrt{ab^2} = \sqrt{a} \cdot \sqrt{b^2}$
$= b\sqrt{a} = 4m\sqrt{2m}$

$$\sqrt{ab^2} = 4m\sqrt{2m}$$

(2) $\sqrt{ab} \times \sqrt{2a^2 b^3} = \sqrt{2a^3 b^4}$
$= \sqrt{a^2 b^4} \cdot \sqrt{2a}$
$= a \cdot b^2 \cdot \sqrt{2a}$
$= (2m)(4m)^2 \sqrt{2(2m)}$
$= 32m^3 \sqrt{4} \cdot \sqrt{m}$
$= 32m^3 \cdot 2 \cdot \sqrt{m} = 64m^3 \sqrt{m}$

$$\sqrt{ab} \times \sqrt{2a^2 b^3} = 64m^3 \sqrt{m}$$

07

Since $\sqrt{20x} = \sqrt{2^2 \times 5 \times x}$,
x must be 5, and
$\sqrt{20 \times 5} = \sqrt{100} = \sqrt{10^2} = 10$

$$x = 5$$

08

$4 < \sqrt{3x+1} < 5$
$4^2 < (\sqrt{3x+1})^2 < 5^2$
$16 < 3x+1 < 25$
$15 < 3x < 24$
$5 < x < 8$

The solutions for x are 6 and 7.
Therefore, there are 2 positive integers.

2. Operations with Radical Expressions

Check Point 1

① $-3\sqrt{5}+5\sqrt{5}=(-3+5)\sqrt{5}=2\sqrt{5}$

② $\sqrt{12}-\sqrt{48}-2\sqrt{3}$
$=\sqrt{4}\cdot\sqrt{3}-\sqrt{16}\cdot\sqrt{3}-2\sqrt{3}$
$=2\sqrt{3}-4\sqrt{3}-2\sqrt{3}$
$=(2-4-2)\sqrt{3}=-4\sqrt{3}$

③ $3\sqrt{2}+\sqrt{75}-\sqrt{50}$
$=3\sqrt{2}+\sqrt{25}\cdot\sqrt{3}-\sqrt{25}\cdot\sqrt{2}$
$=3\sqrt{2}+5\sqrt{3}-5\sqrt{2}$
$=(3-5)\sqrt{2}+5\sqrt{3}$
$=-2\sqrt{2}+5\sqrt{3}$

④ $\sqrt{200}-\sqrt{125}-\sqrt{32}+6\sqrt{5}$
$=\sqrt{100}\cdot\sqrt{2}-\sqrt{25}\cdot\sqrt{5}-\sqrt{16}\cdot\sqrt{2}+6\sqrt{5}$
$=10\sqrt{2}-5\sqrt{5}-4\sqrt{2}+6\sqrt{5}$
$=(10-4)\sqrt{2}+(-5+6)\sqrt{5}$
$=6\sqrt{2}+\sqrt{5}$

Check Point 2

① $\sqrt{15}(\sqrt{12}+4\sqrt{5})$
$=\sqrt{180}+4\sqrt{75}$
$=\sqrt{36}\cdot\sqrt{5}+4\cdot\sqrt{25}\cdot\sqrt{3}$
$=6\sqrt{5}+20\sqrt{3}$

② $(\sqrt{6}-\sqrt{3})(\sqrt{6}+\sqrt{3})$
$=\sqrt{36}-\sqrt{9}=6-3=3$

③ $(\sqrt{6}+4\sqrt{2})^2$
$=\sqrt{36}+2\cdot\sqrt{6}\cdot4\sqrt{2}+16\sqrt{4}$
$=6+8\sqrt{12}+16(2)$
$=6+8\sqrt{4}\cdot\sqrt{3}+32$
$=38+16\sqrt{3}$

④ $(\sqrt{5}+\sqrt{3})(2\sqrt{5}-3\sqrt{3})$
$=2\sqrt{25}-3\sqrt{15}+2\sqrt{15}-3\sqrt{9}$
$=10-\sqrt{15}-9$
$=1-\sqrt{15}$

Check Point 3

① $\sqrt{\dfrac{3}{2}}=\dfrac{\sqrt{3}}{\sqrt{2}}=\dfrac{\sqrt{3}}{\sqrt{2}}\cdot\dfrac{\sqrt{5}}{\sqrt{2}}=\dfrac{\sqrt{15}}{2}$

② $\dfrac{\sqrt{3}}{\sqrt{6}-2}=\dfrac{\sqrt{3}}{\sqrt{6}-2}\cdot\dfrac{\sqrt{6}+2}{\sqrt{6}+2}$
$=\dfrac{\sqrt{18}+2\sqrt{3}}{6-4}$
$=\dfrac{\sqrt{9}\cdot\sqrt{2}+2\sqrt{3}}{2}$
$=\dfrac{3\sqrt{2}+2\sqrt{3}}{2}$

③ $\dfrac{1}{\sqrt{2}+\sqrt{5}}=\dfrac{1}{\sqrt{2}+\sqrt{5}}\cdot\dfrac{\sqrt{2}-\sqrt{5}}{\sqrt{2}-\sqrt{5}}$
$=\dfrac{\sqrt{2}-\sqrt{5}}{2-5}$
$=\dfrac{\sqrt{2}-\sqrt{5}}{-3}=\dfrac{\sqrt{5}-\sqrt{2}}{3}$

Review Exercise

01

(1) $5\sqrt{2}-3\sqrt{2}=(5-3)\sqrt{2}=2\sqrt{2}$

(2) $7\sqrt{7}-2\sqrt{7}+3\sqrt{7}=(7-2+3)\sqrt{7}=8\sqrt{7}$

(3) $4\sqrt{2}-\sqrt{5}-2\sqrt{2}+6\sqrt{5}$
$=(4-2)\sqrt{2}+(-1+6)\sqrt{5}$
$=2\sqrt{2}+5\sqrt{5}$

(4) $\sqrt{45}+\sqrt{27}+\sqrt{12}-\sqrt{20}$
$=\sqrt{9}\cdot\sqrt{5}+\sqrt{9}\cdot\sqrt{3}+\sqrt{4}\cdot\sqrt{3}-\sqrt{4}\cdot\sqrt{5}$
$=3\sqrt{5}+3\sqrt{3}+2\sqrt{3}-2\sqrt{5}$
$=(3-2)\sqrt{5}+(3+2)\sqrt{3}$
$=\sqrt{5}+5\sqrt{3}$

Solutions Manual

02

(1) $5\sqrt{72}-4\sqrt{50}$
$=5\sqrt{36}\cdot\sqrt{2}-4\sqrt{25}\cdot\sqrt{2}$
$=30\sqrt{2}-20\sqrt{2}$
$=10\sqrt{2}$

(2) $\sqrt{98}+\sqrt{8}+\sqrt{18}$
$=\sqrt{49}\cdot\sqrt{2}+\sqrt{4}\cdot\sqrt{2}+\sqrt{9}\cdot\sqrt{2}$
$=7\sqrt{2}+2\sqrt{2}+3\sqrt{2}$
$=12\sqrt{2}$

(3) $2\sqrt{32}-3\sqrt{5}+\sqrt{80}$
$=2\sqrt{16}\cdot\sqrt{2}-3\sqrt{5}+\sqrt{16}\cdot\sqrt{5}$
$=8\sqrt{2}-3\sqrt{5}+4\sqrt{5}$
$=8\sqrt{2}+\sqrt{5}$

(4) $2\sqrt{60}-4\sqrt{24}+\sqrt{135}-3\sqrt{54}$
$=2\sqrt{4}\cdot\sqrt{15}-4\sqrt{4}\cdot\sqrt{6}+\sqrt{9}\cdot\sqrt{15}-3\sqrt{9}\cdot\sqrt{6}$
$=4\sqrt{15}-8\sqrt{6}+3\sqrt{15}-9\sqrt{6}$
$=7\sqrt{15}-17\sqrt{6}$

03

(1) $(\sqrt{5}-1)(\sqrt{5}+1)=\sqrt{25}-1$
$=5-1=4$

(2) $\sqrt{2}(\sqrt{6}-\sqrt{10})=\sqrt{12}-\sqrt{20}$
$=\sqrt{4}\cdot\sqrt{3}-\sqrt{4}\cdot\sqrt{5}$
$=2\sqrt{3}-2\sqrt{5}$

(3) $(2\sqrt{3}-5)(2\sqrt{3}+5)=4\sqrt{9}-25$
$=12-25=-13$

(4) $\sqrt{3}(\sqrt{6}+\sqrt{2})=\sqrt{18}+\sqrt{6}$
$=\sqrt{9}\cdot\sqrt{2}+\sqrt{6}$
$=3\sqrt{2}+\sqrt{6}$

04

(1) $(2\sqrt{5}-\sqrt{3})^2$
$=4\sqrt{25}-2\cdot2\sqrt{5}\cdot\sqrt{3}+\sqrt{9}$
$=20-4\sqrt{15}+3$
$=23-4\sqrt{15}$

(2) $(4+3\sqrt{3})(\sqrt{3}-7)$
$=4\sqrt{3}-28+3\sqrt{9}-21\sqrt{3}$
$=4\sqrt{3}-28+9-21\sqrt{3}$
$=-19-17\sqrt{3}$

(3) $(4\sqrt{2}-2\sqrt{7})^2$
$=16\sqrt{4}-2\cdot4\sqrt{2}\cdot2\sqrt{7}+4\sqrt{49}$
$=32-16\sqrt{14}+28$
$=60-16\sqrt{14}$

(4) $(5\sqrt{2}-1)(2\sqrt{2}+3)$
$=10\sqrt{4}+15\sqrt{2}-2\sqrt{2}-3$
$=20+15\sqrt{2}-2\sqrt{2}-3$
$=17+13\sqrt{2}$

05

(1) $\dfrac{2}{\sqrt{3}}=\dfrac{2}{\sqrt{3}}\cdot\dfrac{\sqrt{3}}{\sqrt{3}}=\dfrac{2\sqrt{3}}{3}$

(2) $\dfrac{15\sqrt{2}}{\sqrt{5}}=\dfrac{15\sqrt{2}}{\sqrt{5}}\cdot\dfrac{\sqrt{5}}{\sqrt{5}}=\dfrac{15\sqrt{10}}{5}=3\sqrt{10}$

(3) $\dfrac{1-\sqrt{3}}{1+\sqrt{3}}=\dfrac{(1-\sqrt{3})}{(1+\sqrt{3})}\cdot\dfrac{(1-\sqrt{3})}{(1-\sqrt{3})}$
$=\dfrac{1-2\sqrt{3}+3}{1-3}$
$=\dfrac{4-2\sqrt{3}}{-2}=\sqrt{3}-2$

(4) $\dfrac{4+3\sqrt{2}}{3+\sqrt{2}}=\dfrac{4+3\sqrt{2}}{3+\sqrt{2}}\cdot\dfrac{3-\sqrt{2}}{3-\sqrt{2}}$
$=\dfrac{12-4\sqrt{2}+9\sqrt{2}-3\sqrt{4}}{9-2}$
$=\dfrac{12+5\sqrt{2}-6}{7}=\dfrac{6+5\sqrt{2}}{7}$

06

(1) $ab=(\sqrt{5}+\sqrt{3})(\sqrt{5}-\sqrt{3})$
$=\sqrt{25}-\sqrt{9}=5-3=2$

(2) $a\sqrt{3}+b\sqrt{5}$
$=(\sqrt{5}+\sqrt{3})\sqrt{3}+(\sqrt{5}-\sqrt{3})\sqrt{5}$
$=\sqrt{15}+\sqrt{9}+\sqrt{25}-\sqrt{15}$
$=3+5=8$

(3) $a\sqrt{5}-2b\sqrt{3}$
$=(\sqrt{5}+\sqrt{3})\sqrt{5}-2(\sqrt{5}-\sqrt{3})\sqrt{3}$
$=\sqrt{25}+\sqrt{15}-2\sqrt{15}+2\sqrt{9}$

$= 5 - \sqrt{15} + 6$
$= 11 - \sqrt{15}$

(4) $ab\sqrt{3} + ab^2 = ab(\sqrt{3} + b)$
$= 2(\sqrt{3} + \sqrt{5} - \sqrt{3}) = 2\sqrt{5}$

07

$\dfrac{\sqrt{2}}{\sqrt{3}} + \dfrac{2}{\sqrt{6}} + \dfrac{\sqrt{3}}{\sqrt{2}}$

$= \dfrac{\sqrt{2}}{\sqrt{3}} \cdot \dfrac{\sqrt{3}}{\sqrt{3}} + \dfrac{2}{\sqrt{6}} \cdot \dfrac{\sqrt{6}}{\sqrt{6}} + \dfrac{\sqrt{3}}{\sqrt{2}} \cdot \dfrac{\sqrt{2}}{\sqrt{2}}$

$= \dfrac{\sqrt{6}}{3} + \dfrac{2\sqrt{6}}{6} + \dfrac{\sqrt{6}}{2}$

$= \dfrac{\sqrt{6}}{3} \cdot \dfrac{2}{2} + \dfrac{2\sqrt{6}}{6} + \dfrac{\sqrt{6}}{2} \cdot \dfrac{3}{3}$

$= \dfrac{2\sqrt{6}}{6} + \dfrac{2\sqrt{6}}{6} + \dfrac{3\sqrt{6}}{6} = \dfrac{7\sqrt{6}}{6} = \dfrac{7}{6}\sqrt{6}$

$\Rightarrow a = \dfrac{7}{6}$ and $b = 6$

Therefore, $ab = \dfrac{7}{6} \cdot 6 = 7$

$ab = 7$

08

(1) $2k\sqrt{3} - 4k + 3 - 4\sqrt{3} = -4k + 3 + (2k-4)\sqrt{3}$

For the expression above to be rational,
$2k - 4$ must be zero. Therefore,
$2k - 4 = 0 \Rightarrow k = 2$

$k = 2$

(2) $(2 - 5\sqrt{2})(3k + 2\sqrt{2})$
$= 6k + 4\sqrt{2} - 15k\sqrt{2} - 10\sqrt{4}$
$= 6k + 4\sqrt{2} - 15k\sqrt{2} - 20$
$= 6k - 20 + (4 - 15k)\sqrt{2}$

For the expression above to be rational,
$4 - 15k$ must be zero. Therefore
$4 - 15k = 0 \Rightarrow k = \dfrac{4}{15}$

$k = \dfrac{4}{15}$

09

Rationalize x first.

$x = \dfrac{2}{\sqrt{6} - 2} \cdot \dfrac{\sqrt{6} + 2}{\sqrt{6} + 2} = \dfrac{2\sqrt{6} + 4}{6 - 4}$

$= \dfrac{2\sqrt{6} + 4}{2} = \sqrt{6} + 2$

Therefore,
$x^2 - 4x + 4 = (x-2)^2 = (\sqrt{6} + 2 - 2)^2$
$= (\sqrt{6})^2 = 6$

$x^2 - 4x + 4 = 6$

3. Radical Equations

Check Point 1

① $\sqrt{6x - 5} - 7 = 0$
$\sqrt{6x - 5} = 7$
$(\sqrt{6x - 5})^2 = (7)^2$
$6x - 5 = 49, \; x = 9$

Check $x = 9$ in the original equation.
$\sqrt{6(9) - 5} - 7 = 0$
$\sqrt{49} - 7 = 0$
$0 = 0 \; \rightarrow$ Solution checks

The solution is $x = 9$

② $\sqrt{x - 3} - x = -5$
$\sqrt{x - 3} = x - 5$
$(\sqrt{x - 3})^2 = (x - 5)^2$
$x - 3 = x^2 - 10x + 25$
$0 = x^2 - 11x + 28$
$0 = (x - 7)(x - 4)$

$x = 7$ or $x = 4$

Check $x = 7$ in the original equation.
$3(\sqrt{7 - 3} - 7) + 15 = 0$
$3(\sqrt{4} - 7) + 15 = 0$
$3(-5) + 15 = 0$

Solutions Manual

$\qquad 0=0 \quad \rightarrow$ Solution checks

Check $x=4$ in the original equation.

$$3(\sqrt{4-3}-4)+15=0$$
$$3(\sqrt{1}-4)+15=0$$
$$-9+15=0$$
$$6 \neq 0 \rightarrow \text{Extraneous solution}$$

The solution is $x=7$

Review Exercise

01

(1) $\sqrt{3x+1}=7$

$(\sqrt{3x+1})^2=(7)^2$

$3x+1=49, \ x=16$

Check $x=16$ in the original equation.

$\sqrt{3(16)+1}=7$

$\sqrt{49}=7$

$7=7 \quad \rightarrow$ Solution checks

The solution is $x=16$

(2) $\sqrt{5x-1}+3=1$

$\sqrt{5x-1}=-2$

$(\sqrt{5x-1})^2=(-2)^2$

$5x-1=4$

$5x=5$

$x=1$

Check $x=1$ in the original equation.

$\sqrt{5(1)-1}+3=1$

$\sqrt{4}+3=1$

$5 \neq 1 \rightarrow$ Extraneous solution

There is NO solution

(3) $8\sqrt{2x-5}-7=3$

$\sqrt{2x-5}=\dfrac{5}{4}$

$(\sqrt{2x-5})^2=\left(\dfrac{5}{4}\right)^2$

$2x-5=\dfrac{25}{16}, \ x=\dfrac{105}{32}$

Check $x=\dfrac{105}{32}$ in the original equation.

$8\sqrt{2\left(\dfrac{105}{32}\right)-5}-7=3$

$8\sqrt{\dfrac{25}{16}}-7=3$

$8\dfrac{5}{4}-7=3$

$3=3 \quad \rightarrow$ Solution checks

The solution is $x=\dfrac{105}{32}$

(4) $2\sqrt{-3x+6}+1=5$

$2\sqrt{-3x+6}=4$

$\sqrt{-3x+6}=2$

$(\sqrt{-3x+6})^2=(2)^2$

$-3x+6=4, \ x=\dfrac{2}{3}$

Check $x=\dfrac{2}{3}$ in the original equation.

$2\sqrt{-3\left(\dfrac{2}{3}\right)+6}+1=5$

$2\sqrt{-2+6}+1=5$

$2\sqrt{4}+1=5$

$5=5 \rightarrow$ Solution checks

The solution is $x=\dfrac{2}{3}$

02

(1) $\sqrt{x-2}+x=4$

$\sqrt{x-2}=4-x$

$(\sqrt{x-2})^2=(4-x)^2$

$x-2=16-8x+x^2$

$x^2-9x+18=0$

$(x-3)(x-6)=0$

$x=3$ or $x=6$

Check $x=3$ in the original equation.

$\sqrt{3-2}+3=4$

$\sqrt{1}+3=4$

$4=4 \quad \rightarrow$ Solution checks

Check $x=6$ in the original equation.

$\sqrt{6-2}+6=4$

$\sqrt{4}+6=4$

$8 \neq 4 \quad \rightarrow$ Extraneous solution

The solution is $x=3$

(2) $\sqrt{x+12}-x=0$
$\sqrt{x+12}=x$
$(\sqrt{x+12})^2=x^2$
$x+12=x^2$
$0=x^2-x-12$
$0=(x+3)(x-4)$
$x=-3$ or $x=4$

Check $x=-3$ in the original equation.
$\sqrt{(-3)+12}-(-3)=0$
$\sqrt{9}+3=0$
$6\neq 0$
$\rightarrow$ Extraneous solution

Check $x=4$ in the original equation.
$\sqrt{4+12}-4=0$
$\sqrt{16}-4=0$
$0=0 \rightarrow$ Solution checks
The solution is $x=4$

(3) $\sqrt{x}-\sqrt{x-5}=2$
$\sqrt{x}-2=\sqrt{x-5}$
$(\sqrt{x}-2)^2=(\sqrt{x-5})^2$
$x-4\sqrt{x}+4=x-5$
$-4\sqrt{x}=-9$, $\sqrt{x}=\frac{9}{4}$
$(\sqrt{x})^2=\left(\frac{9}{4}\right)^2$, $x=\frac{81}{16}$

Check $x=\frac{81}{16}$ in the original equation.
$\sqrt{\frac{81}{16}}-\sqrt{\frac{81}{16}-5}=2$
$\frac{9}{4}-\sqrt{\frac{1}{16}}=2$
$\frac{9}{4}-\frac{1}{4}=2$, $2=2$
$\rightarrow$ Solution checks
The solution is $x=\frac{81}{16}$

(4) $\sqrt{3x+10}=4+x$
$(\sqrt{3x+10})^2=(4+x)^2$
$3x+10=16+8x+x^2$
$x^2+5x+6=0$
$(x+3)(x+2)=0$
$x=-3$ or $x=-2$

Check $x=-3$ in the original equation.
$\sqrt{3(-3)+10}=4+(-3)$
$\sqrt{1}=1$
$1=1 \rightarrow$ Solution checks

Check $x=-2$ in the original equation.
$\sqrt{3(-2)+10}=4+(-2)$
$\sqrt{4}=2$
$2=2 \rightarrow$ Solution checks
The solutions are $x=-3$ and $x=-2$

03

(1) $\sqrt{3x-2}-\sqrt{10-x}=2$
$\sqrt{3x-2}=\sqrt{10-x}+2$
$(\sqrt{3x-2})^2=(\sqrt{10-x}+2)^2$
$3x-2=(10-x)+4\sqrt{10-x}+4$
$4x-16=4\sqrt{10-x}$
$x-4=\sqrt{10-x}$
$(x-4)^2=(\sqrt{10-x})^2$
$x^2-8x+16=10-x$
$x^2-7x+6=0$
$(x-1)(x-6)=0$
$x=1$ or $x=6$

Check $x=1$ in the original equation.
$\sqrt{3(1)-2}-\sqrt{10-(1)}=2$
$\sqrt{1}-\sqrt{9}=2$
$1-3=2$, $-2\neq 2$
$\rightarrow$ Extraneous solution

Check $x=6$ in the original equation.
$\sqrt{3(6)-2}-\sqrt{10-(6)}=2$
$\sqrt{16}-\sqrt{4}=2$
$4-2=2$, $2=2$
$\rightarrow$ Solution checks
The solution is $x=6$

(2) $\sqrt{x+3}-3=\sqrt{2-x}$
$(\sqrt{x+3}-3)^2=(\sqrt{2-x})^2$
$(x+3)-6\sqrt{x+3}+9=2-x$
$6\sqrt{x+3}=2x+10$, $3\sqrt{x+3}=x+5$
$(3\sqrt{x+3})^2=(x+5)^2$
$9(x+3)=x^2+10x+25$

Solutions Manual

$$x^2+x-2=0, \ (x+2)(x-1)=0$$
$$x=-2 \text{ or } x=1$$
Check $x=-2$ in the original equation.
$$\sqrt{(-2)+3}-3=\sqrt{2-(-2)}$$
$$\sqrt{1}-3=\sqrt{4}$$
$$-2 \neq 2$$
$\qquad\qquad\rightarrow$ Extraneous solution

Check $x=1$ in the original equation.
$$\sqrt{(1)+3}-3=\sqrt{2-(1)}$$
$$\sqrt{4}-3=\sqrt{1}$$
$$-1 \neq 1$$
$\qquad\qquad\rightarrow$ Extraneous solution

There is NO solution

Chapter 9 Test Level 1

01
(1) $\sqrt{99x^3}=\sqrt{9x^2}\cdot\sqrt{11x}=3x\sqrt{11x}$

(2) $\sqrt{\dfrac{24x^4}{81}}=\dfrac{\sqrt{4x^4}\cdot\sqrt{6}}{\sqrt{81}}=\dfrac{2x^2\sqrt{6}}{9}$

(3) $3\sqrt{18}\cdot5\sqrt{12}=15\sqrt{18\cdot12}=15\sqrt{36}\cdot\sqrt{6}$
$\qquad\qquad\quad =15\cdot6\cdot\sqrt{6}=90\sqrt{6}$

(4) $\dfrac{3\sqrt{75a^3}}{24\sqrt{5a}}=\dfrac{\sqrt{15a^2}}{8}=\dfrac{\sqrt{a^2}\cdot\sqrt{15}}{8}=\dfrac{a\sqrt{15}}{8}$

02
(1) $\sqrt{50}-\sqrt{32}+\sqrt{18}$
$=\sqrt{25}\cdot\sqrt{2}-\sqrt{16}\cdot\sqrt{2}+\sqrt{9}\cdot\sqrt{2}$
$=5\sqrt{2}-4\sqrt{2}+3\sqrt{2}$
$=(5-4+3)\sqrt{2}=4\sqrt{2}$

(2) $(3-5\sqrt{2})(\sqrt{8}+1)=(3-5\sqrt{2})(2\sqrt{2}+1)$
$\qquad\qquad\qquad\qquad =6\sqrt{2}+3-10\sqrt{4}-5\sqrt{2}$
$\qquad\qquad\qquad\qquad =6\sqrt{2}+3-20-5\sqrt{2}$
$\qquad\qquad\qquad\qquad =-17+\sqrt{2}$

03
$$\sqrt{6}<\ x\ <\sqrt{40}$$
$$\sqrt{6}<\sqrt{x^2}<\sqrt{40}$$
$$6<\ x^2\ <40$$
Since x is positive integer,
$$x^2=9, \ 16, \ 25, \text{ or } 36$$
$$x=3, \ 4, \ 5, \text{ or } 6$$
$\qquad\qquad$ So, there are 4 positive integers

04
$$\dfrac{\sqrt{32}-4}{\sqrt{2}}-\dfrac{\sqrt{12}+\sqrt{48}}{\sqrt{3}}$$
$$=\dfrac{4\sqrt{2}-4}{\sqrt{2}}\cdot\dfrac{\sqrt{2}}{\sqrt{2}}-\dfrac{2\sqrt{3}+4\sqrt{3}}{\sqrt{3}}\cdot\dfrac{\sqrt{3}}{\sqrt{3}}$$
$$=\dfrac{8-4\sqrt{2}}{2}-\dfrac{6+12}{3}$$
$$=4-2\sqrt{2}-6$$

$= -2-2\sqrt{2}$
$\Rightarrow a=-2,\ b=-2,$ and $c=2$
Therefore, $abc=(-2)\cdot(-2)\cdot 2=8$
$$abc=8$$

05

$(1+\sqrt{2}-\sqrt{3})(1-\sqrt{2}+\sqrt{3})$
$=(1+(\sqrt{2}-\sqrt{3}))(1-(\sqrt{2}-\sqrt{3}))$
$=1^2-(\sqrt{2}-\sqrt{3})^2$
$=1-(2-2\sqrt{6}+3)$
$=1-(5-2\sqrt{6})$
$=-4+2\sqrt{6}$

06

$(\sqrt{12}-2)(\sqrt{27}-a+2)$
$=(2\sqrt{3}-2)(3\sqrt{3}-a+2)$
$=6\sqrt{9}-2a\sqrt{3}+4\sqrt{3}-6\sqrt{3}+2a-4$
$=18-2a\sqrt{3}+4\sqrt{3}-6\sqrt{3}+2a-4$
$=14+2a-2a\sqrt{3}-2\sqrt{3}$
$=14+2a-(2a+2)\sqrt{3}$

In order for the expression above to be rational, $2a-2$ must be zero. Therefore,
$2a+2=0,\ a=-1$
$$a=-1$$

07

$a+b=\dfrac{\sqrt{3}-\sqrt{2}}{4}+\dfrac{\sqrt{3}+\sqrt{2}}{4}=\dfrac{2\sqrt{3}}{4}=\dfrac{\sqrt{3}}{2}$

$a-b=\dfrac{\sqrt{3}-\sqrt{2}}{4}-\dfrac{\sqrt{3}+\sqrt{2}}{4}=-\dfrac{2\sqrt{2}}{4}=-\dfrac{\sqrt{2}}{2}$

$(a+b)^2(a-b)^2=\left(\dfrac{\sqrt{3}}{2}\right)^2\left(-\dfrac{\sqrt{2}}{2}\right)^2$
$\qquad\qquad\qquad =\dfrac{3}{4}\times\dfrac{2}{4}=\dfrac{3}{8}$
$$(a+b)^2(a-b)^2=\dfrac{3}{8}$$

08

$x=\dfrac{2}{\sqrt{3}-1}\cdot\dfrac{\sqrt{3}+1}{\sqrt{3}+1}=\dfrac{2(\sqrt{3}+1)}{3-1}$
$=\dfrac{2(\sqrt{3}+1)}{2}=\sqrt{3}+1$

Therefore, we have
$x^3-x^2-2x=x(x^2-x-2)$
$\qquad\qquad\quad =x(x-2)(x+1)$
$\qquad\qquad\quad =(\sqrt{3}+1)(\sqrt{3}+1-2)(\sqrt{3}+1+1)$
$\qquad\qquad\quad =(\sqrt{3}+1)(\sqrt{3}-1)(\sqrt{3}+2)$
$\qquad\qquad\quad =(3-1)(\sqrt{3}+2)$
$\qquad\qquad\quad =2(\sqrt{3}+2)$
$\qquad\qquad\quad =2\sqrt{3}+4$
$$x^3-x^2-2x=2\sqrt{3}+4$$

09

(1) $2\sqrt{-3x+6}+1=5$
$\quad\ 2\sqrt{-3x+6}=4$
$\quad\ \sqrt{-3x+6}=2$
$\quad\ (\sqrt{-3x+6})^2=(2)^2$
$\quad\ -3x+6=4,\ x=\dfrac{2}{3}$

Check $x=\dfrac{2}{3}$ in the original equation.

$2\sqrt{-3\left(\dfrac{2}{3}\right)+6}+1=5$
$\quad 2\sqrt{-2+6}+1=5$
$\quad\quad\ \ 2\sqrt{4}+1=5$
$\quad\quad\quad\ \ 4+1=5$
$\quad\quad\quad\quad\ \ 5=5\ \rightarrow$ Solution checks

The solution is $x=\dfrac{2}{3}$

(2) $\sqrt{x}-\sqrt{x-5}=2$
$\quad\ \sqrt{x}-2=\sqrt{x-5}$
$\quad\ (\sqrt{x}-2)^2=(\sqrt{x-5})^2$
$\quad\ x-4\sqrt{x}+4=x-5$
$\quad\ -4\sqrt{x}=-9,\ \sqrt{x}=\dfrac{9}{4}$
$\quad\ (\sqrt{x})^2=\left(\dfrac{9}{4}\right)^2,\ x=\dfrac{81}{16}$

Solutions Manual

Check $x=\frac{81}{16}$ in the original equation.

$\sqrt{\frac{81}{16}}-\sqrt{\frac{81}{16}-5}=2$

$\frac{9}{4}-\sqrt{\frac{1}{16}}=2$

$\frac{9}{4}-\frac{1}{4}=2$, $2=2$ → Solution checks

The solution is $x=\frac{81}{16}$

Chapter 9 Test Level 2

01

$\frac{4\sqrt{12}}{\sqrt{3}}+\sqrt{6}(\sqrt{24}+2\sqrt{3})-\frac{4}{\sqrt{2}-1}$

$=4\sqrt{4}+\sqrt{6}(2\sqrt{6}+2\sqrt{3})-\frac{4}{\sqrt{2}-1}\cdot\frac{\sqrt{2}+1}{\sqrt{2}+1}$

$=8+12+2\sqrt{18}-\frac{4(\sqrt{2}+1)}{2-1}$

$=20+6\sqrt{2}-4\sqrt{2}-4$

$=16+2\sqrt{2}$

02

$x\sqrt{\frac{2y}{x}}-\frac{4}{y}\sqrt{\frac{y}{2x}}$

$=\sqrt{x^2\times\frac{2y}{x}}-\sqrt{\frac{16}{y^2}\times\frac{y}{2x}}$

$=\sqrt{2xy}-\sqrt{\frac{8}{xy}}$

$=\sqrt{2(2)}-\sqrt{\frac{8}{2}}$

$=2-2=0$

03

$\frac{a}{\sqrt{10}-3}-\frac{b}{\sqrt{10}+3}=\frac{a(\sqrt{10}+3)-b(\sqrt{10}-3)}{(\sqrt{10}-3)(\sqrt{10}+3)}$

$=\frac{a\sqrt{10}+3a-b\sqrt{10}+3b}{10-9}$

$=(3a+3b)+(a-b)\sqrt{10}$

Since $(3a+3b)+(a-b)\sqrt{10}=6+4\sqrt{10}$,

$3a+3b=6 \Rightarrow a+b=2$

and $a-b=4$

Therefore, $a^2-b^2=(a-b)(a+b)=4\cdot 2=8$

$a^2-b^2=8$

04

$a=\frac{1+\sqrt{2}}{1-\sqrt{2}}=\frac{1+\sqrt{2}}{1-\sqrt{2}}\cdot\frac{1+\sqrt{2}}{1+\sqrt{2}}$

$=\frac{1+2\sqrt{2}+2}{1-2}=-3-2\sqrt{2}$

$b=\frac{1-\sqrt{2}}{1+\sqrt{2}}=\frac{1-\sqrt{2}}{1+\sqrt{2}}\cdot\frac{1-\sqrt{2}}{1-\sqrt{2}}$

$=\frac{1-2\sqrt{2}+2}{1-2}=-3+2\sqrt{2}$

$a+b=(-3-2\sqrt{2})+(-3+2\sqrt{2})=-6$

$a-b=(-3-2\sqrt{2})-(-3+2\sqrt{2})=-4\sqrt{2}$

$ab=(-3-2\sqrt{2})(-3+2\sqrt{2})=9-8=1$

Therefore,

$\frac{\sqrt{a}-\sqrt{b}}{\sqrt{a}+\sqrt{b}}=\frac{\sqrt{a}-\sqrt{b}}{\sqrt{a}+\sqrt{b}}\cdot\frac{\sqrt{a}-\sqrt{b}}{\sqrt{a}-\sqrt{b}}$

$=\frac{a-2\sqrt{ab}+b}{a-b}=\frac{-6-2\sqrt{1}}{-4\sqrt{2}}=\frac{2}{\sqrt{2}}$

$=\frac{2}{\sqrt{2}}\cdot\frac{\sqrt{2}}{\sqrt{2}}=\frac{2\sqrt{2}}{\sqrt{2}}=\sqrt{2}$

$\frac{\sqrt{a}-\sqrt{b}}{\sqrt{a}+\sqrt{b}}=\sqrt{2}$

05

$x = \dfrac{4}{3-\sqrt{5}} \cdot \dfrac{3+\sqrt{5}}{3+\sqrt{5}} = \dfrac{4(3+\sqrt{5})}{9-5}$

$= \dfrac{4(3+\sqrt{5})}{4} = 3+\sqrt{5}$

$y = \dfrac{4}{3+\sqrt{5}} \cdot \dfrac{3-\sqrt{5}}{3-\sqrt{5}} = \dfrac{4(3-\sqrt{5})}{9-5}$

$= \dfrac{4(3-\sqrt{5})}{4} = 3-\sqrt{5}$

Since $x - y = (3+\sqrt{5}) - (3-\sqrt{5}) = 2\sqrt{5}$
and $x + y = (3+\sqrt{5}) + (3-\sqrt{5}) = 6$,
we have
$x^2 - y^2 = (x-y)(x+y)$
$= (2\sqrt{5})(6) = 12\sqrt{5}$

$$x^2 - y^2 = 12\sqrt{5}$$

06

(1) $2\sqrt{2x+1} + 4x = -2$

$2\sqrt{2x+1} = -4x - 2$

$\sqrt{2x+1} = -2x - 1$

$(\sqrt{2x+1})^2 = (-2x-1)^2$

$2x + 1 = 4x^2 + 4x + 1$

$4x^2 + 2x = 0$

$2x(2x+1) = 0$

$x = 0$ or $x = -\dfrac{1}{2}$

Check $x = 0$ in the original equation.
$2\sqrt{2(0)+1} + 4(0) = -2$
$2\sqrt{1} + 0 = -2$
$2 \neq -2$
$\rightarrow$ Extraneous solution

Check $x = -\dfrac{1}{2}$ in the original equation.

$2\sqrt{2\left(-\dfrac{1}{2}\right)+1} + 4\left(-\dfrac{1}{2}\right) = -2$

$2\sqrt{0} - 2 = -2$

$-2 = -2$

$\rightarrow$ Solution checks

The solution is $x = -\dfrac{1}{2}$

(2) $\sqrt{2x+9} - x = 3$

$\sqrt{2x+9} = x + 3$

$(\sqrt{2x+9})^2 = (x+3)^2$

$2x + 9 = x^2 + 6x + 9$

$x^2 + 4x = 0$

$x(x+4) = 0$

$x = 0$ or $x = -4$

Check $x = 0$ in the original equation.
$\sqrt{2(0)+9} - (0) = 3$
$\sqrt{9} = 3$
$3 = 3$ $\rightarrow$ Solution checks

Check $x = -4$ in the original equation.
$\sqrt{2(-4)+9} - (-4) = 3$
$\sqrt{1} + 4 = 3$
$5 \neq 3$
$\rightarrow$ Extraneous solution

The solution is $x = 0$

(3) $\sqrt{x} - \sqrt{x+3} = \sqrt{3}$

$\sqrt{x} = \sqrt{x+3} + \sqrt{3}$

$(\sqrt{x})^2 = (\sqrt{x+3} + \sqrt{3})^2$

$x = (x+3) + 2\sqrt{3x+9} + 3$

$-6 = 2\sqrt{3x+9}$

$-3 = \sqrt{3x+9}$

$(-3)^2 = (\sqrt{3x+9})^2$

$9 = 3x + 9$

$0 = x$

Check $x = 0$ in the original equation.
$\sqrt{0} - \sqrt{0+3} = \sqrt{3}$
$-\sqrt{3} \neq \sqrt{3}$ $\rightarrow$ Extraneous solution

There is NO solution

memo

memo

JM EDU Workbook Series

A well-structured workbook plays a critical role in students' learning experience!

CONCEPT & EXAMPLE ▶ **CHECK POINT** ▶ **REVIEW EXERCISE** ▶ **CHAPTER TEST**

Online Math Courses and Books
www.jmeducation.net

YouTube Channel: "Math-Up PLUS"
https://youtube.com/@math-upplus

ISBN 979-11-970670-4-4

JMEDU